Organic Gardening

FOR

DUMMIES®

2ND EDITION

Organic Gardening

FOR

DUMMIES®

2ND EDITION

by Ann Whitman, Suzanne DeJohn,
The Editors of the National Gardening Association

Wiley Publishing, Inc.

Organic Gardening For Dummies,® 2nd Edition

Published by
Wiley Publishing, Inc.
111 River St.
Hoboken, NJ 07030-5774
www.wiley.com

For general information on our other products and services, please contact our Customer Care Department within the U.S. at 877-762-2974, outside the U.S. at 317-572-3993, or fax 317-572-4002.

For technical support, please visit www.wiley.com/techsupport.

Wiley also publishes its books in a variety of electronic formats. Some content that appears in print may not be available in electronic books.

Library of Congress Control Number: 2009920904

ISBN: 978-0-470-43067-5

Manufactured in the United States of America. This book is printed on recycled paper.

10 9 8 7 6 5 4 3 2 1

About the Authors

Suzanne DeJohn describes her fascination with all things botanical as encompassing a curiosity about the natural world and a passion for the science that explains what she sees, all wrapped up in an aesthetic sensibility that inspires her to find beauty in the simplest expressions of nature. "As gardeners, we must take our cues from nature and follow the principles that govern healthy ecosystems. It's the only way we can create an environment that can sustain us now and for generations to come."

Suzanne has worn a variety of hats in her twelve years with the National Gardening Association, including work in the education, editorial, and IT departments. She coordinated NGA's online question and answer service for six years and has answered literally thousands of gardening questions. Convinced that gardeners are curious and love to learn, she was inspired to create the *Exploring the Garden* series of in-depth, online courses that teach the principles of botany in the context of the garden. Suzanne also does Web- and print-based graphic design work for NGA, takes photos for the Web sites, and creates illustrations to accompany articles.

Suzanne's varied background includes a BS in geology from Tufts; university courses in botany, soils, and plant pathology; a stint as a research assistant in plant pathology; and several years as a self-employed artist and graphic designer. She's worked on a landscape crew, as well as on a dairy farm and an organic vegetable farm, and spent several years as a cook at a natural foods store. The common themes running through these seemingly disparate vocations are plants, beauty, nature, and healthy food. Suzanne strives for balance in her life by combining time spent outdoors in her gardens with time spent at the computer, communicating what she has learned about plants and gardening.

Ann Whitman earned a Bachelor of Science degree in Plant and Soil Science at the University of Vermont. She also completed a Master of Arts degree in Landscape Design from the Conway School of Landscape Design in Massachusetts. Ann is the author of *Trees and Shrubs For Dummies* (Wiley Publishing, Inc.) as well as *How-To Landscaping Basics* and *Water Gardens: Simple Steps to Adding the Beauty of Water to Your Garden,* both published by Time Life. She also contributes to several gardening magazines and Web sites. When she's not writing, Ann gardens on fertile river-bottom soil in Vermont where the winters are long and the summers are short, but worth it.

The National Gardening Association (NGA) is committed to sustaining and renewing the fundamental links between people, plants, and the earth. Founded in 1972 as "Gardens for All" to spearhead the community garden movement, today's NGA promotes environmental responsibility, advances multidisciplinary learning and scientific literacy, and creates partnerships that restore and enhance communities.

NGA is best known for its garden-based curricula, educational journals, international initiatives, and several youth garden grant programs. Together these reach more than 300,000 children nationwide each year. NGA's Web sites, one for home gardeners and another for those who garden with kids, build community and offer a wealth of custom content.

To find out more about the National Gardening Association, write to 1100 Dorset St., South Burlington, VT 05403, or visit its Web site at www.garden.org or www.kidsgardening.com.

Dedication

Suzanne dedicates this book to her husband, Dale Lane. "Your wisdom, integrity, generosity, and love inspire me every day."

Acknowledgments

Suzanne would like to thanks Ann Whitman for her incredible work on the first edition of this book. It was an honor, a pleasure, and a challenge to revise — and attempt to improve upon — a book that was so filled with useful information. A big round of applause goes to Tracy Barr, the project editor whose insights greatly improved the organization, clarity, and usability of the book. I'm in awe of the way she kept everyone and everything organized. Thanks, too, to Kathy Simpson, another editor who helped focus my wandering prose, and technical editor David King for scrutinizing the content. Finally, thank you to the National Gardening Association for the opportunity to write about organic gardening, a subject near and dear to my heart.

Publisher's Acknowledgments

We're proud of this book; please send us your comments through our Dummies online registration form located at `http://dummies.custhelp.com`. For other comments, please contact our Customer Care Department within the U.S. at 877-762-2974, outside the U.S. at 317-572-3993, or fax 317-572-4002.

Some of the people who helped bring this book to market include the following:

Acquisitions, Editorial, and Media Development

Project Editor: Tracy Barr

(Previous Edition: Tere Drenth)

Acquisitions Editor: Stacy Kennedy

Copy Editor: Kathy Simpson

Assistant Editor: Erin Calligan Mooney

Editorial Program Coordinator: Joe Niesen

Technical Editor: David King

Senior Editorial Manager: Jennifer Ehrlich

Editorial Supervisor and Reprint Editor: Carmen Krikorian

Editorial Assistant: Jennette ElNaggar

Cover Photos: © The National Gardening Association

Cartoons: Rich Tennant (www.the5thwave.com)

Composition Services

Project Coordinator: Patrick Redmond

Layout and Graphics: Reuben W. Davis, Christin Swinford, Christine Williams

Special Art: Kathryn Born

Proofreaders: Laura L. Bowman, Jessica Kramer

Indexer: Potomac Indexing, LLC

Publishing and Editorial for Consumer Dummies

Diane Graves Steele, Vice President and Publisher, Consumer Dummies

Kristin Ferguson-Wagstaffe, Product Development Director, Consumer Dummies

Ensley Eikenburg, Associate Publisher, Travel

Kelly Regan, Editorial Director, Travel

Publishing for Technology Dummies

Andy Cummings, Vice President and Publisher, Dummies Technology/General User

Composition Services

Gerry Fahey, Vice President of Production Services

Debbie Stailey, Director of Composition Services

Contents at a Glance

Table of Contents

Introduction

This book is for people who want to grow food and maintain their landscape without using synthetic chemical pesticides and fertilizers. Organic gardening is more than just safe food, however, and it's bigger than nontoxic lawns. Organic gardening is also about making conscious decisions and taking responsibility for actions that affect the world outside your back door, past the end of your driveway, and beyond the boundaries of your hometown.

Most people proudly admit to being environmentalists, but not everyone knows how to be a good steward of his or her own yard, let alone the entire planet. This book gets you started on the path to making healthier choices for your own garden and landscape.

About This Book

Organic gardening covers a lot of ground, so to speak — from maintaining a lawn and growing roses to harvesting fresh fruits and vegetables. If you've read this far, you must be curious about how to garden organically in your own yard. This book takes you step by step through building and maintaining healthy soil, encouraging helpful insects and other organisms, choosing problem-free plants, and getting your plants off to the right start. In addition to the basic concepts of organic gardening, it also includes information about how to grow vegetables, herbs, flowers, trees and shrubs, fruits and nuts, roses, and lawns — without harmful pesticides or synthetic chemical fertilizers.

Conventions Used in This Book

When I refer to plant hardiness — a plant's ability to survive the winter extremes — I use the U.S. Department of Agriculture's Plant Hardiness Zone Map, which you can find in Chapter 3. All temperatures are given in degrees Fahrenheit and measurements in feet or inches.

A lowercase *x* in a species name indicates a hybrid cross. *C.* x *lavellei,* for example, indicates the Lavalle hawthorn, a variety of Hawthorn (*Crataegus* species).

When I refer to a *local extension office,* I'm referring to government- or university-sponsored services that offer helpful information on gardening. Look under "Extension office" or "Cooperative extension service" in the phone book. The name of the extension office may also be preceded by the name of your local land-grant college, such as "Ohio State University."

Following are a few more conventions, designed to help you navigate your way through the content:

- *Italic* is used for emphasis and to highlight new words or terms that are defined.
- **Boldfaced** text is used to indicate the action part of numbered steps.
- Monofont is used for Web addresses.

What You're Not to Read

Although we'd like to believe that you want to pore over every word between the two yellow covers, we know that you may be in a hurry or just want the basic information. To help you out, we've made the "skippable" information easy to recognize: It appears in sidebars or is marked by a Technical Stuff icon. While interesting and related to the topic at hand, this information isn't essential for you to know to have success as an organic gardener.

Foolish Assumptions

In writing this book, I made some assumptions about you:

- You want to create a safe, beautiful, and healthful place for your family to work and play.
- You want to harvest the freshest, tastiest, and most nutritious fruits and vegetables possible.
- You care about the environment and are looking for information that helps you care for your landscape in an ecologically sound way.
- You've heard about organic gardening but you need more specifics and 'perhaps some convincing that it's right for you.

Whether you come to this book in total gardening ignorance or have some experience under your fingernails, you'll find plenty of hands-on, how-to information to make your organic garden and landscape the best ever.

How This Book Is Organized

To make navigating through this book easier, it's divided into parts. Each part contains chapters related to the part's general topic.

Part 1: Understanding the Basics of Organic Gardening

If you think you may want to become an organic gardener but aren't sure what that entails, start with Chapter 1. I've provided enough scary statistics there to start you running down the path toward Chapters 2 and 3, which explain the basic concepts of organic gardening, from soil health to planning low-maintenance landscapes.

Part 11: Soil and Fertilizers

Healthy plants and gardens start with the soil. Turn to this part to get started on testing soil; making compost; and buying and using natural, organic fertilizers.

Part 111: Managing Pests

Turn to this part whenever you spot trouble in paradise and need to know what it is and what to do about it. Here you can find everything you need to know about insects, diseases, animal pests, and weeds, including specific control measures and products.

Part 1V: Growing Organically in Your Yard and Garden

The chapters in this part describe how to grow the most popular vegetables, herbs, fruits and nuts, trees and shrubs, roses, flowers, bulbs, and lawns. In each chapter, I offer advice about how to get the best plants, how to plant and maintain them, and where to obtain more information.

Part V: The Part of Tens

Use the handy lists in this part to impress your friends at parties and win them over to an organic lifestyle. I've listed best organic practices and ten ways to have an eco-friendly home and landscape. Go spread the word!

Color photo section

The color photo section near the center of this book shows you some organic gardening techniques you can apply right away. Flip to the photo section for colorful inspiration, examples of organic controls, and details that would be difficult to spot in black-and-white photos.

Icons Used in This Book

This book uses a variety of icons to highlight really neat tips, common pitfalls, and other interesting and helpful information. Here's what they mean:

If I think of something that saves you time or money or that helps you make a better decision, I flag it with this icon. This icon also appears by sources that help you find particular plants, equipment, or help.

This icon alerts you to actions that may be dangerous to you, your plants, or the environment. Proceed with caution!

If it's good for the environment, I've flagged it with this icon. For earth-friendly methods, look here.

This icon flags principles and practices key to organic gardening.

This icon marks more in-depth information for readers who want to dig a little deeper into the subject. If you just want to know the basics, feel free to ignore the info you find here.

Where to Go from Here

This book is designed so that you can jump into any chapter that grabs your attention. New to organic gardening? You probably want to start in Chapter 1. Interested in planting a vegetable garden? Go to Chapter 13. If you don't know where to start, thumb through until something catches your eye, head to the Table of Content for general topics, or go to the index for specific topics.

Part I

Understanding the Basics of Organic Gardening

The 5th Wave   By Rich Tennant

"Organic gardening's become a way of life for us.
I'll tell you more about it once Tom's finished
aerating the soil."

In this part . . .

Not sure what organic gardening is all about? Jump
right into this part for an overview of what *organic*
means. Chapter 1 introduces the foundations of organic
gardening, along with basic techniques you'll use whether
you're growing edibles, flowers, or lawn and landscape
plants. Chapter 2 describes the benefits of gardening
organically, as well as the risks to you and to the environment of using synthetic pesticides. If you need to justify
your organic preferences to naysayers, you'll have plenty
to say after reading this chapter.

Evaluate your landscape conditions, such as sun exposure
and soil moisture, with help from Chapter 3. And if you've
ever wondered about microclimates and plant hardiness,
this chapter is the place to turn. After gathering this information, you can begin planning your organic oasis;
Chapter 3 also explains how to create a landscape map.

Chapter 1

Basic Techniques in Organic Gardening

....

In This Chapter

▶ Understanding the philosophy behind organic gardening

▶ Nurturing the soil

▶ Diversifying your garden

▶ Managing pests

▶ Practicing conservation

....

*E*veryone agrees that organic gardening means avoiding synthetic fertilizers and pesticides. But the philosophy and practice of organic gardening go far beyond that simple concept. Growing organic food, flowers, and landscapes represents a commitment to a sustainable system of living in harmony with nature. For many people, organic gardening is a way of life. This chapter deals with the fundamentals of organic growing, including the philosophy behind organic gardening and the specific techniques that lead to success.

Defining Organic Gardening

The ways that people use — and misuse — soil, water, and air affect the lives and habitats of plants, insects, birds, fish, and animals, as well as humans. Organic gardening is all about preventing and treating problems in the least obtrusive, most nontoxic ways. Dedicated organic gardeners adopt methods that use cultural and natural biological processes to do the following:

✔ **Improve soil health and fertility:** Organic gardeners nurture the soil ecosystem by adding organic matter, such as compost, and avoiding pesticides that can harm soil life. In turn, soil organisms consume and break down the organic matter, making the nutrients it contains available to plants.

- ✔ **Decrease erosion:** Exposed soil is vulnerable to erosion by rain and wind. By covering soil with mulch, cover crops, or other protective materials, organic gardeners preserve the integrity of this precious resource.

- ✔ **Reduce pests and diseases:** Organic gardeners minimize pest problems and reduce the need for pesticides by relying on cultural techniques, such as proper pruning, removing unhealthy plant material, and using row covers.

- ✔ **Encourage plant and animal diversity:** Through diverse plantings and judicious use of pesticides — even organic ones — organic gardeners promote healthy ecosystems that invite beneficial organisms, including pollinators and predators of garden pests, to take up residence.

Organic gardeners take their cues from nature. Instead of relying on the spray schedules promoted by pesticide manufacturers, organic gardeners observe what's going on in their gardens and intervene to prevent pest problems. When you see white butterflies fluttering around your garden, for example, you know it's time to protect your cabbages, broccoli, and cauliflower from cabbage worm. Instead of sprinkling on a pesticide after the caterpillars hatch, you can cover the plants with a special fabric to prevent the butterflies from laying eggs in the first place.

Organic growers view their gardens as living ecosystems and work with nature to produce beautiful landscapes and healthy foods. No matter what plants you're growing — vegetables, fruits, herbs, trees, flowers, grasses — the same basic techniques apply, as the following sections show.

Depleting soil fertility, damaging and polluting ecosystems, and consuming excess water threaten the future of Earth's safe and abundant food supply. The ways that farmers and individual gardeners and homeowners choose to farm, garden, and maintain their landscapes make a difference in whether the land can continue to house, feed, and clothe us. Gardeners around the globe have adopted organic gardening techniques to help nurture the health of the Earth and all its inhabitants. (If you need more convincing that organic is the way to go, turn to Chapter 2.)

Building Soil

Just as a durable house needs a strong foundation, healthy plants require soil that can provide their roots with nutrients, water, and air. Few gardeners are blessed with perfect soil, and even if they were, keeping soil healthy and able to support plants is an ongoing process. Building and maintaining healthy soil is the single most important thing you can do to ensure the success of your garden and landscape plants.

Building soil means providing soil life — microbes, worms, fungi — with the materials and environment they need to do their jobs. Taking from the soil without giving anything back breaks the natural cycle. Harvesting crops, bagging lawn clippings, and raking fallen leaves removes organic material that's ordinarily destined for the soil on which it falls. If the organic material isn't replenished, soil health declines. Substituting synthetic chemical fertilizers for naturally occurring nutrients may feed plants, but it starves the soil.

Adding organic matter is the most common — and most important — part of building soil. Compost is a perfect source of organic matter; other sources include aged manures and crop residues. Maintaining proper soil pH (a measure of acidity/alkalinity) is also vital, because it affects soil life and the ability of plants to use nutrients.

Avoiding things that damage soil is just as important. Compaction from heavy foot or vehicle traffic and misapplied fertilizer and pesticides, for example, can harm the soil's ability to support plant life. Part II tells you everything you need to know about your soil and how to improve it in an organically sound way.

Planting Wisely

Organic gardens strive to maintain healthy, balanced ecosystems. Because plants evolved over millennia to adapt to specific growing conditions, they thrive when those conditions are met. By choosing plants that match a garden site's sun, shade, climate, soil type, and soil moisture, you'll be well on your way to creating a healthy, thriving, pest-free landscape.

The first step in planting wisely is understanding your region's climate, as well as your landscape's particular attributes. Then you can effectively match plants to planting sites. You can find out more about evaluating your landscape in Chapter 3. For specific planting information and the lowdown on growing a wide variety of plants organically — vegetables, fruits, nuts, herbs, and flowers — go to the chapters in Part IV. You can also find information in that part on applying organic principles to lawn care.

The second step is ensuring that your garden cultivates stable plant and animal communities. In nature, plants and animals live in *ecosystems* — communities in which each part contributes to and affects the lives of the other parts. In a balanced ecosystem (see Figure 1-1), each plant and animal species has enough food, water, and *habitat* (place to live).

Figure 1-1:
Plant and animal communities extend above and below ground.

In a balanced ecosystem, the predators have enough prey, and the prey have enough predators. When one part of an ecosystem dies out or becomes too scarce, the plants and animals that depend on its function in the environment get out of balance, too. If honeybees disappear, for example, the plants that need bees for flower pollination won't be able to produce seeds. If predators such as ladybugs become scarce, the insects they normally prey on — aphids — will become so numerous that they will seriously injure or even kill the plants on which they feed.

Ensuring diversity of plant types

Organic gardeners mimic nature by encouraging diversity in their landscapes. Natural plant communities contain many species of trees, shrubs, and perennial and annual plants. This rich diversity helps each plant species survive in many ways:

- **Mixed populations** avoid insect and disease devastation because all the plants of a particular species aren't located next to one another. While pests damage or kill some plants, they overlook others.

- **Deep-rooted plants** often bring soil nutrients to the surface, where they are released by decomposition, benefiting more shallow-rooted species.

- ✓ **Nitrogen-fixing plants,** which can take nitrogen from the air and deposit it in the soil, benefit other species nearby.

- ✓ **Tall, sun-loving species** provide shade, shelter, and support for lower-growing, shade-preferring species.

When plants grow artificially in *monocultures,* which are large colonies of a single species, they lose the benefits of a diverse plant community. Pests and diseases spread easily from one plant to the next, and plants rapidly deplete the soil of nutrients. A good example of the risks of monoculture is the American elm, which was planted as a shade tree along streets across the country. When Dutch elm disease was inadvertently introduced in the late 1920s, its carrier, the elm bark beetle, flew from tree to tree spreading the disease.

Many farmers and gardeners recognize and take advantage of the benefits of *polyculture* — growing more than one crop in a field. Growing plants that mutually benefit one another makes sense and is simple to do in home gardens and landscapes. You can add clover to your lawn, for example, because clover takes nitrogen from the air and adds it to the soil. Also, you can plant shade-loving, ground-covering plants under leafy trees to protect soil and tree roots from erosion.

Encouraging animal and insect diversity

A variety of plants naturally invites a variety of wildlife and insects. Berry-producing trees and shrubs attract birds; nectar-rich flowers draw butterflies and hummingbirds. Why, you may ask, do you want to encourage wildlife and insects in your garden? Answer: Your garden needs them. Beneficial insects and other creatures prey on plant pests and pollinate plants. Some of gardeners' best friends include ladybugs; syrphid flies; and tiny, nonstinging parasitic wasps.

Edible gardens

Since ancient times gardeners have combined plants grown solely for their beauty with those grown for food. Ancient Babylonians mixed ornamentals and edibles in their gardens; so did early American colonists. The trend to separate food gardens from ornamental plantings began in the Victorian era and culminated during the last few generations, when people began relegating food gardens to a corner of the backyard. Some homeowners' associations even forbid food gardens in the front yard! But in the past few years, gardeners have shown renewed interest in *edible landscaping* — using edible plants throughout the landscape, growing vegetables, fruits, and herbs among flowers and shrubs. Organic landscapes invite this mingling; you don't need to worry that the chemical pesticides you've sprayed on your roses will affect the edibles nearby. Refer to Chapter 7 for organic alternatives to synthetic pesticides.

Encourage beneficial creatures by providing a variety of habitats. Plant a variety of flowers so that something is in bloom all season long. Particularly good choices are herbs, such as basil and cilantro; plants with tiny flowers, such as alyssum and thyme; and plants whose small blooms are arranged in flat-topped flower heads, including yarrow and dill. Avoid spraying insecticides, because most of them will harm beneficial creatures too; see Chapter 7 for more information.

Here are some other ways to encourage diversity:

- Provide specific foods for the organisms you want to attract. Plant parsley for the larvae of swallowtail butterflies or milkweed for monarchs, for example.
- Build shelters designed for birds, butterflies, native bees, and toads.
- Mimic nature by creating a layered garden with tall trees, medium shrubs, and lower-growing perennials and annuals.
- Include a variety of different plants, including some evergreens, to provide winter habitat and food.
- Provide a source of fresh water.
- Leave a section of your yard wild, or at least minimally cultivated.

In most natural ecosystems, pests and predators are in a balanced but dynamic relationship. Coyotes and bobcats keep rabbits and rodents in check; without these predators, the rapidly reproducing prey would soon overpopulate, leading to death by starvation. Pests also have a place in your garden because they provide food for beneficial organisms — if food is scarce, the beneficials will starve or leave. The tiny, nonstinging braconid wasp, for example, is a beneficial insect that helps control pest caterpillars called hornworms. The wasp reproduces by laying its eggs on a hornworm. The eggs hatch and the developing wasps slowly devour the caterpillar as they mature. If you kill every hornworm, including the parasitized ones (as evidenced by the white cocoons along its back), you're killing the next generation of beneficial braconid wasps. Tolerating some pests will assure predators that your garden is a good place to hang around.

Using Integrated Pest Management

When faced with pest problems, many gardeners automatically reach for a can or jar of poison. Using pesticides to kill insects deprives the pests' natural predators of food, which causes the predators to decline, necessitating more pesticides to achieve pest control (refer to the preceding section for details). It's a vicious cycle. In addition, pesticides often kill more than just their intended targets. Beneficial insects and spiders that prey on plant pests and pollinate flowers die, too. And if pesticides drift on the wind or water away from their target, fish and birds may be poisoned as well.

Organic gardeners choose a different approach. Instead of fighting pests and disease with chemical warfare, organic gardeners strive to create healthy, balanced ecosystems. If pest problems arise, the gardeners look first for the least toxic, least environmentally disruptive solutions.

Integrated pest management (IPM) combines biological, cultural, physical, and chemical strategies to control pests. In plain English, that means using the easiest, least environmentally harmful, cheapest methods first and using the more expensive, toxic methods only as a last resort.

Managing pests through IPM involves the following steps:

1. **Prevention.**

   Keeping pests and diseases out of the garden in the first place is more than half the battle won. Inspecting new plants, cleaning your tools, eliminating weeds, and using best watering practices help prevent the spread of potential problems.

2. **Crop monitoring.**

   You have to know exactly what pest you're dealing with, when it appears, how many individuals you have, and on what plants.

3. **Cultural controls.**

   Strategies such as rotating crops to avoid planting related plants in the same spot each year and choosing pest-resistant varieties will minimize problems.

4. **Mechanical controls.**

   You can prevent pests from getting on your plants in the first place. Examples include covering plants with special fabrics or using hot water, air, fire, and the heat of the sun to kill pests without poisons. Simply knocking pests into a can of soapy water does the trick too.

5. **Biological controls.**

   Take advantage of nature's law that every organism has a natural control. You can buy and release many of these control organisms, such as ladybugs and beneficial nematodes, or encourage the ones that already exist around your garden.

6. Chemical controls.

Chemicals are the last resort. Start with the least toxic pesticides, choosing kinds that target only the pest and don't affect innocent bystanders, such as bees and spiders.

Part III is devoted to pest management.

Managing Nutrients

Plants need nutrients to grow; flourish; and fend off pests, diseases, and environmental stresses. Giving them what they need is a key to successful organic gardening, but as with humans, overdoing poor food choices spells trouble. The best way to feed plants is to feed the soil. Vast numbers of beneficial organisms call the soil home; nourish them, and you nourish the plants. Adding organic matter, such as compost, provides fungi, bacteria, earthworms, and other soil dwellers both food and a hospitable environment. In turn, they break down this organic matter into nutrients that plants can use.

In some cases, you may need to apply extra nutrients to keep plants healthy. Using organic slow-release fertilizers encourages strong, steady, healthy plant growth. Most organic fertilizers provide a broad range of nutrients, and they won't harm soil life or hurt plant roots.

The synthetic fertilizers that conventional gardeners use provide a few specific nutrients in a form that plants take up immediately. They make plants grow quickly but don't necessarily make them grow strong and healthy because fast-growing leaves and stems are soft and juicy — and very inviting to pests. Plus, any applied nutrients that the plants can't use are wasted, sometimes running off to pollute waterways. Synthetic fertilizers usually come in concentrated liquids or granules that you must dilute in water, and improperly diluted solutions can burn plant roots.

Turn to Chapter 5 for information on soil-building, and see Chapter 6 for information on organic fertilizers.

Conserving Inputs

Most organic gardeners are conservative — in the true sense of the word. We reduce, recycle, reuse, and in general try to limit what we buy. In the garden, conservation means reusing the nutrients contained in plant matter by composting kitchen scraps and garden trimmings. It also means taking care not to waste water and making sure that the products you use in your garden don't put an undue burden on the environment.

Water

Communities across the country are experiencing record drought, and some municipalities are enacting watering restrictions. A well-designed, organic landscape adapts better to restricted watering because the soil has been nurtured and plants are well adapted. Still, even organic gardeners must water once in a while.

The ideal watering system applies moisture directly to the place where it's needed: the roots. Soaker hoses and drip irrigation are best; they apply water slowly, right to the soil, where it can soak in rather than run off. Overhead sprinklers are worst, especially if they're used on a hot, sunny day. Up to one third of the water applied is lost to evaporation, and water inadvertently applied to driveways and sidewalks runs off into storm drains, carrying pollutants with it.

Consider the source

Look at where the products you use in your garden originate. You may be surprised. Is using bagged bark mulch shipped thousands of miles good for the environment, especially if local mulch is available? Does it make sense to buy bat guano from distant caves when a local farm can supply aged cow manure?

As the price of fuel rises, the cost of shipping goods thousands of miles will force consumers to look for products that originate closer to home. You may be surprised by what you can find just down the road: wood shavings from furniture factories; grounds from nearby coffee shops; brewery waste; mulch from municipal Christmas-tree-recycling programs and tree-trimming companies; and small-scale composting operations.

Think creatively! I buy the ends of newsprint rolls from the printer of our daily paper. Instead of laying down individual sheets of newspaper under mulch to prevent weeds — a daunting task on a breezy day — I simply unroll the newsprint and spread mulch as I go. Shredded paper is a good addition to the compost pile.

Chapter 2

Why Garden Organically?

In This Chapter

▶ Keeping your family healthy

▶ Protecting and preserving the environment

Gardeners may choose organic growing techniques for several reasons. Some do so because they believe organic gardens and landscapes are better for their health and the health of their families. Others grow organically because they believe this practice is better for the environment. And some gardeners believe organic gardens are more productive and beautiful. I grow organically for all these reasons and because, when I do so, I become part of the legacy of people who honor the health of the Earth and all its inhabitants by using growing techniques that are safe and sustainable over the long term.

This chapter outlines some of the reasons why gardeners choose organic methods. If you're unsure about committing to organic growing or you need information to help you make the case to naysayers, this chapter can help.

Organic Growing for Your Health

Probably the main reason why many people garden organically is to provide their families with safe, wholesome food and a toxin-free environment. Many gardeners believe that organically grown foods taste better, and recent studies show that organically grown foods may have higher nutrient levels than their conventionally grown counterparts. Organic growers also steer clear of genetically modified plants, the health risks of which are still unclear.

Alternative to synthetic pesticides

When it comes to health and safety, pesticides pose the greatest concern in gardening. Americans use about 4.5 billion pounds of pesticides each year in yards, gardens, homes, farms, and industry, about 1 billion pounds of which are synthetic pesticides. Despite a complex system of rules, regulations, and labeling requirements, thousands of people suffer acute pesticide poisoning each year. Like most gardeners, organic growers may occasionally need to use pesticides, but they choose them carefully, opting for the least-toxic organic sprays as a last resort — only after other control measures have failed.

Many people assume that *organic* means *nontoxic,* but that's not really correct. Some commonly accepted organic pesticides are, strictly speaking, more toxic than some synthetic chemical pesticides. But in general, *organic pesticides,* which are derived from plant, animal, and mineral sources, tend to be less toxic than *synthetic chemical pesticides,* which are created from petroleum and other chemical sources. More important, organic pesticides tend to break down quickly into benign substances, whereas synthetic pesticides can linger in the environment for decades.

Many of the synthetic pesticides used today belong to a group of chemical compounds called *organophosphates.* They're used to control insect pests on fruits and vegetables, to combat termites, and to control fleas and ticks on pets. These chemicals work by interfering with the nervous systems of the pests. Unfortunately, organophosphates can also harm the nervous systems of animals and humans. In fact, they are chemically similar to the World War II–era chemical-warfare agent known as nerve gas. In humans, symptoms of overexposure include nausea, headache, convulsions, and (in high doses) death. Diazinon and chlorpyrifos, two recently banned pesticides discussed in the sidebar "How unsafe pesticides remain on the market," fall into this category. Unfortunately, since diazinon and chlorpyrifos have been phased out, the use of carbaryl, an insecticide that also damages the nervous system, has increased. The EPA classifies this product as a likely human carcinogen.

Despite extensive testing by chemical companies in controlled trials, it's hard to know exactly what pesticides will do out in the real world. Ponder these statistics: The EPA now considers 60 percent of herbicides, 90 percent of fungicides, and 30 percent of insecticides to be potentially carcinogenic (able to cause cancer). A study conducted by the National Cancer Institute found that farmers exposed to chemical herbicides had a six-times-greater risk of developing cancer than farmers who were not exposed. Scary stuff.

No matter what type of pesticide you're using — organic or synthetic — you must follow label directions to the letter. Read all warnings, wear recommended protective gear, and use only as instructed. Taking these precautions isn't just smart, it's also the law.

How unsafe pesticides remain on the market

When the U.S. Environmental Protection Agency (EPA) bans a pesticide, it usually phases it out over several years. In some cases, products already on store shelves or in home garden sheds may legally be sold and used even though they have been banned. (You have to ask yourself why, if a product is worthy of banning, it's also worthy of being sold until the stockpile is used up.) Consider the recently banned pesticides diazinon and chlorpyrifos:

✔ **Diazinon:** The EPA banned residential use of diazinon in 2002, beginning with a ban on using diazinon indoors. Outdoor and garden use was not phased out until two years later.

✔ **Chlorpyrifos:** On June 8, 2000, the EPA announced that many of the currently labeled uses of insecticides containing chlorpyrifos, including Dursban and Lorsban, would be canceled. But selling the products became unlawful only after December 31, 2001 — 18 months later.

The task of removing a chemical from a product is daunting. Manufacturers must change their products, modify packaging, rework their marketing materials, and inform tens of thousands of retailers nationwide to pull products containing the chemical. A comprehensive public relations campaign to inform consumers of the risks as well as safe alternatives is also required. Then any leftover pesticides containing the banned substance must be disposed of safely. When a chemical pesticide comes under suspicion, it can be years before consumers are affected. That's one reason why I avoid these pesticides. I'd rather not take the chance that I'm unwittingly using a dangerous product.

More nutrients in organically grown foods

Most organic gardeners will tell you that the fruits and vegetables they harvest from their gardens taste better than their supermarket counterparts. Are the foods healthier, too? A multi-million-dollar, four-year study of the benefits of organic food, funded by the European Union (EU), suggests that some organically grown foods are more nutritious than their nonorganic counterparts. The study — the largest of its kind — also found that in some cases organically grown foods had higher levels of antioxidants, which are believed to be beneficial in fighting cancer and heart disease.

Why is organically grown food more nutritious? Scientists aren't sure, but here are a couple of tantalizing ideas:

✔ **Nonorganic fertilizers may force rapid plant growth:** Research suggests that the soluble nitrogen fertilizer applied in nonorganic gardens forces rapid but weak plant growth, and that these plants contain fewer of the antioxidants needed to protect their own health — the same antioxidants that protect *our* health.

✔ **Higher nutrient levels in organically grown foods may be linked to healthier soil:** Several studies comparing the nutrient levels in different fruits and vegetables show an apparent decline in food nutrient content over the past 70 years. Studies suggest that this decline may be the result of soils that have been depleted by an industrial agriculture system that relies on synthetic fertilizers rather than on the soil-building techniques favored by organic growers.

Fewer genetically modified organisms

Along with synthetic fertilizers and pesticides, organic growers avoid planting genetically modified organisms (GMOs) — organisms whose DNA has been altered through genetic engineering. Introduced to commercial farmers in the early 1990s, GMOs have raised concerns among health activists and environmentalists.

Historically, plant breeding was confined to cross-pollination: The pollen of a flower from one plant was transferred to the stigma of a flower from another plant. If pollination was successful, the flowers produced viable seeds, and if the breeders were lucky, one of the plants that grew from those seeds had the beneficial traits the breeders were seeking. The plants had to be compatible for pollination to occur; usually, that meant they had to be the same species. Hybrid plants are created through complex, carefully controlled cross-pollination. Genetically modified plants, on the other hand, are created by introducing genes of completely unrelated species. The unrelated species don't even have to be plants!

The U.S. Food and Drug Administration (FDA) proclaims that genetically modified (GM) foods are no different from their hybrid counterparts and therefore needn't be labeled as such. But the public's concern about genetic engineering reflects the notion that mixing the genes of entirely different organisms just isn't right. Food activists coined the term "Frankenfoods," and although the specter of a fish with feathers is evocative, the biggest health risks likely lay in the potential for allergic responses when foreign genetic materials are consumed.

GMOs pose environmental risks, too. Farmers regularly plant GMO varieties of soybean, corn, canola, and cotton. Some of these varieties have been genetically modified with DNA from a soil bacterium to resist the synthetic herbicide glyphosate so that farmers can spray fields to control weeds without damaging crops. The result has been the evolution of "super weeds" that are increasingly resistant to the herbicide. Now researchers are racing to introduce GMOs that are also resistant to dicamba, another synthetic herbicide. How many more genetic mutations and rounds of super weeds do we need before we see that this strategy is flawed?

Similarly, some crops have been altered to contain the bacteria *Bacillus thuringiensis* (Bt), an important biological control used by organic farmers for decades. Pests such as corn earworm are quickly developing resistance to this formerly safe and effective control, leaving organic farmers searching for alternatives.

Although GMOs are currently marketed only to commercial growers, that may not always be the case. And if you live near a farm growing GMOs, pollen from those fields may contaminate your backyard crop. The danger of genetically modified crops is hotly debated, and the EU has placed strong restrictions on growing GMOs.

Organic Growing for the Environment

The Earth's population continues to grow, but the amount of land available for growing food is disappearing rapidly. Erosion, development, pollution, dwindling water supplies, and other human-induced and natural disruptions threaten safe food and water supplies. Plant and animal species continue to disappear at alarming rates as humans damage and encroach on their habitats.

Many gardeners work to improve this grim picture by making personal choices that, at the very least, do as little harm to the environment as possible. The way you choose to grow flowers and food and to maintain the landscape can actually improve the quality of the soil, air, and water, as well as the lives of the organisms that depend on them.

Protecting wildlife

Organic gardeners strive to maintain a balanced ecosystem in which all creatures, even garden pests, play a role. They rely on nontoxic techniques, such as row covers and repellents, to manage pests, not eradicate them. By allowing the presence of some pests, organic gardeners encourage the pests' natural predators to take up residence. And when pests and predators are in balance, everyone wins.

Sometimes, even organic gardeners may choose to use pesticides as a last resort. When they do, they keep in mind that, while pesticides kill pests, they can harm innocent bystanders as well. When possible, organic gardeners choose products that affect only the pest they're trying to control.

Most organic pesticides break down quickly into harmless substances once they're exposed to air, sunlight, and/or water. Many synthetic pesticides, on the other hand, are formulated to keep working — killing — long after the need is passed. These long-lasting pesticides not only continue killing pests, they can also accumulate in the bodies of animals, harming them over a long period. In the case of the infamous DDT, which was banned in the United States in 1972, the chemical accumulated in fish, rodents, and other animals. When predators such as hawks and eagles ate those animals, they accumulated increasingly larger quantities of DDT, too. As a result, they laid eggs with thin shells that broke before they hatched, destroying generations of birds and sending many species to the brink of extinction. Even today, tens of millions of birds are killed each year as a result of pesticide use.

Pesticide contamination of wildlife has serious implications for humans, too. In its report *Chemicals in Sportfish and Game: 2008-2009 Health Advisories,* the New York State Department of Health listed 136 bodies of water with specific fish consumption advisories. The report suggests that women of childbearing age, infants, and children younger than 15 should avoid eating fish from these waters and that others should limit their intake to no more than one meal per month. Pesticides, including chlordane and DDT, are listed as contaminants in some of the lakes and streams. Advisories such as this exist throughout the United States.

Helping pollinators

Pollination occurs when pollen is moved within flowers or from one flower to another of the same species, leading to fertilization and successful seed and fruit production. Some plants, like corn, are pollinated by wind. However, nearly 80 percent of the world's crop plants, including alfalfa, apples, blueberries, cotton, and melons, depend on insects or other pollinators to transfer their pollen. According to the North American Pollinator Protection campaign, 30 percent of the foods we eat require the presence of a pollinating insect.

Although concern for the welfare of pollinating insects has been growing among scientists for decades, it wasn't until a crisis dubbed Colony Collapse Disorder (CCD) caught the media's attention that the general public took notice. During the winter of 2006–2007, U.S. beekeepers reported losses of 50 percent to 90 percent of their hives. Researchers are still trying to determine the cause, but many think that a combination of disease-related and environmental factors may be involved.

Whatever the cause, CCD has awakened us to our utter dependence on the honeybee — a non-native species that was brought here from Europe by early settlers. Before that, plants relied on native pollinators, such as solitary bees, bumblebees, wasps, butterflies, and beetles. Unfortunately, the populations of these native pollinators have dwindled, due at least in part to pesticide use.

Using organic growing practices can help reverse this trend. By growing diverse plants, choosing plants specifically to attract and feed pollinators, and minimizing pesticide use, home gardeners can play an important role in increasing the populations of pollinating insects.

Minimizing water contamination

The U.S. Geological Survey conducted a decade-long study of pesticides in our nation's surface water and groundwater. (*Surface water* includes above-ground sources, such as streams, rivers, lakes, and reservoirs. *Groundwater* flows below ground in cracks in bedrock and between soil particles, collecting in large saturated areas called *aquifers.*) Half of the U.S. population uses surface-water sources for drinking water; the other half gets drinking water from groundwater via dug or drilled wells.

The results, published in 2006, show that at least one pesticide was detected in water from every stream studied. Groundwater fared a bit better. Between one third and one half of groundwater sampled from wells contained one or more pesticides. Although in most cases, the concentration of pesticides was well below levels considered to be harmful to human health, the results show that pesticide contamination is widespread.

Surface waters become polluted from *runoff* — water flows over the ground, carrying pesticides, herbicides, fertilizers, and soil with it. Traces of triazine herbicides, which farmers use on corn and other crops, have been found in more than 90 percent of Midwestern surface waters. Researchers also found triazines in raindrops in 23 states. Even at very low concentrations, these chemicals can harm aquatic life.

Fertilizers pose an additional threat:

- Excess nitrogen and phosphorus fertilizers from lawns, farms, and gardens wash into streams, lakes, and oceans, where they contribute to excess algae growth. Densely growing algae depletes the oxygen in the water, which can kill fish and suffocate the native plant species.

- Nitrogen, the main element in most fertilizers, also moves easily through the soil, especially when mixed with water from rain, snowmelt, or irrigation, and enters the groundwater, contaminating wells and other sources of drinking water. High concentrations of nitrate — a common nitrogen compound — can be toxic to children younger than 6 months old and to other mammals, including cattle, sheep, and horses.

We can't control what commercial farmers spray on their crops. But we can choose to use safe products in our own landscapes and support farmers who grow their crops in environmentally sound ways. As an organic gardener, when you have to resort to using pesticides, you can choose organic alternatives that have less impact on the environment than their synthetic counterparts. Also, you can ask local farms about their pesticide use and purchase from those that espouse the principles you believe in.

Preventing erosion

It takes 500 years to produce 1 inch of natural *topsoil* — the rich matrix of humus, minerals, and microorganisms that plants depend on for growth. Plants in turn hold the topsoil in place with their roots and shelter it with their leaves. Soil without plants erodes easily, washing away with runoff from rain and snow or blowing away in the wind.

When soil washes into streams, rivers, and lakes, it significantly disrupts those ecosystems and pollutes the water. In fact, sediment accounts for nearly 50 percent of all lake pollution and 22 percent of river pollution, according to a 1991 U.S. government report. Erosion devastates farmland, too. The United States loses 2 million acres of *arable land* (land that's suitable for growing crops) each year due to soil erosion. The Iowa Department of Agriculture reported that half of that state's topsoil had eroded by the early 1980s. Experts report that 30 percent of arable land was lost worldwide in the last 40 years of the 20th century, due in part to erosion.

What happens in your own small garden plot may seem insignificant compared with these mind-numbing statistics, but how you garden *does* play a role in the bigger picture. Gardeners can help reduce erosion by keeping plants growing on or covering the soil throughout the year; preserving and encouraging humus formation; and avoiding excessive tilling, disruption, and compacting of the soil.

Conserving water

Fresh, clean water is a scarce and limited resource. Only 1 percent of all the water on Earth is freshwater; the rest is saltwater in the oceans and ice in polar regions. The water cycle is a closed system; the amount of water in the world remains the same but changes its form, from fog to rain to rivers to groundwater.

A typical U.S. household uses about 350 gallons of water per day. Collectively, that's an average of 26 billion gallons of freshwater every day. Up to half the water consumed by many homeowners in summer is used to water lawns and gardens. And when water is applied improperly, much of it runs off into sewers and storm drains, carrying pesticides from lawns, motor oil from driveways, and anything else in its path.

Organic gardeners need to water their gardens, too, but they take steps to minimize use, waste, and contamination. Grouping plants according to water needs, using drip irrigation and soaker hoses, applying mulch, reducing the amount of water-hungry lawn, and watering only when necessary are a few ways to conserve water.

Some gardeners use rain barrels connected to gutters to collect and store water for later use. Others build *rain gardens* — specially landscaped areas designed to collect rainwater and allow it to soak into the ground rather than run off. Conservation of this precious resource just makes sense, and it's especially critical in many regions of the United States that are facing serious drought.

What Constitutes "Organic"? The U.S. Government Gets Involved

When synthetic pesticides and fertilizers became available in the early and middle twentieth century, mainstream farmers embraced them; others bucked the system, remaining committed to what they believed were more ecologically sound farming practices. What began as fringe groups in the United States and Europe evolved into organizations espousing specific practices and certifying farms that practiced them. In the United States, dozens of regional groups created rules and certified farm products as organic. Regional organization made sense, because most organic farms were small, family-run operations that served their local populations.

Things got a bit more confusing when the organic movement gained momentum. Owners of large corporate farms — agribusinesses — realized that consumers were willing to pay a premium for foods labeled organic and began marketing their own produce as organic. But no one could say precisely what the term *organic* meant. To try to clear up the issue, the federal government got involved.

The Organic Foods Production Act

The Organic Foods Production Act (OFPA), enacted as part of the 1990 Farm Bill, set the stage for establishing uniform national standards for the production and handling of foods labeled organic. The Act authorized the creation of a new USDA National Organic Program and established an advisory group called the National Organic Standards Board to help determine the rules.

The USDA National Organic Program (NOP) includes a set of standards for organic growing. Pesticides, fertilizers, and other farm and garden products meeting these standards are acceptable for use in USDA-certified organic farming, production, and processing operations. In a nutshell, here's what's acceptable and what's not under NOP standards:

✔ **Acceptable:** Most horticultural oils and soaps, most copper- and sulfur-based fungicides, seaweed extracts, rock powders, and animal manures

✔ **Not acceptable:** Synthetic fertilizers and pesticides, genetically modified organisms, and sewage-sludge fertilizers

Although some people label the National Organic Program as a watering-down of the principles of organic farming, it does ensure that the products you buy meet certain criteria.

The rules can be a bit confusing and are continually evolving as new products are introduced. Fortunately, there's an easy way to determine whether a product is all right to use in your organic garden: Look for an OMRI logo on the label (see Figure 2-1).

Figure 2-1:
The OMRI
logo.

The Organic Materials Review Institute (OMRI) is a national not-for-profit organization that evaluates products and determines whether they are approved for use in certified organic farming. The OMRI designation on products assures you that the products conform to NOP standards. Learn more about OMRI at www.omri.org.

Must home gardeners abide by the same rules as commercial operations? Of course not. But using OMRI-listed products assures you that the NOP finds them acceptable. Your approach doesn't have to be all or nothing, however. Although I believe that the organic approach is best, you may choose to use a nonorganic fertilizer or pesticide for a particular situation.

New trends in the organic movement

Can a 1,000-acre corporate farm, growing just one or two crops and owned by shareholders who expect the largest return on their investment, truly espouse the heart and soul of organic growing? Will health and the environment end up playing second fiddle to the bottom line of these huge agribusinesses? Some organic gardeners — and consumers — who espouse organic growing primarily because no harmful pesticides are used might say the nationalization of organic agriculture is a good thing, if it means fewer farm chemicals are being used. Those who see organic growing as a holistic endeavor that encompasses techniques to nurture above- and below-ground ecosystems might argue otherwise.

The nationalization of the organic movement has spawned a new movement, one that focuses more on preserving and expanding local agriculture and less on rules and regulations. This *local movement* believes in nurturing the relationship between farmer and consumer. The latest buzzword among gardeners and nongardeners alike is *locavore* — a person who strives to eat locally grown foods. Backyard vegetable gardeners are the ultimate locavores, but most of us can't raise all our own food.

Another buzzword is *sustainable,* which can be defined as the ability of something to continue indefinitely. To me, a sustainable landscape is one in which few, if any, external materials are required. The nutrients in organic matter are recycled and fallen leaves are used as mulch. Energy is provided by good, old-fashioned, elbow grease, rather than petroleum-powered mowers and trimmers. Plants and animals — including humans — exist in harmony.

Here's the U.S. government's definition of sustainable agriculture: "An integrated system of plant and animal production practices having a site-specific application that will, over the long term, satisfy human food and fiber needs; enhance environmental quality and the natural resource base upon which the agricultural economy depends; make the most efficient use of nonrenewable resources and on-farm resources and integrate, where appropriate, natural biological cycles and controls; sustain the economic viability of farm operations; and enhance the quality of life for farmers and society as a whole." That definition isn't quite warm and fuzzy, but even in the language of bureaucrats, it's more a value system than a set of rules.

Pioneers of organic growing

Advocates of natural farming methods eschew the "chemical" way of doing things, believing that that it disrupts the natural ecological order, creating an escalating cycle of dependency on stronger and newer chemicals. Following are a few pioneers of organic agriculture and the systems they created in response to chemical farming:

✔ **Biodynamic agriculture, Rudolf Steiner:** Steiner, an Austrian philosopher, studied the relationships between plants and their environment to develop a holistic growing system called *biodynamic agriculture,* which made use of plants' rates of growth, favored environments, and relationships with other plants. He found, for example, that some plants grow better when grown next to certain other plant species. Biodynamic agriculture is still widely practiced throughout the world. You can learn more about biodynamics from the Biodynamic Farming and Gardening Association (www.biodynamics.com).

✔ **Biodynamic/French intensive method, Alan Chadwick:** Chadwick combined biodynamics with the agricultural practices he learned in France, in which plants grow in wide rows of deeply loosened, compost-fed soil. Chadwick brought his techniques to the United States in the 1960s, when

(continued)

(continued)

he accepted a teaching position at the University of California at Santa Cruz.

- **Biointensive mini-farming, John Jeavons:** In the 1970s, Jeavons combined the methods he learned from Chadwick with sustainable agricultural practices from ancient cultures to create a new organic method called *biointensive mini-farming.* He wanted to find the smallest area needed to produce all his own food, clothing, income, and building materials. Jeavons's techniques allow anyone, anywhere, to produce all the vegetables one person needs for a year with 100 square feet and a four- to six-month growing season. Learn more about biointensive techniques from Ecology Action (www.growbiointensive.org).

- **Polyculture, Masanoba Fukuoka:** Fukuoka, a Japanese farmer, developed a system of agriculture that uses no compost or soil turning; his method uses specific mixes of plants and animals to feed and protect the soil. *Polyculture,* the practice of growing multiple crops together so that each benefits the others, is part of this system. For more information about Fukuoka's techniques, refer to his book *The One-Straw Revolution* (Other India Press, 1992).

- **Permaculture, Bill Mollison and David Holmgren:** Mollison, an Australian ecologist, and his student, David Holmgren, founded permaculture in the 1970s. In a permaculture system, the gardener designs the garden and landscape as a closed system. Collected rainwater irrigates the crops; plant and animal waste returns to the soil; plants and animals benefit one another by serving multiple

purposes. To learn more about permaculture, see Mollison's book *Introduction to Permaculture* (Tagari Publications, 1997) and the Permaculture Institute Web site (www.permaculture.org).

- **Forest gardening, Robert Hart:** Hart, observing the food-growing practices of indigenous peoples in and near forests worldwide, noted that traditional forest gardeners obtained their food from many layers of the forest and surrounding areas. Similar in many ways to permaculture, forest gardening creates an ecosystem that benefits plants and animals as well as humans. Find out more from Hart's book *Forest Gardening* (Chelsea Green Publishing, 1996).

- **Rodale Institute, J. I. Rodale:** While European gardeners were developing and promoting organic gardening techniques in the 1940s and '50s, American publisher J. I. Rodale established an organic farm in Pennsylvania. He called his vision of sustainable food culture *regenerative agriculture* and worked to spread his techniques worldwide. Rodale began publishing *Organic Gardening and Farming* magazine in 1942 and founded the Soil and Health Foundation, now called the Rodale Institute, in 1947. His son Robert took over the reins in the 1970s, buying more farmland and establishing an experimental farm. For information about the institute's many activities, visit its Web site (www.rodaleinstitute.org).

By growing organically, you too can join an international community of gardeners and farmers who are committed to protecting the Earth and growing wholesome, healthful food.

Chapter 3

Planning Your Organic Landscape

· ·

In This Chapter

▶ Knowing plant terms

▶ Understanding climate and microclimate

▶ Evaluating your landscape

▶ Drawing a map

· ·

Design is fundamental to successful organic gardening. Well-placed plants can shelter your house; provide refuge for wildlife; and give you all the fruits, vegetables, herbs, and flowers you desire. This chapter may be the most important one in the book because it's about putting plants in the right places and starting them off on the right foot, so to speak. It provides an overview of designing all types of gardens. For specific information on individual categories of plants, see Chapters 13 through 20.

Factors Affecting Your Design Decisions

Plants come in a huge variety of shapes, sizes, and habits. Knowing something about plant characteristics and getting familiar with descriptive terms makes choosing and using plants easier. Like any hobby, gardening has a vocabulary of its own that allows enthusiasts to communicate effectively. Here's a rundown of terms to understand before you start your garden plan.

Life cycles: Annual, biennial, and perennial

Different plants have different *life cycles* — the amount of time it takes for them to become mature enough to bloom, produce seed, and ultimately die. Plants belong in one of three categories: annuals, biennials, and perennials.

✔ **Annuals:** Annuals complete their life cycle in a single growing season. They typically sprout from seed in the spring, bloom, produce seed, and die before winter comes again. With proper care, most annual flowers will bloom continuously all summer, right up until frost. If you want the most bang for your buck, flowerwise, choose annual plants. Most garden vegetables and many herbs are annuals (or we treat them as such). Because they die in fall, annuals must be replanted every year.

✔ **Biennials:** Biennials live for two growing seasons. In the first year, they sprout and grow leaves and roots. The flowers and seeds come in the second growing season, after which the plant dies. Biennials are relatively uncommon in home gardens.

✔ **Perennials:** Perennials live for at least three seasons, and many live much longer in the right climate (in the wrong climate, they act more like annuals). Perennials can be *herbaceous,* those with stems that die to the ground in the winter and grow back from their roots, or *woody,* those with tough, persistent stems or trunks (think trees, shrubs, and woody vines). Woody perennials create a backdrop for other plants, and provide habitat for wildlife.

Perennial flowers tend to have a distinct bloom period lasting several weeks, although some flower sporadically throughout the summer. By choosing a combination of early-, mid-, and late-season bloomers, you can have continuous color as different flowers bloom and fade.

Deciduous, evergreen, and conifer

Plants are also characterized by whether they keep their leaves year-round, and they fall into these categories:

✔ **Deciduous plants:** These plants grow new leaves each spring. In autumn, those leaves die and fall off, leaving branches bare until spring.

✔ **Evergreen plants:** These plants keep their leaves year-round. Although most shed leaves occasionally, their branches are never bare. Following are two examples of evergreens:

  • **Needled evergreens,** which include pines and spruces. (Think Christmas trees.)

  • **Broadleaf evergreens,** which have non-needle-like leaves. This category includes rhododendrons and most hollies.

Some herbaceous perennials, such as candytuft and hellebore, are evergreen. Others, such as bearded iris, are evergreen in warm climates and deciduous in cold climates; plants like these are sometimes described as *semievergreen.* And sometimes varieties of the same plant differ — evergreen and deciduous daylilies, for example.

✔ **Conifers:** *Conifers* are plants that bear cones. Although most conifers are evergreens, exceptions occur. One exception is larch (also known as tamarack), which is a conifer that loses its needles and is known as a *deciduous conifer.*

Whether a plant drops its leaves is an important consideration in garden design. If you want a year-round screen between your home and your neighbors, make sure that the plants you choose are evergreen. To find out which of these categories a plant fits into, read plant descriptions carefully; don't make assumptions based on generalizations; and try to find information specific to your gardening climate.

Type of leaves, flowers, and roots

This section isn't a botany lesson. The reason you need to know plant parts when you're planning a garden is that it will help you choose plants with flowers and foliage that complement each other from a design perspective, and it will help you foresee challenges such as trying to plant under trees with shallow roots.

Leaves

Each leaf characteristic influences the overall appearance of a plant. I won't bore you with the scores of words botanists have come up with to describe leaves, but here are a few of the most useful categories:

✔ **Color:** Like beauty, color is in the eye of the beholder. Foliage described as black is often dark maroon, for example. (Plant breeders take license when naming new varieties, so try to find photos or live samples.) *Variegated* foliage has leaves with two or more colors in them.

✔ **Size:** Look for actual measurements if leaf size is a concern.

✔ **Shape:** Most descriptions use everyday language, but you may run across botanical terms such as *ovate* (egg-shaped), *lanceolate* (lance-like), and *cordate* (heart-shaped). Figure 3-1 shows some common leaf shapes.

✔ **Surface texture:** Leaves can be shiny and smooth, hairy, fuzzy, or wrinkled.

Flowers

Knowing what a plant's flowers look like can help you find the most complementary place for the plant in your garden. Some plants, like most daffodils, have *single* flowers, which come one to a stem. Others produce clusters of flowers in a wide array of shapes (a variety of which are shown in Figure 3-2).

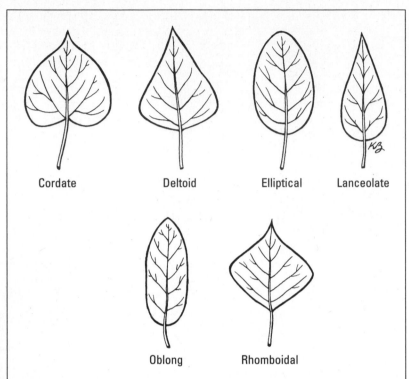

Figure 3-1:
Common
leaf shapes.

Cordate   Deltoid   Elliptical   Lanceolate

Oblong   Rhomboidal

Roots

Roots don't get much attention, but the kind of roots a plant has can give you hints about its culture. Plants generally have one of two kinds of roots:

- **Fibrous roots** are finely branched and grow close to the soil surface. Plants with fibrous roots are easy to transplant and divide into new plants, but are more easily damaged by drought and cold weather.

- **Taproots** usually are thick and long, reaching deep into the soil. After they're established, taproots are difficult to move, but they tolerate temporary drought.

Some plants, such as clematis, have particularly shallow root systems that are easily damaged by cultivation, so use extra caution when weeding around them. Maple trees have extensive surface roots, making it a challenge to grow plants underneath them.

Figure 3-2:
Common flower shapes.

Composite

Panicle

Spike

Unbrel

Plant shapes

When you're planning how to use a plant in your garden or landscape, it helps to know something about how it grows. A garden filled with tall, narrow plants has a very different feel to it than one featuring spreading mounds of foliage. The best garden designs usually include plants with a variety of shapes:

- *Climbing* plants cling or twine around a support as they reach for the sky. Without a support, they sprawl on the ground.

- *Upright* plants stand tall on their own. *Columnar* plants are upright plants that are especially tall and narrow.

- *Mounding* and *shrubby* plants form rounded cushions.

- *Weeping* plants have branches that hang down.

✔ *Prostrate* and *creeping* plants stay close to the ground, and some spread themselves around the garden.

✔ *Pyramidal* plants are wide at the base and narrow at the top, while *vase-shaped* plants are narrow at the bottom and wide at the top.

Plant cold and heat hardiness

The ability of a plant to survive is called its *hardiness.* Plant catalogs often use the term rather loosely to indicate whether you can expect a particular plant to live in a cold-winter climate, but hardiness really is a measure of a plant's ability to survive all the aspects of a particular climate. For a map of U.S. hardiness zones (as well as information about heat zones and sunlight zones), head to the later section "Considering your region's climate."

Cold hardiness

Many things influence a plant's cold-hardiness. It helps to think of all the factors as links in a chain: The weakest link determines the strength of the chain (or, in this case, the hardiness of the plant). Some of the factors have to do with the plant itself, including the following:

✔ **Genetics:** The genetic adaptability of plants to specific climates and soils is called *provenance.* Provenance is a major factor to consider in choosing landscape trees and shrubs, as well as some perennial plants.

✔ **Stage of growth:** The timing of *acclimation,* or winter readiness, varies with each species and depends partly on growing conditions, such as soil moisture and fertility. Soft, new shoots, for example, may suffer frost injury in the autumn, whereas woody stems that grew earlier in the summer remain undamaged.

✔ **Health:** Environmental stressors — such as drought, flooding, storm damage, diseases, and pests — weaken plants and can make them more vulnerable to cold damage.

✔ **Plant parts:** Flower buds are often less cold-hardy than the woody stems of trees and shrubs, and they may be damaged or killed before stem damage occurs. That's why a late-spring cold snap often kills frost-tender flowers but does little harm to other plant parts.

The climate itself also affects plant hardiness. Climatic factors that influence plant survival include the following:

✔ **Duration of winter:** Genetic programming signals some plants to begin flowering and growing after a particular number of hours of cold temperatures followed by warm temperatures. Even before winter really ends, some plants — especially those growing outside their preferred range — break dormancy (begin growing again) and are damaged by spring frost.

✔ **Duration of extreme cold:** Prolonged periods of extreme cold usually cause more damage than a single night of unusually cold temperatures.

✔ **Wind:** Wind increases moisture loss. Unfortunately, plants can't replace lost moisture while the soil is frozen and plants are dormant. Evergreens, which keep their leaves year-round, are especially vulnerable to the effects of drying winds in winter.

✔ **Snow:** Snow provides an insulating blanket that protects plant roots and stems from extreme cold. In areas that receive little snow, the soil temperature gets much colder than in areas with snow cover. (You can use a thick layer of loose mulch to mimic the insulating effect of snow.)

✔ **Sun exposure:** The sun can increase moisture loss from winter foliage and stems. The winter sun can cause frost cracks: The bark on young or thin-barked trees like beech and maples thaws during the day, then freezes at sunset, causing the bark to split.

Heat tolerance

Heat tolerance is a common limiting factor for plants, and in many parts of the country, this factor — not cold-hardiness — is the primary concern. Plants native to desert and tropical regions are naturally heat-tolerant, whereas plants from cooler regions may show little tolerance. Some plants can withstand high daytime temperatures but suffer if nights stay too warm. Sun exposure, humidity, and soil moisture can influence a plant's ability to thrive in a hot climate.

Knowing Your Landscape Conditions

Healthy plants suffer from fewer pest and disease problems, and tolerate drought, flood, and other adverse situations more easily than do struggling plants, so it makes sense to put plants in the right places to encourage their natural resilience. The natural rhythm of the seasons, including the winter low temperatures and the summer highs, sets the most obvious limits within which you garden. Other, subtler factors — including moisture, nutrients, soil, and sun — also influence how and where plants grow best.

Considering your region's climate

The predominating weather conditions of an area, measured over a long period of time, determine a region's *climate*. Factors affecting climate include seasonal temperatures; humidity; timing, amount, and type of precipitation; length of growing season; and wind patterns. Proximity to mountains and large bodies of water, distance above sea level, position on the planet relative to the equator, and *prevailing wind* (the direction from which the wind usually blows) also affect climate. The following sections provide a variety of hardiness maps — for hardiness zones, heat zones, and sunset times.

Don't use geographic proximity alone to evaluate climate. Two places near each other geographically can have very different climates if one is high on a mountainside and the other is on the valley floor, for example. Also, widely separated regions can have similar climates.

USDA Plant Hardiness Zone Map

Low winter temperatures limit where most plants will grow. After compiling weather data collected over many years, the U.S. Department of Agriculture (USDA) divided North America, Europe, and China into 11 zones. Each zone represents an expected average annual minimum temperature.

On the USDA Plant Hardiness Zone Map for North America (see Figure 3-3), each of the 11 zones is 10°F warmer or colder in an average winter than the adjacent zone. The warmest zone, Zone 11, records an average low annual temperature of 40°F or higher. In Zone 1, the lowest average annual temperature drops to minus 50°F or colder. Brrr!

Zones 2 through 10 on some North American maps are further subdivided into *a* and *b* regions. The lowest average annual temperature in Zone 5a, for example, is 5°F warmer than the temperature in Zone 5b. When choosing plants that are just barely hardy in your zone, knowing whether your garden falls into the *a* or *b* category can ease your decision. After a few years of personal weather observation in your own garden, you'll have a pretty clear idea of what to expect for winter low temperatures too.

Return of the native (plants, that is)

Native plants are all the rage in gardens across the country. A *native* plant is one that originated in a particular place and that evolved and adapted over millennia alongside the native insects, fungi, wildlife, and other plants. This longtime association creates a complex web of interrelationships, with plants, insects, and animals depending on one another for food, shelter, pollination, and other needs. Native plants are touted as being universally easy to grow and beneficial to wildlife. In some cases, this description is valid; sometimes, it's just hype.

Some people use *native* to refer to any plant that originates in the United States, but the term is better used to link plants with specific biomes. A "native" cactus from the deserts of the Southwest won't thrive in the upper Midwest, and if it did, the animals and plants there would view it as exotic. The cactus is native to the Southwestern desert biome, not the upper Midwestern biome.

Using an abundance of plants native to your region can benefit native insects and wildlife. Most states have a native-plant society, which is a good place to start your search for true native plants: the ones from your biome.

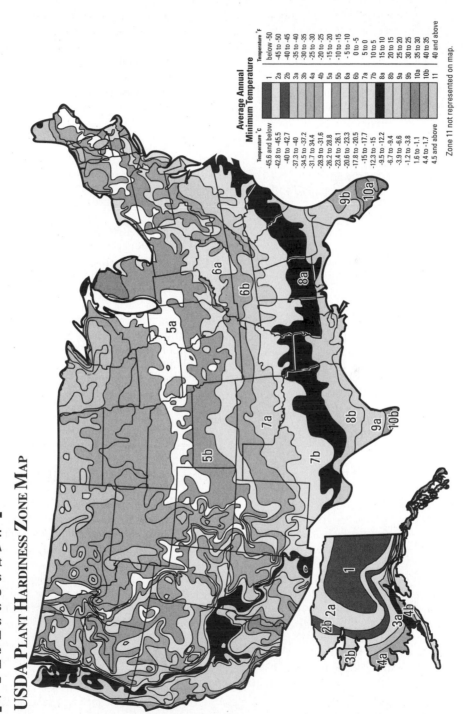

Figure 3-3: The USDA Plant Hardiness Zone Map indicates each zone's expected average annual minimum temperature.

USDA PLANT HARDINESS ZONE MAP

Average Annual Minimum Temperature

	Temperature °C		Temperature °F
1	-45.6 and below		below -50
2a	-42.8 to -45.5		-45 to -50
2b	-40 to -42.7		-40 to -45
3a	-37.3 to -40		-35 to -40
3b	-34.5 to -37.2		-30 to -35
4a	-31.7 to 34.4		-25 to -30
4b	-28.9 to 31.6		-20 to -25
5a	-26.2 to 28.8		-15 to -20
5b	-23.4 to -26.1		-10 to -15
6a	-20.6 to -23.3		- 5 to -10
6b	-17.8 to -20.5		0 to -5
7a	-15 to -17.7		5 to 0
7b	-12.3 to -15		10 to 5
8a	-9.5 to -12.2		15 to 10
8b	-6.7 to -9.4		20 to 15
9a	-3.9 to -6.6		25 to 20
9b	-1.2 to -3.8		30 to 25
10a	1.6 to -1.1		35 to 30
10b	4.4 to -1.7		40 to 35
11	4.5 and above		40 and above

Zone 11 not represented on map.

Most books, catalogs, magazines, and plant labels use the USDA zone system. For a color version, which may be a bit easier to read, visit the U.S. National Arboretum Web site, which offers a map of North America and individual regions at www.usna.usda.gov/Hardzone/index.html.

The USDA map is based on a single factor: a region's average minimum winter temperature. Many other factors affect a plant's ability to thrive in a particular environment, so use the map only as a guideline.

AHS Heat Zone Map

To help gardeners in warm climates, the American Horticultural Society developed the AHS Heat Zone Map. This map divides the United States into 12 zones based on the average number of *heat days* each year — days that reach temperatures of 86°F or higher. Zone 1 has fewer than one heat day per year; Zone 12 has more than 210.

Order your own color poster of the AHS Heat Zone Map by calling the society at (800) 777-7931, ext. 137. Or visit the American Horticulture Society's Web site at www.ahs.org/publications/heat_zone_map.htm for more information and a downloadable map. The site also offers a Heat Zone Finder to locate your particular heat zone by zip code.

Sunset map

In an attempt to take total climate into consideration when evaluating plant hardiness, Sunset Publishing created Sunset's Garden Climate Zones, a map that divides the country into 24 zones. This map is especially useful to gardeners in the western United States, where mountains, deserts, and coastal areas create wildly diverse climates, sometimes within a few miles of each other.

Although most national plant suppliers and references use the USDA zone map, regional garden centers and growers in the western half of the country often refer to the Sunset map. View it at www.sunset.com/sunset/garden/article/1,20633,845218,00.html.

Thinking about your microclimates

Within larger climates, smaller pockets exist that differ somewhat from the prevailing weather around them. These *microclimates* occur wherever a building, body of water, dense shrubs, or hillside modifies the larger climate.

Microclimates may be very small, such as the sunny side of your house or the shady side under a tree, or as large as a village. A town on the shore of Lake Michigan has a different microclimate than a town 20 miles inland, for example. Common microclimates around your property may include the following:

- ✔ **North side of house:** Cool and shady year-round
- ✔ **South side of house:** Hot and sunny all day; often dry
- ✔ **East side of house:** Warm morning sun and cool afternoon shade
- ✔ **West side of house:** Morning shade and hot afternoon sun
- ✔ **Top of hill:** Exposed to wind and sun; soil dries quickly
- ✔ **Bottom of hill:** Collects cold air and may be poorly drained due to precipitation that runs down the slope

No doubt you can find other examples on your site as you closely observe the patterns of sun, water, wind, and temperature throughout the year.

Plan your landscape and gardens to take advantage of microclimates. Use wind-sheltered areas to protect tender plants from drying winter winds in cold climates and hot, dry winds in arid places. Put plants such as phlox and lilac, which are prone to leaf disease, in breezy garden spots as a natural way to prevent infections. Avoid putting frost-tender plants at the bottoms of hills, where pockets of cold air form.

Seasonal sun and shade

When you work out your garden and landscape plans, it helps to know where the sun shines and shadows fall at different times of the year. In the summer, the sun rises higher in the sky, for example, and casts shadows differently than it does in the winter, when it's lower in the sky.

Where you live also affects the sun's intensity. Gardeners in the southern latitudes and at higher elevations enjoy stronger sunlight than gardeners who live in the north and at lower elevations. Garden books use terms such as *full sun* or *part shade* to describe where plants grow best, but full sun in San Diego, California, is not the same as full sun in Eugene, Oregon, or Boulder, Colorado. Plants that grow happily in the sun all day long in Eugene, for example, may prefer a little midday shade in sunny Southern California or mountain-high Boulder.

Figuring out just what kind of sun and shade you have can be confusing. Plant descriptions in this book and many others use the following terms:

- ✔ **Deep or dense shade** occurs on the north sides of buildings and walls, and under trees with low branches and dense leaves. No direct sunlight reaches the ground.
- ✔ **Partial shade** occurs in places that receive direct morning or afternoon sun, but none at midday, from about 10 a.m. to 2 p.m.
- ✔ **Light shade** falls under trees with high branches or sparse foliage.
- ✔ **Full sun** means direct sunlight for at least six hours each day, including some or all of the midday hours.

Do what I do: Combine sun- and shade-loving plants so that one protects the other. In my vegetable garden, for example, I plant leaf-lettuce seeds between the broccoli plants because the broccoli shades the sprouting lettuce, which prefers cooler, shadier soil.

Water

Your climate determines how much water falls on your garden, and the slope of the land and type of soil determine whether that water puddles or runs away. But you can also influence what happens to water after it falls from the sky or flows out of the faucet by designing your garden and landscape to take advantage of natural conditions.

In arid climates where rain falls infrequently, you can grow a lush, colorful garden and landscape — and conserve water too. Here's how:

- **Choose plants that naturally thrive with little rainfall in your climate.** Plant water-hungry exotics sparingly — in containers or as accent specimens only. Seek out plant nurseries that specialize in drought-tolerant species.

- **Protect existing native plants during construction and landscaping projects on your property.** These plants are naturally adapted to the site and require little maintenance. Use them to guide your design plan.

- **Install rain barrels or a cistern to collect and store whatever rain does fall.** Use this water for your garden instead of drawing on municipal services or depleting your well water.

- **Avoid wasteful overhead sprinklers.** Use drip irrigation to deliver water efficiently and directly to the plant roots through a pipe or hose.

- **Alter the slope or make channels to direct the surface water, if you find that rainfall runs off too quickly.** Check local regulations before altering any natural wetland or bodies of water, or affecting water flow onto a neighboring property.

- **Use ground-covering plants to preserve soil moisture and cool the surrounding area.** Avoid heat-reflecting mulches and surfaces, which can increase plants' need for water.

Gardeners who regularly deal with too much moisture, which results in plant disease, have several options as well. Beyond choosing plants that enjoy plenty of water, you can build raised gardens. The soil in a raised garden may drain more quickly than the surrounding soil, especially if you add plenty of organic material. Find out more about raised beds in Chapter 5. You can also install buried drainpipe to carry away excess surface water.

Soil conditions

Nothing you do in your garden is more important than building healthy, fertile, organically rich soil. Soil does much more than simply hold plants in place; it's also the source of nearly all plant nutrition and water. Many of the microorganisms that live in soil benefit plants, too. Soil is so important, in fact, that I devote two entire chapters to the subject. Flip to Chapter 4 for an overview of soils and to Chapter 5 for soil-building techniques.

Getting Started on Your Garden Design

You can find hundreds of garden design books and Web sites, but often, the best place to start planning a design is your neighborhood. What yards strike your fancy as you drive by? Visit public gardens in your region; they're ideal for getting ideas about plants that thrive in your climate. Keep a small camera with you, and snap shots of plant groupings and color combinations that you'd like to replicate in your landscape. Tear pages out of magazines and catalogs, and start a scrapbook.

As you plan your organic landscape, keep the following tips in mind:

- ✔ **Plan for convenience.** Common-sense design features can make garden tasks easier. Make sure that fence openings are wide enough for a lawn mower or wheelbarrow, for example. If you're creating a new garden, install soaker hoses or drip irrigation at planting time, the easiest time to tackle that task.

- ✔ **Plan for diversity.** Choosing plants in a range of types, sizes, colors, and shapes makes for a more interesting landscape; encourages wildlife and beneficial organisms; and minimizes pest problems. See the earlier section "Factors Affecting Your Design Decisions" for more info.

- ✔ **Plan for low maintenance.** Minimize gardening chores with careful planning. Choose hardy, reliable, easy-care plants. Make sure that the mature sizes of trees and shrubs are appropriate to the site so that you'll have to do little pruning. Use easy-care ground covers in place of high-maintenance lawns.

- ✔ **Plan for sustainability.** Think long-term when designing your gardens; consider how plantings will look in five or ten years. (Visit botanical gardens to view mature specimens.) Choose well-adapted, long-lived plants that require minimal supplemental water and fertilizer. Minimize the need for outside sources of fertilizer by composting yard and kitchen waste.

✔ **Plan for abundance.** Think about how your landscape will look in all four seasons, and include plants that will provide interest year-round. Consider all the things gardens can provide. Add a cutting garden for indoor bouquets; plant extra herbs for drying; add gourds and berry-filled shrubs for crafts. Install a cold frame and have fresh produce from early spring to late fall.

✔ **Plan for energy conservation.** Strategically placed shade trees help keep your house cool in summer. Proper landscaping can reduce heating and cooling costs by one third or more. (For details, see "Landscaping for energy conservation," later in this chapter.)

Before you start planning, check local regulations and community covenants for restrictions on things like grass height and types of plants allowed. Some homeowners' associations prohibit vegetable gardens or allow them only in backyards, for example. If you find the rules objectionable, persuade others in your neighborhood to join you in attempting to have them revoked.

Basic design principles for your garden

Mixing and matching plants with creative flair is the part of gardening that gets me excited every winter, when seed and plant catalogs land in my mailbox, and when the soil warms in the spring. Whether you're designing a new landscape or just adding or rearranging existing plants, keep the following design elements in mind:

✔ **Season of bloom:** A big mistake that many gardeners make is buying only what they see blooming in the garden center in the spring. Their gardens end up looking lovely in spring and early summer but lack interest during the rest of the year.

✔ **Color:** Gardeners usually make flower color their top priority when deciding which plants to purchase, but the color of foliage and bark can also add to a garden's overall palette. Consider that many plants bloom for only a few weeks, but you see their foliage and bark at other times of year. Sometimes, the most beautiful gardens have the simplest color schemes. A garden filled with white flowers and silvery-gray foliage, for example, shimmers in the moonlight.

✔ **Scale:** Look for trees and shrubs that complement the scale of your landscape. A huge tree can overwhelm a small yard; a small shrub can look lost in an expanse of lawn. Keep scale in mind in individual gardens, too. You may want to arrange plants by height, putting the shortest ones in the front and the tallest in the back. For gardens that will be viewed from all sides, put the tallest plants in the middle.

Designing with color

Although you really can't go wrong in mixing flower colors, some hues naturally go well together. *Color wheels,* which you can find in the local art supply store, show the rainbow as a circle of colored slices. Color-wheel opposites — such as red and green, orange and blue, purple and yellow — complement each other. Colors that form triangles on the color wheel — such as blue, green–yellow, and red–purple — also make good combinations. A single hue (such as red) has many lighter and darker colors (such as pink and deep red) within its family, and combining these hues make single-color-theme gardens more interesting.

Hot colors — red, yellow, and orange — jump out in the landscape and can appear to be closer than they are. *Cool colors* — blue, green, and purple — blend into the garden and look farther away. Use these colors to achieve certain effects. Cool colors in a small garden can make it appear larger; hot colors draw more attention to streetside plantings. White also stands out in the landscape, especially in dim light, and is useful for planting with more-colorful flowers to brighten or moderate the mix.

✔ **Season-extending attributes:** Some plants offer good-looking seedpods, buds, bark, or growth habits. Poppy seed heads, ornamental grass seed heads, curly willow stems, red osier dogwood shoots, and river birch bark take center stage when foliage and flowers have faded. Plants with an extra-long blooming period or that bloom twice in a season, such as reblooming bearded irises, offer good garden value.

✔ **Growth habit:** Growth habit can make a particular plant more or less suitable for a garden. Climbing vines, for example, they take up little room in the garden and give an extra vertical dimension to the space. Trailing plants, such as creeping thyme and petunia, carpet the ground.

✔ **Cultural considerations:** Look for disease-resistant varieties, especially in species that are vulnerable to particular problems. Phlox, for example, is prone to powdery mildew, but many newer varieties resist the fungus. Look for "disease-resistant" in the descriptions of all plants, but especially for roses, fruit trees, vegetables, and berries.

Types of landscape arrangements

Landscaping can be so much more than just making your yard beautiful. Many plants can serve double duty. For example, a fruit tree planted so it shades your porch will help keep you cool while you savor its delicious fruits. When planning your landscape, consider all the ways in which plants can enhance your daily life.

Landscaping for energy conservation

Before the advent of cheap and readily accessible heating and air conditioning, people used common-sense landscaping to increase the comfort of their homes and to reduce heating and cooling costs. A well-planned landscape can reduce a home's summer air-conditioning costs by 15 percent to 50 percent. Windbreaks can save up to 25 percent on heating costs. Here are a few energy-conservation tips:

- ✔ Plant deciduous trees on the southeast and southwest corners of your house. They'll shade your home from summer sun but shed their leaves in the fall so that the warmth of the winter sun can reach your home. *Note:* Trees on the south side of the house won't provide much cooling in midsummer unless they overhang the roof. Because they block winter sunlight in that position, it's usually best to leave the south side treeless.

- ✔ Plant an evergreen hedge on the north or northwest side of the house (or whichever side is the direction of the prevailing winter winds) to provide a buffer from cold gusts.

- ✔ Plant trees to shade an air-conditioning unit, thereby increasing the unit's efficiency by 10 percent or more. Trim away foliage around the unit to ensure good air circulation.

- ✔ Plant annual or deciduous vines on south-facing exterior walls to help insulate them from hot summer sun. They'll die back or lose their leaves in the fall, letting winter sun reach the walls. Grow vines to shade sunrooms and porches, too.

Some municipalities offer financial incentives to homeowners who use water-conserving landscape plants. Consult your local conservation commission, community conservation district, or state department of natural resources to see whether such a program exists in your area.

An integrated landscape

It's time to rethink the suburban landscape paradigm: a house surrounded by symmetrical evergreen foundation plants; a huge manicured lawn punctuated by occasional flower beds; a vegetable garden relegated to a corner of the backyard.

As an organic gardener, you're uniquely positioned to create integrated landscapes in which edibles and ornamentals share garden space. Why? You don't have to worry about pesticides sprayed on lawns and flowers contaminating your food plants. Why not use blueberry bushes as foundation plants? They're attractive and low maintenance, and the foliage turns a beautiful crimson in fall. Best of all, you can step out your door to a harvest of juicy berries. Rainbow Swiss chard, which has striking orange, pink, red, and yellow stems, is a natural in flower beds and offers a nutritious harvest, too.

It's okay to know the rules of traditional garden design, but it's just as important to know that you can break them!

Putting pencil to paper

Good designers observe and discover how the different parts of the land-scape — home, gardens, and other functional areas of a site — relate to one another, and they use those relationships to direct their designs. Think through each of the following items as completely as you can, using plenty of paper to take notes and scribble ideas:

- **What you want from your landscape:** Your list may include a vegetable garden, herb patch, flowers for bouquets, fruit trees or shrubs, compost bin, tool storage, and recycling bins.

- **How the different items in your list relate to one another:** Consider the distance between places that depend on each other. Does it make more sense to put the vegetable garden at the far corner of the backyard or close to the kitchen and tool-storage area in the garage?

- **How often you will visit each area:** Places that you visit daily, such as the trash, compost, and vegetable garden, should be located closest to the house. An area that needs infrequent maintenance, such as an orchard, can be situated farther away.

- **How many functions each element can fulfill:** Trees can provide shade, fruit, ornament, and windbreak, among other things. Vegetable gardens can be ornamental and also provide food. Flowers attract hummingbirds, color the yard, furnish garnish for salads and bouquets for the table, and provide habitat for beneficial insects.

When you're done brainstorming your list, you're ready to draw up a plan that makes sense on the ground.

Making a map

One of the most important ways that organic gardeners encourage healthy, pest-resistant plants is to plant them where they can naturally thrive. But you have to know something about your site before you can match the plants to their right places. Grab a buddy, the longest tape measure you own or can borrow, and a pencil and paper; then head outside. The next sections lead you through a quick-and-dirty mapmaking exercise.

Step 1: Sketch the major features of your property

Start by drawing the outlines of major features of your property, including buildings and property lines. Use your tape measure and do your best to draw to scale, with everything in the correct proportion to everything else, but don't agonize: Neatness doesn't count.

For long distances, measure the length of your stride, and multiply it by the number of strides it takes you to get from one end to the other.

Sketch the locations of important rooms, windows, and exterior doors of your house. Remember to note permanent features, such as the driveway, paths, deck, and shed. Note the location of water spigots and electrical outlets. Make an arrow on your map to indicate the direction of north; you'll need that information as you plan your garden.

Step 2: Note natural features

Add the following natural features to your map:

- **Sun and shade:** Label the sunny and shady spots around your yard so that you can take advantage of them. If you have lived in the house long enough, note the sun and shade at different times of the day and year.

- **Views:** If you plan to do some landscaping, note the nice and not-so-nice views around your property. Remember to check the views from your windows, too.

- **Soil, slope, and water:** Draw arrows on your map that point down slopes. Circle areas where water pools or runs after a rainstorm. Note places where your soil stays muddy or drains quickly.

- **Wind:** Note the direction and strength of the prevailing winds across your site at different times of the year.

- **Existing plants and natural features:** Use circles to draw existing trees and shrubs that you intend to keep. Record the width of the plant canopy by measuring from one edge of the *drip line* (where rain drips from the foliage to the ground) to the other. Note the locations and sizes of gardens, large rocks, and other features you want to preserve.

Your map may resemble the one shown in Figure 3-4 when you're done. Resist the temptation to add "things to do" to this map at this stage; save that task for the following section.

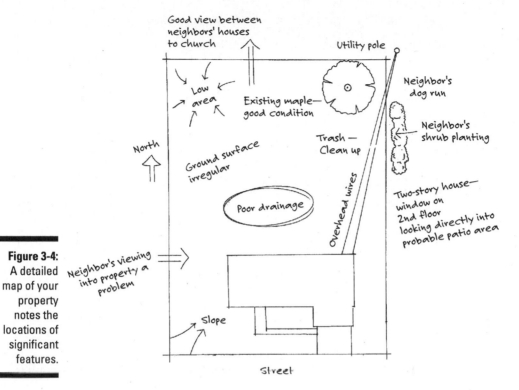

Figure 3-4:
A detailed map of your property notes the locations of significant features.

Putting it all together

Here's where your dreams meet reality. The idea is to take your list of projects and match them to the most appropriate places in your yard. For this project, lay tracing paper over your map or make a bunch of photocopies so that you can doodle ideas at will without messing up the original. As you try out different combinations and placements, keep the following tips in mind:

- ✔ **Prioritize your list of desires.** Put them into a time frame or order of steps. You may have to build a deer-excluding fence before planting an orchard or vegetable garden, for example, and preparing soil comes before planting.

- ✔ **Think long-term.** Some tasks take a day to accomplish; other projects stretch out for months or even years. Break long projects into shorter, prioritized steps.

✔ **Concentrate on the areas closest to the house first.** Put your most intensive gardens and use areas near the house, and plan to install them before you tackle the outlying areas.

✔ **Conserve energy.** Use gravity, sun, shade, wind, and precipitation to your advantage. It's easier to move a barrel of water or a cart of compost downhill than uphill, for example. Note the places where soil warms up first in the spring, and plant your early-season vegetables there.

✔ **Consider maintenance.** Decide how much time you can realistically devote to maintaining your gardens and landscape plants, and plan accordingly. Don't sketch in a 400-square-foot vegetable garden if you have only enough time to weed and harvest a garden half that size.

✔ **Think multipurpose.** Make plants and built-in features serve more than one function. Use a fence or plants to support an ornamental or food-producing vine, screen an unpleasant view, prevent trespassing, enclose a private space, and deflect wind.

✔ **Play matchmaker.** Make a list of plants that you want to grow. Next to each one, write down whether it needs full sun, part shade, or shade. In another column, note soil and moisture preferences. Group plants with similar needs, and look at the places on your map where each group would be happiest.

✔ **Avoid obstacles.** Put trees, shrubs, and perennial plants where they will have room to mature. If you have overhead utility lines, avoid planting trees under or near them. Choose shrubs that won't cover the windows of your house, and plant them so that they won't rub on the siding in five or ten years.

Now, with your plan in hand, it's time to dig in!

Part II
Soil and Fertilizers

In this part . . .

Ready to get down and dirty? This part is the heart of the book, because healthy soil is where organic gardening — and healthy plants — begin.

Chapter 4 explains why soil is more than just dirt. Healthy soil contains minerals, organic matter, and the proper amount of air and water. It's also teeming with microorganisms that help the soil support your garden plants.

Chapter 5 gives you the tools to evaluate the soil you have and good ideas about how to improve it. Compost is king in this chapter, and I get up close and personal with manure, too (whew!). Flip to Chapter 6 for the lowdown on fertilizers that come from plants, animals, and minerals, and find out how to use them.

Chapter 4

Digging beneath the Surface: Soils 101

Soil may not be the most exciting part of gardening, but it's the foundation upon which you build everything else. Healthy soil is alive; it's the most biologically diverse habitat on Earth. A shovelful of rich garden soil contains more species of organisms than you can find aboveground in the entire Amazon rain forest!

What do all those organisms do? They feed on and decompose organic matter and release nutrients for plants to use. Beneficial microorganisms in the soil prey on harmful ones and protect plant roots from diseases and pests. Earthworms and other soil creatures tunnel through the soil, opening spaces for oxygen, water, and nutrients to move freely.

Organic gardeners and farmers encourage this beneficial soil life and improve their soil by adding organic matter, such as compost; by using practices that prevent damage to the soil habitat; and by avoiding synthetic pesticides and fertilizers that destroy subterranean life. To join their ranks, first you need to know what you're dealing with. This chapter has the details.

Soil Components: The Nitty-Gritty

The first step toward improving your soil is understanding what it's made of. If you dig down deeply into the soil, you can see that it's composed of layers, called *horizons,* as shown in Figure 4-1. These layers are, from the bottom up:

✔ **Parent rock:** About half the volume of most soils consists of small mineral pieces that originate in the underlying parent rock. The composition of the parent rock partly determines the type of soil you have; sandstone parent rock yields sandy soil, for example. Impervious parent rock can lead to poorly drained soils, whereas porous or highly fractured parent rock usually contributes to good drainage.

✔ **Subsurface soil (subsoil):** This layer is mineral-rich and largely undisturbed by cultivation and weather. Subsoils contain little organic matter and few microorganisms. Sometimes, a hard, impervious layer called *caliche* or *hardpan* forms in the subsoil; it prevents water from draining properly.

✔ **Surface soil:** This layer, also called *topsoil,* lies above the subsoil, where plows, gardeners, and weather can alter it. Most plant roots and soil microorganisms live in the surface soil. In addition to small mineral pieces, topsoil contains organic matter, air, and water. The proper balance of these components is vital to the health of garden plants.

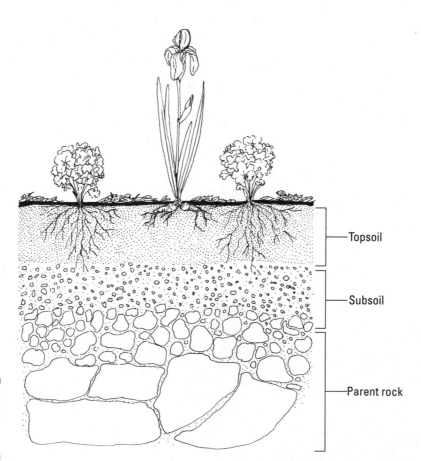

Topsoil

Subsoil

Parent rock

Figure 4-1:
Soil is composed of layers.

It has been said that a nation endures only as long as its topsoil. Without topsoil, little plant life is possible, and without plants, no animals survive. During the Dust Bowl of the 1930s, hundreds of millions of tons of topsoil blew off the land in the southern Great Plains, in part because the deep-rooted native prairie grasses had been replaced by farm fields. It takes 500 years or more for nature to create 1 inch of topsoil from subsoil.

Preserving and improving soil are among the tenets of organic growing. You can't change the type of parent rock in your garden, but you can improve your soil. Most improvement efforts focus on the topsoil, but if this layer is thin, you may need to extend your efforts to the subsoil layer. Find out more about building healthy soil in Chapter 5.

Digging into the Topsoil

As I mention earlier in this chapter, the health of garden plants depends on the soil having the proper balance of mineral pieces, organic matter, air, and water (see Figure 4-2). Understanding the nature of topsoil is key to improving it, and knowing what type of soil you have can help you choose techniques to enhance its good qualities.

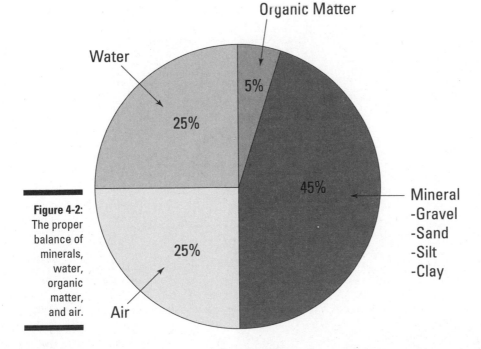

Figure 4-2: The proper balance of minerals, water, organic matter, and air.

Organic Matter — 5%

Water — 25%

Air — 25%

Mineral — 45%
-Gravel
-Sand
-Silt
-Clay

Composition of soil

About half the volume of most soils consists of clay, silt, and sand particles, which differ in size and shape (see Figure 4-3). The relative amounts of these particles determine your *soil texture:*

- **Clay particles,** the smallest soil particles, are microscopic and flat.
- **Silt particles** are more angular and larger than clay but still microscopic.
- **Sand particles** are the largest of the three types. They can be angular or rounded.

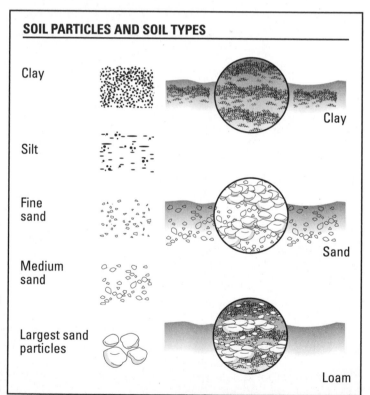

SOIL PARTICLES AND SOIL TYPES

Clay

Silt

Fine sand

Medium sand

Largest sand particles

Clay

Sand

Loam

Figure 4-3: Soil particles differ in size and shape.

REMEMBER

The spaces between soil particles are called *pores.* Nutrient-rich water moves through these pores, as does the air that roots and microorganisms depend on. When the soil contains very little pore space, water and air can't move through the soil. When it has too much pore space, water passes through too quickly.

For most plants, the ideal mixture is approximately 40 percent sand, 40 percent silt, and 20 percent clay. Soil with this makeup is called *loam.* Loamy soil is ideal because it provides a balance of water-holding capacity, drainage, and fertility. Alas, not all soils are loamy. Those composed of mostly one particle type can pose challenges for gardeners:

- ✔ **Clay soils** are naturally fertile, but they can be difficult to work. Clay soil's individual particles are so small and flat that they pack tightly, leaving little room for water and air. On a practical level, this structure means that clay soil drains poorly, stays wet longer than other soils, contains little oxygen, and dries as hard as concrete. A wet spring may mean a delay in planting; a dry summer causes the soil to crack and harden.

- ✔ **Silt soils** have moderate fertility and medium-size particles and pore spaces that hold some water and air. Like clay soils, they can pack tightly, especially when wet. They may get powdery or dusty when dry. Silt particles are easily carried away by runoff and are small enough to be blown away by wind.

- ✔ **Sandy soils** contain few nutrients. Sand particles are large; water drains quickly from the pore spaces, and any nutrients that are present tend to leach out. Sandy soils don't pack tightly like clay and silt soils.

Unfortunately, except by trucking in huge amounts of soil, you have no way to change your soil's texture. You can take advantage of its natural assets, however, and compensate for its challenges by working on the soil structure.

Soil structure

The way that the soil particles align themselves or clump together is called *soil structure.* The best garden soils have a loose, crumblike structure that water, air, and plant roots can penetrate easily. *Unstructured soils,* such as beach sand, don't clump together, which allows water to flow through them too rapidly for most plant growth. *Poorly structured soils,* such as heavy clay, clump together so tightly that little water and air can pass through.

Two of the most important goals for organic gardeners are improving and maintaining good soil structure. Improving soil structure can improve water-holding capacity in sandy soils and improve drainage in clay soils.

Many things affect soil structure, but the most important ones from a gardener's point of view include the following:

- ✔ **Organic matter:** Decayed plants and animals become *humus,* a substance that helps soil particles bind together into crumblike aggregates. Soils that lack enough humus may clump together too tightly or not at all. Adding organic matter improves the structure of both sandy and clay soils. To find out how to add organic matter, head to Chapter 5.

- ✔ **Soil organisms:** As they tunnel through the soil, earthworms, beetles, and other organisms open spaces between soil particles, allowing air, water, and roots to pass through easily. Earthworm *castings* (excrement) are also rich in nutrients. Encourage these beneficial soil organisms by providing food and habitat for them in the form of organic matter.

- ✔ **Rotary-tilling:** Churning the soil through rotary-tiller blades is a good way to break up compact soils and mix in organic matter. Rotary-tilling (also called *rototilling* or just *tilling*) also changes the soil structure.

Although tilling can initially add more air to the soil, be careful not to overtill. Overtilling pulverizes soil aggregates, damages soil life, and promotes too-rapid breakdown and loss of organic matter. Find out more about rototilling in Chapter 5.

- ✔ **Working with wet soil:** Avoid walking on, digging in, or rototilling saturated soil. Wet soil, especially clay, packs together tightly when compressed, forming clods that can bake to potterylike hardness in hot sun. Allow garden soil to drain to the dampness of a wrung-out sponge before working in it. Find out about building raised beds to improve drainage and minimize soil compaction in Chapter 5.

Improving and maintaining soil structure is an ongoing process no matter what type of soil you have. Adding organic matter to your soil every year is an important step, particularly for sandy or clay soils. Organic matter acts like a glue to help sandy soils stick together into aggregates that retain the proper amount of moisture. It also helps clay soils drain better by binding with the tiny particles to create larger ones with more pore space. But even healthy, loamy soils benefit from annual additions of organic matter. Organic matter is vital to soil structure, but it also contributes to soil fertility. Head to the later section "Organic matter" for more information.

Starting from Fertile Ground

If you feed the soil, the soil will feed the plants. For organic gardeners, feeding plants isn't just a matter of pouring on the fertilizer. Instead, gardeners build the natural fertility of their soil by adding organic matter, preserving and improving the soil structure, and modifying the soil pH. (*Fertility* is the capacity of a soil to supply the mineral nutrients that plants need.) Several factors influence soil fertility, as the following sections explain.

Amount of nutrients in the soil

Overall, plants need 16 elements, or nutrients, for proper growth. Different soils contain differing levels of these needed elements. When enough of each element is present, plants grow optimally. If even one element is in short supply, plants can't grow as well. Think of the weakest-link theory, which says that a chain is only as strong as its weakest link. Your soil is only as fertile as its most deficient nutrient.

Nutrients for photosynthesis

The nutrients that plants need in the largest quantities are carbon, hydrogen, and oxygen, which plants use for photosynthesis. During *photosynthesis,* green plants take these nutrients from the air and from the water in the soil to produce sugars — the "food" that fuels plant growth.

Mineral nutrients

Plants generally get mineral nutrients from the soil or from applied fertilizers. Mineral nutrients include nitrogen, phosphorus, and potassium (the familiar N-P-K on fertilizer bags), as well as numerous others. When gardeners talk about feeding plants, they're talking about providing them with extra mineral nutrients.

The term *feeding* is a bit of a misnomer because plants produce their own food — carbohydrates — during photosynthesis. These mineral nutrients (nitrogen, phosphorus, potassium, and others) are more akin to the vitamins we take to supplement our food.

The mineral nutrients needed in the largest quantities are called *macronutrients* and consist of nitrogen, phosphorus, potassium, calcium, magnesium, and sulfur. In addition, plants need smaller amounts of so-called *micronutrients.* The eight micronutrients considered essential for plant growth are iron, manganese, boron, copper, zinc, molybdenum, chlorine, and nickel, all of which occur in very small quantities in most soils. These micronutrients, and other substances found in low concentrations in soils, are sometimes called *trace elements.* Scientists studying plant nutrition may discover additional micronutrients among the many trace elements in soils.

Plants may take up trace elements that they don't need — but that we humans do. The trace elements iodine, fluorine, selenium, cobalt, arsenic, lithium, chromium, silicon, tin, and vanadium, for example, are considered to be essential for animals and humans but not for plants. Brazil nuts usually contain large amounts of selenium, which has no known nutritional value to plants but which is an important antioxidant for human health. The level of selenium in plants varies due to the selenium content in the soil.

Because they are derived from natural sources, many organic fertilizers contain an abundance of trace elements, including important plant micronutrients. Synthetic fertilizers, on the other hand, often contain just nitrogen, phosphorus, and potassium, so they don't replenish or enhance the other nutrients and trace elements. Researchers still have much to discover about soil and the interplay among minerals, organic matter, soil life, and plant health, so it makes sense to choose fertilizers and other soil additives that supply a broad range of nutrients. What's certain is that plant — and human — health depends on healthy soil.

For more on plant nutrients and building soil fertility, see Chapter 5. Look in Chapter 6 for a rundown on organic fertilizers.

Soil particles

The kinds and relative amounts of soil particles you have in your garden soil also affect its fertility. Clay and silt soils tend to hold more nutrients than sand soils do because they have larger surface areas and smaller pore spaces. Sandy soil drains quickly, washing nutrients away. Improving soil structure — the way individual soil particles bind together — can improve fertility. For more information on soil texture and structure, refer to "Soil Components: The Nitty-Gritty," earlier in this chapter.

Organic matter

Organic matter is simply plant and animal matter that is dead and in the process of decay. For gardeners, the most important sources include grass clippings, leaves, hay, straw, pine needles, wood chips, sawdust, and manure. As organic matter decomposes, soil microorganisms consume and break down the material, releasing the nutrients it contains into the soil in forms that plants can use.

Want easy and environmentally friendly ways to add organic matter to your garden (a task you should do every year)? Try the following:

- Till compost into vegetable gardens
- Leave grass clippings on the lawn
- Apply wood-chip mulch to perennial beds

As the organic matter decomposes, it feeds soil organisms, which in turn feed plants. Because organic matter is consumed, it must be replaced regularly. For more information on organic matter, see Chapter 5.

Soil pH

The pH of a soil affects the forms that nutrients take. *pH* is the measure of a liquid's acidity or alkalinity. The pH scale runs from 1 to 14, with 7 being neutral. Anything below 7 is considered to be acidic; anything above 7 is alkaline. If soil is too acidic or too alkaline, nutrients may be present but bound up in compounds unavailable to plants.

Depending on the pH of water in the soil, nutrients form different compounds, some of which plants can't use. Phosphorus, for example, becomes less available for plants at a pH level below 6 and above 7. No matter how much phosphorus the soil actually contains, plants can't use it if the pH is too high or low. The ideal soil pH for most plants is between about 6 and 7. Regions with high rainfall tend to have acidic soils; in dry regions, the soil tends to be alkaline. See Chapter 5 to learn how to determine your soil's pH and modify it, if necessary, for optimum plant growth.

pH facts

The pH scale is *logarithmic,* meaning that values increase (or decrease) exponentially. Therefore, a liquid with a pH of 5 is ten times more acidic than one with a pH of 6; a liquid with a pH of 4 is 100 times more acidic than one with a pH of 6.

Soil isn't the only substance that has a pH value. Take a look at the pH levels of these other things:

Substance	pH Level
Lye	13
Ammonia	12
Milk of magnesia	10.5
Baking soda	8.5
Seawater	8.2
Blood (human)	7.5
Tomato juice	4.5
Apples	3.1
Vinegar	2.5
Battery acid	1

Chapter 5

Building Healthy Soil

*O*rganic gardeners know that if you feed the soil, the soil will feed the plants. Healthy soil supports an abundance of living organisms, including bacteria, fungi, and earthworms, that together create a dynamic soil ecosystem. Many synthetic pesticides and fertilizers destroy this subterranean life, and poor gardening practices can damage the soil environment. The organic techniques described in this chapter will help you improve and maintain a healthy soil environment. Don't treat your soil like dirt!

Knowing Your Soil

Like the aboveground ecosystem of your garden, the underground ecosystem in the soil needs nurturing. Soil improvement isn't a one-time deal; it's an ongoing process of promoting the beneficial organisms your plants depend on.

In the wild, soil life is sustained and nutrients are recycled through natural processes. Microorganisms, earthworms, and other *decomposers* feed on organic matter and transform the nutrients it contains into forms that plants can use. The process is a slow, steady, ongoing one: Plants grow, die, and decompose; the cycle continues.

If you maintain tidy perennial beds or harvest crops from your vegetable garden, you change this natural dynamic. By raking up fallen leaves or picking produce, you're removing organic matter — and the nutrients it contains — from the garden environment. To keep soil healthy, you must put some back, which may mean mulching flower beds with bark mulch or adding compost to vegetable gardens. Most of the soil-building techniques I discuss in this chapter center on nurturing beneficial soil life and maintaining this dynamic underground ecosystem.

The first step to improving your soil is knowing what kind of soil you have. Different soils have different strengths and weaknesses when it comes to supporting plant life. The proper soil-building techniques depend on your soil's fundamental characteristics, such as its water-holding capacity and pH.

Testing your soil type: Sand, silt, or clay?

So how do you know what type of soil you have? Take a small amount of damp soil in your hand, as shown in Figure 5-1, and rub a pinch of it between your thumb and index finger. If the soil feels gritty, it's mostly sand; if it feels slick and slimy, it's mostly clay. If you can form a cylinder, but the material starts to crumble as you roll it, it's mostly silt.

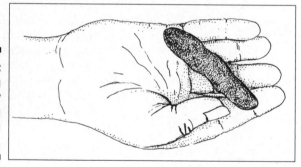

Figure 5-1:
Testing your soil by squeezing a clump in your hand.

For a more accurate measurement of the amounts of clay, silt, and sand in your soil, use the jar test. Here's how:

1. **Collect soil from several places in your garden and mix the samples thoroughly.**

2. **Measure 1 cup of the mixture and remove stones and debris.**

3. **Place the soil in a narrow glass jar (such as a pint canning jar), then fill the jar about two-thirds full of water.**

4. **Seal the jar, and shake it vigorously to mix the contents. Set it down, and start a timer.**

5. **After one minute, measure and mark the level of settled soil. This layer is sand.**

6. **Measure again in two hours, and subtract the sand layer to find the amount of silt.**

7. **After several days, measure again, and subtract the sand and silt to find the amount of clay.**

8. **Divide the height of each level by the total height of the settled soil, and multiply by 100 to find the percentage of each component.**

   If the total settled soil is 6 inches high and the sand portion is 3 inches, for example, the sand content is 50 percent ($3 \div 6 \times 100 = 50\%$)

Testing for drainage

Knowing how well your soil drains helps you determine what to plant, or if you need to take steps to improve drainage. Sometimes, drainage conditions are obvious. Puddles in your lawn a day or two after heavy rains indicate poor drainage, for example. But a layer of clay may lurk underneath a loamy or sandy soil, causing water to linger in otherwise well-drained soil. So before you plant, especially trees and shrubs, dig a hole to see what lies beneath the surface.

Here's how to check for *percolation,* or soil drainage:

1. **Dig a hole 1 foot in diameter and 1 foot deep.**

2. **Fill the hole with water.**

3. **Time how long it takes for the water to drain.**

If the water drains out within 10 minutes or less, your soil drains too fast and probably dries too quickly. In well-drained soils, the water drains within 10 to 30 minutes. If it drains within four hours, the drainage is okay for most plants. If it takes more than four hours, the soil is poorly drained.

Use this information to choose the most appropriate plants for your soil. Keep in mind that adding organic matter, such as compost, to the soil can improve the drainage of both sandy and clayey soils (see "Adding Organic Matter: The Soul of the Soil," later in this chapter).

Testing for pH and nutrients

You need to know your soil's pH and nutrient levels. The *soil pH* measures the alkalinity (sweetness) or acidity (sourness) of the soil. It's important to know whether your soil is acidic (below pH 7 on a scale from 0 to 14) or alkaline (above pH 7), because some nutrients are available to plants only within a specific pH range.

A simple rule is that if your plants are growing, flowering, and fruiting well, the nutrient levels are fine. A high or low pH or unbalanced nutrient levels, on the other hand, can result in yellow, stunted, and unproductive plants. Unhealthy plants are more prone to insects and disease attacks, translating into more work for you and less satisfaction from your garden. That's not what you want!

Testing on your own or sending a sample to the lab

Home test kits give you a basic pH reading and an estimation of the major nutrients in your soil. Nurseries and garden centers sell test kits ranging from extremely simple to elaborate. The more sophisticated tests cost more but give you more accurate results.

You can also send a soil sample to a lab for testing. The nutrient level and pH test results are more accurate and detailed than those provided by home kits. In addition, testing labs can look for things that home kits can't, such as organic matter and micronutrients, as well as heavy metals and other industrial residues. (Soils near heavily traveled roads or on old industrial sites can contain chemicals and metals that you may want to know about before planting a vegetable garden.)

Lab reports also offer specific recommendations about which nutrients to add to your soil (and in what quantity) for your plants' optimum growth. Many state-university extension services offer free or low-cost soil test kits. To find the extension office nearest you, consult the U.S. Department of Agriculture's Cooperative State Research, Education, and Extension Service Web site at www.csrees.usda.gov/Extension.

The soil ecosystem changes constantly, so a soil test is just a snapshot of your soil at the time you gather the sample. Although the soil pH and many nutrient levels are relatively stable, other nutrient levels (such as nitrogen) can change forms depending on precipitation, temperature, and crop cover. Use your soil test results as guidelines, but focus on building a healthy ecosystem rather than on simply adding nutrients.

Your soil's pH results

Most plants grow best in a pH range between 6 and 7, with 6.5 to 6.8 considered ideal. Some plants, however, such as blueberries and rhododendrons, like a highly acid soil (pH below 5), so you may need to adjust the pH to individual plants.

Generally, soils in areas with low rainfall often are alkaline; those in high-rainfall areas usually are acidic because rain leaches calcium from the soil. To paint a broad stroke, if you live east of the Mississippi River, you probably have acidic soil; if you live in the arid Western states, your soil is probably alkaline. Testing your soil to be sure is a good idea, however.

Nutrient test results

A soil test also shows the quantities of soil nutrients that are available to plants, especially the three nutrients that plants use in the greatest amounts: nitrogen, phosphorus, and potassium. Soils also contain many other nutrients, such as magnesium and calcium, that plants need in smaller amounts. If any nutrient is insufficient, plants don't grow to their maximum potential.

Soil test recommendations may not follow organic principles. They may suggest, for example, that you add specific synthetic fertilizers to boost certain nutrient levels. You may need to look for organic alternatives to provide these nutrients.

Adjusting your pH

If your soil is too acidic, you'll need to add lime to raise the pH. The term *lime,* or *limestone,* refers to crushed calcium carbonate (calcite or calcitic limestone) rock. Soils that test low in magnesium benefit from dolomitic limestone (calcium–magnesium carbonate). The finer the dust, the faster it dissolves and begins to raise soil pH.

Look for pelleted lime, which consists of very finely ground limestone formed into easy-to-apply pellets. Avoid slaked or hydrated lime, which acts so quickly that it can harm soil life. How much lime you need to add depends on the type of soil you have and its current pH. The soil-testing lab will make a specific recommendation based on that information.

If you have alkaline soil, applying sulfur will lower the pH. Usually, the best product to use is 100 percent finely ground sulfur, sometimes called elemental sulfur. Soil bacteria convert sulfur to sulfuric acid, which lowers the soil pH. Again, soil-testing lab results offer guidelines.

When adding lime or sulfur to your soil, be sure to wear gloves and a dust mask, because the material can be very dusty and irritating if inhaled. You can spread the material by hand or use a drop spreader made to spread grass seed on a lawn. In the garden, work the lime or sulfur into the top few inches of soil with a rake or shovel after spreading.

Don't expect results from the addition of lime or sulfur right away. Most limestone or powdered sulfur products take a few months to react with the soil enough to change the pH to the desired levels — another good reason to prepare your soil a season before you plan to plant.

Adding Organic Matter: The Soul of the Soil

"Organic matter" is the mantra of the organic gardener and farmer. It's the soul of the soil and a universal component of healthy earth. Organic matter basically is dead plant and animal stuff: grass clippings, leaves, hay, straw, pine needles, wood chips, sawdust, manure, and anything else that used to be alive. It's a miracle worker that improves soil in several vital ways:

- **Feeds microorganisms and other soil life:** Beneficial bacteria, protozoa, fungi, beneficial nematodes, and other soil microbes consume organic matter (and one another) and excrete that matter in a form plants can use for growth. Earthworms, beetles, and other creatures also eat organic matter and tunnel through the soil, creating beneficial air spaces and excreting nutrients.

- **Decreases harmful disease organisms:** Beneficial microbes prey on and control harmful, plant-damaging nematodes and fungi.

- **Improves the soil structure:** Organic matter helps sandy soils stick together better and hold water and nutrients. It also helps open spaces between small, sticky clay particles so that clay soil drains better and contains more oxygen.

- **Increases reserve of soil nutrients:** Soil microbes store nutrients in their bodies; they release those nutrients as they die or are consumed by other microbes. The more microbes the soil contains, the more nutrients it can store.

Add organic matter to your plantings any time you can, whether you use straw mulch between vegetable garden beds, compost around perennial flowers, or bark mulch around trees or shrubs.

If you mix uncomposted, carbon-rich materials such as sawdust or straw into the soil, you'll get a flurry of microbial activity. As the organisms reproduce in response to the influx of food, they tie up other nutrients, especially nitrogen. Plan to wait at least a month before planting; otherwise, your plants may show signs of nutrient deficiency. After the microbes do their work decomposing the carbon-rich material, they die; then the nitrogen and other nutrients tied up in their bodies return to the soil and become available to plants again. Carbon-rich materials applied on the surface of the soil as mulch decompose slowly and won't tie up nutrients.

One of the end products of organic matter decomposition is *humus,* a chemically stable material that contributes to good soil fertility and structure. Humus is a sticky, shapeless substance in which no identifiable organic matter (leaves, stems, and so on) is present. The actual properties of humus are still a bit of a mystery to soil scientists, but they agree that it is an important part of a healthy soil ecosystem. Humus helps soil particles stick together to form aggregates and acts like a sponge to absorb and hold water and nutrients. People sometimes use the terms *humus* and *organic matter* interchangeably, or describe good soil as humus, but technically, humus is just one component of healthy, biologically active soil.

Sometimes, even the healthiest soil can't provide all the nutrients garden plants need, and a boost of fertilizer is called for. For information on buying and using organic fertilizers, turn to Chapter 6.

Dung ho!

If you're not yet a connoisseur of manure, think of it as processed organic matter that has already begun decomposing. It does wonders for soil health and plant growth. You can add the droppings of different farm (and sometimes wild) animals to your garden, giving the soil all the benefits of organic matter plus a boost of nutrients. Like a fine wine, however, manure is best when it's aged before using.

Fresh manure contains concentrated nitrogen. It may be too potent for tender plants and can "burn" roots — similar to the way that a too-concentrated solution of synthetic fertilizer can burn roots. Let manure age for six months to a year before using it, or compost it for faster results (see "Compost: The prince of organic matter," later in this chapter). Some garden resources refer to aged manure as well-rotted manure, which is the same thing.

Table 5-1 shows animal manures that you may find locally or bagged at your garden center, along with their relative nutrient values (dry weight) of nitrogen, phosphorus, and potassium, as well as some additional comments.

Table 5-1	Common Animal Manures	
Animal	*Percentage N-P-K*	*Tips*
Chicken	3-1-1	Strong smell. Don't use fresh on young plants.
Cow	3-0.5-2	Can be very moist.
Horse	2.5-0.5-1	May contain lots of weed seeds.
Llama, alpaca	4-0.6-2	Compost before using.
Rabbit	5-3-2	Strong smell. Compost before using.
Sheep	3.5-0.5-2	Mild smell.

If you live near a zoo, you may have access to the manures of wild animals, such as elephants and giraffes. You can also use water from your freshwater aquarium or pond.

Keep these rules in mind when using manures:

- ✔ **Select manure from the oldest pile at the farm.** Many farm manure piles contain lots of additional organic matter, such as sawdust from horse or chicken bedding. Manure mixed with bedding and aged for a year or more can be used directly on your garden.

- ✔ **Use bagged manures.** Bagged products usually are composted and ready to use. If you need lots of manure, however, buying bags can be costly.

- ✔ **Avoid cat, dog, pig, and human manures.** These substances can carry diseases that affect humans.

- ✔ **Apply composted manure annually.** In general, add a 2- to 3-inch layer of manure to garden beds and around perennial plants at least once a year. If you want to use fresh manure, add it to your garden in the fall (or whenever you can leave that part of the garden unplanted for six months or so), and mix it into the soil so it can slowly decompose.

A few people have become ill after handling fresh manure. Wear gloves and shoes when working with raw manure, and wash your hands and clothing afterward to be on the safe side. If the manure is dry and dusty, wear a dust mask. The National Organic Program rules state that raw animal manure must be composted or incorporated into the soil at least 120 days before the harvest of a crop whose edible portion has contact with the soil (such as root and leafy crops). Some experts recommend avoiding the use of uncomposted manure on edible crops.

Green manures and cover crops

Another great way to get organic matter into your garden is to grow your own. *Green manures* are plants that you grow specifically to cut down and mix into the soil to add organic matter and nutrients.

Although the terms are sometimes used interchangeably, *green manure* usually refers to crops that are planted during the regular growing season specifically to add organic matter and nutrients, and *cover crop* refers to plants grown during the dormant season — winter in most regions; summer in hot, dry climates — to help prevent erosion, loosen compacted soil, and control weeds, besides adding organic matter.

In addition to providing these benefits, green manures and cover crops do the following:

- ✔ **Maintain high levels of soil microorganisms:** When the plants are incorporated into the soil, they feed the essential microbes that make nutrients available to plants. The plant residues also provide surfaces on which the microbes can live.

- ✔ **Attract beneficial insects:** Some green manures and cover crops, such as clover and buckwheat, have flowers that beneficial insects love. These insects help with pollination and pest control in your garden.

The best type of plant for your green manure or cover crop depends on what you're trying to accomplish, your climate, and the planting time. Plants that are often grown as green manures or cover crops include legumes, such as clover, vetch, cowpea, and fava bean; grasses, such as winter rye, wheat, oat, and barley; and buckwheat.

 Farm supply stores usually offer a good selection, and the proprietors can suggest the best ones for gardens in your region. Mail-order catalogs offer the widest selection, but even small garden centers may sell the most common ones. Consult the package or catalog description for the amount of seed you need to sow per square foot.

Planting green manures

Using green manures is an ideal way to prepare the soil in new garden beds or beds that you intend to leave fallow (unplanted) for the growing season. Rototill the area, broadcast the seed, and let the green manure crop grow through the gardening season. At the end of the growing season, before the plants go to seed, mow the area and rototill to incorporate the material into the soil. Don't let the plants produce mature seed if you want to prevent plants from returning next season. The garden will be ready for fall planting, or you can sow a fall cover crop. Buckwheat is a popular green manure because it grows quickly in summer.

Planting cover crops

Plant cover crops after the harvest when garden beds would otherwise be bare. Plant seeds a month or more before your dormant season. (Sow seeds in fall in the North, early summer in the Deep South and Southwest.) The seeds will sprout, begin to grow, and then slow down during the dormant season. When temperatures moderate, the plants grow again.

Winter rye, barley, and wheat are good choices for winter cover crops in areas where winter is the dormant season. In hot, dry climates in which summer is the dormant season, good choices are buckwheat and cowpeas. A few weeks before planting, mow the cover crop, till it into the soil, and allow the plant matter to begin decomposing.

Compost: The prince of organic matter

The best and most refined of organic matters is *compost,* which is organic matter and/or manures that have decomposed until they resemble loamy soil.

Whether you make your own compost (see the "Compost Happens: Making Your Own" section, later in this chapter) or buy it ready-made, you can add finished compost to the garden or around plants at any time. I pile a 2- to 3-inch layer annually around my plants and on my garden beds.

Why not just add raw organic matter to your garden instead of composting it? When you compost the materials first, the final product is uniform in color, nutrients, and texture; is odor free; and contains fewer viable weed seeds and potential disease organisms (depending on how it was composted). Your plants will be happy with you for treating them so well.

As gardeners have become more aware of the value of compost, more sources of it have become available. You can buy compost in bulk (back the truck right up) or bagged, depending on where you live. The following sections explain these options. For many gardeners, making their own compost is the best solution. For information, head to the section "Compost Happens: Making Your Own."

Buying bagged compost

Bagged compost is the easiest form to buy, especially if you have a small yard or container garden. Look for the words "certified organic," the "OMRI Listed" seal, or some other indication that the contents are approved for organic growing and don't come from contaminated sources, such as sewage sludge. (OMRI — the Organic Materials Review Institute, or OMRI — certifies products that meet the National Organic Standards. Find out more in Chapter 2.)

Buying compost in bulk

For larger quantities of compost, buy in bulk. The price is less in quantity, and you can check the quality of the compost as well. Many private companies, municipalities, and community groups make and sell compost. Often, they even deliver the compost to your yard for a fee.

Use these tips to evaluate bulk compost:

- ✔ **Consider the source.** Before buying the compost, ask about the primary, organic-matter sources that were used to make the compost. Compost made from yard waste (leaves and grass clippings) is considered to be the safest and best. Other compost may contain ingredients that had contaminants, such as herbicides from agricultural crop residues and heavy metals from municipal wastes, which may affect the growth of your plants or accumulate toxins in your soil. Ask if the finished product is tested for contaminants.

- ✔ **Look at the color and texture.** Finished compost should look dark and have a crumbly texture without any large pieces of undecomposed organic matter, such as branches or pieces of wood.

- ✔ **Squeeze it.** If water oozes out when you squeeze a handful of the material, it's too wet; if it blows away easily, it's too dry.

- ✔ **Give it a whiff.** The smell should be earthy, without a strong ammonia or sour smell.

Compost Happens: Making Your Own

Making your own compost is probably the simplest way to ensure high-quality compost and save some money. The process really isn't as complicated as you may think; the many commercial composting bins and containers on the market make composting a mess-free, hassle-free process.

When you make compost, you create a pile of material to be composted, mix the materials thoroughly at the correct ratios of carbon (brown stuff) and nitrogen (green stuff) — explained in detail in "Maintaining proper ratios," later in this chapter — and keep the pile watered just enough to keep it moist but with enough air to breathe. Using this method, you can enjoy finished compost a month or two after you start.

Why not just pile the material in the backyard somewhere and let it rot on its own? A pile just thrown together and not maintained may dry out too much for microbes to flourish, or it may stay so wet that the wrong microbes take over. Anaerobic bacterial thrive in saturated conditions, and their presence results in a slimy, sour-smelling pile. Anaerobes don't produce as much heat as aerobic bacteria (see the following section), so they won't kill the weeds and pests, and the pile will take much longer to decompose.

Getting your compost pile started

A well-constructed and well-maintained pile provides the proper amount of water and oxygen for aerobic bacteria, which are the best decomposing microbes; they work quickly, generating heat as a byproduct of their activity. This heat helps material break down quickly and kills many diseases, insects, and weed seeds. Containing your compost pile makes it look neater, helps you maintain the correct moisture, and prevents animals from getting into it.

Here's what you need to know to build a good compost pile:

1. **Choose a shady location that's out of the way but still within view so that you don't forget about the pile.**

   The soil under the site should be well drained.

2. **Make (or buy) a bin.**

   You can build your own (see Figure 5-2) or buy a commercial home composting unit, like those shown in Figure 5-3.

3. **Add dry materials.**

   Add a 6-inch layer of dry (brown) organic matter — such as hay, straw, old leaves, or sawdust — to the bottom of the container.

4. **Add fresh materials.**

   Add a 2- to 3-inch layer of fresh (green) organic matter — such as grass clippings, manure, table scraps, or even high-nitrogen fertilizer such as cottonseed meal — on top of the dry layer. For advice on choosing your ingredients, go to "Choosing materials to compost," later in this chapter.

5. **Keep adding these layers, watering each one as you go, until the pile is 4 to 5 feet tall and fills the bin.**

   A smaller pile won't heat up well enough to break down the materials, and a larger pile can be difficult to manage.

6. **In two days, mix the layers thoroughly.**

   Particle size should be varied; smaller particles hasten decomposition.

7. **Cover the pile with a tarp to keep rain away and preserve moisture.**

   If the pile gets too soggy or too dry, it won't heat up.

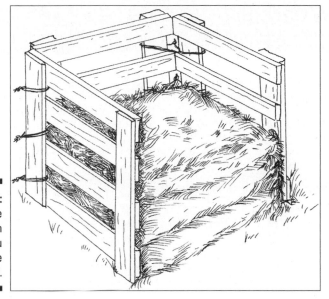

Figure 5-2:
A simple
wooden
bin you
can make
yourself.

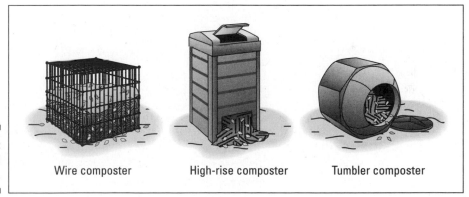

Figure 5-3:
Commercial
composters.

Wire composter   High-rise composter   Tumbler composter

Keepin' it cookin'

The pile will start to cook within a week. Now you need to keep it cooking. After all, a hot pile is a happy pile. Here's the procedure:

1. **Keep the pile moist by watering it periodically.**

   Dig into the pile about 1 foot to see whether it's moist. If not, water the pile thoroughly, but not so much that it's soggy.

2. **Turn the pile when it cools down.**

   Using a garden fork, remove the outside layers and put them aside. Remove the inside layers into another pile and then switch. Place the outside layers in the center of the new pile and the inside layers along the outside of the new pile. Loosen any matted clumps.

3. **Let it cook again.**

   How hot it gets and how long it cooks depend on the *C/N ratio,* or *carbon-to-nitrogen ratio,* of materials in the pile and whether you have the correct moisture levels. For information on C/N ratios, see "Maintaining proper ratios," later in this chapter.

4. **When the pile is cool, turn it again.**

   You should have finished compost after two to three turnings. The finished product should be cool and crumbly, with a dark color and earthy smell.

Sometimes, a compost pile never heats up, smells bad, or contains pieces of undercomposed materials. Chances are that one of the following conditions occurred:

✔ The pile was too wet or dry.

✔ You added too many carbon materials and not enough nitrogen materials.

✔ The pieces of material were too big or packed together. Shred leaves, branches, and pieces of wood to help them decompose more quickly.

✔ The pile was too small.

You can find lots of compost aids on the market. *Bioactivators* — packages of concentrated microbes — are among the most popular because they can speed the decomposition process. These microbes occur naturally, however, and many are already present in a well-constructed compost pile.

Choosing materials to compost

What you put in the compost pile is up to you; just remember that it needs to be from an organic material. Here's a short list of possibilities:

✔ Hay, straw, pine needles, leaves, yard trimmings, and weeds

✔ Kitchen scraps (eggshells, old bread, and vegetable and fruit scraps)

✔ Manure (except dog, cat, pig, or human)

✔ Sawdust and wood chips

✔ Shredded newspaper

Avoid adding the following to your compost bin:

- ✔ Kitchen scraps containing meat, oil, fish, dairy products, and bones (They attract unwanted animals, such as rats and raccoons.)
- ✔ Weeds that have gone to seed or that spread by their roots, such as quack grass
- ✔ Diseased or insect-infested vegetable or flower plants
- ✔ Herbicide-treated grass clippings or weeds
- ✔ Dog, cat, pig, or human feces

Maintaining proper ratios

In composting corners, you often hear about the *C/N ratio* or *carbon-to-nitrogen ratio.* All organic matter can be divided into carbon-rich (brown stuff) and nitrogen-rich (green stuff) materials. Using the right mixture of brown to green stuff when building a compost pile encourages the pile to heat up and decompose efficiently.

Table 5-2 shows which common compost materials are high in carbon and which materials are high in nitrogen. Notice that the soft, fresh materials, such as fresh grass clippings, tend to be higher in nitrogen than hard, dry materials, such as sawdust. Mix these materials to form a pile with an average C/N ratio of 25:1 to 30:1, and you'll be well on your way to beautiful compost. *Note:* Use the ratios in Table 5-2 as guidelines. Actual ratios vary depending on the sources of the materials and other factors.

Speaking of sources, make sure that your compost materials haven't been contaminated with pesticides or other chemicals.

Table 5-2	Carbon/Nitrogen Ratios of Various Materials
Material	*C/N Ratio*
Fresh alfalfa hay	18:1
Grass clippings	19:1
Old manure	20:1
Fruit and vegetable scraps	25:1
Cornstalks	60:1
Dried leaves, straw	80:1
Newspaper	170:1
Fresh sawdust	500:1
Wood	700:1

Quick and easy compost recipes

To make the most compost in the shortest time, try some of these proven recipes. For each recipe, mix the ingredients thoroughly, and follow the directions in "Keepin' it cookin'," earlier in this chapter. Depending on the weather and compost ingredients, you should have finished compost within one to two months.

✔ **Recipe 1:** Use 4 parts kitchen scraps from fruits and vegetables, 2 parts chicken or cow manure, 1 part shredded newspaper (black ink only), and 1 part shredded dry leaves.

✔ **Recipe 2:** Use 2 parts kitchen scraps, 1 part chicken manure, and 1 part shredded leaves.

✔ **Recipe 3:** Use 2 parts grass clippings, 1 part chicken manure, and 1 part shredded leaves.

Turning Your Soil

Whether to use a rotary tiller is an ongoing philosophical debate among gardeners, with promoters and detractors arguing the issue. Rotary tillers, often called *tillers* for short, are machines with blades or *tines* that chop into the soil, churning (or *tilling*) it and blending everything in the top 6 to 12 inches of soil. Following are some of the factors to consider and arguments on both sides of the fence:

✔ Tilling is an easy way to incorporate soil amendments, such as lime, compost, and green manure crops into the soil.

✔ Tilling turns weeds under, facilitating their decomposition. But it can also bring weed seeds to the surface of the soil, where they can germinate readily. It can also chop and disperse roots of perennial weeds, facilitating their spread.

✔ Tilling can kill some insects and diseases that may be lurking around the soil surface. But it can also kill earthworms and other beneficial soil creatures.

✔ Tilling makes for a clean garden bed that's easy to plant. But it can also damage soil structure, increasing the risk of creating a poorly drained and hard-to-work soil, especially if the area is tilled when the soil is still too wet.

✔ Tilling hastens the breakdown of desirable organic matter, so you have to add organic material more frequently and in greater quantities.

✔ Tilling promotes erosion, especially when you're gardening on a slope or in a windy area.

✔ Repeated tilling can create a compacted layer just below the tilled layer.

An alternative to tilling that's easier on the soil and gives you more exercise is using a turning tool such as a garden fork, shovel, or U-bar (shown in Figure 5-4). These tools work especially well in small, raised beds that don't have a lot of earth to turn. A few weeks before planting, add any compost or amendments, and use these tools to turn the soil over. Then rake the bed smooth, and plant to your heart's content.

If you have a large garden or are breaking new ground, a powerful tiller can save time and effort. To minimize damage, till as little as possible, using hand tools to do the rest of the work.

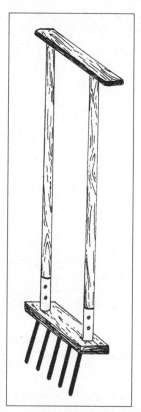

Figure 5-4:
A U-bar tool.

No-till gardening

Because tilling can be so disruptive to the soil ecosystem, some gardeners use a no-till system. If you're patient, you can create a garden without disturbing the soil at all by using sheet composting. Follow these steps:

1. **Cut existing vegetation close to the soil line.**

2. **Cover the area with layers of newspaper or cardboard, and begin adding layers of organic matter, using the same ratios suggested for compost piles.**

3. **Continue adding layers to a depth of a foot or so.**

4. **Cover the entire area with a few inches of straw.**

5. **Wait.**

   In six months to a year, depending on the climate and time of year, you should be able to dig through the pile into the native soil and begin planting.

Maintain your no-till garden by keeping unplanted areas covered with a thick layer of organic mulch.

Raised beds

A *raised bed* is soil that has been mounded to form a large flat surface. Raised beds are commonly used in vegetable gardens, but the principles apply to other types of plantings too. These structures offer many advantages, especially if you have poorly drained or clayey soil:

- ✔ **Faster soil drainage:** Water drains quickly from the loose, mounded soil.

- ✔ **Faster soil warmup in the spring:** Drier soil warms more rapidly than water-saturated soil.

- ✔ **Prevention of soil compaction:** Because you don't step on raised beds, the soil doesn't compact as much, and the roots grow better.

- ✔ **Concentration and conservation of fertilizer and water in the growing zone:** Materials are applied only to the beds, rather than broadcast over the entire garden, including paths.

- ✔ **Efficient and more productive plants:** More ideal growing conditions allow you to space plants a little closer together than normal, thereby reducing watering and weeding.

You can build two types of raised beds: contained and freestanding. *Contained* raised beds have permanent walls around them made of wood, bricks, or stone. These beds look neat and tidy and are good for permanent plantings. *Freestanding* raised beds don't have walls made from other materials, so you can modify their shape and size.

Limit the width of raised beds to 3 to 4 feet so that you can reach in to tend plants without stepping on the soil. The height of raised beds is up to you; a height of 6 to 12 inches provides all the benefits listed in this section.

You can make a raised bed by raking existing soil into a mound or by bringing in extra topsoil. When you have the bed, amend the soil with compost each year to replace nutrients removed by harvesting. Work the compost into the top 12 inches of soil with a garden fork, and smooth the top of the bed with a garden rake, as shown in Figure 5-5.

Figure 5-5:
Rake the soil flat and smooth on top of raised beds before planting.

Chapter 6

Using Organic Fertilizers

*P*lants need nutrients to grow; flourish; and fend off pests, diseases, and environmental stresses. Giving them the nutrients they need is key to successful organic gardening. Healthy soil that contains plenty of compost or organic matter goes a long way toward providing essential nutrients for plant growth, but your plants may still need additional nutrients to grow to their full potential. In this chapter, I give you the lowdown on *organic fertilizers* — those derived from natural plant, animal, and mineral sources — and how to use them.

Fertilizers 101

In contrast to soil amendments that improve the overall soil environment, fertilizers are formulated to provide specific plant nutrients in specific amounts.

It's a myth that all plants need repeated fertilizing throughout the growing season. Plants growing in healthy soil — soil that has the proper pH and is amended regularly with organic matter — may thrive just fine without supplemental feeding. Trees, shrubs, and perennials especially adapt well to slow, steady growth. The fast growth stimulated by heavy fertilizing, on the other hand, can result in weak, succulent plant tissue that's more susceptible to attack by insects and diseases and to damage from severe weather.

Vegetables often benefit most from fertilizing. We expect these plants — whether they're broccoli or corn or zucchini — to put on fast growth and produce abundantly, and when we harvest, we remove nutrient-rich plant material, so we need to replace those nutrients in the soil. Annual flowers also thrive with supplemental feeding, especially those growing in containers. The continuous flowering we expect from our petunias and impatiens requires a reliable supply of nutrients.

Garden centers, farm stores, and catalog suppliers offer fertilizers in so many forms that you may get confused about which ones to choose. Make your decision based on the cost of the actual nutrients, the ease of application, and how quickly you want the nutrients to become available to the plants.

Organic versus synthetic fertilizers

Organic fertilizers generally come from plants, animals, or minerals. Most organic fertilizers contain a broad range of nutrients, including important trace elements; many add organic matter to the soil and enhance the soil ecosystem. By contrast, synthetic fertilizers have specific chemical formulations and often contain only three nutrients: nitrogen, phosphorous, and potassium. These products don't do anything to enhance soil life, and they don't add organic matter.

Organic fertilizers have other benefits over synthetic fertilizers for both soil and plants:

- ✔ They release their nutrients more slowly in the soil, when the plants need them, so they last longer.

- ✔ The nutrients are contained in complex molecules that won't leach away with the first rain.

- ✔ They are less likely to burn the young roots of seedlings. Synthetic fertilizers are made from mineral salts that can kill roots as well as soil microbes if applied improperly.

- ✔ They enhance soil health by nurturing (or at least not harming) the soil microbes that help make soil nutrients available to plants.

In general, organic fertilizers are a kinder, gentler way to give plants the nutrients they need.

Fast release versus slow release

Applying nutrients in a form that plants can use immediately may seem logical, but often, that strategy isn't the best one. The nutrients in fast-release, or highly soluble, fertilizers are ready to use as soon as you apply them. The problem is that plants may not be able to use all the nutrients right away, so any excess nutrients can leach away or run off, possibly leading to stream or groundwater pollution. Later, when the plant is ready to use the nutrients, they're gone.

Most organic fertilizers provide a slow, steady supply of nutrients. Often, the nutrients are bound in organic molecules that require the ongoing action of soil microbes to release them. This process gives plants a limited but steady supply of nutrients, mimicking nature's processes. (Many fertilizer manufacturers are now creating slow-release formulas of synthetic fertilizers. Sometimes, these fertilizers are bound into little pellets that dissolve slowly in the soil. Although they're a step up from fast-release synthetic fertilizers, these fertilizers don't offer all the benefits of organic alternatives. They still may contain only nitrogen, phosphorous, and potassium, for example, and they do nothing to improve the soil environment.)

Some organic fertilizers are relatively fast-release. Liquid seaweed/fish emulsion blends, for example, contain a supply of readily available nutrients. They're perfect when plants need an extra boost, and they contain a broad range of trace elements too. Slow-release organic fertilizers such as rock powders, on the other hand, break down slowly in the soil environment, releasing their nutrients over months or years.

Before adding fertilizer, take a soil sample to a soil-testing lab or use a home test kit to find out the soil pH and to see exactly which minerals your plants need and in what quantities. Even if your plants show signs of a nutrient deficiency, your soil may need a pH adjustment instead of fertilizer (as discussed in Chapter 5). Also note that some plants have special pH and nutrient requirements. Check the plant descriptions in Part IV to find out more.

The big three

Nitrogen, phosphorous, and potassium are the three nutrients plants need in the largest quantities; they're sometimes referred to as the *primary* nutrients. They each play a critical role in plant growth and development. Healthy, fertile soil naturally contains these three elements, and plants can easily take them up. But if your soil is deficient or if you're growing vegetables, fruits, or other demanding crops, you may want to supplement the soil's nutrients with fertilizers.

Complete fertilizers contain nitrogen (N), phosphorous (P), and potassium (K), but don't let the term *complete* fool you. It doesn't mean that the fertilizer has all the nutrients that plants need — just that it contains three of the major ones. (In case you're wondering, the scientific symbol for potassium, K, comes from the Latin word *kalium*.) Bags of complete fertilizers are labeled with three numbers, such as 5-3-3. Each number represents the percentage of N, P, and K in that bag, in that order, as measured by weight. A bag of 5-3-3 fertilizer, then, contains 5 percent nitrogen, 3 percent phosphorous, and 3 percent potassium.

You need to know the actual percentages of nutrients in the bag because a soil test often recommends pounds of actual N, P, or K to add to your garden. To determine the amount of each nutrient in the bag, multiply the weight of the bag (say, 20 pounds) by the percentage of each nutrient — for example, 20 pounds × 5% (.05) = 1 pound of nitrogen. If the soil test recommends 2 pounds of actual nitrogen per 100 square feet, you want to evenly distribute two 20-pound bags of this 5-3-3 fertilizer over each 10-x-10-foot section of garden.

Nitrogen (N)

Nitrogen is responsible for the healthy green foliage of plants, as well as protein and chlorophyll development. (*Chlorophyll* is the pigment that makes plants green and is a vital component of photosynthesis.) Nitrogen moves easily in the soil and leaches out rapidly, especially from sandy soils and in high-rainfall areas or irrigated gardens.

Plants use lots of nitrogen during the growing season, so nitrogen is commonly the most deficient element. If you add too much nitrogen, however, plants have dark green, leafy growth but less root development and delayed flowering or fruiting. Also, pests may target the overly vigorous growth stimulated by excess nitrogen. Symptoms of nitrogen deficiency include slow growth and yellowing leaves, especially in older foliage.

Phosphorous (P)

Plants need phosphorus for strong root growth; fruit, stem, and seed development; disease resistance; and general plant vigor. Phosphorous doesn't move in the soil as easily as nitrogen does, so you don't have to add it as frequently.

Depending on where you live, your soil may have plenty of phosphorous, but that nutrient may be unavailable to plants. Phosphorus availability depends on soil temperatures, pH range, and the soil levels of other nutrients (such as calcium and potassium). Maintain the soil pH between 5 and 7 to keep phosphorous available. Work phosphorous-rich fertilizers into the soil around the root zone at planting time to make the nutrient readily accessible to plant roots. Deficiency symptoms include stunted plants with dark green foliage, reddish-purple stems or leaves, and fruits that drop early.

Potassium (K)

Potassium, sometimes called *potash,* is essential for vigorous growth, disease resistance, fruit and vegetable flavor and development, and general plant function.

Potassium doesn't move around in the soil, so work the fertilizer into the root zone. Potassium also breaks down slowly, so you won't need to add it often. Annual applications of organic matter may supply enough potassium, but a soil test is the surest way to determine need. Avoid adding too much potassium fertilizer because it can make other nutrients (such as magnesium) unavailable.

Deficiency symptoms include yellow areas along the leaf veins and leaf edges, crinkled and rolled-up leaves, and dead twigs. Fruit trees growing in potassium-deficient soils may have poorly developed or bland-tasting fruit. In conifers, the needles on the tree become dark blue-green and then turn yellow to reddish brown. (Note that some conifers, mainly pines, normally shed older, yellow needles.) Florida palms are especially prone to deficiency of this nutrient: Their leaves develop yellow to orange spots on the oldest foliage first, and then the leaf edges turn brown and die.

Secondary nutrients

Calcium, magnesium, and sulfur are called *secondary* elements. They're essential not only for plant growth, but also for adjusting and maintaining soil pH — the measure of acidity and alkalinity of the soil (see Chapter 5). These nutrients are also vital to plant functioning, and excessive or deficient levels can upset plants' ability to use other nutrients in the soil.

Although it's rare for home garden soils to be deficient in these nutrients, keep your eye out for these deficiency symptoms:

- ✔ **Calcium:** Calcium-deficient plants may have twisted, dark green new leaves and leaf-tip burn. Flowers may have weak stems, and fruit may develop rotten spots on the bottom (opposite the stem end).

- ✔ **Magnesium:** Magnesium-deficient plants have curled leaf edges and discolored older leaves.

- ✔ **Sulfur:** Sulfur deficiency results in slow growth and small, spindly plants.

Limestone, which contains calcium, and dolomitic limestone, which contains calcium and magnesium, are used to raise the pH of acid soils toward neutral, where most plants grow best. In alkaline soils, sulfur helps lower the pH to the optimum level.

Micronutrients

The essential nutrients that plants need in the smallest quantities are called *micronutrients,* and they include iron, manganese, boron, copper, zinc, molybdenum, chlorine, and nickel. Fortunately, organic matter usually supplies adequate amounts of these nutrients, because adding too much of any one of these micronutrients can cause more problems than adding none at all.

Micronutrient deficiency is often hard to spot because plants vary in their specific needs and symptoms. Too little iron, for example, can cause blueberry leaves to turn yellow between the veins; too little boron can cause black spots on beet roots.

If your plants have a micronutrient deficiency, the best solution may be to adjust the pH to the level that those specific plants prefer rather than to apply micronutrient fertilizers. Blueberries, for example, require acidic soil; at a pH of 4.2 to 5, the plants usually can take up all the iron they need from the soil. If blueberry plants show symptoms of iron deficiency, check the soil pH, and adjust it if necessary. Beets, on the other hand, prefer a soil pH between 6.5 and 7. If the pH is too low or too high, they can't take up the boron they need. It's better to adjust the pH than to add boron-rich fertilizers, because too much boron can harm other types of plants.

It pays to research the plants you're growing so that you can provide them the basic growing environment they require. You'll save time, aggravation, and money spent on unnecessary — and possibly detrimental — micronutrient fertilizers.

Some fertilizers contain *chelated* micronutrients. In the process of chelation, the nutrients are chemically bound to other molecules so that the plants can absorb them more easily. Usually, chelated micronutrient fertilizers are used to provide a quick, short-term fix for mineral deficiencies.

Application methods

Application methods simply come down to spraying, spreading, or sprinkling. Here's how to apply some common types of fertilizer:

✔ **Granular:** Among the most common and easily applied forms, granular fertilizers are also among the most economical. Sprinkle by hand or broadcast them with a lawn spreader around plants or over the lawn. Many organic fertilizers come in granular form.

✔ **Powder:** Some fertilizers, such as limestone and rock powders, are so finely ground that they readily blow in the wind. When applying them in your garden, choose a windless day, and wear a dust mask. As an alternative, look for pelletized forms of these fertilizers.

Granular and powder fertilizers take time to break down and release their contents to the soil and plants, so apply them a few weeks before planting vegetables and flowers, and use them as long-term sources of nutrients for trees, shrubs, lawns, and perennials. Generally, the smaller the particles, the more quickly the fertilizer becomes available to plant roots.

✔ **Liquid:** Liquid fertilizers give plants a quick nutrient boost. Common liquid fertilizers include fish emulsion and seaweed extract, as well as homemade "tea." (You can find a recipe for manure and compost teas in the sidebar "Tea, anyone?" later in this chapter.) Liquid fertilizers are good candidates for *foliar feeding*, that is, being applied directly to plant leaves.

To apply nutrients during the growing season, *side-dress* plants by applying granular or liquid fertilizer to the soil about 6 inches from plant stems. For even faster results, apply liquid fertilizers directly to plant leaves (called foliar feeding). Mix foliar fertilizers with water with neutral pH (7.0), and apply only when air temperatures are below 85 degrees Fahrenheit. One or two side dressings or foliar feedings during the active growing season should be plenty for most garden vegetables and flowers. Container-grown plants may need monthly fertilizing for best growth.

Types of Organic Fertilizers

Commercially formulated fertilizers list specific nutrient levels on the package, but bulk products, such as compost and manure, have widely variable contents. The nutrient levels I mention for each fertilizer type in this section are approximate, because levels vary somewhat depending on the product and supplier.

Plant-based fertilizers

Fertilizers made from plants generally have low to moderate N-P-K values, but their nutrients quickly become available in the soil for your plants to use. Some of them even provide an extra dose of trace minerals and micronutrients. The most commonly available plant-based fertilizers include the following:

- ✔ **Alfalfa meal:** Derived from alfalfa plants and pressed into pellet form, alfalfa meal is beneficial for adding nitrogen and potassium (about 2 percent each), as well as trace minerals and natural growth stimulants. Roses in particular seem to like this fertilizer; they benefit from up to 5 cups of alfalfa meal per plant every ten weeks, worked into the surface of the soil. Add some to your compost pile, too, to speed the decomposition process.

- ✔ **Compost:** As I discuss in Chapter 5, compost is beneficial mostly for adding organic matter to the soil. Although it supplies some nutrients, its most important roles are enhancing soil life and helping make nutrients available to plants.

- ✔ **Corn gluten meal:** Derived from corn, this powder contains 10 percent nitrogen fertilizer. Apply it only to actively growing plants, because it inhibits the growth of seeds. The manufacturer recommends allowing one to four months after using this product before planting seeds, depending on the soil and weather conditions. Use it on lawns in early spring to green up the perennial grasses and prevent annual weeds like crabgrass from sprouting.

- ✔ **Cottonseed meal:** Derived from the seed in cotton bolls, this granular fertilizer is particularly good at supplying nitrogen (6 percent) and potassium (1.5 percent). Look for organic cottonseed meal; traditional cotton crops are sprayed heavily with pesticides, some of which can remain in the seed oils.

- ✔ **Kelp/seaweed:** Derived from sea plants, this product comes in liquid, powder, and pellet forms. Although kelp/seaweed fertilizer contains only small amounts of N, P, and K, kelp adds valuable micronutrients, growth hormones, and vitamins that help increase yields, reduce plant stress from drought, and increase frost tolerance. Apply it to the soil or as a foliar spray.

- ✔ **Soybean meal:** Derived from soybeans and used in pellet form, soybean meal is prized for its high nitrogen (7 percent) content and is used as a source of phosphorous (2 percent). Like alfalfa meal, it is particularly beneficial to nitrogen-loving plants, such as roses.

- ✔ **Humus:** When looking at organic fertilizer products, you'll invariably come across those containing humus, humic acid, or humates. *Humus* is a stable end product of organic-matter decomposition that's believed to increase microbial activity in soil, improve soil structure, and enhance the root development of plants. Although it doesn't necessarily add nutrients directly, humus may help plants take up the fertilizers you apply. If you add compost to your garden regularly, you're already adding humus, so it's probably not worth purchasing it. If you're not using compost, it may be a useful amendment.

Other plant-based organic fertilizers include cocoa meal (may be toxic to pets), coffee grounds, molasses, and peanut meal.

Animal-based fertilizers

Whether by land, by sea, or by air, animals, fish, and birds all provide organic fertilizers that can help plants grow. Following are some of the most commonly available kinds:

- **Manures:** Animal manures provide lots of organic matter to the soil, but most have low nutrient value. A few, such as chicken manure, do have high available nitrogen content. In general, use only composted manures, because fresh manures can burn tender roots. You can find much more information on manures and the many available types in Chapter 5.

- **Bat/seabird guano:** Yes, this product is what it sounds like — the poop of bats and seabirds. Guano comes in powdered or pellet form and is high in nitrogen (10 to 12 percent). Bat guano provides only about 2 percent phosphorous and no potassium, but seabird guano contains 10 to 12 percent P, plus 2 percent K. The concentrated nitrogen in these products can burn roots if they're not used carefully. Use them to make manure tea, as described in the sidebar "Tea, anyone?" They tend to be more expensive than land-animal manures.

- **Blood meal:** It's a bit gruesome, but blood meal is the powdered blood of slaughtered animals. It contains about 14 percent nitrogen and many micronutrients. Leafy, nitrogen-loving plants such as lettuce grow well with this fertilizer. Reportedly, blood meal also repels deer (but may attract dogs and cats).

- **Bonemeal:** A popular source of phosphorous (11 percent) and calcium (22 percent), bonemeal is derived from animal or fish bones and is commonly used in powdered form on root crops and bulbs. It also contains 2 percent nitrogen and many micronutrients. It may attract rodents.

- **Fish products:** Fish byproducts make excellent fertilizers, and you can buy them in several forms:

  - **Fish emulsion** is derived from the fermented remains of fish. This liquid product can have a fishy smell (even the deodorized version), but it's a great complete fertilizer (5-2-2) and adds trace elements to the soil. When mixed with water, it's gentle yet effective for stimulating the growth of young seedlings.

  - **Hydrolyzed fish powder** has higher nitrogen content (12 percent) than fish emulsion; it's mixed with water and sprayed on plants.

  - **Fish meal,** which is high in nitrogen and phosphorus, is applied to the soil.

  Some products blend fish with seaweed or kelp (refer to "Plant-based fertilizers," earlier in this chapter) for added nutrition and growth stimulation.

Other animal-based organic fertilizers include crab meal, dried whey, earthworm castings, feather meal, and leather meal.

TIP

Tea, anyone?

You can use animal manures and compost to make liquid fertilizers called *manure tea* and *compost tea*. The brewing process yields nutrients that are readily available for plant use, and the teas are gentle enough to use on young plants and to spray on plant foliage for a quick boost. Here's how to make manure or compost tea:

1. Place a shovelful of aged manure and/or compost in a burlap bag (or other porous cloth bag), and secure the top.

2. Submerge the bag in 10 to 15 gallons of water, and let it steep for one week or until the liquid takes on the color of strong brewed tea.

3. Pour off the liquid, and dilute it until it's the color of weak brewed tea.

4. Use the diluted tea to water around plants.

5. Dilute it again to half strength for use on young seedlings and as a foliar spray.

Using composted human waste (euphemistically called *night soil*) to fertilize gardens has been a common practice in countries such as China for generations. In many Western countries, our version of this practice is using composted sewage sludge as fertilizer. Modern sewage treatment plants, however, receive waste from many sources, including industries. Although sludge has fertilizer and soil-building value, sewage sludge is *not* generally considered to be an organic fertilizer, because it may contain toxic heavy metals that accumulate in the soil. Although you can buy granular fertilizers made from sludge, organic gardeners generally avoid them.

Rock on with mineral-based fertilizers

Most rock fertilizers decompose slowly into soil, releasing minerals gradually over a period of years. Organic gardeners use many different minerals to increase the fertility of their soils, but fertilizing with minerals is a long-term proposition. Because some of these products take months or years to break down fully into forms that plants can use, one application may last a long time. Following is a list of rock powders, the nutrients they supply, and application tips:

- **Chilean nitrate of soda:** Mined in the deserts of Chile, this highly soluble, fast-acting granular fertilizer contains 16 percent nitrogen. It's also high in sodium, though, so don't use it on arid soils (in which salt buildup is likely) or on salt-sensitive plants. Because it is so fast-acting, this product can harm soil life; certified organic farms may use it to supply only 20 percent of a crop's nitrogen.

✔ **Epsom salt:** Epsom salt helps tired feet — and it's a fertilizer too! Containing magnesium (10 percent) and sulfur (13 percent), Epsom salt is a fast-acting fertilizer that you can apply in granular form or dissolve in water and spray on leaves as a foliar fertilizer. Tomatoes, peppers, and roses love this stuff! Mix 1 tablespoon of Epsom salt in a gallon of water, and spray it on plants when they start to bloom.

✔ **Greensand:** Mined in New Jersey from 70-million-year-old marine deposits, greensand contains 3 percent potassium and many micronutrients. It's sold in powdered form. Greensand breaks down slowly, so it's used to build long-term reserves of soil potassium.

✔ **Gypsum:** This powdered mineral contains calcium (20 percent) and sulfur (15 percent). It adds calcium to soil without raising the soil pH. Some gardeners claim that it helps loosen heavy clay soils.

✔ **Hard-rock phosphate:** This mineral powder contains 20 percent phosphorous and 48 percent calcium, which can raise soil pH; avoid it if your soil is already alkaline. It breaks down slowly, so use it to build the long-term supply of phosphorous in your soil.

✔ **Soft-rock phosphate:** Often called *colloidal phosphate,* soft-rock phosphate contains less phosphorus (16 percent) and calcium (19 percent) than hard-rock phosphate, but the nutrients are in chemical forms that plants can use more easily. This powder breaks down slowly, so one application may last for years in the soil. It also contains many micronutrients.

✔ **Limestone:** This mined product has various nutrient levels, depending on its source. It's used primarily to raise pH. *Calcitic* limestone is high in calcium carbonate (usually above 90 percent). *Dolomitic* limestone contains both calcium (46 percent) and magnesium (38 percent). These powders are often available in easier-to-spread granular forms. Conduct a soil test (see Chapter 5) for pH and for magnesium to find out which kind of lime, and how much, to add to your soil.

✔ **Rock dusts:** These powders, which are mined from various rocks, often contain few major nutrients but are loaded with micronutrients and other essential elements that plants need in small quantities. One dust, called Azomite, supplies more than 50 trace minerals; another, granite dust, breaks down very slowly and contains about 3 to 5 percent potassium plus trace elements. Use these products as supplements in regular soil-building and fertility programs.

✔ **Sul-Po-Mag:** Also known as K-Mag, this mineral source provides plants readily accessible potassium (22 percent), magnesium (11 percent), and sulfur (22 percent). Use it to add magnesium to high-pH soils without raising the pH.

✔ **Sulfur:** This yellow powder contains 90 percent elemental sulfur, which is used not only as a nutrient for plant growth, but also to lower the pH. Go easy on the application, however, because overuse can decrease soil-microbe activity.

Finding a Sustainable Source

Organic gardeners striving to build a sustainable landscape must take into account the sources of the materials they use. Many organic fertilizers and soil amendments are bulky and heavy, and some are shipped hundreds or thousands of miles to reach garden centers. Consider the amount of nonrenewable petroleum needed to transport these products.

Start your search for fertilizers in your own backyard and neighborhood. You may be able to satisfy all your plants' nutrient needs by using green manures and homemade compost, and by finding sources of fertilizer close to home: coffee grounds from local coffee shops, for example, and waste from various manufacturing processes such as breweries and dairy processors. If you live near an ocean, seaweed (rinsed of salt) may be an option.

You can find most of the fertilizers discussed in this chapter in local garden centers and home-and-garden supply stores. If you can't find what you want, here are some of my favorite mail-order companies:

- ✔ **Dirt Works,** 1195 Dog Team Road, New Haven, VT 05472; phone 877-213-3828; Web site www.dirtworks.net.

- ✔ **Fedco Seeds,** P.O. Box 520, Waterville, ME 04903–0520; phone 207-873-7333; Web site www.fedcoseeds.com.

- ✔ **Gardener's Supply Co.,** 128 Intervale Rd. Burlington, VT 05401; phone 800-876-5520; Web site www.gardeners.com.

- ✔ **Gardens Alive!,** 5100 Schenley Place, Lawrenceburg, IN 47025; phone 513-354-1483; Web site www.gardens-alive.com.

- ✔ **Harmony Farm Supply & Nursery,** 3244 Highway 116 North, Sebastopol, CA 95472; phone.707-823-9125; Web site www.harmonyfarm.com.

- ✔ **Peaceful Valley Farm & Garden Supply,** P.O. Box 2209, 125 Clydesdale Court, Grass Valley, CA 95945; phone 888-784-1722; Web site www.groworganic.com.

- ✔ **Worm's Way,** 7850 N. State Road 37, Bloomington, IN 47404; phone 800-274-9676; Web site www.wormsway.com.

For a longer list of suppliers plus a wealth of other information, check out the Organic Trade Association Web site at www.ota.com. This important organization's Web site also lists state organic farming associations and much more.

Part III
Managing Pests

The 5th Wave   By Rich Tennant

"I used an all natural method of pest control, but we're still getting an occasional vacuum cleaner salesman in the garden."

In this part . . .

Just as you expect ants at a picnic, you can count on weeds in a garden and bugs on the plants. But these pests don't have to spoil your fun or your gardening success. Instead of reaching for a pest-killing potion, turn to this part for environmentally safe and effective solutions.

For an overview of organic pest control, look to Chapter 7. You'll learn how to prevent many pest problems and diagnose those that do arise. When you know what's "bugging" your garden, read on to learn about the many organic pest control products.

Chapter 8 is all about insects — good and bad. If you can identify and nurture the good guys, they'll help keep pests in check. Turn to Chapter 9 to learn about diseases and to Chapter 10 for information about animal pests. Weeds can be among the biggest headaches for organic gardeners; Chapter 11 gives you the tools you need to take control.

Chapter 7

Pest Control and Pesticide Safety 101

. . . .

. . . .

Most discussions of garden pests are full of warfare terms such as *battle, enemy,* and *defeat.* It's easy to understand this attitude when you see your rose blossoms ravaged by Japanese beetles or your cabbages full of cabbageworm holes. Then, even the most eco-friendly gardener is tempted to reach for the nearest insecticide! But for organic gardeners, pest management isn't just about killing pests. It's also about taking steps to prevent pest problems and choosing nontoxic pest control methods before resorting to sprays.

This chapter introduces you to integrated pest management and explains how you can use it to create a healthy, productive garden. And because many pesticides — even organic ones — can be harmful if misused, there's a section on using pesticides safely.

Dealing with Pests the Organic Way: Integrated Pest Management

Spraying pesticides to get rid of pests may be satisfying in the moment, but the long-term effects can include poisoning soil and water; creating an unhealthy environment for yourself, your family, and your pets; eliminating beneficial organisms; and wasting money on unnecessary products. Organic gardeners take a different approach: They strive to maintain a healthy balance of organisms, and they treat problems only when treatment is clearly warranted. The goal is to manage pests, not annihilate them.

When it comes to pest management, organic gardeners heed two basic tenets:

- ✔ **Pesticides aren't always the answer:** Organic gardeners consider whether it's really necessary to control the pests they find. A few aphids on your hibiscus aren't likely to cause any major damage if your garden is a haven for beneficial insects that dine on aphids. As a matter of fact, organic gardeners try *not* to eliminate all insect pests, because if all the pests disappear, so will the insects, birds, and spiders that feed on them. By tolerating a small number of pests, you can keep their predators around in case your garden has a sudden pest-population explosion.

- ✔ **Not all problems are pest problems:** Avoid the temptation to assume that all problems are caused by pests. Other factors may be at fault: excessive heat, not enough or too much sun, lack of or too much moisture, herbicide drift, freezing temperatures, hail, wind, air and water pollution, and mower and string-trimmer injury, for example. These problems are especially likely in plants growing in unfavorable environments — shade-loving plants in full sun, for example. Plants stressed by these factors are also more vulnerable to insect and disease attack. Eliminating the environmental stress solves the underlying problem, which in turn may make pesticides unnecessary.

When problems arise in your garden, you need a methodical and environmentally sound way to deal with them. That's where the concept of integrated pest management (IPM) comes in. Although not strictly an organic approach, IPM outlines logical steps that you can use to keep your garden and landscape healthy.

In IPM, farmers and gardeners follow a series of graduated steps, starting with good growing practices and establishing acceptable levels of damage. Control starts with least-toxic methods and moves to more-toxic or invasive steps only when needed.

Start with pest-resistant plants

Plant breeders work constantly to introduce more *varieties,* or plant selections, with characteristics different from those of the original species. One of the most important factors that breeders look for in a variety is *disease resistance* — the ability of a plant to remain unaffected (or only slightly damaged) by a particular disease. Many modern plant varieties resist devastating plant diseases, such as the potato blight that led to the Irish famine of the mid-nineteenth century and the apple scab fungus that disfigures fruits and foliage.

Breeders have introduced resistance to insect pests, too. If squash borers are a problem in your garden, for example, look for squash varieties listed as resistant or tolerant to this common pest. If deer repeatedly ravage your garden, look for plants touted as deer resistant (although deer will eat almost anything if they're hungry enough).

It helps to know which pests are most likely to affect the plants that you want to grow. I mention these potential problems in the plant descriptions in Part IV. Catalog write-ups often mention pest resistance as well, because it's a good selling point.

Make the garden less inviting to pests

Your garden may be rolling out the red carpet for pests unintentionally. Most pests are opportunists that take advantage of weak or stressed plants and take up residence where the eating is easy.

Put the right plant in the right place

Choose the best location for each plant, taking into account its particular needs for water, sunlight, and nutrients. Plants emit a chemical signal when they are weakened, and pests get the message loud and clear. Although experts continue to debate the degree to which stress affects human health, in the plant kingdom, no such quibbling exists. When plants don't get their needs met, they become stressed, and the longer the stressful situation continues, the greater the decline in plant health. Even a healthy plant can fall prey to pests, of course, but it will be better able to survive the attack than a plant that is already weakened by stress.

Confuse pests with mixed plantings

Insects have chemical receptors that help them zero in on their favorite foods, making your 50-foot row of squash plants look like a giant billboard flashing the message "Squash plants here; come and get 'em!" So plant smaller patches of each crop and scatter the patches throughout the garden or yard. Combining different types of plants in your garden instead of planting each crop in large blocks makes it harder for insects to find all the plants. Diseases are less likely to spread in mixed plantings, too.

Keep time on your side

Young plants, with their tender, succulent stems, are easy prey for pests. As plants mature, their tissues become more fibrous and less prone to damage. Use this to your advantage: Plant a crop so that it's growing strong by the time the predominant pest insect hatches. In some regions of the North, for example, early plantings of corn can avert corn earworm and fall armyworm, which migrate from the South and arrive in the North later in the season. You can also time your plantings for a couple of weeks *after* the pest eggs hatch so that the young larvae will die from lack of food before your plants are up and growing.

Pests emerge earlier in the season if local temperatures have been high and later if temperatures have been cool. Farmers and other agriculture experts use these temperature records to predict the *emergence* of key pests — when the pests emerge from their winter hiding places. Talk to local growers and your local extension office about pest-emergence predictions and recommended planting times. Some extension Web sites offer weekly pest-emergence updates during the growing season.

Avoid opening wounds

Like an open skin wound, damaged bark or foliage provides an ideal entry point for diseases and insects. Even torn leaves caused by a thunderstorm provide an opening for invasion. Although you can't lessen the ravages of weather, you can protect plants from mechanical damage caused by string trimmers and rotary tillers. Encircling trees, shrubs, and perennial beds with a wide band of mulch helps keep power equipment away from the plants. Make sure that mower blades are sharp so that they make straight, clean cuts, rather than leaving ragged edges on grass blades.

Rotate crops

Moving each vegetable crop to a new location in the garden every year can help foil pests. At the end of the season, many insects leave eggs or pupae in the soil near their favorite host plants. If the young emerge in the spring and find their favorite food there again, they will have a feeding frenzy. If, on the other hand, their food is now on the other side of the garden, they may starve before they find it. Also, diseases can build up in the soil to infect the same crops each year. Crop rotation is easy with annual flowers and vegetables that you replant each year.

Don't overfertilize

It's easy to end up applying too much fertilizer in the mistaken belief that if a little is good, more is better. Unfortunately, excess nutrients are as harmful to plants as nutrient deficiency is. Excess nitrogen, for example, causes stems and leaves to grow rapidly, producing juicy growth that's a delicacy for aphids and spider mites because it's easy to puncture and consume. An imbalance of phosphorus encourages egg production in spider mites.

The easiest way to prevent nutrient imbalances is to provide nutrients in the form of organic matter and organic fertilizers, which make nutrients available gradually. Refer to Chapter 6 for information on organic fertilizers.

Clean up debris

Fallen leaves, dropped fruit, and other debris can harbor insects and diseases, so during the season and at season's end, pick up and destroy fallen fruit, and turn plant residues into the soil or add them to your compost pile. Dispose of diseased plants in the trash or add them to a compost pile that reaches 160 degrees Fahrenheit. Cultivate the soil to work in any debris that could shelter insects through the winter. Cultivating also exposes hiding pests to cold temperatures and predators.

Invite beneficial organisms

Spiders, birds, toads, and a whole host of insects prey on garden pests. Make your garden and landscape an attractive place for them, and they'll do much of your pest-control work for you. Find out more about beneficial organisms later in this chapter.

Identify culprits

Even the most accomplished and diligent organic gardeners face pest problems. The first step in managing a specific pest is identifying it.

Just because an insect shows up on a plant doesn't mean that it's a pest. Ants and spiders, for example, may take up residence on plants, but they're generally harmless. Always take the time to research pests and make a positive ID. Use a field guide to identify insects so that you don't inadvertently destroy beneficial ones.

If you think your plant is being attacked by a pest, give the entire plant a once-over. Where is the damage? Is it all over or confined to one area? Is discoloration all over the plant, or does the damage occur in distinct locations? What type of plant is it? Are nearby plants also affected? If so, what types?

Next, examine the plant up close. Check the tops and bottoms of leaves, looking for insects, caterpillars, and egg masses. Look carefully at the new growth — a common gathering place for insect pests. As you touch the leaves, watch for scurrying or flying insects. Examine the plants at different times of day, and try to catch the pests in action. Jot down notes, take photos, or collect samples so that you can research possible culprits.

Do you see lesions on the leaves? A disease may be the cause. Note the size, color, and shape of the spots. Look at the spots' margins. Are the edges of the spots distinct or fuzzy? Note whether the lesions are on the top or bottom of leaf surfaces, and whether they're all over the plant or confined to one area. Are the flowers and fruit also affected?

If only the lower leaves on a plant are chewed, you may be dealing with an animal pest. Different animals can reach different heights, so measure how high up the plant the damage occurs.

Chapters 8 through 11 identify common garden pests, so you may find your culprit in those chapters. If not, consult regional field guides and extension publications. After you identify the pest, learn as much as possible about when it appears and on which plants, what factors contribute to its abundance, what kind of damage it does, and at what life stage it is easiest to control. Controls are more effective if you catch the pest in the most vulnerable part of its life cycle.

Establish thresholds

One of the most challenging steps in integrated pest management is determining whether control of a pest is really necessary. Resist the temptation to react immediately with a pesticide; analyze the situation first. Do you see a few scattered insects or a cast of thousands? After you spot a particular pest or symptoms of its damage, examine similar plants in your garden to determine the extent of the population and its distribution. Is the damage located on the leaves of a plant you'll be harvesting in a week or two? Is the damage purely cosmetic? Control measures may not be warranted.

In IPM, this process is called *establishing damage thresholds,* and it's fundamental to organic gardening. Small populations of pests may not cause enough damage to warrant control, and they may provide a consistent supply of food for the predators that keep them in check. Kill all the pests, and their predators will leave too. When the next population of pests arises, the predators will be gone.

Some pests multiply quickly, however, so keep a close eye on plants so that pests don't get out of hand. Aphids, for example, are remarkably prolific: a single aphid, for example, can produce 5.9 billion offspring in 6 weeks. That's a lot of aphids!

Choose a control method

Once you decide to take action, you need to choose your control method. Organic gardeners use a variety of techniques to manage pests, starting with the least toxic and least disruptive to the garden ecosystem. The following sections provide an overview of the various controls available to organic gardeners. In Chapters 8 through 11, you find more details on controlling specific pests.

Physical controls

One of the simplest ways to keep pests from attacking plants is to keep the two apart. The following control methods involve preventing pests from reaching plants and removing the ones that do take up residence:

- **Barriers:** Use barriers as your first line of defense against pests. They keep pests away from plants before they can do any damage. Fences are the obvious solution for animal pests such as deer and woodchucks. Row covers protect young crops from insect attack. Bird netting keeps birds from eating your berries. The color insert shows barriers in action.

- **Handpicking:** For some gardeners, removing pests, such as Japanese beetles and slugs, by hand is a satisfying endeavor, not to mention an easy, nontoxic solution. For the squeamish, battery-powered, handheld bug vacuums are available.

- **Hosing off:** Small insects such as aphids and spider mites are easily dislodged by a spray from the hose. Often, washing plants every few days is enough to keep these pests in check.

- **Repellents:** You can keep pests at bay by using substances that are unappealing to them. Deer, for example, may avoid trees in which bags of human hair or fragrant soaps are hanging, and neem oil is reputed to repel Japanese beetles. You may need to try several repellents or rotate them to keep pests away.

- **Scare tactics:** Shiny Mylar balloons may frighten birds, at least long enough for you to gather your fruit harvest. Motion detector-activated sprinklers can scare off raccoons, deer, and cats.

- **Trapping:** You can use traps in two ways: set them out to detect the first appearance of a pest so you can start preventive measures, or use them to reduce pest populations. Popular traps include sticky red spheres for apple maggots and hanging traps for Japanese beetles.

Biological controls

Biological controls use living agents to control pests. Although the term can technically refer any organism that kills pests, it most often refers to products containing microscopic organisms (usually bacteria or fungi) that we apply to plants. Larger predators of garden pests, such as ladybugs and toads, are usually called "beneficials" and are addressed in the following section, "The Benefits of Beneficials."

Most organic gardeners are familiar with Bt (short for *Bacillus thuringiensis*), a strain of bacteria used to control pest caterpillars. Other biological controls include milky spore disease and parasitic nematodes, both of which are used to control Japanese beetle grubs. Some of the biggest innovations in pest control are coming in the field of biological controls. Manufacturers have introduced products containing *Streptomyces griseoviridis,* a species of soil bacteria that colonizes roots and helps prevent disease organisms from infecting the plants. In light of recent bans on common synthetic pesticides, we're likely to see more and more biologically based pesticides introduced.

Other controls

A huge range of pesticide sprays and dusts is available to gardeners. Organic growers choose products that are the least toxic and most targeted to the pests they want to control. Insecticidal soap and horticultural oil are two mainstays. Look for more detailed information on pest-control products in Chapters 8 through 11.

The Benefits of Beneficials

Sometimes, the best control is right under your nose. Many familiar garden denizens are voracious eaters of the pests we're trying to control. We just need to invite them to dine. The following sections help you sort out the good from the bad and give you tips for keeping the good guys where you want them: in your garden.

Identifying beneficial insects

Insects that prey on or parasitize insect pests are called *beneficial* insects. Whether you know it or not, you rely on these allies to help keep the insect balance from tipping too far in the destructive direction. If you familiarize yourself with these good guys, you can encourage their presence in the garden and avoid killing these innocent bystanders just because they happen to be the insects you spy on your favorite dahlias.

You can buy many of these beneficial insects from mail-order catalogs to increase your local populations. See the "Sources of beneficial insects" sidebar, later in this chapter.

The following beneficial insects are worth befriending:

- **Big-eyed bug:** These fast-moving, ⅛- to ¼-inch bugs have tiny black spots on their heads and the middle part of their bodies, as shown in Figure 7-1. They dine on aphids, leafhoppers, spider mites, and some small caterpillars. Because these bugs aren't commercially available, look for them on nearby weeds, such as goldenrod or pigweed, and relocate them to your garden.

- **Braconid wasps:** Several species of braconid wasps, shown in Figure 7-2, parasitize pest insects. Both the slender adults and tiny, cream-colored grubs feed on a range of pests, including aphids, cabbageworms, codling moths, and corn borers. Purchase these ⅒- to ½-inch wasps from suppliers and plant some dill, fennel, and other parsley-family flowers to help keep them around. Adults require carbohydrate food, such as the *honeydew* secreted by aphids, tree sap ooze, or flower nectar.

- **Centipedes:** Indoors and out, multilegged centipedes feed on many insect pests. Most species don't bother humans (unless you count the screech with which they are frequently greeted), and while some southwestern species do inflict a temporarily painful bite, none are dangerous. You can't do much to encourage their presence, but if you can leave them alone to do their job, you'll have fewer insects around.

- **Damsel bugs:** These slender, ⅜- to ½-inch bugs have strong-looking front legs. They prey on aphids, caterpillars, leafhoppers, and thrips. Damsel bugs are common in unsprayed alfalfa fields, where you can collect them in a net for relocation to your yard.

- **Ground beetles:** Many beetle species live in or on the soil, where both their larval and adult stages capture and eat harmful insects. They vary in color (black, green, bronze) and in size. Although most live close to the ground, feeding on aphids, caterpillars, fruit flies, mites, and slugs, the 1-inch-long caterpillar hunter beetle climbs trees to feed on gypsy moths and other tree-dwelling caterpillars.

Because these beetles aren't available commercially, the best thing you can do to encourage their presence is to avoid using herbicides and insecticides. Also, learn to distinguish them from unwanted insects. Most of the helpful ground beetles are large, dark, and fast moving. They often have nasty-looking mandibles and eyes on or near the fronts of their heads.

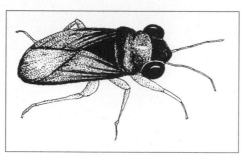

Figure 7-1:
Big-eyed
bug.

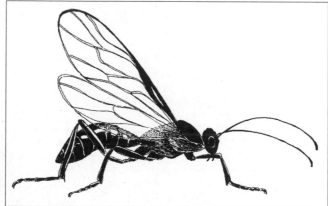

Figure 7-2:
Braconid
wasp.

✔ **Hover flies:** These insects get their name from the adults' habit of hovering around flowers. The adults, resembling yellow jackets, are important pollinators; the brownish or greenish caterpillar-like larvae have an appetite for aphids, beetles, caterpillars, sawflies, and thrips. If you grow an abundance of flowers, you're likely to see hover flies.

✔ **Ichneumonid wasps:** Ichneumonid wasps are valuable allies in controlling many caterpillars and other destructive larvae. The dark-colored adult wasps (see Figure 7-3) vary in size from less than 1 inch to 1½ inches, and they have long antennae and long egg-laying appendages — called *ovipositors* — that are easily mistaken for stingers. The adults need a steady source of nectar-bearing flowers to survive.

✔ **Lacewings:** The delicate green or brown bodies and transparent wings of these ½- to ¾-inch insects, shown in Figure 7-4, are easy to recognize in the garden. Adults live on nectar. The spindle-shaped, alligator-like, yellowish or brownish larvae feed on a wide variety of soft-bodied pests, such as aphids, scale, thrips, caterpillars, and spider mites. Each of the distinctive, pale green, oval eggs sits at the end of its own long, thin stalk on the underside of a leaf. You can purchase lacewings as eggs, larvae, and adults. To keep the welcome mat out for the adults, allow some weeds to flower nearby.

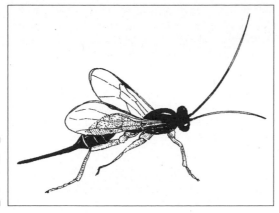

Figure 7-3:
Ichneu-
monid wasp.

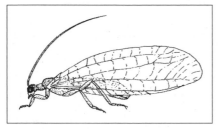

Figure 7-4:
Lacewing.

✔ **Lady beetles:** The convergent lady beetle, also called a lady bug, is what most people think of when they praise lady beetles' appetite for aphids. Both adults and larvae prey on soft-bodied pests, including mealybugs and spider mites. The convergent lady beetle larvae look like small, black, segmented pillbugs with rows of knobby or hairy projections and four orange spots on their backs. (This species is distinguished from her damaging pest cousin, the Mexican bean beetle, by two converging white lines on the *thorax* — the segment between the head and the abdomen. The number of spots varies widely.)

If you plan to purchase and release lady beetles, prevent them from flying away by setting out another food source, such as an artificial yeast/sugar or honeydew mixture, which is available from commercial lady beetle suppliers. See the "Sources of beneficial insects" sidebar, later in this chapter.

✔ **Minute pirate bugs:** These bugs have an appetite for soft-bodied insects, such as thrips, corn earworms, aphids, and spider mites. A single bug can consume 30 or more spider mites a day! The adults are ¼ inch long, somewhat oval-shaped, and black with white wing patches. The fast-moving, immature nymphs are yellow-orange to brown and tear-drop-shaped. You can purchase them for release in your yard.

✔ **Predatory mites:** Similar in appearance to pest mites, predatory mites are tiny (smaller than $\frac{1}{25}$ inch) and quick. They feed primarily on thrips and pest mites, and are widely used to control these insects in commercial orchards and vineyards. They are available to home gardeners as well, from the places listed in the "Sources of beneficial insects" sidebar, later in this chapter.

✔ **Praying mantises:** Because these curious-looking insects eat as many beneficial insects as pest insects, they're not among the most useful of the beneficial insects. Other beneficials that target specific pests usually are more effective.

✔ **Rove beetles:** These beetles have the distinctive habit of pointing their abdomens upward as they walk. Decaying organic matter is their home, where they feed on soil-dwelling insects, such as root maggot eggs, larvae, and pupae (especially those of cabbage and onion maggots). In mild, wet climates, they also eat slug and snail eggs.

✔ **Soldier beetles:** The favorite diet of both the adults and larvae of these common beetles consists of aphids, caterpillars, corn rootworms, cucumber beetles, and grasshopper eggs. The adults, shown in Figure 7-5, are slender, flattened, and $\frac{1}{3}$ to $\frac{1}{2}$ inch long. The larvae are the same shape and covered with hairs. They spend much of their life cycle in the soil, so they will be more prevalent in areas where the soil is undisturbed.

✔ **Spiders:** All spiders are predators, ridding the garden of many common pests. You can provide good habitat for spiders by mulching with hay and straw, which has been found to reduce insect damage by 70 percent due solely to the numbers of resident spiders.

✔ **Spined soldier bugs:** Adult spined soldier bugs dine on the larvae of Colorado potato beetles, Mexican bean beetles, and sawflies, as well as European corn borers, cabbage loopers, and tent caterpillars. The adults, shown in Figure 7-6, resemble tan, shield-shaped stinkbugs with prominent spurs on their shoulders immediately behind the head. They pierce their victims with a harpoon-like mouth. You can purchase them for release in your garden.

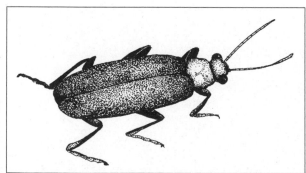

Figure 7-5:
Soldier
beetle.

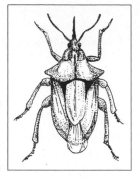

Figure 7-6:
Spined
soldier bug.

✓ **Tachinid flies:** These large flies feed on tent caterpillars, armyworms, corn borers, cutworms, stinkbugs, and other pests. The adult fly is about the size of a housefly and may hover above squash plants in search of prey. It has a bright orange abdomen, black head and thorax, and a fringe of short black hairs on the hind legs. Coriander, coyote brush, evergreen euonymus, fennel, goldenrod, and white sweet clover attract these flies to your yard.

✓ **Tiger beetles:** A variety of brightly colored and patterned, ½- to ¾-inch beetles fall into this group, and they all have distinctively long legs. They feed on a wide range of soil-dwelling larvae. If you use an electric bug-zapper light, you're inadvertently killing these garden allies.

✓ **Trichogramma wasps:** Tiny as pencil points, these parasitic wasps inject their eggs inside the eggs of more than 200 species of moths, and the developing larvae consume the host. Buy these wasps commercially, and release them during their hosts' peak egg-laying times. Suppliers can give you more specific directions on release times.

✓ **Yellow jackets:** I know it's hard to think of these annoying insects as beneficial, but they do help rid your garden of flies, caterpillars, grass-hoppers, and many larvae by taking them home to their young. Yellow jackets are fond of white sweet clover and ivy, so expect to see them near your house if you have either type of plant nearby.

Attracting beneficial insects

You can take important steps to welcome beneficial insects to your yard and encourage those you purchase to stick around:

✓ **Wait to release beneficials until you've seen their favorite prey in the garden.** If beneficials don't find any food in your garden, they move else-where. You can purchase food for lady beetles (from the companies that sell the beetles) to encourage them to stay even after aphid populations decline, for example.

✔ **Grow some plants that attract beneficial insects.** With a constant supply of nectar, adult beneficial insects can live much longer than they would without it. Shallow-throated flowers are easier than deep-throated flowers for many of the tiny beneficials to feed from. Goldenrod is a favorite, attracting more than 75 species of beneficial insects. Include this and other plants from the parsley and sunflower families, such as alyssum, artemesia, aster, coriander, cumin, daisy, dill, Florence fennel, gazania, goldenrod, marigold, sunflower, yarrow, and zinnia.

To make it easier for gardeners to attract beneficial insects, many suppliers offer seed mixtures for plants that provide nectar and pollen for beneficial insects. See the "Sources of beneficial insects" sidebar, later in this chapter.

✔ **Include a diversity of plants in your yard to attract a variety of insects.** Choose a mix of species, including evergreens, and plants of different sizes and shapes. A mixture of trees, shrubs, perennials, and annuals in the yard provides a lot of options for food and hiding places. Try to have something in bloom throughout the growing season.

✔ **Avoid using broad-spectrum insecticides, which kill a wide range of insects, including beneficials.** Even some organic insecticides, such as pyrethrin, are toxic to beneficials. Often, beneficials are even more susceptible to the insecticide than pests are, because as predators and parasites, they must move quickly over leaf surfaces and thus come into contact with insecticides more readily. Many insecticides are also toxic to bees. If you must use a chemical as a last resort, spray only in the evening, when bees have returned to the hive.

✔ **Provide a water source for beneficial insects.** Fill a shallow birdbath or bowl with stones and water, and place it near the garden. Change the water frequently to discourage breeding mosquitoes.

Encouraging other insect predators

Many creatures depend on insects for food, and you can enlist them in your pest-control efforts. Birds, bats, frogs, toads, lizards, and even small mammals can eat surprisingly large numbers of insects. Offer them the habitat they enjoy, and let them get to work:

✔ **Bats:** Bats aren't exactly a welcome sight around most homes, especially if you've ever awakened at night to hear their flapping wings above your head. But bats are often underappreciated. Their steady diet of insects — beetles, moths, and (of course) mosquitoes — makes them worth a gardener's tolerance.

Sources of beneficial insects

Buying bugs through the mail may seem like a strange idea, but gardeners need all the natural help they can get! Contact one or more of these suppliers to find the best beneficial insects for your bug-eat-bug garden. Note that some Web sites offer good color photos of beneficial insects and their prey.

✔ **Gardens Alive!** has been helping home gardeners for years, and its Web site is an excellent reference, complete with photographs of pests, diseases, and controls. For a catalog, phone 513-354-1482 or visit the company online at `www.garden salive.com`.

✔ **Harmony Farm Supply & Nursery** sells a variety of organic gardening and irrigation supplies. For a catalog, call 707-823-9125 or visit the Web site at `www.harmony farm.com`.

✔ **IPM Laboratories** is a great source for gardeners with large acreage or greenhouses. Visit its Web site at `www.ipm labs.com` or call 315-497-2063.

✔ **Peaceful Valley Farm & Garden Supply** offers beneficial insects and far more on its Web site at `www.groworganic.com`. For more information, phone 888-784-1722.

Consider putting up a bat house to help keep bats nearby. Bat houses, which look like birdhouses with entrance slots in the bottom, are available at many garden-supply outlets, including Gardener's Supply Co. (`www.gardenerssupply.com`), Peaceful Valley Farm & Garden Supply (listed in the "Sources of beneficial insects" sidebar), and Bat Conservation International (`www.batcon.org`).

✔ **Birds:** If you've ever watched a mother bird feeding her young, you know that her nestlings are nonstop insect feeders. Granted, birds do snare valuable, soil-enriching earthworms, but they also consume huge numbers of insects. A house wren, for example, can gobble more than 500 beetles, grubs, and insect eggs in an afternoon. Welcome birds to your yard by providing food, such as fruiting trees and shrubs, birdseed, suet, water from birdbaths, and shelter that includes a diversity of trees and shrubs (including evergreens). Put up birdhouses to encourage your favorite feathered friends to raise their families nearby.

✔ **Toads:** If you're lucky enough to have a resident toad in the garden, consider him an ally. He'll consume up to 100 insects — cutworms, grasshoppers, grubs, slugs — every night during the gardening season. He may even hang around for years if you make your yard hospitable. Toads lay their eggs in water, so a water garden or pond will ensure future generations. You can easily provide drinking water by setting a low dish or birdbath on the ground near some tall plants that offer shelter.

✔ **Lizards:** The five-lined skink is common in the eastern United States and eats a variety of insect pests, including roaches, grasshoppers, flies, and grubs. The Mediterranean gecko, another insect-eating lizard, is found in Texas and throughout the southeastern United States. Attract these lizards to your yard by leaving wild areas that include some brush and rock piles.

Using Pesticides Safely

Many gardeners rely on pesticides to achieve beauty and bounty in their landscapes. Although as an organic gardener you'll choose the least toxic controls, you still must follow all the safety precautions recommended on the label when you apply organic products. This chapter outlines important safety information about buying and using pesticides.

Types of pesticides

Pesticide is a catchall term that describes materials used to kill pests. The three most commonly used by gardeners are

✔ **Insecticides,** which are materials used to kill insects

✔ **Fungicides,** to control fungal diseases

✔ **Herbicides,** for killing weeds

Other pesticides include *bactericides* to control bacterial diseases, *molluscicides* to control slugs and snails, and *miticides* or *acaricides* to kill mites.

I may seem to be stating the obvious, but make sure that you're applying the right control for the problem. An insecticide won't control fungal diseases, and vice versa. Some pesticides are nontoxic to all but the intended pest, whereas others affect multiple organisms. Pesticides that kill a wide range of insects are called *broad spectrum;* they should be used only as a last resort, because they kill beneficial organisms as well as harmful ones.

Many people mistakenly believe that *organic* and *nontoxic* mean the same thing, so I must lay this myth to rest. *Organic* simply means that the product came from naturally occurring sources, such as plants, animals, and soil minerals. Some organic pesticides — nicotine, for example — are highly toxic and every bit as dangerous to humans and other animals as they are to insect pests. Whether you grow plants organically or not, use the least toxic pesticides possible.

Active versus inert ingredients

The ingredients in a pesticide that are responsible for killing, repelling, or otherwise controlling pests are called *active ingredients*. The rest of the formulation — up to 99.9 percent — is made up of *inert ingredients*. Inert ingredients are added for a variety of reasons, such as to make the pesticide easier to apply, to help the material cling to leaves, or to improve shelf life.

Manufacturers aren't required to list the individual inert ingredients, but that doesn't mean they aren't toxic. In 1997, the U.S. Environmental Protection Agency began encouraging (but not requiring) pesticide manufacturers to use the term *other ingredients* on their labels because a survey found that consumers assumed "inert" meant "harmless."

Pesticide toxicity

All pesticides are toxic, but some are more toxic than others. *Acute toxins* poison immediately upon exposure. *Chronic toxins* may accumulate in body fat and organs, and reach toxic levels after repeated exposure.

Acute pesticide toxicity is determined by feeding the material to *(orally)* or applying the material to the skin of *(dermally)* laboratory rats, mice, or rabbits, and determining the dosage — milligrams of product per kilograms of body weight — at which 50 percent of the animals die within 14 days. The acute toxicity is expressed as lethal dose, or *LD50*. The lower the LD_{50}, the more acutely toxic the pesticide is. The LD_{50} doesn't measure chronic toxicity. Pesticides are categorized and labeled according to their acute oral and dermal toxicity as follows:

- ✔ **Class I:** The most highly toxic pesticides have an oral LD_{50} below 50 mg/kg or a dermal LD_{50} below 200. Their labels always bear a skull-and-crossbones symbol and the words *DANGER* and *POISON.* A special license is required for their use.

- ✔ **Class II:** Moderately toxic pesticides have oral and dermal LD_{50} levels of 51 to 500 and 201 to 2,000 mg/kg, respectively. Their labels always say *WARNING.*

- ✔ **Class III:** Slightly toxic pesticides have oral and dermal LD_{50} levels of 501 to 5,000 and 2,000 to 20,000 mg/kg, respectively, and their labels must say *CAUTION.*

- ✔ **Class IV:** Considered to be the least toxic, these pesticides have LD_{50} levels above 5,000 mg/kg oral and 20,000 mg/kg dermal, and their labels may say *CAUTION.*

In addition, the lethal inhalation dose is determined by exposing test animals to the chemical dust or vapors, and this toxicity is expressed as LC_{50} (parts per million). Many chemicals are more acutely toxic when inhaled because they enter the bloodstream more quickly.

Toxicity varies from one person to the next and depends greatly on how a person is exposed to the chemical. Some chemicals have low toxicity if ingested but cause severe lung damage if inhaled. Other chemicals cause bodily harm other than acute poisoning. Treat all pesticides with respect, and always read the label completely before using.

Protecting yourself, the plants, and the environment

As an organic gardener, you have already made the commitment to eliminate synthetic chemical pesticides from your garden and yard. Many of the insect, weed, and disease controls that organic gardeners use, however, are still toxic, especially if improperly used. Broad-spectrum botanical insecticides such as pyrethrins — used by many organic growers — if used improperly will harm beneficial insects and aquatic animals, and can injure pets and people. Knowing when, where, and how to apply these chemicals is part of responsible gardening.

Personal safety

Before you grab that spray bottle or can of dust off the shelf and head out to the garden, pause to check your personal attire. No matter how innocuous the pesticide, you must protect yourself from potential harm. Here's what you need:

- **Long sleeves:** Cover your arms and legs completely. If you're spraying trees, wear a raincoat with a hood for extra protection.

- **Shoes:** No sandals, please, and don't forget the socks.

- **Hat:** Your scalp absorbs chemicals easily. Also remember to cover your neck.

- **Gloves:** I use disposable rubber gloves, especially when measuring and mixing concentrated pesticides with water.

- **Goggles:** Eyeglasses aren't enough. Use safety goggles that enclose your eyes and protect them from spray.

- **Dust mask or respirator:** Protect your lungs and sensitive membranes from damage. Use a special respirator with filters (available from garden centers, farm supply outlets, and mail-order catalogs) when spraying pesticides. A dust mask is helpful only when you're applying nontoxic dusts to prevent inhalation.

Other toxic chemicals

Many chemicals — both natural and synthetic — are toxic to one degree or another. The following table shows the oral LD_{50} of some common household and garden chemicals. The lower the LD_{50}, the more toxic the substance. Note the range for some chemicals, which can depend on the sensitivity of different test animals and on the way the pesticide is formulated. *Note:* The ones marked with an asterisk (*) are considered to be acceptable for use in organic gardens.

Chemical	Acute Oral LD50 (mg/kg Body Weight)
Nicotine	10
Copper sulfate	11 (human) to 472 (rats)
Kerosene	50
Chlorpyrifos (Dursban)	96 to 272
Phosmet (Imidan)	150
Ryania	150 (dogs) to 2,500 (guinea pigs)
*Caffeine	200
*Pyrethrins	200 to 2,600
Carbaryl (Sevin)	246
Aspirin	1,200
*Sabadilla	2,500 to 4,000
Table salt	3,320
*Azadirachtin (neem)	3,500
Glyphosate (Roundup)	5,400
*Bacillus thuringiensis	>5,500
*Insecticidal soap	>5,500
*Sulfur	>5,500

Sources: The Extension Toxicology Network (EXTOXNET) and *Ball Pest & Disease Manual,* by Charles C. Powell and Richard K. Lindquist (Ball Publishing).

Most pesticide injuries occur during mixing, while you're preparing to spray. Put on your gear before you get started. Always mix and pour chemicals, including organic pesticides, in a well-ventilated area where accidental spillage won't contaminate or damage food or personal property. Even something as nontoxic as diatomaceous earth can irritate your lungs, and spilled oil can ruin your clothes. Following are other points to keep in mind:

✔ Don't use your kitchen measuring cups and spoons; buy a separate set for garden use.

✔ Clear all toys and other stuff out of the area you plan to spray, including the areas where the spray may drift (check the wind direction).

✔ Don't allow pets or other people into the area while you're spraying, and keep them out for the duration recommended on the product label.

Plant safety

Read the pesticide label carefully, and apply the chemical only to listed plants. Consider weather and overall plant health, too. Some chemicals more easily injure drought-stressed and insect- or disease-weakened plants. High temperatures or intense sunlight can also increase the chance of plant damage.

Relatively harmless pesticides can injure some plants. Horticultural oil, for example, isn't safe to use on Colorado blue spruce and many thin-leafed plants. Protect them from harm if you spray other nearby plants.

Environmental safety

One of the reasons I choose to garden organically is to keep the environment safe for the wild critters that live around me. Some botanical pesticides, such as pyrethrins, are very toxic to fish and beneficial insects. When you apply chemicals, follow the label directions very carefully. Never spray or dump pesticides near bodies of water; never pour them into the sink or down the storm drain. Mix up only as much as you need.

Also check the weather. Don't spray or apply dust in breezy conditions, because the chemical may drift away from the target area and harm nearby plants or animals. If you expect rain, don't bother to apply pesticides that will wash off before doing their job.

Keeping records

Use a calendar with plenty of space on it to write notes and record everything that affects your garden. Seed-planting and first-harvest dates, rainfall amounts, unusual temperatures and weather events, the appearance of pests and diseases — everything goes on the calendar. Also note which fertilizers and pesticides you used and on which plants.

After keeping calendars for a couple of years, you may see patterns emerging that help you anticipate problems and keep them from becoming too troublesome. Good records show you what works and what doesn't, allowing you to make informed changes in your gardening practices. Keeping records is one of the easiest and most important organic gardening practices that you can undertake.

Chapter 8

Managing Insect Pests

*M*ost of the insects in your garden and yard won't harm your plants, but the ones that do are enough to keep you on your toes. As an organic gardener, you've made a commitment to protect the good guys and innocent bystanders from harm while eliminating the bad guys. To do that, you have to know a little about insects themselves and about organic insect-control methods. In this chapter, I describe the major insect pests (as well as nematodes, slugs, snails, and spider mites, even though they're not technically insects) and explain what you can do as an organic gardener to control them all.

Understanding Insects

Each insect has its preferred foods and methods of feeding. Some primarily eat only certain plants; others are less fussy. Some chew only roots or the youngest new leaves; others tunnel through stems or pierce holes in their host and suck plant sap.

Insects also pass through several life stages, each often looking very different from the last. At different stages, they live in different places. A beetle, for example, may spend parts of its life in the soil, on tree bark, and on leaves. In addition, insects are more vulnerable to attack by predators, parasites, or pesticides and traps during some life stages than during others. Knowing how to identify all the life stages gives you more ways to control it. Here's what to look for:

✔ **Eggs:** Each insect species has unique times, places, and methods for laying its eggs. Colorado potato beetles, for example, lay clusters of orange eggs underneath plant leaves. Plum curculios and the apple maggot fly lay their eggs inside fruit.

✔ **Larvae, grubs, nymphs, maggots, and caterpillars:** When the eggs hatch, they become immature insects. This immature stage, during which the insect eats and grows rapidly, is often the most plant-destructive period of an insect's life. Plant symptoms include holes or tunnels in leaves, fruits, bark, and stems, as well as stunted and deformed growth.

The name of this life stage depends on the kind of insect you're describing. Immature moths and butterflies are called caterpillars, for example, whereas young beetles are called grubs.

✔ **Pupae:** Many insects — including beetles, moths, butterflies, and flies — go through a stage between larva and adult when they form a cocoon or hard shell around themselves. They don't eat or cause damage at this stage and don't succumb easily to predators or pesticides. The transformation of a larva into an adult is called *pupating.*

✔ **Adults:** Adult insects are ready to mate and lay eggs. Most have wings and are at their most mobile life stage. Some adult insects, such as thrips, feed on plants by piercing or rasping holes and sucking or sponging up the plant juices. Others, such as Japanese beetles, chew on plant parts. Adult butterflies and moths don't damage plants and actually help pollinate flowers.

Many insects spend part of the year, usually winter, in plant debris and fallen fruit. Sometimes the easiest way to control these insects is to rake up debris thoroughly and destroy it. Other insects need access to their hosts only during a very short period; using barriers and traps at just the right time may prevent them from doing damage or laying their eggs. Get to know your pests, and you may find easy ways to control them.

Managing Insect Pests

Sharing your vegetables, flowers, trees, shrubs, and lawn with insects is a balancing act. On one hand, you want a safe, attractive landscape and a bountiful, pesticide-free harvest. On the other hand, armies of marauding insects and other pests may seem intent on destroying your dreams. What's an organic gardener to do?

The answer is *integrated pest management,* called *IPM* for short. Success with IPM depends on careful and regular observation of your plants, the weather, soil conditions, and other factors that influence plant and insect growth. Refer to Chapter 7 for an overview of how you can use IPM to manage all types of garden pests. In the following sections, I outline techniques and products specifically for controlling insect pests.

Removing pests manually

Getting rid of insects can be as simple as handpicking or even vacuuming them. You can incorporate some of these easy techniques into a stroll around your yard.

- **Handpicking insects:** When I go out to tend my plants, I'm never without a can of soapy water — the future final resting place for any Japanese beetle I encounter. Beetles are as sluggish as I am in the early morning, so they can be easily picked or knocked off your plants into a can. You can make this an after-dinner routine as well, when the beetles have slowed down and settled in for the night. Use this technique on many other insects as well. As an alternative to the catch can, spread plastic under plants and shake the plants to dislodge insects. Then pour the insects from the plastic into a pail of soapy water.

Tiny insects are difficult to pick off, but a little judicious pruning can remove masses of them. Aphids tend to cluster near flower buds and growing tips, so cutting off those portions will help reduce the population and control damage spread. Pick off leaves that have leaf miners and other insects, and remove portions of branches infested with tent caterpillars.

- **Vacuuming the leaves:** Pest insects tend to congregate on the upper portions of plants, whereas beneficials frequently hide on the lower leaves and branches. You can use these tendencies to your advantage by vacuuming the upper leaves with a low-suction vacuum (you don't want to lose the leaves too) whenever you see pests accumulating. Afterward, dispose of the vacuum bag so that insects can't crawl back out.

- **Giving plants a brisk shower:** Simply knocking the insects off can greatly reduce their damage, especially if you spray plants every day or two, before the insects have time to make the journey back up onto the plant. I use this technique on houseplants too. Avoid spraying leaves in the evening, because wet foliage at night can encourage disease organisms to spread.

An estimated 70 percent of all insect pests spend part of their life cycle in the soil, which is why birds flock to bare soil looking for food. Whenever you cultivate the soil, you help bring larvae and eggs to the surface, where they can be picked off by birds and other creatures. Keep in mind that cultivating also warms the soil faster in the spring and encourages insects to emerge from the soil sooner. I let chickens roam free in my gardens after the final harvest and again after turning the soil in the spring. They do an excellent job of cleaning up insects and leftover vegetables.

Barriers, repellents, and traps

Insect pests can't damage your plants if they can't get to them. Block their access with simple but effective barriers around your plants, such as those explained in the following sections.

Particle barriers

Substances made up of fine grains or powders can create a physical barrier between plants and pests.

- **Diatomaceous earth:** Called *DE* for short, this widely used white powder consists of the fossil remains of microscopic water creatures, called *diatoms,* and is mined from areas where ancient oceans or lakes once existed. The particles pierce an insect's exterior cuticle and cause dehydration. The sharp particles also injure and deter slugs and snails. DE kills beneficial as well as harmful insects, so it may not be the best choice in all situations. Apply the dust to damp foliage to control soft-bodied insects, or spread a 6-inch band of DE on the soil around each plant stem to control crawling pests. Some DE products contain non-toxic bait that attracts pests and induces them to eat the dust, which is also fatal. Wood ashes and limestone can have the same effect. These powdery materials work best when dry and need to be reapplied after a rain.

- **Particle films:** Particle films are mixed with water and sprayed directly onto plants. One brand, Surround, is made from very fine kaolin clay, a naturally occurring mineral. Treated plants look like they've been dusted with a fine layer of talcum powder, so this product is best used on vegetable and fruit crops rather than ornamental plantings. The material sticks to insects and discourages them from feeding. At harvest time, the white film is easily washed or rubbed off.

Row covers

These lightweight air- and water-permeable fabrics were developed to raise the temperature around plants and extend the growing season. They can also keep plants relatively safe from insect pests — such as cabbage maggots, Mexican bean beetles, and squash bugs — if you spread them over your plants early enough in the season. If you wait too long before covering your plants, the insects will have a chance to set up housekeeping in the garden, and they'll thrive under the protective covering.

Floating row covers are so lightweight that you can simply drape them loosely over seedlings (to allow room for the plants to grow). Secure the edges in the soil or with boards to keep opportunist insects from slipping in through the sides. You can use light- or medium-weight row covers to form *low tunnels* — row covers supported by hoops (go to the color insert to see a row cover in action).

If you live in a cool climate, you may be able to keep the covers on all season long without overheating your plants; warm-climate gardeners need to remove the covers when temperatures rise. Remove the covers from plants, such as squash, that depend on insects for pollination when the plants bloom.

Cutworm collars

If you've ever come out to the garden and found transplants flat on the ground with their stems chewed off at soil level, you've seen the handiwork of cutworms. Their name is quite descriptive of their damage. These caterpillars emerge hungry from the soil in the early spring, and your plants will be dinner unless their stems are protected. You can make cutworm collars from empty toilet-paper or paper-towel cores, cut into 2-inch cylinders, or from strips of newspaper that encircle the stem completely (but not tightly) and extend 1 inch into the soil. Place the collars around transplants when you put them in the ground.

Tree protectors

Caterpillars and other insects crawl up the trunk en route to the leaves, and crawl back down the trunk to rest or pupate in the soil. Catch them during their travels with strips of cardboard or fabric that encircle the tree and form a barrier. Some insects, such as the codling moth, like to hide under corrugated cardboard, especially in the fall as they prepare for winter. To trap these insect pests, cut old boxes into long strips and wrap the strips around the tree trunk, with the ridges facing the tree. Destroy the infested cardboard strips before spring and replace them with fresh ones.

You can also wrap 18-inch-wide burlap strips, folded in half, around the trunk, with string securing the burlap to the tree at the inside of the fold. Insects become trapped under the fold as they head upward. Even simple wide burlap strips wrapped around the trunk collect some caterpillars underneath. These traps are only a temporary detour for most insects, so you need to check the traps frequently and dispose of the insects.

Copper bands

Copper has the unique ability to repel slugs and snails, whose slimy coatings react chemically with copper, generating a toxic reaction — similar to an electric current — that sends them elsewhere. You can use copper sheet metal to fashion permanent edging around your garden beds, or staple copper-backed paper (available from garden centers) to the sides of wooden planter beds.

You can also make a tree band out of copper. Cut a 3-inch-wide strip of copper sheet metal long enough to encircle the tree trunk. Punch holes in the ends for string to tie the strip together when you wrap it around the trunk.

Repellents

Just like there are tastes most humans don't like, there are substances that insect and animal pests avoid. Like barriers, repellents are a good way to prevent pest problems:

- ✔ **Neem:** Neem does not poison insects outright. Instead, when insects eat the active ingredient, it interrupts their ability to develop and grow to their next life stage or lay eggs. It also deters insects from feeding and is effective against aphids, thrips, fungus gnats, caterpillars, beetles, leaf miners, and others. Amazingly, plants can absorb neem so that any insects that feed on them may be killed or deterred from feeding. Neem breaks down in the presence of sun and soil within a week or so. To discourage insects from eating your plants, spray neem before you see a large infestation.

- ✔ **Citrus oils:** The oils from the skins of citrus fruits kill a broad range of insects on contact. The oils continue to repel pests such as fleas, ants, and silverfish for weeks, and are safe around people and pets. The *active ingredient* — the chemical that does the damage — is d-Limonene; look for it on the label.

- ✔ **Hot pepper wax sprays:** The chemical capsaicin causes the heat in hot peppers and is the active ingredient in these botanical products. In low doses, as in ready-to-use sprays, hot pepper wax repels most common insect pests from vegetables and ornamental plants. It doesn't cause the fruit or vegetables to become spicy hot but stays on the surface of the plant, where it remains effective for up to three weeks. Hot pepper wax is even reportedly effective in repelling rabbits and tree squirrels.

 Avoid using cayenne or other hot pepper powder from your spice rack. If the material gets into animals' eyes, it can cause excruciating pain. Use waxy sprays, which stick to plant material and are more likely to act as deterrents to feeding.

- ✔ **Other plant extracts:** Many herbs, spices, and plants — including tansy, nasturtium, garlic, onion, marigolds, rue, mint, rosemary, sage, and geranium — contain chemicals that repel or kill insects. Garlic is one of the best-known and most-effective extracts against thrips and other leaf-eating insects: The strong odor disguises the true identity of the host plant, so pests pass them by.

Traps

You can use traps in two ways: You can set them out to detect the first appearance of a pest so you can start preventive measures, or you can use them to reduce pest populations. The following sections discuss several common types of traps.

Sticky traps

Wrap a piece of fabric around a tree trunk and paint it with a sticky coating to trap crawling insects. You can make your own sticky coating by mixing equal parts mineral oil or petroleum jelly and liquid dish soap. Or purchase premade sticky substances such as Tanglefoot at hardware stores or garden centers. A sticky substance can damage bark, so always apply it to another material.

You can take advantage of insects' color preferences in making traps. If you have some scrap wood, paint it yellow, cover it with a sticky coating, and place it in the garden to lure aphids, imported cabbageworms, fungus gnats, and several types of flies (including whiteflies). Codling moths prefer white traps. Trap thrips with sticky blue cards. To make cleanup easier, cover the trap with plastic wrap before applying the sticky coating.

Apple maggot traps

Apple maggot traps are sticky traps (see the preceding section) that go a step further by mimicking the color and shape of the apple maggot's favorite fruit. These sticky red spheres lure adult females searching for apples in which to lay their eggs. You can make your own trap by painting any apple-size ball red, covering it with a sticky coating, and hanging it in an apple tree. The larger the tree, the more traps you'll need. Set out the spheres in early to mid-June, just after the petals have fallen.

Pheromone-baited traps

These traps are baited with a *pheromone* — the scent released by a female insect to attract a male of the same species. The artificial pheromone in the trap lures male insects, and a sticky coating or the trap's configuration prevents them from leaving after they realize that they've been hoodwinked. Codling moths, oriental fruit moths, and Japanese beetles are some of the insects easily captured in this type of trap.

Some evidence exists that putting up a Japanese beetle trap can attract more trouble than you bargained for. The beetles move so freely from yard to yard that your trap may solve your neighbors' beetle problems and worsen yours. To avoid being the neighborhood lure, place traps at the edge of your property and buy traps for your neighbors, too! Japanese-beetle control needs to include large areas, such as whole neighborhoods, to be most effective.

Biological controls

Everybody gets sick at one time or another — and that includes bugs. You can help them along the path to their destruction with a variety of infectious microorganisms, or *microbes,* that target specific pests. The beauty of these disease-causing microbes is that they are completely harmless to most beneficial insects, humans, and other animals. Microbes take time to work but often remain active in the environment long after you apply them.

Bacteria

Several insect-infecting bacteria, or *Bacillus* species, that exist naturally in most soils have become important tools in the battle against damaging caterpillars, beetles, and other pesky bugs:

- **Milky spore:** Milky spore disease controls Japanese beetles and other closely related beetles. It affects the soil-dwelling larvae or grubs. After the grubs eat the bacteria, they become ill and stop feeding, dying within days. They often darken in color when infected. When the insects die, the disease organism spreads in the soil, where it can infect other insects.

  It takes several years for the bacteria to spread and achieve good control, however, and they are less effective in very cold winter climates. In warmer climates, one treatment can remain effective for at least ten years. For best results, entire neighborhoods should participate in spreading the milky spore product.

- **Bt:** *Bacillus thuringiensis,* known as Bt for short, infects many insect pests, especially in their larval stages. Different strains or varieties of the bacteria affect different kinds of pests. One of the most widely used products contains the strain Bt kurstaki or Bt aizawai, which infects and kills young caterpillars, including many major pests of vegetables, ornamentals, and trees.

  The strains Bt tenebrionis and Bt san diego infect leaf-eating beetles, such as Colorado potato beetles. The bacteria are most effective against young larvae because the bacteria more easily rupture their stomach linings. Another strain, Bt israelensis, is effective against mosquitoes, fungus gnats, and blackflies.

- **Spinosad:** The active ingredient in this relatively new insecticide is derived from a naturally occurring soil-dwelling bacterium called *Saccharopolyspora spinosa.* It is an effective control for caterpillars as well as for beetles, leaf miners, thrips, Colorado potato beetles, and fire ants.

All bacteria-containing pesticides degrade when exposed to sunlight and high storage temperatures. Also, insects must eat the pesticide to become infected.

Fungi

Many naturally occurring fungi infect and kill insect pests, and you'll likely see new fungal-based insecticides introduced.

- **White muscadine fungus:** One of the most promising fungal-based insecticides for farm and garden use is *Beauveria bassiana,* commonly known as the white muscadine fungus. The fungus lives in the soil and affects aphids, caterpillars, mites, grubs, whiteflies, and others. Insects don't have to consume the fungus; mere exposure can lead to infection. For this reason, avoid using it whenever bees and beneficial pollinators can be affected. It may also be toxic to fish and shouldn't be used around fish-containing waters. To encourage the native *Beauveria* population in your garden, avoid using fungicides.

✔ **Endophytic grasses:** The word *endophyte* literally means *within plants.* In this case, it describes a mutually beneficial relationship between a fungus and a grass; the fungus lives entirely within the grass plant. Some lawn-grass mixes touted as low maintenance include "endophyte-enhanced" species. These grasses tend to be more drought-tolerant and better able to compete with weed species, and they are able to repel insect feeding.

Nematodes

Not to be confused with pest nematodes, *beneficial nematodes* are microscopic, wormlike organisms that live in moist soil. Naturally occurring throughout the world, they prey on many soil-dwelling pests, including ants, fleas, sod webworms, raspberry cane borers, and cutworms. They are especially useful for controlling Japanese beetle grubs. You can purchase beneficial nematodes from garden centers and mail-order suppliers.

Because they're living organisms, nematodes must be stored and applied properly. Beneficial nematodes are most effective in moist soil and at soil temperatures between 60 and 90 degrees. They can be killed by exposure to the sun, so they're best applied in early evening or on cloudy or rainy days when the soil temperature is at least 55 degrees.

Viruses

Two other groups of promising microbes include *granulosis virus* and *nuclear polyhedrosis virus,* which infect many caterpillar pests. Although still unavailable for home gardeners, granulosis virus is proving to be an important tool for commercial orchardists. These viruses can control codling moths, armyworms, gypsy moths, oriental fruit moths, and cabbageworms.

Soap and oil sprays

Insects breathe through pores in the cuticle that surrounds their bodies. If you plug up the pores, the insects suffocate and die. That's where soaps and horticultural oils enter the picture. Disrupt the cuticle with these sprays, and — poof! — the insects can't maintain their internal moisture. Soaps and oils kill a wide range of pest insects but affect beneficial insects, too. Use them with caution to avoid harming beneficial insects.

Horticultural oils

Horticultural oils are made from refined mineral or vegetable oils. Although oils effectively kill any insect that they cover — including eggs, larvae, pupae, and adults — they don't differentiate between good and bad bugs. Horticultural oils come in two types:

✔ **Dormant oil:** Dormant oil is a heavy grade of oil usually used in late winter or early spring to suffocate overwintering insects such as aphids, mites, and scales, including their eggs, on dormant fruit and ornamental trees and shrubs.

✔ **Summer oil:** Lighter oil, sometimes called *summer oil,* is sprayed during the growing season to control aphids, mites, lace bugs, corn earworms, mealybugs, leaf miners, and many others, including tough-to-kill scale insects.

Read labels carefully to make sure that you have the right oil for the job; then mix and spray as directed.

Oils do have several drawbacks. Don't use them when temperatures are likely to rise above 90 degrees Fahrenheit, when plants are suffering from drought stress, or if you have applied or plan to apply sulfur fungicide within 30 days. Oils also remove the bluish waxy coating from Colorado blue spruce, so avoid using it on that species. Follow all precautions on the label.

Some products combine oil with ingredients such as insecticidal soaps or botanical insecticides, which make them even more effective. Oil helps these other ingredients stick to the plant or penetrate the insect's cuticle.

Insecticidal soaps

Insecticidal soaps contain the active ingredient *potassium salts of fatty acids,* which penetrate and disrupt the cuticle that holds moisture inside insects' bodies. When sprayed with soap, many soft-bodied insect pests, such as aphids, dry out and die. Some pests, especially beetles with hard bodies, remain unaffected, however. To make soaps more effective, some products combine soap with pyrethrins, a botanical insecticide that's described later in this chapter.

Insecticidal soap is nontoxic to humans and other animals, and breaks down quickly in the environment. If you use a concentrated product, dilute it with soft water before use for the best effect. Hard or mineral-rich water decreases its effectiveness.

The downside to insecticidal soap is that it also disrupts the waxy cuticle on some plants, making it toxic to young and thin-leafed plants, especially tomatoes. If you aren't sure of the plant's sensitivity to the product, always test it on a leaf or two, and allow a couple of days to pass before spraying a whole plant. Follow the label directions carefully.

Botanicals: Plant-based insecticides

Insect and disease killers that come from plant extracts are called *botanical pesticides* or *botanicals*. Although derived from natural sources, botanicals are not necessarily safer or less toxic to nonpest insects, humans, and animals than synthetically derived pesticides. In fact, most botanicals are broadspectrum insecticides, which kill both good and bad bugs indiscriminately. Some botanicals cause allergic reactions in people; others are highly toxic to fish and animals; and some may even cause cancer.

Use all pesticides, including botanicals, only as a last resort and only after thoroughly reading the label on the package. See Chapter 7 for information on how to use pesticides safely.

Pyrethrins

These insecticidal compounds occur naturally in the flowers of some species of chrysanthemum plants. The toxins penetrate the insects' nervous system, quickly causing paralysis. In high-enough doses or in combination with other pesticides, the insects die. The compound breaks down rapidly when exposed to sun and air, and becomes less effective if stored for longer than one year. Many commercial products contain pyrethrins.

Powerful synthetic compounds that imitate the natural chrysanthemum compounds are called *pyrethroids*. Pyrethroids are not approved for use in organic farms and gardens. Also avoid any pyrethrins that list piperonyl butoxoid on the label. This additive is not approved for organic use.

Although relatively harmless to humans, pyrethrins are highly toxic to fish and bees and moderately toxic to birds. They kill both beneficial and pest insects. To keep bees safe, spray pyrethrins in the evening after bees have returned to their hives for the night, and avoid spraying blooming plants.

Ryania and sabadilla

Ryania and sabadilla are botanical pesticides historically used by organic gardeners to control a variety of insects. Because of their toxicity to beneficial insects, fish, birds, and mammals, these pesticides are becoming increasingly hard to find.

Seek other pest controls before resorting to these substances. Rotenone was once a popular organic insecticide, but because of its extreme toxicity to fish, it has fallen out of favor. Although it may be available from garden and farm suppliers, no rotenone products are approved for organic production.

A Quick Guide to Getting Rid of Common Pests

The following list of vegetable, flower, tree, shrub, and fruit pests includes the worst offenders. Many more insects cause damage, of course, and you can get more information about the ones to watch out for from your local extension office:

- ✔ **Aphids:** These pear-shaped pests, shown in Figure 8-1, pierce holes in plant tissue and suck the juices. Their sizes range up to ⅛ inch, and color varies depending on the species, from black to green, red, or even translucent. Aphids leave behind sticky sap droppings called *honeydew* that attract ants and may turn black if covered with sooty mold. Aphids can proliferate quickly on weakened plants and tend to congregate on the newest leaves and buds. Blast them off with a hose; control them with beneficial green lacewings, ladybugs, or sticky yellow traps; or spray them with insecticidal soap.

- ✔ **Apple maggots:** Slightly smaller than houseflies, these pests spend the winter in soil and then appear in June or July, mainly in northern climates, to begin laying eggs in apples, crabapples, plums, and other fruits. Maggots hatch and tunnel through the fruit, ruining it (see Figure 8-2). Rake up and dispose of infested fruit in the fall before the maggots emerge and become established in the soil for the winter. Trap adult flies with red, apple-like spheres coated with sticky goo (refer to "Apple maggot traps," earlier in this chapter) and baited with a special apple-scented lure. Begin trapping three weeks after the petals begin falling from the blossoms in spring and continue through August, cleaning and refreshing the sticky stuff as needed. Use one to two traps in young or small, 6- to 8-foot-high fruit trees, and six traps in mature 10- to 25-foot trees. Apply a spinosad-based insecticide.

- ✔ **Ataenius spretulus:** These ¼-inch-long black beetles lay eggs in turfgrass in the spring. The eggs hatch into small white grubs, which feed on grass roots until midsummer. After pupating, new adults emerge from the soil and mate; then they prepare for winter by burrowing an inch or so deep into the soil. Discourage the pest by reducing lawn thatch and encouraging predatory and parasitic beneficial insects.

- ✔ **Bagworms:** Bagworms are the larval stages of moths. After hatching in late spring, bagworm caterpillars use pieces of plant debris to construct dangling 1- to 2-inch-long, baglike structures for themselves. The small caterpillars feed on the leaves and twigs of many trees and shrubs, especially arborvitae and juniper. Cut the bags loose, removing the silk that wraps around the stem, and destroy them. Spray with *Bacillus thuringiensis* (Bt) or a spinosad-based insecticide in early spring, or trap adults with sticky pheromone traps.

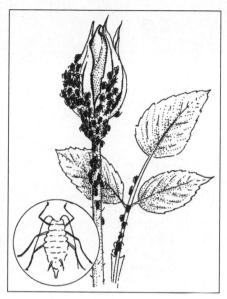

Figure 8-1:
Aphids.

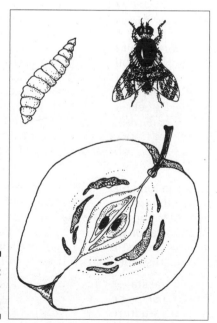

Figure 8-2:
Apple mag-
got larvae.

✔ **Bean leaf beetles:** Adult beetles, shown in Figure 8-3, chew large holes in
bean leaves, and the larvae attack the roots. Control by covering plants
with row-cover fabric. Spray with the organic pesticide neem as a last
resort.

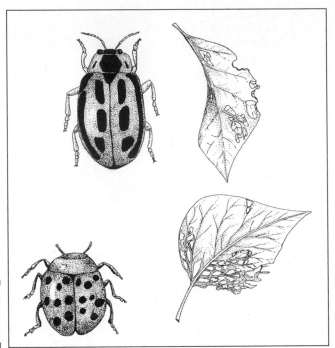

Figure 8-3:
Adult bean
leaf beetles.

✔ **Billbugs:** The adult beetles have long snouts and eat turfgrass leaves, while the grubs consume the grass roots and lower stems. They're especially fond of zoysia and Bermuda grasses. Control by planting tall fescue and perennial ryegrass varieties that contain endophytes.

Don't use these grasses where horses, cattle, and sheep will graze, because endophytes produce a toxin that affects animals as well as insect pests.

✔ **Black vine weevils:** Both adults and larvae of this snout-nosed beetle species damage fruit and ornamental plants. The ⅛-inch-long black adults emerge from the soil in early summer and lay eggs near the soil on host plants. When the eggs hatch, the larvae burrow into the soil and eat the roots. Meanwhile, the adults eat crescent-shaped notches in the leaves. Control by covering crops with floating row-cover fabric to screen out adults or by knocking the adults off the plants onto a drop-cloth in the evening. Use beneficial nematodes for the larval and pupal stages.

✔ **Borers:** Some beetle and moth larvae tunnel into the wood, canes, and stems of raspberries, roses, rhododendrons, squash, fruit trees, and other ornamental trees and shrubs, as shown in Figure 8-4. The tunneling weakens the plant and makes it more disease-prone, and can cut off sap circulation, causing wilting and twig or cane death. Prevent borers by choosing plant species that are less susceptible, wrapping the trunks of young trees to prevent sunburn or other wounds where borers can attack, and covering susceptible vegetable crops with floating row-cover fabric. Watch for signs of damage, including dead bark, sawdust piles, dead or wilted canes and limbs, and poor performance. Control by slitting open affected stems and killing the larvae or pruning off and destroying stems. If you find borers or bark beetles, cut off and destroy the severely infested limbs, inject beneficial nematodes into the remaining borer holes, and remove dead or dying trees and plants.

✔ **Cabbage loopers:** The 1-inch-long, gray, adult moths lay eggs on cabbages, broccoli, cauliflower, and similar types of crops in late spring to early summer. The bright green caterpillars have white stripes down each side of their bodies and move with a looping motion. Control by handpicking the caterpillars, encouraging beneficial wasps, and spraying Bt.

✔ **Chinch bugs:** Both the immature nymphs and the black-and-white, ⅛-inch-long, winged, adult bugs cause significant damage to lawns and grain crops by sucking the juice from grasses. Irregular patches of lawn turn brown, and you may detect a foul odor from crushed bugs when you walk over the affected areas. Control by planting endophyte-containing grasses and encouraging beneficial predator insects by allowing clover to grow in your lawn.

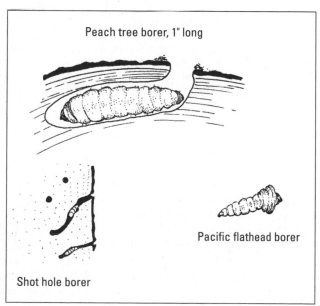

Figure 8-4:
Stem-boring insects.

Peach tree borer, 1" long

Pacific flathead borer

Shot hole borer

✔ **Codling moths:** This ½-inch-long brown moth lays its eggs on the leaves and twigs of apples and other fruits, starting when the trees' flower petals begin falling in the spring and continuing through the summer. When the caterpillars hatch, they tunnel through the center of the fruit, as shown in Figure 8-5. Control adult codling moths by trapping, killing, or confusing them with sticky pheromone-baited traps. Immature larvae spend the winter under the loose bark of fruit trees and in fallen apples. Spray trees with horticultural oil in early spring before the leaves emerge to smother the larvae. You can also trap the larvae by wrapping corrugated cardboard around the tree trunks in summer and then destroying it after the insects crawl inside. Monitor and replace every one to two weeks.

✔ **Colorado potato beetles:** The yellow- and black-striped adults, shown in Figure 8-6, emerge from the soil in early summer, mate, and lay orange eggs on the undersides of potato-family leaves, such as potato, eggplant, tomato, tomatillo, and nightshade. Both adults and larvae defoliate potato-family crops quickly. The reddish grubs devour the plant leaves and then develop into beetles, which lay a second generation of eggs later in the summer. The adults spend the winter in the soil and in plant debris. Control by encouraging spiders, lady beetles, predatory stink-bugs, and tachinid flies. Cover plants by applying a floating row cover or straw mulch, handpicking adults, crushing egg clusters, and spraying Bt san diego or a spinosad-based insecticide on very young grubs.

✔ **Corn earworms and tomato fruitworms:** This caterpillar is one and the same critter, but its name changes depending on the crop it's damaging. The adult moths emerge in spring to lay their eggs on plant leaves and corn ears. The caterpillars burrow into the fruit or eat the leaves for up to a month before dropping to the soil to pupate. Control in corn by choosing resistant varieties with tight husks on their ears or by applying soybean oil mixed with Bt or spinosad to the corn silks. Handpick from other fruits and vegetables, encourage beneficial bugs and wasps, or spray with neem. In warm regions, the pupae overwinter in the soil; light tilling exposes them to predators. In colder regions, the moths migrate in fall.

✔ **Cucumber beetles:** Striped and spotted cucumber beetle species, shown in Figure 8-7, cause significant damage by chewing large holes in the leaves, roots, and fruit of vegetables such as squash, corn, beans, and peas. They can also carry viral and bacterial wilt diseases, spreading the diseases throughout your garden. Both adults and larvae feed on plants. Control by covering plants with row covers until they flower to prevent adults from laying eggs. Remove plant residue from the garden to eliminate winter hiding places. Use beneficial nematodes to control grubs in the soil; use a particle film barrier like Surround WP to confuse the adults and discourage feeding.

Figure 8-5:
Codling
moths.

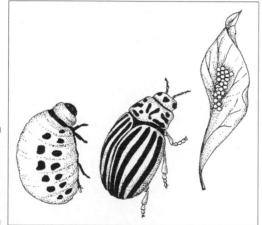

Figure 8-6:
Colorado
potato bee-
tle adults
and larvae.

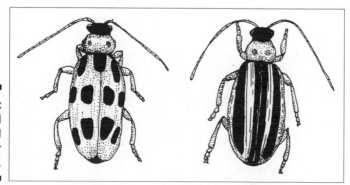

Figure 8-7:
Striped and
spotted
cucumber
beetles.

✔ **Cutworms and armyworms:** The 1- to 2-inch-long cutworm caterpillars, shown in Figure 8-8, chew through the stems of young plants at night, killing them, and then spend the day curled in the soil nearby. Armyworms also feed at night, usually in early summer, stripping the leaves from grasses, grains, and vegetable crops. Control by picking the caterpillars from the soil near decimated seedlings and spraying Bt or spinosad to kill caterpillars. Spray horticultural oil in midsummer to kill the eggs on host plants. Remove plant debris from gardens to prevent overwintering by adults. Wrap the stems of young vegetable plants with 2- to 3-inch-wide strips of newspaper so that half the paper extends below the soil surface.

✔ **Flea beetles:** The highly mobile, shiny blackish beetles are only $\frac{1}{10}$ inch long, but they tend to feed in large groups, skeletonizing leaves in a few days' time. Adults emerge in spring and do most of their damage by midsummer. Eggs, laid in the soil, hatch into larvae that eat plant roots until late summer. Control by covering vegetables and susceptible flowering plants with row-cover fabric or delaying plantings until the beetles subside. Beneficial nematodes attack the grubs. You can also vacuum them up with a small handheld vacuum cleaner early in the morning, while they're still sluggish. A particle film barrier like Surround WP may discourage feeding.

✔ **Gypsy moths:** The adult moths lay masses of eggs under a fuzzy covering on trees and other surfaces in autumn. The caterpillars are 2 inches long, and are gray with brown hairs and distinctive red and blue spots (see Figure 8-9). They emerge in spring to eat the foliage on several species of shade trees, including oaks. This pest spreads across the country as the caterpillars and egg clusters hitchhike on cars, campers, trains, and trucks. Catch caterpillars as they attempt to crawl up tree trunks by using a sticky pest barrier wrapped around the tree. Spray the caterpillars with Bt, spinosad, or neem. If the pests are severely damaging any trees that are too tall for you to treat yourself, call an arborist for help.

✔ **Imported cabbage moths:** The white moths have a distinctive black dot on each wing. They flutter around your garden, laying yellow eggs on the undersides of leaves of cabbage, broccoli, and other cole crops in the spring and early summer. The fuzzy green caterpillars hatch and quickly begin feeding on leaves and developing flower buds, leaving piles of green excrement. Control by covering crops with floating row covers or by handpicking and crushing eggs and caterpillars. Spray with Bt or spinosad, if necessary. Yellow sticky traps attract the adults.

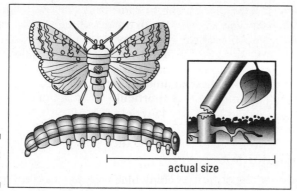

Figure 8-8:
Cutworms.

actual size

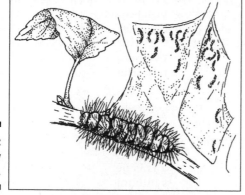

Figure 8-9:
Gypsy
moths.

✔ **Japanese beetles:** Found mostly east of the Mississippi River, the fat, white, C-shaped, ¾-inch-long larvae live in the soil under turf, where they consume grass roots from early spring to early summer. The adults — ½-inch-long, metallic blue-green beetles with coppery backs — emerge from the soil in midsummer and attack plants with gusto, stripping leaves, buds, and flowers. Inspect your garden in the evening or early morning for the beetles, shown in Figure 8-10, knocking them off plants into a can or bucket of soapy water. To control the larvae, treat your lawn with milky spore disease, which takes several years to spread through the lawn, or with beneficial nematodes, a quicker-acting helper. Neem sprays may discourage feeding.

✔ **Lace bugs:** These ⅛-inch-long insects suck the sap out of the undersides of foliage, giving the leaves a whitish or yellow blotchy appearance. Look under the leaves for their sticky brown droppings. Ornamental plants including firethorn, mountain laurel, cotoneaster, and rhododendron are vulnerable, as well as vegetables and flowers. Hose off insects or spray with horticultural spray oil to suffocate the pests, concentrating on the undersides of the leaves. Use insecticidal soap or neem on heavy infestations.

✔ **Leaf miners and sawflies:** The larvae of tiny sawflies, moths, beetles, and flies, these pests tunnel through the leaves of trees, shrubs, flowers, and vegetable plants (honeysuckle, tomato, holly, pine, boxwood, birch, and lilac), leaving discolored patches on the foliage. Control by planting vulnerable crops in a new place each year and covering with row-cover fabric in spring. Remove and destroy infested leaves, shown in Figure 8-11, and rake up any that fall. Eliminate host weeds, especially lamb's-quarter and dock, but encourage parasitic wasps with carrot-family plants. Spray with neem in spring, when adults begin to lay eggs. Leaf-miner damage is mostly cosmetic.

✔ **Leafhoppers:** These small, wedge-shaped adults jump from plant to plant, especially when disturbed. The adults and immature nymphs suck plant juices, distorting plant growth and spreading plant diseases. Many beneficial insects prey on and parasitize the nymphs. You can also try spraying plants with strong blasts of water to dislodge the immature insects. Spray neem if necessary.

✔ **Nematodes:** Plant-damaging nematodes are microscopic, wormlike creatures that live in the soil. (They're different species from the beneficial parasitic nematodes.) They usually attack plant roots, causing abnormal growths and decreasing the plant's ability to take up water and nutrients. Some nematodes also attack stems and leaves. Control by rotating vegetable crops, and avoid planting susceptible crops in the same place each year. *Solarizing* the soil — covering it with clear plastic and letting it bake in the sun — also provides some control. Planting certain types of marigolds can discourage nematodes. The marigold *(Tagetes patula)* variety called Single Gold, also sold as Nema-gone, has proved most effective in Dutch trials. Many nematodes are beneficial, however, and actually attack the harmful kinds.

✔ **Oriental fruit moths:** These small, slim moths produce several generations of larvae each year in the North and as many as seven generations in the South. In the spring, the first larvae tunnel into the new twigs of fruit trees, causing wilting and twig death. The midsummer generations burrow into the fruit, leaving sticky residue on the surface. Late-summer larvae tunnel into the stem ends of the fruit, leaving no visible signs but destroying the inside of the fruit. Larvae spend the winter in tiny cocoons on tree bark and surrounding plant debris. To control, work the soil shallowly around infested trees in early spring to kill the larvae, and spray trees with horticultural oil spray. Use pheromone traps to catch adult males and disrupt mating. Attract parasitic wasps and flies with flowering plants nearby.

Figure 8-10:
Japanese
beetles.

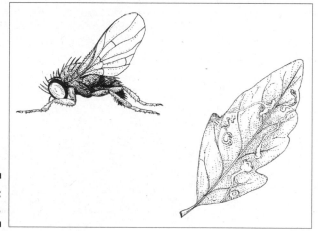

Figure 8-11:
Leaf miners.

✔ **Plum curculios:** Occurring east of the Rocky Mountains, these ¼-inch-
long weevils, shown in Figure 8-12, cause significant damage to apple,
pear, and cherry fruit. The female beetles make crescent-shaped cuts
in young fruit right after the petals fall from the flowers and then lay
their eggs in the wound. When the grubs hatch, they eat through the
fruit, causing it to drop from the tree. The larvae pupate in the soil and
emerge as new adults in mid- to late summer. To control the adult beetles, spread out a tarp or old sheet underneath the tree, shake the tree
to knock the beetles off, and then step on them. Rake up and destroy
fallen fruit, which may contain larvae. Keep plant debris out of orchards
to eliminate hiding places for overwintering adults. If you happen to
have a flock of chickens, as I do, let them forage for insects under the
trees.

Figure 8-12:
Plum curcu-
lio weevils.

✔ **Root maggots:** Small flies of several species lay eggs in the soil near host plants or on the base of the plant. When the maggots hatch, they burrow into the roots, killing or stunting the plant. Onions, leeks, vegetables in the cabbage family, radishes, and carrots are common targets. Onion maggots can kill significant numbers of onion seedlings, especially in cool, wet weather. Control by covering susceptible crops with floating row-cover fabric or apply beneficial nematodes.

✔ **Rose slugs:** The ½-inch-long sawfly larvae and adults eat the undersides of rose leaves and related plants in spring and early summer, quickly stripping them to skeletons. Handpick small infestations, or spray with insecticidal soap or horticultural oil.

✔ **Sawflies:** The caterpillar-like larvae of the sawfly, shown in Figure 8-13, hatch in early spring and devour the foliage of needle-bearing ever-greens, especially pine, hemlock, and spruce. They pupate in the soil, emerging as adults in the fall. Adults lay eggs in cracks in tree bark. Many natural predators eat the larvae and pupae. Control by spreading a dropcloth under infested trees and collecting the larvae as they drop to the ground in late summer. Spray trees with horticultural oil in early spring to smother eggs and newly hatched larvae. Avoid using oil on blue spruces, however, because it will permanently discolor the foliage.

✔ **Scales:** Adult scale insects, shown in Figure 8-14, may have a hard or soft shell-like exterior that resembles bumps on plant stems and leaves. These pests suck plant sap and can weaken and even kill plants if present in large numbers. Many species secrete sticky honeydew that encourages fungus. Control is difficult on large trees and shrubs; your best bet is to release and encourage predatory beetles and wasps. Remove and destroy badly infested stems, and spray with horticultural oil. Indoors or on small plants, clean off light infestations with a cotton ball soaked in soapy water.

Figure 8-13:
Sawfly
larvae.

✔ **Snails and slugs:** These pests feed on the tender leaves of many ornamental, fruiting, and vegetable plants during the cool of night or in rainy
weather. Sometimes they're hard to spot: All you see are the slime trails
they leave behind and the holes they chew in leaves and fruit. They
proliferate in damp areas, hiding and breeding under rocks, mulch,
and other garden debris. Control by placing boards, cabbage leaves, or
other hiding places in the garden. In the early morning, lift the traps and
destroy the slugs by sprinkling with a 50/50 mix of ammonia and water.
Shallow pans of beer also attract and drown these pests. Surround
plants and gardens with copper barriers — metal strips that seem to
shock slugs if they attempt to crawl across them. Diatomaceous earth
and wood ash also deter them but must be refreshed periodically. Look
for nontoxic baits that contain iron phosphate.

✔ **Spider mites:** These tiny arachnids, shown in Figure 8-15, are almost
microscopic, but when they appear in large numbers, you can begin to
see the fine webs that they weave. Use a magnifying glass to identify
them. They suck plant sap, weakening plants and causing leaf discoloration. They're especially active in arid conditions. Favorite hosts include
fruit trees, miniature roses, citrus, pines, and houseplants. To control,
wash plants with a strong blast of water, use dormant oil in early spring,
or use light horticultural oil or insecticidal soap in summer. Encourage
beneficial insects, many of which prey on spider mites.

✔ **Spruce budworms:** These caterpillars cause significant damage to
spruce and fir forests throughout North America and can severely disfigure and kill landscape trees, too. In midsummer, moths lay eggs, which
hatch into small, orange-yellow to brownish caterpillars. The caterpillars
hibernate until the following spring when they emerge to eat the mature
and newly developing needles. Symptoms include dead shoots and
chewed needles and cones. Control the pest by spraying with Bt in late
summer as the newly hatched larvae emerge and again in early spring.
Release and encourage parasitic Trichogramma wasps. Avoid planting
spruce and fir trees in areas where the pest is prevalent.

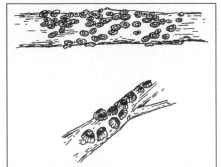

Figure 8-14:
Scale
insects.

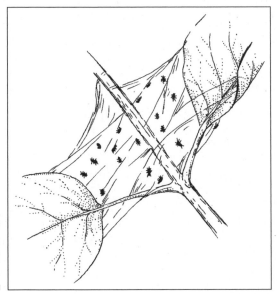

Figure 8-15:
Spider
mites.

✔ **Squash bugs:** These brown, green, or gray ½-inch-long bugs and their
nymphs attack the leaves of squash and pumpkins, causing the leaves
to die. They become a problem when their population swells in late
summer. Control by handpicking the bugs, growing vines on trellises,
rotating crops, and cleaning up plant debris before winter.

✔ **Squash vine borers:** The adult lays an egg at the base of the stem in
spring to early summer. After hatching, the larvae tunnels into the stem,
causing the plant to wilt and eventually die. Control by covering plants
with floating row covers early in the season. Remove the row covers at
blossom time. Remove larvae from infested stems and cover the stem
with soil, allowing it to root. Butternut squash resists this pest.

- ✔ **Tarnished plant bugs:** Among the most destructive pests of strawberries and other crops, plant bugs pierce the tissues of vegetable, flower, and fruit plants, and suck the sap. Their feeding damages the plants, causing swelling, dead spots, bud drop, and distorted growth. The brownish, flattened oval bugs, shown in Figure 8-16, move quickly when disturbed and spread plant diseases. Control by covering crops with floating row covers and encouraging or releasing predatory insects. Knock insects off plants into soapy water in cool morning or evening hours, when bugs are sluggish. Spray with neem or pyrethrins if necessary.

- ✔ **Tent caterpillars:** Adult moths lay eggs in midsummer in hard, dark-colored, shiny masses that encircle twigs of deciduous trees. Caterpillars emerge in the spring and form colonies in large tentlike webs on their host trees. Large infestations can defoliate an entire tree. Control by seeking out and destroying the egg masses in late summer, especially on apple, cherry, and aspen trees. In spring, break up the tents with a long pole, and before the caterpillars disperse, spray them with insecticidal soap. Knock caterpillars off severely infested branches with a broom and destroy. Encourage beneficial insects by planting carrot-family plants. Spray with Bt or spinosad in spring.

- ✔ **Thrips:** These tiny, slender-bodied flying insects damage all soft parts of ornamental and vegetable plants, including leaves, flowers, and roots. Infested flowers and young fruits look distorted. Leaves have silvery or white discolored patches on them, sometimes speckled with black. Use a magnifying lens to identify them. Encourage or release lacewings and other predatory beneficial insects. Spray with horticultural oil or hang blue sticky traps.

- ✔ **Tomato hornworms:** Once you see these caterpillars, you never forget them. The bright green larvae grow up to 4 inches long and as big around as your little finger, with white diagonal stripes along their sides and a black horn on their tail end. When disturbed, they may rear up and make a clicking sound. Handpick them and drop into soapy water, or spray small ones with Bt or spinosad. The large, gray-brown adult moths are 4 to 5 inches across and fly at night.

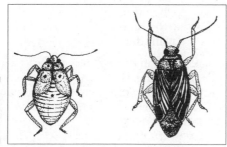

Figure 8-16:
Tarnished
plant bugs.

✔ **Webworms:** This group includes several moth species whose caterpillars spin webs or cocoons around themselves and their host leaf, which they devour. Fall webworms attack trees and shrubs in late summer; garden webworms prefer vegetables and strawberries; and turf webworms go after grass. Control by handpicking; breaking up nests; and spraying with insecticidal soap, Bt, or spinosad. Encourage beneficial insect predators.

✔ **White grubs:** Many beetle species lay eggs in the soil, which hatch into root-eating grubs. Common species of white grubs (see Figure 8-17) include June beetles, Japanese beetles, and rose chafers. Control with beneficial nematodes applied to the soil.

✔ **Whiteflies:** Resembling tiny, white moths, these insects (shown in Figure 8-18) congregate on the undersides of leaves, sucking plant sap and spreading plant diseases. Infested plants may release clouds of them when disturbed. Control whiteflies with insecticidal soap or light horticultural oil, or by trapping them with yellow sticky traps. Be sure to treat leaf undersides, where whiteflies and their larvae reside. Encourage parasitic wasps and predatory beetles.

✔ **Wireworms:** These 1-inch-long, copper-colored worms tunnel through plant roots and tubers, causing significant damage and opening wounds that encourage plant disease. Control the larvae by cultivating frequently and destroying the exposed insects. Chickens do a good cleanup job in my garden before planting time. You can also trap worms with pieces of cut potato placed in the soil. Check the potatoes for worms every few days and discard.

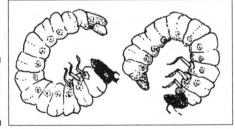

Figure 8-17:
White grubs.

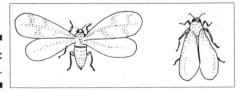

Figure 8-18:
Whiteflies.

Chapter 9

Battling Plant Diseases

*W*hen it comes to diseases, prevention is the name of the game. You can do your part to prevent disease through thoughtful garden and landscape planning and maintenance. But what do you do when disease does strike? How can you tell whether the problem is a disease or some other malady?

In this chapter, I explain the most ecologically friendly ways to prevent and manage diseases. Then I describe the most common diseases, including environmental problems that are sometimes mistaken for diseases.

What's Wrong with My Plant?

The symptoms of many diseases, environmental stresses, nutrient deficiencies, and insect attacks may look similar at first glance. Even something as simple as wilting has several possible causes, including too little water, stem or root disease, high temperature, and stem-boring insects. Fortunately, most problems have more than one symptom, which helps you pinpoint the trouble. Boring insects, for example, often leave a pile of sawdust or droppings at the entrance of the wound. Digging into the soil may reveal decaying or nematode-infested roots. So before you jump to any conclusions, look at all the possibilities. (Refer to Chapter 7 for an overview of evaluating plant problems.)

The first step in diagnosing a disease problem is gathering all the facts. Start by looking at overall conditions:

- ✔ **Environment:** Check soil moisture and pH (see Chapter 5); recall any fertilizers or other amendments you've used recently (see Chapter 6); rule out unusually hot or cold temperatures; consider wet or dry weather; and look for mechanical damage, such as severed roots, leaves torn by high winds or hail, or string-trimmer injury. If you applied a herbicide recently, consider whether it could have drifted onto the affected plant.

- ✔ **Insect activity:** Examine leaves and stems for obvious pests and sticky residue or droppings. Dig gently around the roots for grub and nematode damage. Refer to Chapter 8 for descriptions of insect pests and the damage they cause.

- ✔ **Comparison with healthy plants:** Note specific differences between healthy specimens and troubled ones. Check leaf color and size, as well as overall plant vigor. Look at the bark and stems.

Typical symptoms of disease include discoloration and spotting; sudden death of stems or twigs; and soft, watery plant tissue. If you suspect that your plant is affected by disease, compare the symptoms with those described in the "Curing Common Garden Diseases" section, later in this chapter.

Understanding Plant Diseases

Several kinds of organisms cause diseases in plants, just as they do in people. Viruses are the toughest ones because they're incurable; all you can do is try to prevent them. Bacteria are nearly impossible to eliminate, too, after the plant is infected. Fortunately, fungi cause most plant diseases, and effective control chemicals are available, although prevention is still the best course of action.

The following sections give you an overview of diseases caused by pathogens — bacteria, fungi, viruses — and the ways you can prevent and control them. Later in the chapter, I describe specific diseases and environmental conditions that can mimic disease symptoms.

The fungus among us

Fungi play an important role in our lives and in garden ecosystems, and the number of species that cause problems is relatively small. "Good" fungi are responsible for much of the decomposition that takes place in your compost pile. Also, without fungi we'd have no yeast bread (yeast is a fungus) and no beer!

If you take the time to study them, you'll find that fungi are fascinating. They range in size from a single cell to the largest known living organism on the planet: a 3½-mile-wide underground fungus in Oregon that consists of a huge tangled mass of threads called mycelium. Occasionally, the fungus reveals itself in mushrooms at the bases of dead trees.

Like all living organisms, fungi have distinct life cycles that vary from species to species. Most fungi have very exacting requirements that allow them to live and spread, and knowing these requirements will help you predict and prevent problems in your garden.

Plant pathologists (scientists who study plant diseases) use the phrase *disease triangle* to illustrate the fact that plant diseases result from an interaction among a pathogen (disease-causing organism), a plant, and an environmental condition. Most fungus species infect a single plant species, called the *host plant,* and most require the presence of water to spread. If you can interrupt any step of the process, you can prevent the spread of disease.

Most plant-disease fungi spread by releasing huge numbers of dustlike spores. The spores are dispersed in many ways: on the wind, in water droplets, in your clothing as you brush by infected plants. If a spore lands on the species' host plant and the environmental conditions are right (usually, moisture is present), the spore germinates and begins to grow. Fortunately, gardeners can take many steps to minimize the spread of these fungi in their gardens.

Bacteria and viruses

Bacteria have colonized nearly every habitat on Earth. They are remarkably durable and able to withstand environmental extremes that would kill other organisms. Bacteria cause more plant problems in tropical regions than temperate ones; most require warmth and moisture to spread. Symptoms include spotting of leaves, stems, or fruits, as well as *soft rots,* which make plant tissues watery or slimy. Although bacterial plant diseases can be controlled by the same types of antibiotics used in animals, this strategy usually isn't practical, so gardeners must rely on prevention.

Plant diseases caused by viruses are often named for the symptoms they cause. Tobacco mosaic virus (TMV), for example, affects tobacco-family plants and causes leaves to become mottled. Viruses are transmitted on infected seed, through wounds such as pruning cuts, and via insects, such as aphids and leafhoppers.

Plant viruses can't be treated — only prevented.

Preventing Problems

Some diseases, especially of trees and shrubs, are incurable and the plant values are high, so prevention is critical. Fortunately, your gardening methods can go a long way toward keeping diseases out of your vegetable and flower patch, and away from your fruits and landscape trees. Because the presence of moisture is required for most diseases to spread, you'll see that many of these techniques involve keeping plant foliage dry.

 Inspect your plants frequently. You have a better chance of preventing a serious outbreak if you catch it early. Look for stem and leaf wounds and damage, off-color foliage, wilting, leaf spots, and insects whenever you work among your landscape and garden plants.

Making wise plant selections

When choosing plants for your garden, choose disease-resistant varieties. Many popular flowers, vegetables, perennials, turfgrasses, trees, and shrubs come in varieties that resist common diseases and even some pests. Liberty apple, for example, resists apple scab fungus, and the President Lincoln lilac resists powdery mildew. One of my favorite tomatoes, Celebrity, is resistant to verticillium and fusarium wilts, nematodes, stem canker, and mosaic virus.

Also make sure to choose plants that are adapted to your climate and site. Avoid plants that struggle in your climate, moisture, sunlight, or soil conditions. If your soil drains poorly, for example, don't plant shrubs that require well-drained soil. See Chapter 3 for more about designing your garden and landscape for success.

Keeping plants dry and mulched

Most diseases described in this chapter thrive on moist leaves but not on dry foliage. To keep the leaves dry, follow this advice:

- **Space and prune plants to provide good air circulation.** Fresh air helps leaves dry quickly and thwarts diseases.

- **Water the soil, not the plants.** Soaker hoses and drip irrigation are better choices than sprinklers because they apply water directly to the soil. If you must use sprinklers, early-morning watering is best, because the sun will evaporate any water on the leaves. Avoid evening watering; the foliage will stay wet all night, giving fungus spores a chance to grow and infect plants.

> ✔ **Avoid working with wet plants, because diseases spread easily when the foliage is wet.** Many diseases spread through splashed water. Beans, strawberries, raspberries, and other plants are particularly susceptible.

Another way to keep your plants healthy and prevent disease is to mulch. A thick layer of organic mulch around your garden plants and shrubs keeps weeds from gaining an upper hand. It also helps maintain consistent soil moisture and temperature, which keeps plant roots healthy and better able to resist disease. Soil- and water-borne diseases, such as black spot on roses, have a harder time infecting plants when mulch prevents muddy water from splashing onto leaves. To discourage fungi that attack tree trunks and stems, however, keep mulch a few inches away from plants.

Other ways to prevent disease

Add the following techniques to your gardening routine and you'll be well on your way to preventing most disease problems.

> ✔ **Avoid excess nitrogen fertilizer.** Nitrogen makes plants grow fast and juicy. As a result, the outer layers of the leaves and stems that protect the plant are thinner than usual (similar to human skin) and more susceptible to insect damage. Use organic fertilizers that release their nutrients slowly to avoid encouraging insects. See Chapter 6 for fertilizer suggestions.
>
> ✔ **Keep your yard clean.** Dispose of diseased leaves, fruit, and wood in the garbage, not in the compost pile.
>
> ✔ **Keep your tools clean.** If you prune diseased plants, sanitize your pruning shears between cuts by spraying with isopropyl alcohol. Oil your shears regularly; it helps them cut easier and makes them a snap to clean. Also clean your digging tools.
>
> ✔ **Keep your shoes clean.** Knock the dirt off your shoes to keep pests and diseases from traveling from one garden to another.
>
> ✔ **Practice crop rotation.** Many diseases live in the soil from one year to the next, waiting for their favorite host plants to return. Foil them by planting something different in each spot each year. This method is especially effective for annual vegetables.
>
> ✔ **Control insects.** Many insects — including aphids, bark beetles, and tarnished plant bugs — can spread diseases between plants. Keep them under control, and you'll help prevent disease. Refer to Chapter 8 for information.

Disease-Control Techniques and Products

Preventing plant stress and environmental imbalances are the most important first steps in controlling disease. Beneficial microbes, especially in the soil, usually keep the populations of plant-disease-causing organisms in check, but environmental factors can tip the balance in favor of the bad guys. High humidity and soil moisture encourage diseases to spread. Stress from transplanting, pruning, and insect infestation can weaken plants and make them more vulnerable to infection from fungi, bacteria, and viruses. And sometimes the pesticide you use against one problem can make another problem worse. Broad-spectrum fungicides (copper and sulfur, for example) kill beneficial fungi as well as harmful ones.

The only plant diseases you can control effectively after the plants become infected are those caused by fungi. Except for solarization and copper, the following control methods target mainly fungi. (See Chapter 7 for information on pesticide safety.)

- **Solarization:** Discussed in detail in Chapter 11 as a weed control, solarization captures the sun's heat under a sheet of clear plastic and literally bakes the soil, killing fungi and bacteria as well as weeds. Unfortunately, it also kills both good and bad microbes. Use this technique in gardens where disease has been a problem in the past.

- **Particle films:** Particle films, which are relatively new products, are made from fine clay particles that are mixed with water and sprayed directly on plants. Treated plants look like they've been misted with white spray paint, so particle films aren't the best choice for ornamental plantings. In addition to reducing disease infection, the material deters insect feeding, and helps protect plants against heat stress and sunburn. One brand is Surround.

- **Botanical sprays:** Some organic fungicides contain citric acid and mint oil. They are broad-spectrum products, killing a range of fungi and bacteria. One brand is Fungastop.

- **Antitranspirants:** These waxy or oily materials are designed to help evergreens maintain leaf moisture during winter months. By coating the leaves, they also prevent fungus spores from attacking. Look for Wilt-Pruf and similar products, and follow the instructions on the label.

- **Potassium bicarbonate:** This natural chemical controls powdery mildew and some other diseases in roses, grapes, cucumbers, strawberries, and other plants. It also supplies some potassium fertilizer when sprayed on foliage, which strengthens plants' cell walls and makes them harder for pests and diseases to penetrate. Follow label directions carefully, spraying all leaf surfaces thoroughly to ensure contact with the fungus.

✔ **Fungal fungicides:** Some of the newest fungicides are fungi themselves. These good guys grow in the soil and into roots, protecting the plants from harmful root-rot fungi (see "Curing Common Garden Diseases," later in this chapter). Apply them to the soil before planting or water them into lawns and gardens. You can also apply these fungicides to foliage. These products contain viable fungi, so you must store them properly and use them according to label instructions for best results.

✔ **Bacterial fungicides:** Two fungicides derived from naturally occurring bacteria are Serenade (derived from *Bacillus subtilis*) and Sonata (derived from *Bacillus pumilus*). They work by boosting the plants' natural immune systems as well as by inhibiting fungal germination and growth. They work best when sprayed early in the growing season as a preventive measure, before diseases have spread.

Another bacterial fungicide called Mycostop is made from the soil bacteria strain *Streptomyces griseoviridis*. It's applied at planting time and colonizes plant roots to help prevent infection.

✔ **Neem oil:** This multipurpose pesticide thwarts black spot on roses; it also prevents powdery mildew and rust fungi, as well as insects and mites. Several formulations are available, so read the label to be sure that the product is labeled for the plant you want to treat, as well as for the pest you're trying to control.

✔ **Sulfur:** Useful for controlling nearly all fungus diseases on leaves and stems, sulfur is one of the oldest pesticides known. You can dust the powder directly on leaves or mix finely ground dust with water and a soapy wetting agent that helps it adhere to leaf surfaces.

Sulfur can cause leaf damage if it's applied within a month of horticultural oil, however, or when temperatures exceed 80 degrees Fahrenheit. It also lowers soil pH and harms many beneficial insects. Inhaled dust can cause lung damage. Take precautions to protect yourself. Lime–sulfur sprays are also available; the addition of lime reduces the possibility of leaf damage.

✔ **Copper:** Copper sulfate is a powerful fungicide that controls a wide range of leaf diseases, including fungal and bacterial blights and leaf spots, but it is much more toxic to humans, mammals, fish, and other water creatures than most synthetic chemical fungicides. It also can build up in the soil and harm plants and microorganisms. Use copper-containing products only as a last resort, and take full precautions to avoid poisoning yourself and others.

Some gardeners have found that repeated sprays of compost teas seem to minimize disease problems, in addition to providing nutrients. Find out more about making and using compost tea in Chapter 6.

Sources of information

As consumers and farmers demand more organic methods of disease control, alternatives to chemical pesticides are becoming more common. To keep up with the latest information, visit the following Web sites:

✔ Appropriate Technology Transfer for Rural Areas (ATTRA) offers in-depth information on many home, garden, and agricultural crops, and focuses mainly on sustainable growing methods (`www.attra.org`).

✔ Ohio State University maintains PlantFacts, a database of information from 46 North American universities and government agencies (`http://plantfacts.ohio-state.edu`).

Curing Common Garden Diseases

Many names of plant diseases describe the symptoms they cause — powdery mildew, leaf curl, and club root diseases, for example. Some diseases attack only one plant part, whereas others can affect the entire plant. The following list describes some of the most common diseases of trees, shrubs, vegetables, flowers, and fruits:

✔ **Anthracnose:** This group of fungi can attack many plants (beans, vine crops, tomatoes, and peppers) and trees (dogwoods, maples, ash, and sycamores). Look for small, discolored leaf spots or dead twigs. The disease can spread to kill branches and eventually the whole plant. You can spread it easily by splashing water and walking through wet plants. Many plant varieties are resistant to anthracnose fungi; choose them whenever you can. Prune off affected plant parts, if possible, and dispose of the debris in the trash, not in the compost pile. Fungicides containing copper can help.

✔ **Apple scab:** This fungus attacks apple and crabapple trees, producing discolored leaf spots and woody-brown scabs on the fruit. The leaf spots start out olive-colored, eventually turning brown. Plant scab-resistant varieties. Rake up and destroy fungus-infected leaves to prevent the fungus from reinfecting the trees in spring. Spray with copper- or sulfur-based fungicides during wet spring and summer weather.

✔ **Armillaria root rot:** This fungus infects and kills the roots and lower trunk of ornamental trees, especially oaks. Symptoms include smaller-than-normal leaves, honey-colored mushrooms growing near the base of the tree (see Figure 9-1), and declining tree vigor. Trees may suddenly fall over when the roots weaken and decay. Keep trees growing vigorously, and avoid damage to their roots and trunks. If you live in an area where the disease is prevalent, plant resistant tree species. Consult local nursery or local extension-office experts for information.

Mycelial plaques

Armillaria on tree bark

Figure 9-1:
Armillaria
root-rot
fungus.

✔ **Black spot:** This fungus causes black spots on rose leaves, as shown in Figure 9-2. Yellow rings may surround the spots, and severe infections can cause the shrub to lose all its foliage. The disease spreads easily in splashing water; it overwinters in fallen leaves and mulch around the plant. Remove old mulch after leaf fall in the autumn, and replace it with fresh mulch. Prevent black spot by choosing disease-resistant roses and by cleaning up and destroying any diseased leaves that fall to the ground. Avoid wetting the foliage when you water.

Neem oil (not neem extract) is the best organic fungicide against black spot. Use it at the first signs of the disease, but spray either early or late in the day to avoid harming beneficial insects. Fungicide sprays containing copper, sulfur, or potassium bicarbonate can also offer some protection.

✔ **Botrytis blight:** This fungus attacks a wide variety of plants, especially in wet weather. It causes watery-looking, discolored patches on foliage that eventually turn brown. Infected flowers — especially roses, geraniums, begonias, and chrysanthemums — get fuzzy white or gray patches that turn brown, destroying the bloom. Strawberry and raspberry fruits in particular develop light brown to gray moldy spots, and the flesh becomes brownish and water soaked. Discourage botrytis by allowing air to circulate freely around susceptible plants, and avoid working with wet plants. Remove and destroy any infected plant parts. Try a citric acid/mint oil fungicide or the bacterial fungicide Mycostop.

Figure 9-2:
Black spot
fungus.

✔ **Cedar-apple rust:** Rust diseases, including this one, often have complicated life cycles in which they infect different plant species and exhibit very different symptoms in each, depending on their life stage. Cedar-apple rust fungus appears as bright orange spots on the leaves and fruit of apples and crabapples. On its alternative hosts — juniper and red cedar — it develops yellow to orange jellylike masses in the spring. The fungus needs both hosts to reproduce and spread.

Prevent the disease by planting resistant apple varieties and keeping the alternative hosts several hundred yards away from susceptible trees. A related fungus, pear rust, affects pears similarly.

✔ **Club root:** This fungus infects mainly cole crops (such as cabbage, broccoli, and collards) and grows best in acidic soils. Symptoms include stunted growth, wilting, poor development, and swollen lumps on the roots. Practice good garden hygiene by keeping tools clean and picking up plant debris. Raise the soil pH to 7.2, and avoid planting susceptible crops in infected soil for at least seven years. Some vegetable varieties are immune.

✔ **Corn smut:** You can't miss this fungus disease, which causes large, mutant-looking, white to gray swellings on corn ears. When the swellings burst open, the fungus spreads. Prevent the disease by planting resistant corn varieties and rotating crops so that you don't grow corn in the same place year after year. Dispose of infected plant parts in the trash.

✔ **Cytospora canker:** Cankers appear as oozing, sunken, or swollen areas on the bark of susceptible trees, such as peaches, apples, maples, spruces, and willows. The new shoots turn yellow, wilt, and then die back. The disease attacks the woody stems of susceptible plants, forming cankers that can kill infected branches. Plant resistant or less-susceptible plants, and keep them growing vigorously. Avoid bark injuries that provide an entrance for infecting fungus. Remove and destroy infected branches, cutting back to healthy wood that doesn't contain any black or brownish streaks.

✔ **Damping off:** A problem mostly in young plants and seedlings, this fungus rots stems off near the soil line, causing the plant to keel over and die. Prevent damping off by planting seeds and seedlings only in pasteurized planting soil and avoiding overwatering. Air circulation helps prevent the fungus, too. Clean your tools in isopropyl alcohol to prevent the spread of damping off.

✔ **Fusarium wilt:** This fungus is fatal to many vegetable crops. The first symptoms are yellowing leaves and stunted growth, followed by wilting and plant death (see Figure 9-3). In melons, the stems develop a yellow streak, which eventually turns brown. Choose Fusarium-resistant varieties. After plants are infected, no cure is possible. If you build your soil's health so that it contains lots of beneficial microorganisms, you should rarely be bothered with this disease.

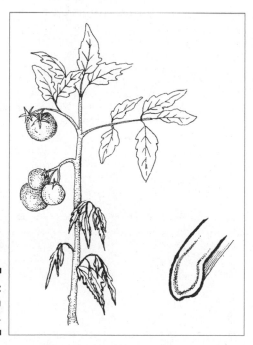

Figure 9-3:
Fusarium
wilt.

✔ **Galls:** Galls appear as swollen bumps on leaves, stems, and branches. Gall wasps, aphids, and mites infest oaks and other landscape trees and shrubs, causing unsightly swellings on leaves and twigs. In other cases, bacteria and fungi are the culprits. Usually, the damage is simply cosmetic and not life-threatening to the plant. Control depends on what's causing the problem. Take a sample of the damage to a plant expert at your local extension office, or contact your local Master Gardener program.

✔ **Leaf spots and blights:** Several fungi show up first as circular spots on leaves of tomatoes, potatoes, peppers, and other vulnerable vegetables, flowers, and ornamental plants. The spots increase in size until the leaves die and fall off. The fungi spread easily in damp weather and in gardens where overhead watering wets the foliage, especially late in the day. The best control is to remove all plant debris at the end of the gardening season, clean tools between uses, practice crop rotation, buy disease-resistant varieties, and avoid contact with wet plants. Try botanical and biological fungicides first, using copper-based fungicides only as a last resort.

✔ **Mildew (downy and powdery):** These two fungi produce similar symptoms: a white, powdery coating on leaves. They infect a wide variety of plants, including roses, vegetables, fruit trees, strawberries, raspberries, and lilacs. A different species of mildew attacks each kind of plant. A mildew that attacks lilacs, for example, won't harm roses. The fungi disfigure plants but may not kill them outright. Instead, they weaken their hosts, making them unattractive and susceptible to other problems. Downy mildew attacks during cool, wet weather. Powdery mildew (shown in Figure 9-4) appears during warm, humid weather and cool nights, especially when the soil is dry.

Many vegetable and flower varieties are resistant to mildew; read package and catalog descriptions carefully. Remove infected plant debris from the garden, and avoid getting the leaves wet. Use potassium bicarbonate, superfine horticultural oil, or neem oil to treat infected plants. Try botanical and biological controls, using copper- and sulfur-based fungicides as a last resort.

✔ **Root rot:** This broad term covers several fungal root diseases that cause susceptible plants to turn yellow, wilt, and sometimes die. Nearly all plants are susceptible under the right conditions, such as excessive soil moisture, poor soil aeration, and wounding. The fungi can survive in the soil for many years without a host. Prevent root rot by building healthy, well-drained soil. Microbial fungicides can help foil many root-rot diseases.

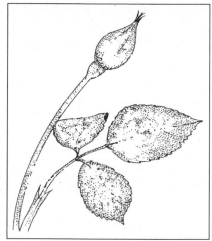

✔ **Rust:** Many fungi cause rust, and the symptoms of this disease vary widely, depending on the kind of plant they infect. Usually, the symptoms include yellow to orange spots on the leaf undersides, with white or yellow spots on the upper leaf surface. Susceptible plants include brambles, hollyhocks, roses, pines, pears, bluegrass and ryegrass lawns, wheat, barberry, and beans. Each rust species infects a specific plant species, so the rust on roses can't infect beans, for example. Some rusts, such as white pine blister rust, have complicated life cycles and must infect two different plants — in this case, white pines and *Ribes* species, such as currant and gooseberry. Symptoms of this disease include yellow, orange, reddish-brown, or black powdery spots or masses on leaves, needles, or twigs.

Rust fungus: Rust fungus, shown in Figure 9-5, forms yellow or orange bumps on leaf undersides and is most prevalent in humid and damp conditions. Provide good air circulation to keep foliage as dry as possible, remove and destroy infected parts, and keep your tools clean. Plant disease-resistant varieties.

✔ **Slime flux:** This bacterial rot inside infected trees — usually, elms, maples, and poplars — causes oozing and often bad-smelling sap running from old wounds or pruning cuts. No control is possible after the symptoms appear.

Figure 9-5:
Rust fungus.

✔ **Verticillium wilt:** This fungus affects many plants, including tomatoes, eggplant, potatoes, raspberries, strawberries, roses, Japanese maples, olives, and cherries. Look for wilting and yellow leaves, especially older ones. In some plants, the leaves curl up before falling off. Prevent future infections by cleaning up all garden debris, cleaning tools thoroughly with disinfectant, and avoiding susceptible species. Choose resistant varieties, and practice crop rotation.

✔ **Viruses:** This group of incurable diseases infects vegetables, brambles, strawberries, trees, and flowering plants. Usually, the leaves develop mottled yellow, white, or light green patches and may pucker along the veins. Flowers may develop off-color patches, and fruit ripens unevenly. Aphids, leafhoppers, nematodes, and whiteflies spread the virus as they move from plant to plant. Viruses often live in wild bramble plants and weeds. Smoking or handling tobacco products around susceptible plants can spread tobacco mosaic virus, which infects tomatoes, eggplants, peppers, petunias, and other plants. Prevention is the only strategy. Buy only virus-free plants and keep pests in check. Eradicate wild brambles near your garden.

Rooting Out Environmental Problems

Plants live intimately with their environment, which means that air, water, and soil quality, weather, and animals can take their toll. The way plants respond to environmental damage often mimics disease caused by micro-organisms or insect pests; at other times, the culprit is fairly obvious. Look through the following sections of probable causes before you start blaming innocent viruses, aphids, and fungi.

Air pollution and ozone

Automobile exhaust and other pollutants contain gases that injure susceptible plant leaves. Ozone gives foliage a white speckled appearance. Another common pollutant in urban areas is peroxyacyl nitrate (PAN), which causes silvery damage to leaf undersides. Sulfur dioxide, an industrial air pollutant, turns leaves yellow, especially between the veins. Beans, lettuce, spinach, tomatoes, sugar maples, pines, and English ivy are especially vulnerable to air pollutants.

Herbicide injury

Weed-killing sprays can drift on the wind to affect nearby plants. If a section of plant turns brown seemingly overnight, try to determine whether anyone in the area has used a herbicide. You can't fix the damage, but if you prune off damaged foliage, the plant may recover. Some herbicides are systemic and move within the plant to kill it, roots and all, so you'll have to wait and see.

Lawn-mower and string-trimmer damage

Mechanical damage to the bark and stems of trees and shrubs poses a serious threat to their health. Water and nutrients flow through the stems just under the bark, and breaking the bark interrupts this flow, causing stress, wilting, and even death. Even small wounds open the plant to insect and disease invasion. Maintain a wide weed- and grass-free area around trees, shrubs, and gardens so that you don't have to mow or weed-whip close to them. Hard plastic or wire mesh tree guards also offer protection.

Leaf scorch

When the edges of leaves turn yellow and then brown, as shown in Figure 9-6, suspect environmental damage from drought or heat. Trees in paved areas where heat rises from the pavement are vulnerable, as are any plants in very dry soil or unusually hot weather. Avoid planting susceptible trees, such as maples, in hot, dry locations.

Figure 9-6:
Leaf scorch.

Nutrient deficiency

Although most natural soils contain enough nutrients to support healthy plants, disturbed soil around new homes and in improperly maintained gardens may have some nutrient shortages. Each nutrient has specific deficiency symptoms, but some symptoms resemble others or mimic other problems or diseases. Nitrogen-deficient plants have yellow older leaves and stunted growth; lack of potassium causes yellow leaf margins; and phosphorus-deficient leaves usually have purplish streaks or an overall purplish appearance. Iron deficiency, caused by high pH, is especially prevalent in acid-loving plants such as azaleas, blueberries, oaks, and hollies. The leaf veins remain dark green, but the rest of the leaf becomes yellow. Conduct a soil test (see Chapter 5) and flip to Chapter 6 for more information about specific nutrients.

Salt damage

Salt used to de-ice roads poses a serious threat to perennials, trees, and shrubs. As water drains off the roads, salts in the water accumulate in the soil, burning foliage and roots, and killing plants. Salt spray from passing cars can also damage or kill trees and shrubs. Injury appears as stunted growth, brown needles on conifers, and wilting. You can leach road salts out of the soil with heavy irrigation, but a better solution is to avoid planting within 20 feet of a frequently salted road and to divert drainage water from the road away from plants. If you live in a coastal area where salty air and soil are the norm year-round, choose salt-tolerant plants recommended by your local nurseries.

Winter and frost injury

Cold temperatures, frost, wind, and frozen soil combine forces to damage plants in several ways. Late-spring and early-autumn frosts injure tender plants as well as hardy plants that aren't sufficiently dormant and, therefore, able to withstand cold temperatures. Young, succulent, actively growing shoots and expanding flower buds usually are the most vulnerable. Avoid fertilizing and pruning plants in late summer, which can promote new growth that won't mature before freezing occurs. Injury symptoms include wilted brown leaves, stems, and flowers. Protect vulnerable plants in spring and fall by covering them with row covers or cold frames, as described in Chapter 13.

Low winter temperatures cause the most damage to plants growing in containers, in areas where they are marginally hardy, and in places where winters bring little snow cover (snow insulates the soil and prevents the soil temperature from dropping dangerously low). Even the roots of the hardiest shrubs and trees die at temperatures between 0 and 10 degrees. Here are some symptoms of injury caused by low temperatures:

- **Root damage:** Root damage may appear later in the growing season, when plants either fail to grow or sprout leaves but die suddenly in late spring. Spread 4 to 6 inches of loose mulch over the roots of perennials, strawberries, and vulnerable shrubs after the ground freezes in late autumn.

- **Sunscald:** *Sunscald* is the cracking of tree branches and trunks caused by sudden and dramatic temperature fluctuations. The sun heats trees' bark during winter days, but the temperature drops rapidly at sunset. To protect vulnerable trees, such as citrus, paint trunks with whitewash made from a 1:1 mix of water and white water-based latex paint, wrap them in light-colored tree wrap, or use clay particle film like Surround.

- **Dried-out evergreen leaves and needles:** The leaves and needles of evergreens face the challenge of drying out in the winter without being able to replace their lost moisture. When the soil freezes, the roots can no longer take up water to transport to the leaves. Winter sun and wind take their toll, and symptoms include bronze or brown needles and leaves. Wrap vulnerable shrubs with burlap, plant them in protected places, or spray them with an antitranspirant that prevents them from drying out. See the "Disease-Control Techniques and Products" section, earlier in this chapter, for more information.

- **Split trunks and branches:** Snow and ice can accumulate on tree and shrub branches and split them from the trunk, toppling whole trees. Protect shrubs by wrapping them with burlap and heavy twine to hold the branches together or by covering them with plywood A-frames, especially if they are near a building where snow can slide off the roof or where snowplows dump their loads. Prune damaged limbs immediately to prevent further damage from bark tearing.

Woodpecker holes

These birds eat insects that live in and around trees, and they often make holes in the bark in pursuit of their prey. Some bird species also enjoy the sap of some trees and drill holes to get at it. The holes usually are small, round, and drilled in neat rows in the trunk. Unfortunately, you can't do much after the damage is done. Wrapping the tree may prevent further damage, but don't fill the holes or paint over them.

Chapter 10

Outwitting Critters

- -

In This Chapter

▶ Observing symptoms and signs

▶ Determining the cause

▶ Controlling the culprits

- -

A discussion of garden pests wouldn't be complete without considering the animals that may plague your gardens: deer, rabbits, groundhogs, and the like. Although insect feeding is subtler and causes incremental damage over time, some of these larger critters can quickly eliminate an entire plant — or row of plants. This chapter looks at the most common animal pests and the steps you can take to minimize the damage they cause. *Note:* For the most part, the animals have been ordered from most to least damaging to a garden. Deer, rabbits, and woodchucks can consume a whole garden. The smaller creatures cause specific problems but they don't eat everything overnight. Of course, whatever critter is eating your garden is the most serious at that moment!

Most of these animals do their work under the cover of darkness, so you're unlikely to catch them in action. Instead, to figure out what's doing the damage, you'll have to look at the plant and scout for signs that tell you which animal was there. After all, there's no use putting up a 3-foot rabbit fence when deer are the culprit, or installing an expensive 8-foot deer fence to keep out groundhogs.

Oh, Deer!

Deer are among the most troublesome of garden pests. They live in wooded areas but also in suburban and urban locales, and in many places their numbers are increasing. When food is scarce, they eat just about anything. A deer or two can ravage an entire garden overnight. Deer eat plants but also trample vegetation, and bucks rub their antlers on young trees to remove the "velvet" and to mark their territory.

Deer tend to travel the same routes day after day. If your yard is in the path of their customary travels from sleeping quarters to a water source, you'll be spending some evenings discussing deer-repellent strategies.

Identifying deer damage

To identify deer damage, look closely at affected plants. Deer don't have upper front teeth, so when they eat, they tear plant tissue rather than cutting it, leaving ragged edges. Deer prefer tender new growth when it's available, but eat buds and twigs in winter. They tend to feed on the edges of wooded areas so that they can duck for cover if threatened.

Deer can reach as high as 6 feet, so if you see damage at eye level, you're probably dealing with a deer, not a mutant rabbit. Look for telltale hoofprints and piles of deer scat (usually rounded pellets with a dimple on one end, about the size and shape of a chocolate-covered peanut or small black olive). Deer are most likely to visit gardens when other food sources are scarce, especially in late winter and early spring.

Keeping deer out of your garden

Deer have some quirky tendencies that gardeners can use to their favor. Try some of the remedies discussed in the following sections.

If you continually use the same deterrent, the deer will get used to it and ignore it. So vary your methods, try different products, and combine them now and then. You can use predator urine (which repels by scent) along with a bad-tasting hot pepper spray, for example.

Repellents

Several types of repellents may keep deer out of your yard:

- **Soap:** Hang bars of soap from low tree branches or from stakes so that the bars are about 30 inches off the ground. Fragrant, tallow-based soaps such as Irish Spring work best.

- **Hair:** Ask your barber or hairdresser if you can have some hair trimmings. Human hair hung in mesh bags about 3 feet off the ground may deter deer.

- **Spray:** Use spray repellents on foliage. One recipe: Mix three raw eggs in a gallon of water and spray the mixture on plants. This substance apparently smells worse to the deer than it does to you.

   For best results, spray plants before the deer develop their feeding habits and reapply most sprays after heavy rain.

Avoid spraying fruit and vegetables, because you don't want to eat the stuff yourself. If you use commercial repellents, follow the label instructions carefully.

Row covers

In early spring, spread row-cover fabric over tender new growth, supporting the covers with wire cages or hoops if necessary. These row covers can deter the deer long enough to give your plants a head start and allow time for wild food plants to become plentiful. Refer to Chapter 8 for info on row covers.

Scare tactics

Motion-detector-activated sprinklers may deter deer for a short time. (Just be sure to turn them off before you venture into the garden.) Playing a radio in the garden at night may work for a few days, but the deer will catch on quickly, and if they're hungry enough they won't care.

Stringing fishing line between posts scattered through your garden sometimes confuses deer enough that they go elsewhere. You'll have to remember that the fishing line is there, however, or you'll keep walking into it too. This option is better for less frequently visited gardens than for your vegetable garden.

Fencing

The only surefire way to keep deer out of your garden is to put up a tall fence. Deer have been known to jump 10-foot fences, but an 8-foot fence will deter most intruders unless they're very hungry.

To ensure the success of your fence, use deer tendencies to your advantage. Apparently, deer are intimidated about jumping when they can't tell how much distance they have to clear. For that reason, they're less likely to jump a fence over a narrow, long garden than a fence that surrounds a large, wide garden. The two long sides appear to be too close together for the deer to see a place to land. You can create the same illusion by installing a fence so that it slants outward away from the garden. This technique can intimidate the deer by making the fence appear wider than it really is. You can even make a 5-foot-fence more deerproof by using taller posts and attaching strands of wire above the fence, such as at 7 feet and 10 feet.

Place a circle of 4-foot-tall wire fencing around young trees, especially fruit trees. Make sure that the diameter of the fence is large enough that the deer can't reach over to eat the twigs.

If all else fails, you may need to resort to low-voltage electric fencing, as shown in Figure 10-1. Place an electrified strand 3 feet high and 3 feet outside your other fence. Bait the strands of wire with peanut butter to encourage the deer to take a taste and get the message.

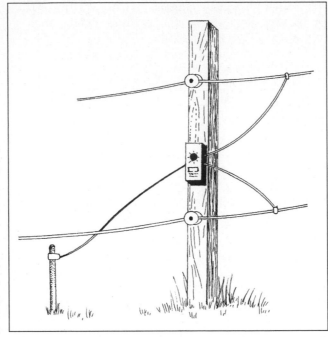

Figure 10-1:
Low-voltage
electric
fencing may
be the only
solution to
foiling deer,
raccoons,
and other
persistent
pests.

Deer- resistant plants

Many plants are touted as deer resistant, but if deer are hungry enough, they'll eat just about anything. Still, if you live in an area where deer pressure is high, including deer resistant plants like catmint, hellebore, and yarrow increases the likelihood that at least something in your garden will survive.

Wascally Wabbits

Rabbits are homebodies. They tend to stake out a rather small territory — 10 acres or less — and not wander elsewhere. They make their homes in natural cavities in trees, in other animals' abandoned burrows, in brush piles, and under buildings. They nibble the foliage of almost any plant, returning again and again, day and night, to finish the job.

Unlike deer, rabbits have both upper and lower front teeth, and you can identify their damage by a clean, angled cut on the ends of leaves and twigs. If you suspect rabbits, look for their droppings, which are round or slightly flattened; think marbles or M&Ms. The individual pellets are smaller and rounder than the more elongated deer scat.

Rabbits tend to eat vegetables and flowers in spring and summer; sprouting tulips are a favorite spring treat. In fall and winter, they favor twigs and bark and can cause considerable damage to landscape trees and shrubs. Wild rabbits may strip bark off of young trees up to a height of 2½ feet off the ground; snow cover allows them to reach higher. If they remove the bark around the entire trunk or stem, girdling it, any plant parts above that portion won't be able to get nutrients and will die.

Here are some techniques to foil their feeding:

✔ **Fencing:** The best way to keep rabbits away from your plants is to fence them out. Because they burrow, a fence must also extend underground. Choose a 4-foot-high, chicken-wire fence with 1-inch mesh. Bury the bottom foot of the fence, bending the lowest 6 inches into a right angle facing outward.

✔ **Trunk protectors:** Protect tree trunks with a cylinder of ¼-inch hardware cloth or other wire mesh. (Larger mesh works for rabbits, but the ¼-inch size protects trees from gnawing mice, too.) The material should be a few inches away from the trunk and extend high enough that rabbits standing on snow can't reach above it. You can also get commercial tree guards (see Figure 10-2).

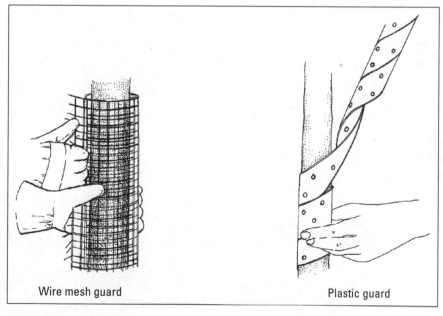

Figure 10-2:
Wire or plastic tree guards protect bark from rabbits and gnawing rodents.

Wire mesh guard

Plastic guard

✔ **Repellents:** I've had good luck repelling rabbits with hair gathered from hair salons and dog groomers. I sprinkle it around the boundary of a garden and replenish it every few weeks. You can also purchase commercial repellents that are made to spray on the ground or directly on plants. Because most of these sprays repel by taste, use them only on ornamental plants, and follow label directions carefully.

Groundhogs

These slow-moving rodents, also called woodchucks and whistlepigs, live in an extensive system of underground dens and tunnels, and they defy you to find all their tunnel entrances. A tunnel can extend nearly 70 feet. If you see a mound of excavated earth surrounding a foot-wide hole, you're probably looking at the entrance to a groundhog tunnel.

Groundhogs generally stay within about 100 feet of their dens, venturing out morning and evening to find food: your tender veggies. They favor beans, squash, and peas, and they can mow down a row of seedlings overnight. They also gnaw and claw woody plants.

If you suspect groundhogs, scan your landscape in the morning and evening hours. The animals are relatively bold, and you may catch a culprit red-handed. Here are some deterrents:

✔ **Fencing:** Groundhogs can climb up almost as well as they can dig down, so use a sturdy 4- or 5-foot fence, and bury the bottom 18 inches underground. Bend the top of the fence outward so that a groundhog falls over backward if it attempts to climb over. Two strands of electric fence — one 4 inches above the ground and the other 8 inches high — may also keep them out.

✔ **Repellents:** Hot pepper wax sprays may act as deterrents; groundhogs don't seem to be fazed by other repellent sprays.

✔ **Traps:** You can use a Havahart trap to capture a live groundhog and then release it into the wild. Groundhogs can't survive in wooded areas, so know that you're probably giving the creature a death sentence unless you release it in a suitable habitat: an open grassy field. In most cases, this habitat is likely to be someone's backyard or a farm field, and the property owner probably won't appreciate your gift.

Be sure to check with local and state ordinances about restrictions on the live trapping and release of wild animals.

Groundhogs can carry rabies and are aggressive, so use caution around them.

Gophers

These burrowing rodents live in underground tunnel systems extending as far as 200 yards. They feast underground on plant roots and bulbs, occasionally emerging to eat aboveground parts of those plants located near the tunnel openings. Most gopher species live in the western two thirds of the country; one species is native to the Southeast. If you live in New England, don't blame your garden problems on gophers.

The telltale sign of gophers is a collection of fan-shaped soil mounds, with new mounds appearing daily. You won't see a tunnel entrance; the critters keep the entrances plugged with soil.

Gophers are difficult to scare or repel. Castor oil sprayed on the garden may repel them. If gophers are a serious problem, you may want to go to the trouble of lining the sides and bottom of your garden (at a depth of 2 feet) with hardware cloth to keep the gophers out. Gopher-resistant wire baskets, which can be placed in planting holes before planting, are commercially available. For persistent problems, use traps.

Research has shown that vibrating devices such as large whirligigs stuck in the ground near tunnels have little effect. Apparently, gophers in a home landscape get used to the sounds and vibrations of mechanical equipment like lawn mowers. So don't waste your money on these devices.

Mice and Voles

Mice and voles look similar. Both are small rodents, but the tail of a vole is much shorter than that of a mouse. Mice are fond of young seedlings, especially those that are growing in a warm house or greenhouse on a cold winter day; they're omnivores, though, and eat almost anything. Voles, on the other hand, are almost exclusively herbivores and are the more troublesome pest for gardeners.

Both mice and voles cause damage to plants in the wintertime, when food is scarce and the bark of your favorite tree makes an easy meal. Fruit trees are especially at risk. Even during the summer, if you have a thick layer of mulch surrounding the tree right up to the trunk, the rodents can hide in the mulch and feed undetected. To guard against giving them sanctuary and to deter feeding, leave a space of several inches between the trunk and the mulch. If necessary, remove all the mulch around trees and shrubs in the winter, because the animals don't like to feed out in the open, where predators can find them. Snow cover also provides a hiding place. Where voles are a problem, wrap the trunks of young trees with a tree guard made of wire or plastic.

Voles create extensive networks of tunnels that, if located under your garden or lawn, can cause root damage. Chewed root vegetables probably are the work of voles. Look for the tiny, ⅛-inch-wide chisel marks left by their incisors. Damage to stored vegetables, on the other hand, probably is the work of mice.

Voles are hard to control, but you can discourage them by keeping your yard free of weeds and keeping grass mowed. Surround valuable plantings with a fence made of ¼-inch hardware cloth buried 6 inches deep and rising at least a foot off the ground. Keep the perimeter mowed and free of plant debris.

Moles and Skunks

These critters are the innocent bystanders or innocent burrowers of the garden-pest realm. Unlike voles, moles are carnivores and don't eat plants. They simply love to burrow in search of grubs, earthworms, and other insects. In the process, they inadvertently expose plant roots to air or push the plants out of the ground, in both cases killing the plants.

Moles produce two types of tunnels: tunnels that lie just beneath the surface and appear as raised ridges in your lawn, and tunnels that go much deeper, connecting the surface tunnels. It's when they're digging the deep tunnels that moles create the characteristic round, volcano-like mound of soil. Field mice or voles may also use the tunnels to forage for plant roots and flower bulbs. The best strategy for controlling moles is to control the grubs they're hunting by using some of the strategies discussed in Chapter 8.

Like moles, skunks will dig up a lawn in search of grubs. Look for their distinctive 3- to 5-inch-wide pits or cone-shaped holes. They may also remove or roll back sections of sod in their quest. Skunks will scavenge fallen fruit, slugs, and even pet food. To discourage them from their nocturnal visits, pick up pet food at night, keep garbage cans tightly closed, and treat your lawn for grubs. Skunks love eggs, so you may be attracting them inadvertently if you put eggshells in your compost.

Squirrels

Squirrels are so bold, it's likely that you'll catch them in the act of digging in your garden. These agile, fearless creatures can cause quite a problem, especially in newly planted bulb beds; crocus and tulip bulbs are like candy to them. They're also likely to eat fruits, nuts, berries, seedlings, and bark.

You can't get rid of squirrels permanently. If you evict your current residents, new ones will come to take their place. You can try deterrents like spraying bad-tasting sprays on favorite plants, however.

To protect your bulbs in fall, cover newly planted beds with chicken wire; the bulbs will grow right through it in spring. Be sure to plant bulbs at the proper depth, too, and take care not to leave any bulb debris (such as pieces of the papery outer covering) on the soil surface to attract squirrels. Motion detector–activated sprinklers can offer short-term help.

Don't use mothballs in the garden. You don't want this potential carcinogen contaminating your soil.

Raccoons

Raccoons like to eat pretty much anything. They seem to appear out of nowhere to pilfer your fruit and corn just before you get out to harvest it. They also eat grubs and, like skunks, dig up your lawn to find them, damaging plants in the process.

Repellents and motion detector-activated sprinklers may provide enough protection to allow your crops to ripen. Controlling grubs in the lawn (using the techniques described in Chapter 8) can also help. A low, two-strand electric fence, described in the "Groundhogs" section earlier in this chapter, may keep them out of vegetable gardens.

Armadillos

Armadillos are awfully cute until they decide to tear up your lawn in search of insects and grubs. These creatures can climb and burrow, but you may be able to exclude them from your yard with a fence that slants outward and extends 1 foot into the soil and 2 feet aboveground.

Your garden is my litter box

Roaming cats enjoy loose soil and mulch, and frequently use gardens and landscaped areas as litter boxes. Laying rough-textured or chunky bark mulch or ornamental rocks on the soil may repel them, because these materials are uncomfortable to soft paws. You can also lay chicken wire on the soil and cover it with mulch.

Cats don't like the smell of dog hair or anise oil, so try spreading these substances on the soil. Shredded lemon and grapefruit peels also deter cats. If you prefer using a commercial product, try one like Bad Cat, which contains citrus oils.

Armadillos have poor eyesight but an acute sense of smell. Try deterring them by sprinkling human hair around the garden or by using a low electric fence, described in the "Groundhogs" section.

Birds

Birds in the yard are a mixed blessing. You appreciate their appetite for insects, but when they nibble on the tomatoes and devour the ripe blueberries, they cross the line into nuisance territory. You can keep birds away from your plants by draping bird netting or row covers over them, but this solution isn't always practical.

Noise, fluttering objects, and anything resembling a predator can startle birds. Try bordering your garden with strings tied to stakes and fastening aluminum pie plates or unwanted CD disks to the string. The noise and flashing of the sun on the shiny surfaces can scare birds away. Or instead of string, use only a thin nylon line, which will vibrate and hum in the breeze.

You can use the modern version of the scarecrow: balloons and kites with images of predators, such as owls and hawks. Place them in the garden to convince birds that their enemy is on guard.

Birds catch on quickly, so change your scare tactics regularly.

Chapter 11

Weed It and Reap!

· ·

· ·

Controlling weeds is one of the biggest challenges for all gardeners, but especially for those of us trying to grow organically. Weeds compete with your lawn and garden plants for food, water, and sun; they harbor injurious pests and diseases; and they run amok, making the yard look unkempt.

The organic weed-control methods described in this chapter offer new hope of winning the battle against weeds without poisoning the environment. But *wild plants,* as I prefer to call weeds, also offer an opportunity. They give observant gardeners clues about the soil in which they grow and provide habitat for helpful insects as well as harmful ones. And some so-called weeds are actually valued garden plants in other regions: One man's trash is another man's treasure.

Winning the Weed Wars

Weeding is not a favorite gardening activity; it's just not glamorous. I don't know about you, but I prefer almost any other chore to crawling around on my knees in the dirt and pulling weeds. And although my tool shed is festooned with quite a number of very effective weeding tools, I've learned by experience that it's better to prevent them from sprouting in the first place.

Use the techniques in the following sections to prevent and control weeds in your landscape and garden. Choose the methods that match your needs, whether you're starting a new garden or maintaining an established planting.

Mulching

Just like other plants, weeds need air and light to grow, and if you deprive them of these crucial requirements, they die. One of the best ways to keep weeds in the dark is to put mulch over them. *Mulch* is anything that covers the soil for the purpose of preventing weeds, conserving moisture, or moderating the soil temperature.

Many materials make good mulch. The ones you choose really depend on what's locally available, how much you want to spend, the appearance factor, and where you plan to put it.

Decomposing mulches

The best mulch materials for organic gardens and landscapes also feed the worms and add organic matter to the soil as they decompose. Usually, 2- to 4-inch layers are sufficient to do the job, depending on the density of the material. Take a look at the following popular mulches and their uses:

- ✔ **Tree bark:** Tree bark is the ubiquitous landscape mulch. Available in shreds or chunks of various sizes, bark lasts a long time (depending on the particle size) and gives your landscape a finished look. Be sure you're buying real bark, however, by checking the bag label or asking the seller for the content. Wood chips that are dyed to look like bark are becoming prevalent in some areas.

- ✔ **Wood chips, sawdust, and shavings:** Although suitable for mulch, these products break down more quickly than bark and compete with your plants for nitrogen as they decompose. If you use these substances around food and landscape plants, be sure to add an additional nitrogen source, such as those described in Chapter 6. Fine materials like sawdust can compact so tightly that water can't penetrate.

Never use materials from pressure-treated wood. Although the green-hued, CCA (chromated copper arsenate), pressure-treated wood was phased out in 2004, the newer types of pressure-treated wood may still contain substances that you don't want in your gardens.

- ✔ **Shredded leaves and pine needles:** These materials are among the best sources of free, attractive, and nutrient-rich mulch for flower beds, fruits, and vegetables. Be sure to shred leaves before using to prevent matting in the garden. I run over fallen leaves with the lawn mower, discharging them into easy-to-rake mounds.

Pine needles and the leaves of oak and some other trees acidify the soil. Use these freely around acid-loving plants, but monitor the soil pH around less tolerant plants. Some plants are sensitive to the chemicals in certain tree leaves. Cabbage-family plants, for example, don't like oak leaves, and many plants, including tomatoes and blueberries, are incompatible with walnut leaves.

Choose plants with staggered bloom periods so you have something in bloom from spring to fall, not only for beauty, but also to attract beneficial insects and pollinators.

Freshly harvested organic fruits, vegetables, and herbs taste better and may contain more nutrients than their conventionally grown counterparts.

Bumblebees are important pollinators; invite them to your garden with nectar-rich flowers such as these ornamental oregano blooms.

Many vining plants thrive on trellises, where good air circulation minimizes diseases and the plants take up less garden space.

Choosing diverse plants for your landscape invites beneficial insects and discourages pests from running rampant.

Adding composted manure to garden beds increases soil organic matter and promotes a healthy soil ecosystem.

This unusual purple-streaked eggplant thrives in an organic garden.

Sow seeds of fall greens in compost-rich soil for harvesting into early winter.

Don't assume all problems are caused by pests! These leaves were damaged by hail.

Once you've tasted organically grown heirloom tomatoes you'll never go back to supermarket fare.

Install a bird feeder to encourage insect-eating birds like this indigo bunting to take up residence in your landscape.

Create season-long interest by combining plants with a variety of flower and foliage textures and colors.

A mulch of pine straw controls weeds in this garden filled with a variety of herbs, flowers, and vegetables.

Attract beautiful butterflies by planting nectar-rich flowers like this tithonia.

Harvest squash like this pattypan when they're young and tender.

Soaker hoses, like the one under this pepper plant, provide a slow, steady supply of water right at the root zone and use water more efficiently than overhead sprinklers.

This organically grown mixed perennial border attracts beneficial insects and butterflies and provides bountiful flowers for bouquets.

The rich soil in these raised beds allows the gardener to grow an abundance of food in a small space.

Assess your landscape and choose plants that thrive in your climate and specific garden conditions.

The row cover on the left keeps flea beetles off eggplant seedlings. On the right, powdery Surround, a particle film barrier, deters caterpillars on cole crops.

Fertilize seedlings with a dilute solution of liquid organic fertilizer, such as a seaweed/ fish emulsion product.

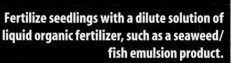

The mulch in this woodland garden suppresses weeds and keeps the soil moist and cool, providing a perfect habitat for shade-loving plants.

Conserve water by using soaker hoses and mulching plants with straw, bark chips, or pine straw.

Beautiful and nutritious, these vegetables, herbs, and flowers were all grown organically and harvested at their peak.

One of the easiest crops to grow organically, greens like these are not only beautiful, but they're also nutritious.

- **Seed hulls and crop residue:** These attractive, locally available, light-weight materials include cocoa bean, buckwheat hulls, ground corncobs, and other substances left over from processing an agricultural crop. Use on top of newspaper or other sheet mulch to increase suppression of weeds.

  If you decide to use cocoa mulch, take care: It can be toxic to dogs.

- **Straw and hay:** Although straw and hay are traditional mulches for vegetables and strawberries, beware! Hay contains weed seeds that can add to your problems. Straw from grain crops, such as oats and wheat, contains fewer seeds and is a better choice as weed-suppressing mulch. Allow the soil to warm up in the spring before putting mulch around tomatoes and other heat-loving crops; otherwise, the straw will insulate the soil from the sun's warmth.

- **Lawn clippings:** Clippings cost nothing and work best in flower and vegetable gardens, where they decompose quickly. Allow the clippings to dry on the lawn before raking them up. Fresh clippings may mat down and become slimy as they decompose. If you're getting clippings from a well-meaning friend, be sure that the clippings don't come from a chemically treated lawn.

- **Newspaper and cardboard:** Use cardboard or several layers of whole newspaper sheets in pathways or around landscape plants to smother weeds. (Avoid using the colored glossy pages.) Cover with a thick layer of loose mulch, such as bark, shredded leaves, or straw. Depending on rainfall, you may have to replace newspaper during the growing season.

  If you have lots of ground to cover, ask your local newspaper printer whether you can have or buy the ends of paper rolls left over from printing. It's easy to roll out a section, moisten the paper with a hose, and apply mulch, and then continue unrolling the paper for the next section.

Some organic mulches can go sour if they get too wet and packed down, and begin to decompose without sufficient air. If your mulch smells like vinegar, ammonia, sulfur, or silage, mix and aerate it with a garden fork. Don't apply sour mulch around flowers, vegetables, fruits, or young shrubs and trees; its acidity can damage or even kill the plants. Cover unused mulch piles with a tarp.

No matter what kind of organic mulch you use, keep it away from direct contact with plant stems and trunks. Pull it several inches away from the plants to prevent moisture buildup around the trunks and to deter insects, slugs, rodents, and diseases. Be sure to loosen mulch with a rake periodically to allow water to penetrate easily.

Nondecomposing mulches

Some mulches don't decompose but have other special uses that make them useful in some situations:

✔ **Gravel and stone** are best for landscapes in fire-prone areas and around buildings where termites and carpenter ants pose problems. They don't add significant nutrients to the soil, however, and usually need landscape fabric (see the following paragraph) under them to prevent weeds. Avoid sand, which attracts cats, ants, and weed seeds.

✔ **Landscape fabrics** allow water to pass through but shade the ground and prevent weeds from coming up. They also prevent organic material from reaching the soil, however, and I find that shallow-rooted plants such as blueberries grow roots into the landscape fabric, making it difficult to remove later.

Although the synthetic fabric lasts a long time, it may need to be replaced at some point. Use it around trees and shrubs or under decks where you don't want weeds, but avoid using landscape fabrics in gardens. There are new paper versions of landscape fabric that can be used anywhere.

✔ **Plastic sheeting** is commonly used to cover soil under heat-loving crops like tomatoes and squash. Black and colored plastics heat the soil; white plastic keeps it cool. Plants growing in plastic mulch need careful and frequent irrigation because rain won't reach the soil. Don't use plastic sheeting around landscape plants, because it prevents water and air from reaching roots.

Many specialty plastic mulches are available now, in addition to the basic black and clear plastic that you find in the hardware store. Here are two examples:

- **IRT (infrared transmitting) plastic** lets in the warming rays of the sun but blocks the rays that stimulate seed growth.

- **SRM (selective reflective mulches)** warm the soil, increase some crop yields, and may repel some pests. But their unique benefit is that they reflect specific wavelengths of light back to the plants, stimulating growth.

Some organic gardeners avoid plastic mulches despite their benefits because as they age they become brittle and break into pieces but never truly biodegrade.

✔ **Mulch mats** are made from a variety of materials, including cocoa fiber and recycled rubber. Most of these mats are designed to look like bark mulch but last much longer. Circular mats are designed to be placed around trees; the long strips are for edging beds.

Solarizing

One of the niftiest ways to beat the weeds is to *solarize* — use the heating power of the sun. The concept is simple: Capture the sun's heat under a sheet of clear plastic and literally bake the weeds and their seeds to death. Use solarization to clear existing plants from new gardens. If the soil gets hot enough, solarization also eliminates some soil-dwelling pests and diseases.

This technique takes several weeks in warm, sunny climates. If you garden in a cool, cloudy climate, try it during the warmest or sunniest times of year, and allow up to 8 weeks for the process to work. Here's how to do it:

1. **Mow closely or till the ground to remove as much of the existing vegetation as you can.**

   Solarization works best on bare ground.

2. **Dampen the soil.**

   Moisture helps speed the process.

3. **Spread a sheet of heavy-gauge clear plastic over the area.**

   Stretch it taut to keep it close to the ground, as shown in Figure 11-1.

4. **Anchor with stones.**

   Place a few stones or other weights on the plastic to keep it from blowing around and to hold it near the soil.

5. **Seal the edge of the plastic to hold in the heat by covering it all the way around with soil or boards.**

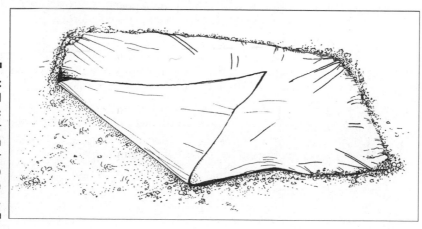

Figure 11-1: Spread clear plastic and anchor it with stones or boards to solarize the soil.

Avoid tilling the soil after solarization; otherwise, you may bring new seeds to the surface.

Cover cropping

Open ground is an open invitation for weed seeds to take root and for creeping plants to expand their territory. You can prevent and smother weeds, protect the soil from erosion, and enrich the soil at the same time by planting crops that you can till into the soil later. Thickly planted cover crops prevent weed seeds from sprouting and crowd out the ones that do. When the cover crop has done its job, you simply rototill it into the soil, where it decomposes and adds organic matter. (Cover crops grown primarily to add nutrients are sometimes called *green manures,* which I discuss in Chapter 5.)

Unlike some other weed-control measures, cover cropping requires you to plan ahead.

Legumes, grasses, and buckwheat

Cover crops fall into two broad categories. Within each group, some crops live for a single season and others are *perennial,* coming back year after year:

- **Legumes:** Plants that can convert nitrogen from the air to nitrogen in the soil are called *legumes.* These plants increase the fertility of the soil while they grow and add rich organic matter when they're rotary-tilled under. Some of them, especially alfalfa, have deep roots that bring water and other nutrients to the surface.

  Legumes provide an excellent source of nectar for bees as well as habitat for numerous beneficial insects. Legumes for cover crops include several types of clover, hairy vetch, soybeans, and alfalfa.

- **Grasses and buckwheat:** These cover crops grow quickly, allowing you to till under some of them just a few weeks after planting; others can remain in place for months. Either way, they add large amounts of organic matter to the soil.

  Buckwheat flowers are valuable for bee nectar. Other cover crops in this group include annual ryegrass, oats, winter rye, and Sudangrass.

Ways to use cover crops

Cover crops can serve your garden needs in different ways, depending on your goals and time frame:

✔ **New garden preparation:** The year before you intend to plant a vegetable, fruit, or flower garden, turn over the soil and sow a thick cover crop. Depending on the crop used and on whether you have time, turn under the first cover crop and grow another before tilling the garden for food or flowers.

✔ **Between gardening seasons:** After you harvest the last of your vegetables and remove the crop residue from the garden, sow a cover crop for the winter. If you live in a cold-winter climate, choose a fast-growing grass and plant it at least several weeks before the ground freezes. Turn it under in the spring. In warmer climates, prevent the cover crop from going to seed; otherwise, it can become a weed itself.

✔ **During the garden season:** Some cover crops, especially white clover, are useful as permanent ground covers in orchards and in the aisles between permanent planting beds. Clover encourages beneficial insects and adds nitrogen to the soil while preventing noxious weeds.

Farm supply stores usually are the least expensive sources of cover-crop seed. Their knowledgeable staff can help you choose the best crop for your climate and particular need. If you don't have a farm supply store nearby or just need a small amount of seed, buy it from a seed catalog that specializes in organic supplies. Read more about cover crops in Chapter 5.

Flaming

Among the latest and most effective weed killers to hit the market are propane-fueled flamers, which make quick work of weeds. These devices don't actually set plants on fire; they have special nozzles that work by literally boiling the sap inside the plants and bursting their cells.

The least expensive flamer costs little more than a high-quality rake and is a worthwhile investment for a large garden, yard, or orchard. Expect to pay $30 to more than $100 for a flamer hose, fittings, nozzle, and valves. The gear attaches to any standard propane tank, such as the kind used for barbecue grills. The most expensive models allow you to wear the fuel tank as a backpack and include convenient squeeze-control valves. You can purchase flamers at farm and garden supply stores and from mail-order companies.

For the most effective control, use your flamer when weeds are small (see Figure 11-2). Large weeds and tough perennials may need repeat treatments.

Avoid using flamers in windy or dry conditions, especially if you live in an arid region. Keep a hose or other water source handy to douse unexpected flames.

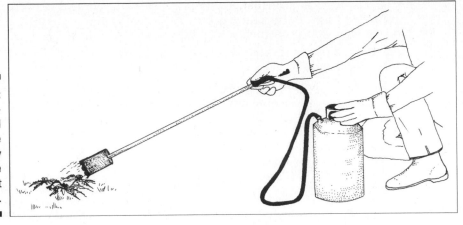

Figure 11-2: Propane-powered flamers are especially effective against weeds.

Flamers use a nonrenewable resource, propane, to generate the heat. Gardeners striving for a sustainable landscape may want to limit the use of propane, which is a fossil fuel.

Pulling and cultivating

Good old-fashioned hand pulling and hoeing aren't among gardeners' favorite garden chores, but they work, especially if you follow these two basic rules:

✔ **Disturb the soil as little as possible.** This first rule is really important, because many weed seeds lie dormant in the darkness just under the soil surface. When you churn up the soil, you expose the seeds to the light and air they need to sprout and attain pest status.

✔ **Get them while they're small.** Small weeds with fragile roots and stems take little effort to destroy. Large weeds take more work, disrupt more soil, and potentially contribute to the seed population in your soil if you leave them long enough to go to seed. Also, the longer the weeds live, the more water and nutrients they rob from your food and landscape plants.

Weeding techniques

If you'll be pulling by hand, moisten the soil thoroughly first, preferably the day before so that the soil can drain. The weeds will be much easier to pull and you're more likely to get the whole root than you would in dry soil. You can leave small pulled weed seedlings in the garden to decompose; remove larger ones to the compost pile.

Weed your garden in sections. When you complete a section, immediately cover the soil with a layer of organic mulch to prevent more weeds from invading. Any weeds that do manage to grow through the mulch will be easier to pull. To keep lawn grass from invading perennial beds, install edging that extends several inches into the soil.

Weeding tools

With so many different weeding devices on the market, you may have a difficult time choosing the most effective tools for the job. The kinds of weeds that you're dealing with affect your choice. For plants with long taproots (dandelions and burdock, for example), you need a tool that reaches down into the soil and pulls out the entire root without disturbing your lawn too much. I use a *dandelion weeder,* also called an *asparagus knife* or *fishtail weeder,* which consists of a 12-inch-long metal rod with a forked tip and wooden handle.

Most weeds don't require such a specialized tool, however. The most effective and all-around useful weeding tools disturb very little soil as they work. The best hoes for weeding, shown in Figure 11-3, have sharp blades that slice the plants just below the soil surface:

- ✔ **Collinear hoe:** The collinear hoe allows you to stand up straight as you weed.

- ✔ **Stirrup hoe:** I use the stirrup hoe frequently because it cuts on both the push and pull actions.

- ✔ **Swan-neck hoe:** The swan-neck hoe gets into tight spots easily.

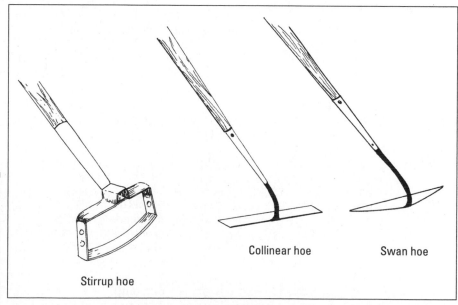

Figure 11-3: Weeding hoes slice plants off just below the soil surface.

Stirrup hoe

Collinear hoe

Swan hoe

Smaller hand tools and those with shorter handles are available too; they allow you to weed raised beds or weed while sitting or kneeling.

All weeding hoes need occasional touching up with a sharpening stone.

Organic herbicides

When all else fails, gardeners can turn to herbicides to kill the weeds. Before you accuse me of blasphemy, allow me to introduce you to some organic weed-control chemicals. As with any chemical treatment — organic or synthetic — use the most powerful ones only as a last resort.

Herbicides work in several ways that depend on a particular plant's life stage or characteristics to be effective:

✔ **Pre-emergent herbicide:** Sprouting seeds send out roots first, followed by the stem and first leaves. This vulnerable time is the best and easiest stage in which to knock them out. Pre-emergent herbicides kill these tiny seedlings as they sprout and are especially useful on lawns and in other places where mature weeds are difficult to remove.

One relatively new organic pre-emergent herbicide is corn gluten meal, a highly concentrated corn protein extract. It can control weeds for up to six weeks if applied in early spring and again in late summer, and as a bonus, it's high in nitrogen.

✔ **Herbicidal soap:** Plants have a waxy coating on their leaves that prevents moisture loss. Herbicidal soap damages the waxy layer, allowing the plant to dry out and die. This type of herbicide works best on young, tender, actively growing weeds in hot, dry weather. It's less effective on mature plants and perennial weeds.

Plants are sensitive to changes in pH. Some products use acetic acid (derived from vinegar) or pelargonic acid (derived from fruit) as their active ingredient. These acids damage the plants' protective waxy coating, killing the sprayed plant parts in a matter of hours.

Regular kitchen vinegar is only 5 percent acetic acid; though it may kill weed seedlings, it has little effect on mature plants. Commercial formulations of up to 20 percent acetic acid are available. Although these substances are more potent weed-killers, they're also more hazardous to use. Follow label directions, wear gloves and goggles when applying, and store them as you would any other garden chemicals.

These products are acceptable for spot treatments but shouldn't be used extensively, because they also kill beneficial organisms and lower soil pH. New formulations made from a combination of vinegar and citrus, cinnamon, and/or clove oils have been introduced recently.

Home Sweet Home

As if weeds themselves weren't bad enough, they also contribute to the two other major headaches that gardeners face: pests and diseases. Knowing which insects and diseases the wild plants around your garden harbor can help you decide whether to encourage their growth or eradicate them.

For insects, both good and bad

Wild plants provide habitat for a wide range of insects, but not all bugs are bad bugs. Some insects (such as the beneficial insects discussed in Chapter 7) actually help your garden, and many of them depend on wild plants for habitat — places to lay their eggs, forage for food, and spend the winter months.

Wild plants with small flowers — yarrow, goldenrod, pigweed, and wild carrots — attract many beneficial insects. In addition, wasps that prey on aphids, caterpillars, and other pests also enjoy pollen and nectar-rich flowers, such as dandelions, daisies, clover, nettles, and coneflowers. Leave these plants in the wild places outside your garden, but remove their spent flowers before they go to seed and spread beyond their allotted space.

Some wild plants not only provide habitat for beneficial bugs, but also create a haven for damaging insects. Carrot rust flies live on both wild and garden-variety carrots, for example, and wild apple trees harbor curculio, apple maggots, and codling moths that move into your nearby orchard. Consider eliminating these wild plants near your garden if you have trouble with the pests they perpetuate.

Another way that some wild plants benefit your garden is by attracting pests that would otherwise discover and damage your crops. I'm perfectly happy to encourage the wild grapes and other so-called *trap plants* that Japanese beetles like to munch if they leave my roses alone! In some cases, you may wait to until these wild weeds have attracted a load of pests and then destroy them, taking care of two problems at the same time. Flowering mustard, for example, attracts cabbage worms and harlequin bugs. When the wild plants contain plenty of pests, pull them up and destroy them — killing two birds with one stone, so to speak.

For diseases that spread to related plants

Wild plants often suffer the same diseases that affect cultivated plants and gladly spread their misery around. Related plants such as those in the nightshade family — including deadly nightshade, horsenettle, potatoes, tomatoes, and eggplants — can infect one another with verticillium wilt and other diseases. Wild brambles share viruses with strawberries and cultivated brambles. Insects that feed on these plants often spread diseases as they travel and forage, and the soil remains contaminated even after the diseased weeds are gone. Avoid planting vulnerable plants in the same soil where related species grew within the past few years, and control insects that spread diseases.

See Chapter 9 for more on diseases and Chapter 8 for insect identification and control.

Part IV
Growing Organically in Your Yard and Garden

The 5th Wave   By Rich Tennant

"Plenty of sunshine, organic matter, and the right soil will keep them bright and colorful. And what that won't do, a box of fluorescent felt tip markers will take care of."

In this part . . .

Chapter 12 provides general information on sowing seeds, choosing healthy plants, and setting plants out in the garden. Each subsequent chapter in this part is devoted to a special segment of your garden or landscape. Chapter 13 walks you through the vegetable garden, and Chapter 14 gives you great growing tips for herbs. If you're leaning toward fruits and nuts, I've got you covered in Chapters 15 and 16.

For a tiptoe through the tulips — or daylilies or zinnias — prance over to Chapter 17. Think you can't grow organic roses? Think again after reading Chapter 18.

Make your landscape the envy of the neighborhood with the tips on trees and shrubs in Chapter 19 and lawns in Chapter 20. This part lists the most pest-free, low-maintenance trees, shrubs, and turf grasses for your growing conditions.

Chapter 12

Planting How-To

· ·

· ·

Whether you're planting vegetables, fruits, herbs, or trees and shrubs, it's important to know a little something about each plant, such as when to plant it and how it grows. This chapter gives you an overview of the various types of plants and describes planting techniques. Look to Chapters 13–20 for more specific information on different types of garden and landscape plants.

Types of Plants

Garden and landscape plants can be divided into categories — annuals, biennials, and perennials (both herbaceous and woody) — based on their life cycles. I describe all four types of plants in the following sections. (Refer to Chapter 3 for more information about plant types, hardiness, and climate zones.)

Annual plants

Annual plants complete their life cycles in one growing season and must be replanted each spring. Most vegetables and some flowers and herbs are annuals. You plant annual crops in spring, and harvest in summer and autumn; then the plants die. The following spring, you start over. Tomatoes, peppers, corn, and melons fall into this category. So do herbs like dill and basil, and flowers like sunflowers and zinnias.

You can purchase annuals as young plants growing in containers — sometimes called *transplants* or *starter plants* — or start them yourself from seed. Some plants are easier to start from seed than others; see "Starting from Seed," later in this chapter.

Biennial plants

Biennial plants complete their life cycles in two years. Because they flower in their second year, by planting biennials every year you'll always have some in bloom. Biennials, such as parsley, that are grown for their leaves are often grown as annuals and replanted each spring (see the preceding section).

If you purchase or sow biennial flowers, make sure the plants are hardy in your area because they'll need to overwinter, then bloom in the second growing season.

Herbaceous perennials

Herbaceous perennials are plants that live for more than two years. Each autumn the aboveground parts die back. If a perennial is hardy in your region, the roots remain alive and resprout the following spring. Many flowers and herbs are herbaceous perennials, as are a few familiar vegetables and fruits, such as asparagus, horseradish, and strawberries. Perennial herbs include thyme, oregano, and sage. The thousands of perennial flowers include coneflower, black-eyed Susan, and peony.

Perennial plants are sometimes started from seed but are more commonly sold growing in containers or as bare-root plants. *Bare-root plants* are sold during their dormant season and are packaged without soil around their roots. Instead, the roots are packed in moist newspaper or sawdust. Asparagus and strawberries are commonly sold in bare-root condition.

Woody perennials

Woody perennials are plants whose aboveground parts persist throughout the winter and are more commonly called trees and shrubs. Most landscapes include trees and shrubs, most of which are grown for their ornamental properties. Landscape designers sometimes describe these woody plants as forming the *bones* of the landscape. They provide a year-round framework and backdrop for other garden plants.

Woody plants are sold growing in containers, bare root, or balled and burlapped. *Balled and burlapped* plants are dug from the field with a ball of soil around their roots; then this ball of soil is wrapped in burlap or plastic.

Why bare root?

If properly stored and shipped, bare-root plants grow as well as, or better than, container-grown plants. Bare-root plants are often less expensive, and you may find a greater selection of varieties than in container-grown plants, especially from mail-order companies.

These plants must be kept cool so that they don't break dormancy until they're planted. If you purchase plants through the mail, be sure to keep them cool upon arrival and plant them within a day or two.

Avoid buying bare-root plants that have been sitting on store shelves and have begun to sprout. They are no longer dormant and will struggle to get established in your garden.

Starting from Seed

You can start many plants from seed, but annual flowers and vegetables are the most common types. Starting your own plants from seed has many benefits:

✔ **Seeds usually come in greater variety than plants.** A store may offer a half-dozen varieties of tomato plants, for example, but hundreds of tomato varieties are available by seed. The same is true of many flowers.

✔ **You control what's sprayed on plants.** Growers and garden centers may use nonorganic pesticides; if you start from seed, you can manage pests organically.

✔ **You can provide plants the optimum conditions to thrive.** Purchased plants are often grown in hot, humid greenhouses and given a daily dose of synthetic fertilizer to promote fast growth. By the time they reach store shelves, they're often root-bound, with the roots completely filling the pot. In the garden, these plants may struggle to adapt to the harsher conditions, and their small root systems are so used to synthetic nutrients that they may not be able to take up nutrients from the soil efficiently.

✔ **Some plants grow best from seed.** Although you can purchase squash and nasturtium as starter plants, for example, these varieties grow so quickly from seed that seed-grown plants often outperform transplanted ones that need time to acclimate after planting.

✔ **It's fun!** Perhaps this is the best reason.

You have two ways to grow plants from seed: direct sowing and starting plants in containers. I discuss both methods in the following sections.

Sorting out seed types

When choosing varieties of seeds to plant, you may come across the terms *open pollinated, heirloom, hybrid, and genetically modified.* The first three types are important for home gardeners; the fourth is a new type that, to date, applies mainly to commercial farmers.

✔ *Open-pollinated* varieties produce offspring that are similar to the parents. The flowers are pollinated naturally rather than in a plant-breeding lab. Some genetic variability occurs among the plants, so when growers save seed from their best-performing plants, those traits are passed to the offspring. Many open-pollinated varieties are locally adapted and have unusual colors, shapes, and flavors. Gardeners have relied on these varieties for generations because they can save the seeds for replanting.

✔ *Heirloom* seeds are varieties that have been planted for several generations — perhaps 50 years or more, although there's no specific longevity required to qualify as an heirloom.

✔ *Hybrid varieties* have been around since the 1920s. Researchers found that breeding different corn varieties together resulted in offspring with better traits than either parent, and they grew more vigorously and uniformly. Many hybrid varieties exhibit improved disease resistance. Hybrid seeds are a result of controlled cross-pollination of specific parent plants. For this reason, plants grown from seed collected from hybrid plants may not resemble the parent plant closely. If you plant seeds from a hybrid tomato, for example, you'll get a tomato plant, but its fruit may not taste nearly as good as does the parent plant's.

✔ *Genetically modified* plants (sometimes called genetically modified organisms, or GMOs) are created through gene splicing, wherein genetic material from unrelated plants or even other organisms is inserted into a plant. These varieties generally are available only to commercial farmers. Genetically modified plants may offer some benefits, but many questions still exist about the long-term health risks and environmental safety of manipulating the gene pool so dramatically and quickly. GMOs are not allowed in organic growing. Read more about GMOs in Chapter 2.

Which type of seeds to plant is a personal decision, and your decision doesn't have to be all or nothing. Many organic growers plant hybrids; others opt for open-pollinated varieties so that they can save seeds for replanting. If you know that tomatoes commonly suffer from *Fusarium* in your area, for example, go ahead and plant some flavorful but susceptible heirloom Brandywine tomatoes — but include a few *Fusarium*-resistant hybrid plants too, just in case the disease is especially bad this year and your Brandywines succumb. The key is to experiment in your garden with a range of varieties to find the ones that grow, produce, and taste best.

Sowing seeds directly

Some plants grow best when their seed is sown directly into the garden. In some cases, the plants grow so quickly that direct sowing is the most efficient method. In other cases, the seedlings' roots are so sensitive that they don't like to be disturbed.

Corn, beans, peas, carrots, sunflowers, larkspur, and morning glories all grow best when their seeds are planted directly in the garden.

Preparing the soil

Well-prepared soil is the key to successful growing, especially with seeds that you sow directly in the garden. Remove golf-ball-size or larger rocks and clods of soil; rake the bed flat. For more about preparing your soil, see Chapter 5.

Sowing the seeds

Whether you're planting flower or vegetable seeds, the general rule is to plant seeds twice as deep as the seeds are wide. For big seeds, such as beans, that means about 1 to 2 inches deep; small seeds, such as lettuce, should be planted only ¼-inch deep. Heed the planting depth guidelines on seed packets, because seeds planted too deeply may not grow.

Seed packets also provide specific planting information. Some seeds require light to germinate, for example, and should be pressed into the soil surface rather than buried.

Label the beds, noting the plant type, planting date, and days to germination (also listed on the seed packet).

Tending the soil and the sprouts

After planting, keep the soil evenly moist, especially the soil surface. If the surface dries out, it can form a crust that prevents seedlings from emerging. In hot weather, a daily light sprinkling may be necessary.

You should see signs of life within a few days for quick sprouters or in two weeks or more for slow growers. Be patient — as long as you used fresh seed labeled for the current year, the plants should come up. In unusually wet and cold or hot and dry soil, however, seeds may rot or fail to sprout. Keep track of the days to germination, and if that period passes with no signs of sprouting, replant when the weather improves.

Starting seeds indoors

In many parts of the country, the growing season is too short to grow slow-maturing plants from seed sown in the garden. Tomatoes, peppers, petunias, and pansies are examples of plants that must be started indoors or in a heated greenhouse. By the time the weather warms up, the plants will be several inches tall and will have a good head start.

In regions with long winters, starting seeds indoors is a great way to beat the winter blues as well as to get a jump on the gardening season.

What you need

To start seeds indoors successfully, you need some specific equipment:

- **Sterile soilless seed-starting mix:** Purchased planting mix has the proper balance of drainage and water-holding capacity, and it's sterile to minimize disease problems. Avoid using garden soil to start seeds indoors; it often drains poorly and may harbor organisms that can damage germinating seeds. *Note:* Some seed-starting mixes contain synthetic fertilizers, so choose carefully.

- **Containers:** Any small vessel with drainage holes will suffice, but most gardeners use purchased plastic flats or peat pots set into a waterproof tray.

- **Light source:** Although some seeds can be started on a sunny windowsill, you'll have better success if you provide supplemental light. You can purchase commercial indoor light gardens or rig up a set of fluorescent lights over a table. Raise the lights (or lower the table) so that the lights remain close to, but not touching, the growing plants.

Planting your seeds

Before you begin, moisten the seed-starting mix with warm water. Then fill each container with mix, firming it gently. Sow seeds at the depth recommended on the seed packet. Label containers with the type of seed, the planting date, and the days to germination; then set the containers in a warm place. Check the containers daily, and as soon as you see the first sprout, place the containers under lights.

Caring for the emerging plants

To care for your growing plants, follow this advice:

- **Watering:** Plants growing in small containers may need watering daily. Strive to keep the soil evenly moist — think wrung-out sponge. Too much moisture can lead to root rot; too little moisture will wilt the plants.

- **Fertilizing:** Begin fertilizing your seedlings when they have two sets of true leaves (the first set of leaves is called *seed leaves*). One option is to use an organic fertilizer diluted to half strength once a week. Some gardeners use ¼-strength fertilizer at every watering.

- **Transplanting:** Depending on the type of plant, the size of the container, and the length of time until you set the plants out in the garden, you may need to transplant seedlings into larger containers. Do the transplanting when the roots are starting to fill out the container but before they begin to wrap around the perimeter and grow out the drainage holes.

When should you start different kinds of seeds? Create a planting calendar, as described in Chapter 13.

Keep seed packets so that you can refer to them during the season for information such as spacing guidelines. Also, if a crop performs especially well or a flower is particularly beautiful, having the packet allows you to track the source of the seeds.

Buying Plants

Few gardeners grow all their plants from seed; most of us buy some plants. These days, it seems as though everyone sells plants, from the traditional greenhouse/nursery to the drugstore. You can also order plants from a catalog or on the Internet. Wherever you purchase them, it pays to buy the best-quality plants that you can find.

Knowing your sources

Here are some pros and cons of different sources:

- **Locally owned garden centers:** They usually offer the best varieties for your area and can give you advice on growing them. Plants grown on-site haven't been subjected to shipping stress. Usually, the size-to-price ratio is excellent. Although the selection may not be as large as a mail-order catalog offers, I often find a good blend of favorite "bread-and-butter" varieties and newer, more exotic offerings.

- **National chain stores:** Garden centers attached to home improvement and mass-market department stores are known for their cheap prices and vast quantities of merchandise, but watch out for neglected plants. For the best-quality plants, show up when the delivery trucks do. Be sure that the perennials, trees, and shrubs you buy are truly hardy in your climate. The staff may or may not have a clue.

- **Mail-order catalogs and Web sites:** The glossy pictures look perfect and enticing, and the descriptions sound like dreams come true. Due to shipping costs, however, the plants usually are smaller and more expensive than locally grown specimens. The plants also have to undergo the rigors of hot or cold and bumpy travel. Catalogs, however, expand the universe of available plant varieties and offer a cornucopia for the specialist and the connoisseur.

Buying your plants from any specific source matters less than choosing vigorous, healthy specimens. When you buy your plants by mail, you're at the mercy of the supplier, so when you find a reliable source, you may want to stick with it rather than simply look around for the best deal.

Picking winners

When you're shopping for plants locally, it helps to know what qualities to look for. Here's how I pick the winners from the losers:

- ✔ **Look for disease-free foliage.** Avoid plants with yellow, brown, or black spots or with wilted, yellow, or mottled leaves. See Chapter 9 for more on diseases.

- ✔ **Check for pests.** Pass your hand gently over a flat of seedlings. If a cloud of whiteflies or tiny gnats swirls up out of the foliage, pass the plants by. Peek under leaves for aphids, thrips, and spider mites, and check stems for scale insects. See Chapter 8 for pest descriptions.

- ✔ **Watch for mechanical damage.** Look for broken stems or bruised leaves, which can indicate rough handling.

- ✔ **Choose plants whose compact growth is in proportion to pot size.** If the top of the plant appears to be too big for the pot, the roots may be squished and/or the plant has been pushed into vigorous growth with lots of fertilizer. Both conditions compromise the plant's health and ability to adapt to life in the garden.

- ✔ **Small is beautiful.** Large plants make a more immediate impact in your garden, but they cost more and recover from transplanting more slowly than smaller ones do. Small perennials and annuals often catch up in growth to larger plants within a few weeks and may even surpass them by season's end. And although they're tempting, avoid flowers that are already in full bloom. Instead, look for compact plants with healthy foliage.

 It goes without saying that buying wilted plants is a no-no. Plants need water to survive, and even a short drought when they are small and growing rapidly can affect how they perform in your garden in the coming months. If you see widespread wilting in the nursery, take your business elsewhere.

 When you transport your plants from the store to your planting site, protect them from wind, heat, and cold. Never carry them uncovered in the back of a truck — conditions in the bed of a moving truck are the equivalent of a hurricane — and don't leave them to cook in a closed vehicle. When you get them home, keep them in a cool, shady place, and water as needed until planting time.

Preparation and Planting

After you get your plants home from the nursery (or, if you planted them from seed, when you decide that they've grown enough), you can pop them right in the ground, right? Not so fast. Plants have a better chance of survival if you follow this advice first:

✔ **Check the calendar and the weather forecast.** Be sure that the temperatures are warm enough for the type of plant. If there's a threat of temperatures dropping into the 40s, heat-loving plants are going to be shocked and unhappy about their plight.

✔ **Prepare plants for outdoor life.** If you're planting indoor- or greenhouse-grown plants, you need to give them time to toughen up gradually so they can adjust to the natural wind and sun conditions in your garden. Introduce them to the great outdoors on cloudy, calm days, and bring them inside at night. Gradually allow them more direct sun and wind over a period of seven to ten days. Allow the soil to dry between waterings, but don't let the plants wilt. This process is called *hardening off*. When the plants can tolerate full sun and wind, they're ready for the garden. (Be sure to cover tender plants if frost threatens.)

✔ **Time your planting to coincide with seasonally cool and damp weather.** Transplanting invariably damages some roots, so plants may not be able to take up water fast enough to endure hot, sunny weather. If you must plant when it's hot, provide some shade and keep plants well watered until they can survive on their own.

✔ **Prepare the soil.** The perfect garden soil is weed free, well drained, loosened, and fertile. See Chapter 5 for more on soil.

When the weather is cooperative, the ground is ready, and your plants are hardened off, you're ready to go. The following sections tell you what to do.

Planting container-grown perennials, annuals, and vegetables

Whether your plants are purchased or homegrown, the act of putting plants in the ground is pretty straightforward, and most plants are quite forgiving. Water the plants a few hours before planting and then follow these simple steps to get your potted plants off to a good start:

1. **Dig a hole that's twice as wide as the pot.**

   Use a shovel or trowel, and make the hole deep enough to keep the plant at the same soil level that it occupied in its container.

2. **Gently remove the plant from the pot.**

   Cup your hand around the stem of the plant and tip the pot gently, supporting the soil with your fingers and the heel of your hand, and protecting the stem and leaves from bruising. Push or tap on the bottom of the pot if the plant resists, but don't pull on the stem.

   If the plant is large, lay the container on its side on the ground, and slide the plant out. Squeeze or roll the pot if necessary to dislodge the root ball; if you can't loosen it, cut the pot away.

3. **Put the plant into the hole.**

   In most cases, the *crown* of the plant — where the roots meet the top of the plant; usually the soil level in the pot — should be at or slightly above ground level. Add soil to or remove soil from the hole so the plant sits at the proper height.

4. **Backfill with soil.**

   Gently fill around the roots, firming the soil around the roots while keeping the crown at the proper level.

5. **Water the plant.**

   Saturate the soil gently, being careful not to displace the soil. Add more soil to the hole if needed.

   If water appears to be running off rather than soaking in, create a berm of soil in a circle around the plant to create a shallow basin (see Figure 12-1). Fill the basin with water, and allow it to soak in. To prevent stem rot, remove the berm during prolonged wet weather and after the plant is established.

Figure 12-1: Make a raised ring or berm of soil around the planting hole, and fill with water.

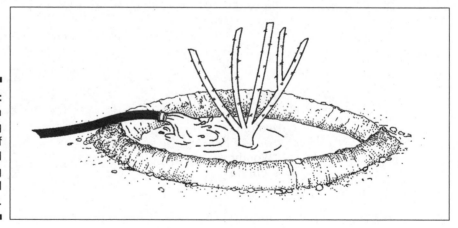

Planting bare-root plants

Plant bare-root plants as soon as possible after purchasing or receiving them through the mail. Immediately unwrap the plants from the packaging, and make sure that the packing material — usually sawdust or shredded paper — is moist. If you must delay planting for a few days, keep the plants moist and in a cool, dark location.

Don't store bare-root plants with any ripening fruit, such as in a refrigerator or root cellar, because the fruit gives off ethylene, which harms growing plants.

Here's how to get your bare-root plants off to a good start:

1. **Prune any damaged or dead roots and stems, and prune back extra-long roots so that they're even with the others.**

2. **Soak the root system**.

   Place the roots in a bucket of tepid water for about an hour before planting.

3. **Dig a planting hole that's twice as wide as your plant's root spread.**

   Follow the instructions that come with the plant to determine how deep to dig the hole. In many cases, the plant's crown should sit at the soil level, but the level varies depending on the type of plant.

4. **Make a mound of soil in the bottom of the hole and then set the plant on top of this mound, spreading the roots evenly around it.**

5. **Fill the planting hole half way and then add water to settle and moisten the soil around the roots.**

6. **Finish backfilling and then water the plant thoroughly.**

   If necessary, create a berm of soil in a circle around the plant to keep water from running off (refer to Figure 12-1).

Planting trees and shrubs

Trees and shrubs are often expensive, and it pays to take special care in planting them. Most woody plants are sold in containers or are balled and burlapped (refer to "Woody perennials," earlier in this chapter). Be sure that the soil is moist, but not sopping wet, at planting time to make handling easier. Prune any damaged, dead, or broken stems before planting.

In some circles, the proper way to dig a hole is controversial. What's the big deal, you ask? Plenty, if you ask someone who installs trees for a living. If you plant trees and shrubs too deep or too high, or crowd the roots into a small hole, they'll fail to thrive. People who study these things have also discovered that adding peat moss and other amendments to the planting hole is not only unnecessary but also can contribute to trouble in the long run: Roots tend to stay where the soil is most fertile and may not venture outside the walls of the original hole. The resulting plants have small root systems, are more prone to drought stress, and are likely to blow over in a strong wind.

Here's the right way to plant a tree or shrub:

1. **Measure the diameter of the root ball or root spread, and multiply the result by 3 to find the diameter of the hole you need to dig.**

   If the root ball is 1 foot wide, for example, you need a 3-foot-wide hole.

2. **Measure the depth of the root ball and dig a hole no bigger than this result.**

   The idea is to set the root ball on undisturbed soil. If it's sitting on loosened or amended soil, the tree or shrub may sink over time.

3. **Check the planting depth.**

   Test the depth by setting the tree in the hole. The *trunk flare* — where the trunk widens near the base — should be at the soil surface or slightly above it, as shown in Figure 12-2. Shrubs should be at or slightly above the soil depth at which they previously grew.

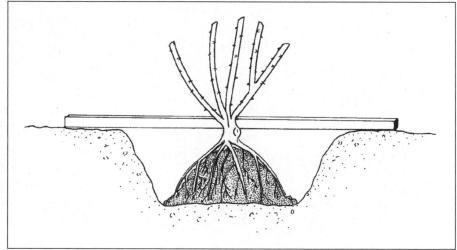

Figure 12-2: Position the tree so that the trunk flare is at the soil surface.

4. **Prepare the roots.**

   Lift the plant out of the hole and slip it out of its pot or remove the plastic burlap from the root ball. (You can leave natural burlap on the root ball because burlap degrades in the soil, but you should slice it off carefully and roll it down to help the decay process.) Prune broken roots and gently unwind tangled roots, preserving as many roots as possible.

5. **Put the plant back in the hole.**

6. **Backfill the hole until it is about three quarters full.**

   Fill the hole with the soil you removed from the hole, working it gently around the roots and holding the tree in position.

7. **Add water.**

   Fill the hole with water to settle the soil around the roots. Allow it to drain.

8. **Finish filling the hole with soil.**

9. **Make a watering basin.**

   Build a low ring of soil around the perimeter of the planting hole to hold water for the first few months (refer to Figure 12-1). Knock it down when the tree begins growing actively.

10. **Mulch and water again.**

    Spread a 2-inch-thick layer of bark or shredded leaf mulch over the planting area. Pull mulch 3 to 4 inches away from the trunk, however. Then water the tree again.

After planting your tree or shrub, water it only when the soil dries out to a depth of 4 to 6 inches. When you do add water, apply it slowly and gently, making sure that it soaks in rather than runs off. Moisten the soil down to the depth of the root ball.

What's at stake?

Unless your tree has a trunk greater than 3 inches in diameter or you live in a windy area, you probably don't need to stake it. Trees develop stronger roots and trunks if they're allowed to move in the wind. If you must stake a tree, follow these steps:

1. Place two stakes opposite each other and perpendicular to the prevailing wind.

2. Cut the stakes equal to half the height of the tree plus 18 inches.

3. Loosely attach loops made from strips of soft cloth to the tree and stakes so that the tree can gently sway in the wind.

4. Remove the stakes and ties after a year.

Chapter 13

Raising Organic Vegetables

For most people, growing chemical-free vegetables is what organic gardening is all about. As more and more news comes out about the dangers of chemical pesticides and fertilizers, more people are choosing to grow their own food — and are finding that homegrown vegetables are fresher and taste better than the store-bought kind.

In the first half of this chapter, I talk about designing and starting your vegetable garden, and give you some tips to make your garden more productive. The second half of the chapter describes the most popular home-garden vegetables and varieties, tells you how to grow and harvest them, and describes which pests you can expect to show up for dinner.

Planning Your Vegetable Garden

You may dream of a big garden filled with all types of fresh and inviting vegetables, but getting to that stage takes experience and preparation. For the first-timer, small is beautiful; take time to get it right on a small scale before launching a market-garden-size project. Keep the following ideas in mind to save yourself a lot of work and frustration later in the season:

  ✔ **Start small.** Little plants and seeds turn into a big commitment as they grow. A 10-x-20-foot garden is plenty to grow a variety of vegetables, such as lettuce, beans, carrots, tomatoes, and peppers. If you want to grow vining crops or space hogs such as corn or pumpkins, you can expand it to 20 x 30 feet. Planting too large a space to keep well tended probably is the number-one cause of gardener frustration and burnout.

✔ **Make it convenient and inviting.** Place the garden in a location where you'll see it daily. Mine is right outside the dining-room window, and my garden gets more attention now than it did when it was in the corner of our backyard. Your garden is more likely to thrive when you visit it regularly.

✔ **Put the garden in full sun.** Vegetable plants need at least six hours of full sun each day. Orient and plan the garden so that tall plants such as corn and tomatoes don't cast shade on shorter plants such as beets and cabbage.

✔ **Choose a well-drained spot.** Vegetables are more prone to disease in soggy soil. Consider building raised beds. See Chapter 5 for how to test and amend soil for proper drainage.

✔ **Grow a mix of crops.** Planting a variety of vegetables ensures that something will produce. Also, diversity in the garden encourages good insects and helps reduce problems from harmful ones.

Choosing varieties

For some vegetables, dozens — or even hundreds — of varieties are available. How do you choose? Try these tips:

✔ **Consider taste.** Some varieties are relatively mild; others are more strongly flavored. Romano beans, for example, are described as having a pronounced beany flavor, and purple asparagus varieties are sweeter than green varieties.

✔ **Look for disease resistance.** The letters *VFFNT* in Celebrity tomato descriptions, for example, denote resistance to verticillium wilt, two strains of fusarium wilt, nematodes, and tobacco mosaic virus. Look for scab-resistant potatoes, powdery mildew–resistant squash, and downy mildew–resistant lettuce, too.

✔ **Note days to maturity.** If you live where summers are short or plan to grow a succession of crops, look for relatively fast-maturing varieties.

✔ **Grow the unusual.** Consider planting unusual crops or varieties — those that aren't readily available in markets. Regular white potatoes are easy to find and inexpensive, but fingerling and blue potatoes are harder to find, and when you do find them they're often expensive.

✔ **Consider plant size.** Look for varieties described as compact if space is at a premium.

Deciding what goes where

You can be as creative or traditional as you like in your vegetable-garden design. Plant everything in straight rows or create imaginative curved raised beds. My vegetable garden is oddly shaped, so I frequently make rounded and triangular beds. I even made a heart-shaped raised bed one year and planted it with red-leaf lettuce and carrots!

Draw your garden plan on graph paper, laying out rows and raised beds with a ruler and pencil. To figure out how many plants will fit into a row or bed, follow the guidelines on the seed packets and make little dots or circles to indicate the larger veggies, such as broccoli, tomatoes, and squash.

When you plan your vegetable garden, leave room for walking paths at least 24 inches wide that allow you to harvest and work the beds easily. And don't be afraid to mix in herbs and flowers. The more color and variety a garden has, the more beautiful it is, and the more likely it is to strike an ecological balance with birds and beneficial insects that help keep harmful pests in check.

For even more garden success, try a few of the techniques I use in my garden. They may help you grow better and more vegetables, too:

- ✔ **Spread the wealth.** Don't plant all the same type of vegetables in one spot. I plant two small patches of beans in different places in the garden, for example, so that even if animals or insects destroy one patch, they may not find the other.

- ✔ **Rotate crops every planting season, if possible.** Follow crops that use lots of nitrogen, such as sweet corn and tomatoes, with crops that add nitrogen to the soil, such as beans and peas. Avoid planting crops from the same family, which tend to have the same insect pests and diseases, in the same spot — for example, tomatoes, eggplants, and potatoes or cabbage, broccoli, and kale. Allow at least three years before planting a vegetable family in the same spot again.

- ✔ **Use succession planting.** Some crops, such as lettuce and beans, are quick to mature, so you can plant them several times throughout the growing season for a constant supply of tender new vegetables. This technique works best when you plant small patches of each vegetable every two weeks. That way, you won't ever have a glut of lettuce, and you can extend the growing season.

Determining a planting date

Most vegetables are *annual plants* that die after one season of growth. They generally fall into two groups:

- **Warm-season vegetables** — such as tomatoes, peppers, sweet corn, melons, and cucumber — grow best in hot weather. Plant them one to two weeks after the last frost date for your area or when the soil is at least 60 degrees Fahrenheit. These plants don't like the cold, so don't rush to plant them before the soil warms up. Contact your local weather service, your cooperative extension office, or a gardening neighbor to determine your average last spring frost date, if you aren't sure when it usually occurs.

- **Cool-season vegetables** — including broccoli, spinach, lettuce, carrots, and potatoes — grow best during cool weather. You usually can plant them in the garden one to two weeks before the last frost date. These crops not only tolerate cool weather, but also need it to grow and mature properly. You can even plant some cool-season crops, such as peas and lettuce, in midsummer to late summer for a fall harvest.

Winter is the quiet time between gardening seasons in most parts of the country. But in mild-winter and hot-summer areas of the country — such as Southern California, Texas, and Florida — you plant warm-season crops in spring and late summer, and cool-season crops in winter. Summer is the time for you and the veggies to take a break from the hot weather. In rainy, mild areas, you can grow some crops year-round, especially those that enjoy cool weather.

You can get vegetable plants started in your garden in two ways. Some crops — such as beans, peas, carrots, and squash — normally are sown directly in the garden soil, where they'll grow. Other plants — such as tomatoes, peppers, and eggplants, which take a long time to mature their crops — grow best if they're transplanted (in fact, they're called *transplants*). These plants get an early start in a greenhouse or in your house four to six weeks before you set them in their permanent garden location. This head start is critical in cold areas that have short summers. Find out more about starting seeds indoors in Chapter 12. Other vegetables, like cucumber, broccoli, onion, and lettuce — go either way. Base your decision on how much time you have and on whether your favorite varieties are more readily available as transplants or as seeds.

The easiest way to organize your planting schedule is to make a calendar. Begin by marking your average last spring frost date; then fill in the planting dates for different crops. You could write "Plant peas" two weeks before the last frost date, for example. If you do most of your gardening on weekends, fill in the nearest weekend date. Use your calendar to guide your indoor seed-starting, too. If you plan to grow your peppers indoors for eight weeks, and you intend to plant them in the garden a week after the last frost date, count back seven weeks from the last frost date and write "Start peppers indoors." A calendar like this will simplify your planting and ensure you don't forget anything.

Sowing seeds and setting out transplants

The general rule for planting seeds is to plant them twice as deep as the seeds are wide, but your best bet is to follow the guidelines on the seed packet. Keep the soil evenly moist after planting. If you're unsure what the crop seedlings look like, plant seeds in rows. That way, you'll be able to differentiate and remove weed seedlings between and within the rows.

If you're transplanting plants that were started indoors or in a greenhouse, give them at least a week to *harden off* (become acclimated to harsher outdoor conditions) before planting them outside. Use your planting calendar to help you time your transplants. Find out more about sowing seeds and growing your own transplants, hardening off, and planting techniques in Chapter 12.

When you plant vegetable transplants in the garden, you can set some types deeper in the soil than they grew in their pots. I plant peppers, eggplants, tomatoes, and cabbage-type plants right up to their first set of *true leaves,* the ones that look like miniature adult leaves. Planting more deeply gives plants stability, and some plants form roots along the buried stem.

At planting time, loosely wrap a strip of newspaper 2 to 3 inches wide around each vegetable seedling's stem to prevent cutworms from chewing through it. The paper should extend at least an inch above and below the soil.

Feed me: Fertilizing

When seeds are up and growing, and the transplants are planted, some gardeners give them all a dose of fertilizer. Mild liquid organic fertilizers, such as fish emulsion and seaweed mix, provide nitrogen and other essential nutrients for early growth. Follow label directions for dilution rates.

Depending on the health of your soil, you may also consider applying a granular organic fertilizer, such as 5-3-3, to keep plants growing strong. (See Chapter 6 for more on organic fertilizers.) *Heavy-feeding* vegetables — such as corn, tomatoes, and broccoli — may need monthly doses of fertilizer to perform their best, whereas *light feeders* — such as beans, radishes, and peas — may need little or no additional fertilizer.

Apply fertilizer according to the label instructions. Sprinkle granular fertilizer 6 to 8 inches from plant stems, and scratch it gently into the soil. Water the soil to dissolve and disperse the fertilizer. Use a watering can to apply liquid fertilizer around the bases of the plants.

If you have healthy soil you may not need to fertilize. Even organic fertilizers can accumulate in the soil, causing a harmful salt buildup that damages plant roots. Also, excess fertilizer can run off into streams, causing water pollution. If you give your plants too much nitrogen at the wrong time, you may even prevent some vegetables from forming fruit. Tomatoes, peppers, and egg-plants, for example, may grow loads of lush foliage but few flowers or fruit.

Weeding and watering

As soon as you see signs of vegetables germinating — or even before — you'll likely see weeds too. Get familiar with what your vegetables will look like when they're small so that you don't pull them out instead of the weeds. Planting in rows and marking seedlings carefully will help you distinguish crop from weed.

The best way to control weeds is to hand-pull or slice them off with a hoe when they're young; you disturb less soil that way, and the weeds are easier to pull at that time than when they're more mature. When you finish, mulch around the vegetables to conserve moisture and help control weeds. (Head to Chapter 11 for more about weeding and mulching.)

Watering is critical during the early stages of plant growth, but it's also essential when the plants are forming and ripening fruits. Mulching is an excellent way to conserve soil moisture, but you may need to do some supplemental watering, depending on your weather and where you live. Rather than water with overhead sprinklers or with your garden hose, consider using soaker hoses to apply water directly to the soil. You'll minimize disease problems and waste less water.

Garden tricks and season extenders

Experienced gardeners pick up a few methods along the way that make certain crops grow better. Consider trying these nifty tricks to save space, produce better-quality veggies, and extend your growing season beyond the first and last frost dates.

A trifecta of tactics: Trellises, fences, and cages

If you're short on space in your garden or want to plant more than you really have room for, go vertical! You can save space and energy by trellising, fenc-ing, or caging certain vegetables. Climbing vegetables, such as peas and pole beans, need fences or poles to grow on. These devices save space; also, these crops produce best when they're allowed to climb. Set up a teepee of 6- to 8-foot poles, attach chicken wire to fence posts, or train the plants on an A-frame. (If you use the teepee method, wind some twine around the poles at 6-inch intervals to give the vines something to cling to or wind around.)

Cucumbers, melons, and even some squash love to vine and ramble. You can direct their energy by growing them on a trellis. Place the trellis on an angle, such as an A-frame design (shown in Figure 13-1), instead of straight up and down.

If you're growing vines with heavy fruits, such as melons or squash, make sure that the trellis is very sturdy.

Tomatoes, peppers, and eggplants all can be caged or staked with a pole to keep them growing upright, elevate their fruits off the ground (which can help prevent disease and damage from slugs, mice, and other ground-dwelling critters), and give you more produce in less space. Commercial growers tie wire or twine between fence posts and weave the growing tomato plants through it. Also, 4- to 5-foot-high wire cages made of hog fencing or concrete reinforcing wire work well. Secure the cages with a tall stake pounded into the ground to prevent them from blowing over.

Figure 13-1:
An A-frame.

Floating row covers

Floating row covers are among the best things ever to happen to veggie gardeners. The material, which is like cheesecloth, is lightweight and lets air, light, and water through it, but it blocks insects that can attack vegetables. Also, when row covers are used on newly sown plants in the spring, they keep the air and soil a little warmer, thereby helping seeds germinate faster and young plants grow more quickly.

I use floating row covers on my peppers in spring to ensure an early harvest of fruits, because pepper flowers need warm air temperatures. The row covers help at the other end of the season, too, by holding in heat and moderating the cool autumn-night temperatures.

For vegetables that require pollination by insects, such as pumpkins and squash, remove row covers as soon as you see the first flowers. For crops that don't need pollination by bees, such as lettuce and broccoli, you can leave the row cover on throughout the growing season — as long as it doesn't hold in too much heat. The row cover prevents cabbage moths, aphids, and other pests from getting to your vegetables. You can support a row cover with wire hoops or just lay it right on the top of vegetables. It's so lightweight that the veggies will lift it as they grow.

Staying warm with cold frames

A clever way to start your growing season earlier in the spring and keep it going long into the frosty fall is to make or buy a cold frame. *Cold frames* are bottomless, insulated boxes made of wood, hay bales, metal, or plastic; they work like miniature greenhouses. The lid of the box is angled slightly to increase its exposure to the sun; its plastic or glass top keeps the inside much warmer than the outside air temperature. Even in the coldest climates, you can use a cold frame to grow food year-round.

In the spring, grow a crop of lettuce in a cold frame, and get your other warm-season crops off to an early start. In the fall and winter, try cold-tolerant spinach, kale, and leeks.

You can make your cold frame large enough to fit over a raised bed in the garden, or keep it small and portable to move around as needed. Cold frames are also handy for hardening off seedlings before transplanting them to the garden.

The key to using cold frames is ventilating them as needed by propping open the sash or top window. Even on very cool but sunny days, the inside of the box really heats up, much like a car with its windows rolled up. Automatic vent openers, available from greenhouse suppliers, raise and lower the top automatically without electricity, depending on the air temperature. For more on gardening with cold frames, get a copy of Eliot Coleman's excellent book *Four-Season Harvest* (Chelsea Green Publishing Co.).

Harvest time

Picking is one of my favorite activities, second only to eating. The temptation is to go out and harvest as soon as I see something growing. This technique works well for crops that taste best when they're harvested young, including beans, summer squash, cucumbers, lettuce, and peas. The more you pick of these crops, the more they produce! In fact, if you allow some vegetables to become too mature on these plants, they may stop producing altogether.

For many other crops, however, you have to be patient. Tomatoes, peppers, carrots, and beets taste best when they're allowed to ripen and grow to maturity in the soil or on the plant. When in doubt, take a bite. If the flavor doesn't suit your taste buds, wait a few days before you try again.

Most vegetables taste sweetest and are most tender when they're freshly picked. In our house, I start the water boiling on the stove before I head outside to harvest the corn for supper. Peas, summer squash, and string beans are also sweet and juicy if they're picked just before eating. Other vegetables, such as most varieties of winter squash, need a week or two at 60 to 70 degrees Fahrenheit to cure after harvest to develop their full flavor. Read the next section to get more specifics on each vegetable.

Vegetables from A to Z

Seed catalogs have so many delicious veggies to choose from that you may have a tough time knowing where to start — and stop! If you're growing your first garden, grow just a few of your favorite vegetables, and stick to one variety of each. As you gain experience, add more kinds, and experiment with one or two new crops each year. If something doesn't work out the way you expected it to, try a different variety or growing method, or abandon it and give the garden space to another crop. For me, that's one of the beautiful things about vegetable gardens — you get to start with a clean slate each year and get the chance to improve and change your garden based on last year's experiences.

In the following descriptions of vegetables, I include some choice varieties, planting and care recommendations, harvest tips, and specific pests you need to watch out for.

Many organic gardeners prefer to buy seeds and young transplants that were produced organically. More and more seed companies are offering organic seeds, and some specialize in them (refer to Chapter 12). Support your local organic growers by buying vegetable transplants from them if they offer transplants for sale.

Alliums: Onions, shallots, garlic, and leeks

Onions, garlic, shallots, and leeks belong to a group of pungent plants called *alliums*. These plants generally form bulbs or enlarged below-ground stems. Many members of the allium family make lovely additions to the flower garden.

- ✔ **Planting:** Alliums like well-drained, fertile, loose soil and appreciate raised beds. They grow well in cool weather and can take a light frost. Sow onion and leek seeds indoors 8 to 10 weeks before transplanting the plants into the garden. Keep the tops trimmed to about 3 inches high until transplant time.

  In moderate climates, sow seeds in fall for a spring harvest. Plant shallot and onion sets in the spring for a late-summer harvest. Cloves of garlic are best planted in fall, even in cold climates, to overwinter and mature the following summer.

- ✔ **Care:** Keep your alliums weed free, well watered, and fertilized with a high-phosphorous fertilizer (such as bonemeal) to promote large bulb growth.

- ✔ **Harvesting:** When the tops begin to yellow, onions usually are ready for harvest. After pulling them out of the ground, either use them fresh or allow them to cure in a warm, airy room for a few weeks before storing in a cold basement. Use sweet onion varieties within a few weeks.

  Shallots, pungent onions, and some garlic varieties, however, can last for months in storage.

  Pull leeks as needed in fall, after cool weather sweetens their taste. Many varieties can withstand 20-degree Fahrenheit temperatures. When temperatures drop below that, mulch leeks with a blanket of straw, pulling it aside to harvest into winter.

- ✔ **Pests and diseases:** Onion maggots probably are the worst pests of allium-family crops, feeding on onion roots and bulbs. Mulching, crop rotation, and row covers help reduce the risks from these pests.

Onions

Choosing an onion variety is more complicated than choosing most other vegetables, because onions fall into different groups based on sulfur content and the day length they need to form bulbs. *Pungent* varieties contain more sulfur, which makes them keep longer in storage and produce more tears when you cut them. *Sweet* varieties don't have as much sulfur and need to be used sooner after harvest. Adverse growing conditions — weed competition, drought, and poor fertility, for example — can increase onions' sulfur content, even in the sweet varieties.

Onions are also referred to as short-day, long-day, and intermediate:

- **Short-day** varieties form bulbs when they receive 11 to 12 hours of daylight. If you live south of 35 degrees latitude (from northern South Carolina through Oklahoma and Arizona to central California), choose short-day varieties.

- **Intermediate** varieties require days that are 12 to 14 hours long to form bulbs and are good for middle latitudes.

- **Long-day** varieties need 14 to 16 hours of daylight and are best for northern climates.

When in doubt, try a widely adapted, day-neutral variety such as Candy.

You can start onions from seeds, transplants, and *sets,* which are small dormant bulbs.

Garlic

Garlic varieties come in two types: soft-neck and hard-neck. *Soft-neck* kinds produce 12 to 18 small cloves and are best for long-term storage. *Hard-neck* types produce 6 to 12 large cloves and don't keep as long in storage. Dozens of gourmet garlic varieties differ in climate preference, size, storage life, and pungency. Ask around at farmers' markets for advice on the best varieties for your region.

Don't plant regular supermarket garlic; it may have been treated with a post-harvest sprout inhibitor to keep it from growing more. Planting store-bought organic garlic should be safe, though, because it should sprout normally when planted.

Shallots and leeks

Shallots are mild-tasting small onions and the easiest to grow of all the edible alliums. Another onion relative, the leek, is indispensable in European cooking and is easy to grow in raised beds.

Asparagus

Asparagus plants are either female or male, and the best varieties of asparagus are the ones dubbed *all-male.* The female plants produce seeds, which reduces the amount of energy they put into producing spears. The males don't produce seeds and, therefore, produce more edible-size spears. Good all-male varieties include the Jersey series. UC 157 is a good one for California. Purple Passion produces large, sweet, purple spears.

- **Planting:** Asparagus is a perennial vegetable that can live for 20 years, so take special care to create a proper planting bed. Choose a sunny location with well-drained soil. Dig a 1-foot-deep trench, and add 6 inches of compost or well-rotted manure. Form 8-inch-high mounds 18 inches apart in the trench, and lay the spiderlike asparagus roots over the mounds, as shown in Figure 13-2.

The crowns (where the roots meet the stems) should be about 5 to 6 inches below the soil surface. Cover them with 2 inches of soil and gradually backfill the trench, an inch or two at a time over the course of several weeks as the asparagus spears grow, until the trench is level with the surrounding soil.

✔ **Care:** Fertilize the bed each spring with compost and a complete fertilizer. Keep the bed weed free and well watered.

✔ **Harvesting:** Don't harvest any asparagus spears for the first year after planting. Let the crowns build up strength. The second year, harvest in spring only those spears larger than a pencil diameter for 3 to 4 weeks. In subsequent years, harvest spears for up to 2 months. Then allow the remaining spears to grow to rejuvenate the crown.

✔ **Pests and diseases:** Asparagus beetle is a hard-to-kill pest of asparagus. The adults damage the spears, and larvae eat the fernlike leaves. Control them by removing the ferns in late fall, and spray with pyrethrins in spring at first signs of this pest. Foraging hens can also help keep the pest in check.

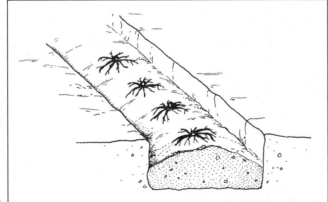

Figure 13-2:
Planting
asparagus
in trenches.

Cole crops: Broccoli, cauliflower, cabbage, and company

These closely related plants have the same growing requirements, diseases, and pests. All these vegetables thrive in cool spring and autumn weather, and tolerate frost. Check days to maturity, which can vary widely among varieties.

In addition to the familiar broccoli varieties, such as Premium Crop and Packman, consider including some broccoli raab and rapini, which have smaller stems and a stronger flavor. Try one of the new orange, purple, or green cauliflowers, which contain more vitamins and antioxidants than regular white varieties. Some new cabbage varieties produce smaller heads that are easier to use and store. Consider including savoy, red, and Chinese cabbages too. Kale is considered to be one of the most nutritious vegetables, so be sure to include a few varieties. Other cole crops to try include Brussels sprouts, kohlrabi, and collards.

- ✔ **Planting:** Sow seeds directly into the ground or start transplants indoors 4 to 6 weeks before transplanting them outside. Take advantage of cool weather by sowing cole crops in early spring for an early-summer harvest or in late summer for a fall harvest. Some cole crops can be grown through the winter in mild-winter areas for harvest in spring.

- ✔ **Care:** Cole crops need a moderate amount of fertilizer and water throughout the growing season to grow well; they also like well-drained soil. Fertilize at planting and 1 month later with a complete fertilizer. Place organic mulch such as straw around plants after transplanting to help keep the soil cool and moist.

- ✔ **Harvesting:** Harvest broccoli when the heads (clusters of flowers) are tightly packed and still green, cutting just below the head. In most cases, new but smaller broccoli heads will grow farther down the stem. If the yellow flowers begin to open, the taste becomes bitter, and the plant will stop producing more heads.

  Harvest cabbage when it's firm to the squeeze. Cut the plants as described for broccoli. To harvest white or *blanched* cauliflower, wrap the upper plant leaves around the developing 3- to 4-inch heads. Harvest within 4 to 10 days. Harvest Brussels sprouts after cool weather in fall when the sprouts are still firm by twisting them off the stem. Pick kale and collard leaves as needed.

- ✔ **Pests and diseases:** Cabbageworms and cabbage loopers are the two primary pests of cole crops. The larvae feed on the leaves, decimating the plant quickly. Handpick the caterpillars, or spray *Bacillus thuringiensis* (Bt) to control them (refer to Chapter 8). Cabbage maggots attack the roots of cole crops. Place row covers over the plants to prevent the flies from laying eggs at the base of the plant. Also, black rot and club root damage the roots and heads of cole crops; crop rotation is the best control for these diseases.

Eggplant

Eggplant, like its cousins peppers and tomatoes, loves hot weather, plenty of water, and full sun. Eggplants come in many size and color varieties. In addition to the dark purple, oval types, try lavender-streaked Rosa Bianca, long and narrow Ichiban and Thai Long, and round Easter Egg and Turkish Orange.

- ✔ **Planting:** Start seeds indoors 8 weeks before transplanting outside. Wait until the soil has warmed to at least 60 degrees before transplanting. In colder climates or small gardens, consider planting eggplants in large containers to save space and encourage them to grow faster. Eggplants in containers also are very ornamental and look great as decorative plants. Here in cool Vermont, I grow the best eggplants by covering them with a floating row cover to hold in the heat.

- ✔ **Care:** Eggplants like moderate fertility and water, so fertilize monthly and mulch with black landscape fabric. But go easy on the nitrogen fertilizer; otherwise, you'll have too much foliage and too few flowers and fruits.

- ✔ **Harvesting:** Harvest eggplants when they've reached the desired size for eating. Harvest before the skin color becomes dull-looking — a sign of overmaturity and mushiness.

- ✔ **Pests and diseases:** Verticillium wilt disease is a main problem for eggplants. This disease causes the entire plant to wilt and die in summer. The easiest solution for this soil-borne disease is planting eggplants in containers filled with sterilized potting soil. Colorado potato beetles also love eggplant leaves. Handpicking adults, crushing eggs, and spraying with Bt san diego control the larval stage of this pest. See Chapter 8 for more on *Bacillus thuringiensis* varieties.

Leafy greens: Lettuce, Swiss chard, spinach, and friends

Leafy greens are easy crops to grow because you don't have to wait for the flowers or fruits, as you do with cucumbers or tomatoes — you just eat the leaves!

Lettuce varieties are categorized by the way their leaves grow. *Head lettuces,* such as iceberg types, form compact balls of leaves. *Loose-leaf lettuces,* at the other end of the spectrum, have loosely arranged leaves that don't form tight heads. Other types — such as butterhead, romaine, and oakleaf — fall somewhere in between.

Consider planting loose-leaf lettuce seed mixes, which contain several varieties and are beautiful in both the garden and the salad bowl. Other leafy vegetable garden staples include Swiss chard, spinach, and an array of less well-known salad and cooking greens. Some Swiss chard varieties are ornamental and edible, such as red-stemmed Ruby and multicolored Bright Lights. In regions where temperatures warm quickly in spring, look for spinach varieties described as slow to bolt, such as Space, Tyee, and Bloomsdale Longstanding.

In the specialty greens category, grow arugula, dandelion, cress, chicory, mache, and mustard to give salad a zippy flavor. Many of these greens are blended in mixes called *mesclun.* Mescluns may be spicy or mild flavored, but I guarantee that they have more flavor than just a simple bowl of lettuce.

For Asian cooking, grow bok choi, tatsoi, and mizuna. You can add these leafy vegetables to stir-fries or mix them into the salad bowl. Bok choi forms a loose cluster of juicy stems and dark green leaves. Tatsoi grows in a low rosette of spoon-shaped leaves that regrow if you cut them. Mizuna has slender stalks and fringed leaves.

- **Planting:** Most greens are cool-season crops, so sow seeds or set transplants outdoors a few weeks before the last frost date. You can start some leafy greens, such as lettuce, indoors 3 to 4 weeks before you set them outdoors, giving plants a jump on the growing season. Stagger your crops of greens by planting small patches a couple of weeks apart throughout the season. These plants mature quickly, and you'll want a consistent harvest of greens.

- **Care:** Leafy greens need nitrogen first and foremost. Add compost before planting, and add a supplemental nitrogen fertilizer such as fish emulsion every few weeks. Mulch the plants after they're established with an organic hay or straw mulch to keep the soil cool and moist and to prevent soil from splashing onto leaves. Keeping the plants well watered will help prevent leaf-tip burn on lettuce.

- **Harvesting:** Harvest lettuce and greens when you're hungry and whenever leaves are big enough to eat. Pick off the lower leaves first so that new, younger leaves continue to grow from the center of the plant. When greens such as arugula and lettuce *bolt* (send up a flower stalk), the leaves probably are too bitter for most tastes; you should pull up and compost the plants.

- **Pests and diseases:** Snails and slugs can devour a patch in no time. You can trap them; set up barriers; bait them; and, of course, handpick them to keep the populations low. Rabbits and woodchucks can also be a problem — fencing is the best cure for them. Leaf-miner insects, especially on spinach, can ruin individual leaves. Just pick them off and destroy the damaged leaves, and the plant will be fine. See Chapters 7 and 8 for more information on managing pests.

Legumes: Peas and beans

You have hundreds of bean varieties to choose from. Dry beans in particular have colorful regional names and histories.

Beans enjoy warm weather; wait until after the last spring frost, when the soil has warmed to at least 60 degrees, to sow seeds in the garden. Bean plants grow by forming low bushy plants or climbing up a pole or trellis. In some cases, you can find pole and bush versions of the same variety. You can eat beans fresh or allow the pods to mature for dry beans used in cooking.

Peas produce better in cool weather, so plant them as soon as the soil has dried out in spring. Pea varieties fall into two camps: those with edible pods and those grown just for fresh or dried seeds, called *English peas*. Peas with edible pods either have flat pods (snow peas) or fat, juicy pods (called snap or sugar peas).

- **Planting:** Legumes are easy to grow because the seeds are so large and easy to plant. Sow directly in well-drained soil.

- **Care:** After they're growing, pole beans need poles for support, whereas tall pea varieties need a fence to climb on. Keep the beds well weeded and watered. Legumes generally don't need supplemental fertilizer because they have the unique ability to make their own nitrogen fertilizer through a relationship with soil-dwelling bacteria called *rhizobia*.

- **Harvesting:** Harvest beans when the pods are about 6 inches long, before the pods get bumpy from the seeds forming. Harvest dry beans after the pods have yellowed and withered. If they don't dry in the garden, you can pull up the whole plants and hang them to dry in an airy garage.

  Harvest snap and English peas when the pods fill and are firm to the squeeze. Keep checking and tasting when the pods begin to size up to be sure that you harvest at the peak of sweetness. Harvest snow peas at any point after the pods form.

- **Pests and diseases:** The Mexican bean beetle causes the most trouble. Handpick them or use predatory insects such as soldier bugs to control them. Pea aphids attack pea plants and are easy to kill with just a stream of water from a hose. Watch out for rabbits and woodchucks — fences work best. Rust fungal disease attacks beans and spreads quickly, especially if you work in the bean patch while the leaves are still wet. The plants and beans develop yellow spots, which can kill the plant. Clean up plant debris in fall, and stay away from the bean patch in wet weather. See Chapters 8 through and 10 for more about managing pests and diseases.

Peppers

Peppers are warm-weather crops that come in a rainbow of colors. Peppers generally are grouped according to their taste: hot or sweet.

Capsaicin gives hot peppers their heat. Use care when handling hot peppers; take care not to rub your eyes or an open wound, because the capsaicin can cause painful burning. (Researchers are also studying capsaicin's antimicrobial properties, its ability to relieve pain, and its potential to prevent cancer.)

Peppers are sometimes rated in Scoville heat units (SHU) based on the amount of capsaicin they contain. Sweet peppers contain no capsaicin and get a rating of 0; medium-hot jalepeños, a rating around 4,000; and fiery-hot habañeros, a rating of 200,000 or more. How much capsaicin a pepper contains depends on factors other than variety, such as water availability, so use the scale as a general guideline to help you choose varieties.

Peppers are also great plants for container growing. Some varieties are very ornamental, such as Pretty in Purple, which has colorful purple to red fruit and purple-tinged stems and leaves.

- ✔ **Planting:** Start seeds indoors 8 weeks before setting plants outside. Wait until the soil has warmed to 60 degrees before transplanting.

- ✔ **Care:** Peppers need fertile soil and plenty of water to grow well. In cool areas, consider growing them in black fabric mulch to heat the soil and keep weeds away. Fertilize monthly with a complete fertilizer, and add 1 tablespoon of Epsom salt to the water to help the peppers grow better. Don't overfertilize peppers with nitrogen fertilizer, though; you'll get more foliage than flowers and fruits.

- ✔ **Harvesting:** Pepper fruits turn a rainbow of colors, depending on the variety, as they mature. The beautiful part about peppers is that you can pick them at the green stage or allow them to mature, when they reach their sweetest flavor. Hot peppers also can be harvested at any stage, but the flavor is hotter and better developed when the peppers are allowed to mature.

- ✔ **Pests and diseases:** The pepper maggot is among the most frustrating pests of sweet peppers. The adult fly lays an egg on the developing fruits; the egg hatches into small, white worms that tunnel into the fruit; the tunneling causes the fruit to rot. Cover the plants with row covers early in the season to discourage adults from laying eggs. Sprays are of little use because the worm is inside the fruit.

  Fruitworms and wilt disease also cause trouble; consult Chapters 8 and 9 to learn more about these pests.

Potatoes

Look for early-, mid-, and late-season potato varieties to stretch out your harvest. Early potatoes are ready to harvest about 65 days after planting — perfect for summer potato salads. Midseason varieties mature in 75 to 80 days, and late ones take 90 days or more to harvest. The later varieties keep longer in storage.

Potatoes are also roughly divided into baking and boiling varieties. Baking potatoes have drier, more mealy-textured flesh; boiling potatoes are moist and waxy. Look for colorful varieties such as All Blue, All Red, and lavender-skinned Caribe.

If you're looking for something new to try, plant some fingerling potatoes. These varieties produce long, slim, tasty tubers and tend to yield more per pound planted than regular potatoes. My favorites include Russian Banana, which has yellow flesh and skin, and French Fingerling and Rose Finn Apple, which have pink skin and yellow flesh.

✔ **Planting:** Potatoes are another cool-season root crop that can be planted a few weeks before your last frost date. They grow rather unpretentiously and without much maintenance until late summer, when you dig the roots. Potatoes grow best in loose soil that hasn't been amended with fertilizer. Too much nitrogen fertilizer in particular can lead to poor tuber formation.

Purchase *seed potatoes* (small tubers), cutting the largest ones into smaller pieces with at least one "eye" or bud. Avoid planting supermarket potatoes, because they may have been sprayed with a sprout inhibitor. (Store-bought organic potatoes are okay to plant.) Place them in 1-foot-deep trenches about 1 foot apart. Fill in the trench with soil as the plants sprout and grow, eventually mounding or hilling around the tops of the plants with soil, as shown in Figure 13-3. Hilling the soil around the plants allows the roots to form more potatoes, kills weeds, and protects the tubers from the light. Tubers exposed to light turn green and have an off flavor.

✔ **Care:** Keep the soil moist by watering or applying organic mulches such as hay or straw.

✔ **Harvesting:** When the potato tops turn yellow and begin to die back, it's time to dig up the tubers. With a shovel or iron fork, carefully dig around the potato plants, and lift up the tubers. Let them cure in a dark, airy, 50-degree room for a few weeks; then store them in a cool basement at about 40 degrees. Eat any damaged potatoes immediately.

Never store potatoes and apples near one another. Apples give off ethylene gas, which causes potatoes and other vegetables to spoil.

✔ **Pests and diseases:** The Colorado potato beetle is the most famous pest. This yellow- and black-striped beetle lays orange eggs on the undersides of leaves; these eggs hatch into voracious orange-red larvae that devour potato and eggplant leaves. Handpick the adults and crush the eggs. Spray Bt san diego to control the larvae.

Wireworms tunnel into potato tubers, causing them to rot. They're a problem mostly in new gardens created from lawns.

Fungal diseases, such as potato scab and blight, can ruin a crop. Your first defense is to buy resistant varieties. Control potato scab by lowering the soil pH to below 6, and avoid using manure fertilizer. Control blight by planting your potato crop in a new place every year, buying certified disease-free tubers, mulching, and keeping weeds under control. See Part III for more information on managing pests and weeds.

Figure 13-3:
Hill soil around young potato plants.

Root crops: Carrots, beets, and radishes

Root crops provide good eating well into the fall and winter, and they're easy to grow. Raised beds filled with loose, fertile, stone-free soil provide just the right environment. In addition to the usual orange carrots, consider growing white, yellow, and purple varieties. If your soil is heavy or rocky, try shorter, stubbier varieties like Danvers Half-Long and Parisian Market. Beets come in a range of colors in addition to the common dark red, including white, orange, and red-and-white-striped Chioggia. Like hot peppers, radish varieties differ in how hot or pungent they are, so choose varieties according to your taste preference.

- ✔ **Planting:** Directly sow root crop seeds a few weeks before the last frost date for your area. Sow the seeds lightly and cover them with sand, potting soil, or grass clippings to keep them moist. Radishes germinate within a few days; carrots may take 2 weeks. I usually mix radish and carrot seeds to help mark the row and harvest the radishes before the carrots need the space.

- ✔ **Care:** Root crops generally need loose soil well amended with compost, weed-free growing conditions, and consistently moist soil to thrive. Thin the seedlings so the eventual spacing is about 2 to 4 inches apart, depending on the crop. If you don't thin root crops when they're young, they won't get large enough to eat. You can eat the thinned beet greens.

- ✔ **Harvesting:** Pull up radishes when the roots get large enough to eat. Leave carrots and beets in the ground to harvest as needed. Their flavor gets sweeter after the soil cools. You can even cover carrots in late fall with a cold frame, fill it with hay mulch, and harvest carrots all winter.

- ✔ **Pests and diseases:** Other than four-legged critters such as rabbits, which love to eat the carrot and beet tops, the biggest pest of carrots is the rust fly. The adult fly lays an egg near the carrot, and the small larvae tunnel into the carrot root. Cover the crop with a row cover to prevent the flies from laying eggs. Swallowtail butterfly larvae also like to munch on carrot tops, so try to grow enough for all of you!

Sweet corn

As soon as you harvest corn, the sugars in the kernels begin to turn to starch, making the corn less sweet as time goes by. But many new sweet-corn varieties stay sweeter longer after harvest because plant breeders breed them to contain *supersweet* characteristics. These varieties — which include Bodacious (yellow), Honey N'Pearl (bicolor), and How Sweet It Is (white) — must be planted at least 25 to 100 feet from other, non-supersweet varieties. If another variety pollinates a supersweet variety, the kernels may be tough and starchy. Another way to separate varieties is to stagger the planting dates so only one type of corn is in flower at a time.

If you're satisfied with regular, old-fashioned varieties, choose those with yellow, white, or both-colored *(bicolor)* kernels. If you plant yellow and white varieties in close proximity, you may get bicolor corn anyway. Some of my favorites include Silver Queen (white) and Early Sunglow (yellow).

- ✔ **Planting:** Sow seeds in blocks of 4 to 5 short rows after the soil has warmed to 65 degrees. Separate blocks of different corn varieties by at least 25 feet so that no cross-pollination occurs.

- ✔ **Care:** Sweet corn needs well-drained, highly fertile soil and warm weather to grow well. Hoe soil up around the plants when they're 8 inches tall to support them during windy days and to destroy young weeds that compete with the corn plants. Fertilize at planting (with compost) and again when the corn is knee-high (with a high-nitrogen fertilizer such as soybean meal). Fertilize a final time with the same fertilizer when the silk emerges at the tips of the ears.

- ✔ **Harvesting:** Start checking for maturity when the corn ears feel full and the silks are brown. You can take a peek under the husks at the corn ear tip to see whether the kernels have matured. Pick the ears on the young side for the sweetest flavor.

- ✔ **Pests and diseases:** Major corn pests include the corn earworm and corn borer. The earworm larvae tunnel into the tip of the corn ear, causing only cosmetic damage; the ear is still edible. Either spray Bt on the silks or apply a few drops of mineral oil when ears are young to kill the earworm larvae. Varieties with extra-tight husks, such as Tuxedo, resist damage.

  Corn-borer larvae cause more major damage to a plant by tunneling into the leaves and stalk. Bt sprays and crop rotation can help lessen the problems from corn borers.

  Raccoons are the other major corn pests. Raccoons love corn and seem to know when it's ripe. An electric fence is the best — and maybe the only — defense against these clever animals.

Tomatoes

Easily the most popular garden vegetable, the tomato comes in a variety of sizes, shapes, and colors. The plants, however, fall into two categories. *Determinate* varieties stop growing taller when they reach a certain height and need minimal support, making them ideal for containers. *Indeterminate* varieties just keep on growing taller and taller, like Jack's beanstalk! Indeterminate tomatoes require trellising but yield more fruit per square foot of garden space.

Most gardeners grow tomatoes for three main purposes: slicing, snacks, and sauce. Some of my favorite standard, round, slicing tomato varieties include Celebrity and Early Girl (red), Brandywine (pink), Lemon Boy (yellow), Big Rainbow (striped yellow and red), and Big Beef (red). For snacking, I like cherry-tomato varieties Sun Gold (gold), Super Sweet 100 (red), Sweet Million (red), and Yellow Pear (yellow). My favorite plum tomatoes, which I use to make sauce, include Amish Paste, Roma, Bellstar, Heinz 2653, and Viva Italia.

✔ **Planting and care:** Tomatoes grow best when transplanted into 60-degree soil and kept warm. Plant tall and leggy tomato transplants up to within 4 inches of their tops in a deep hole, or lay them on their side in a trench (see Figure 13-4), and the stem will root. Place a tomato cage or trellis support around the plants at planting time. Tie or wind indeterminate varieties around their supports as they grow, and prune off extra side shoots to keep the plant from getting too bushy.

✔ **Care:** Mulching with black landscape fabric in cool areas helps speed the growth of tomato plants. Tomatoes need fertile soil, so amend the soil with compost before planting and then side-dress plants monthly with a complete fertilizer. Keep the plants mulched and well watered to prevent blossom-end rot (discoloration and decay on the end opposite the stem) as fruits mature.

✔ **Harvesting:** Allow the fruits to turn red (or yellow, gold, or whatever the mature color). The longer you leave them on the vine, the deeper the color, and the sweeter and fuller the fruit flavor. Even if you pick too early, however, fruits continue ripening if they're placed in a warm, airy room.

✔ **Pests and diseases:** The main insect pests are tomato hornworms and tomato fruitworms. Both of these caterpillars can be controlled with Bt, although you can easily handpick hornworms because they're so large. Nematodes can also attack tomato roots, causing the roots to be deformed and the plants to be stunted and unproductive. Choose nematode-resistant varieties if these microscopic soil pests are a problem in your area.

Leaf blight diseases often start as small spots on leaves and then expand to yellow areas, killing leaves and the plant if unchecked. To control these diseases, clean up crop debris at the end of the growing season, rotate crops, and mulch to prevent the disease spores from splashing onto leaves during rains. Wilt diseases, such as verticillium and fusarium, can cause plants to wilt and die in midseason. Purchase plants that are wilt resistant (usually indicated in the variety description), and remove and destroy infected plants as soon as you can to prevent the disease from spreading.

Vining crops: Cucumbers, squash, pumpkins, and melons

All these crops have the common trait of growing their fruits on long, trailing vines, although some varieties now grow in more compact bushlike patterns. Many of these species can pollinate one another, too, making it nearly impossible to get seeds that grow fruit resembling the original varieties.

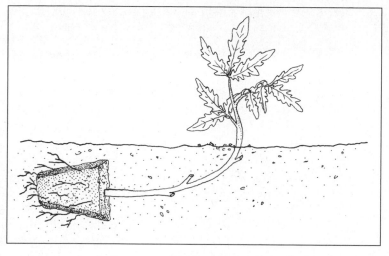

Figure 13-4:
Plant leggy
tomato
transplants
horizontally
in a trench.

Cucumbers are classified as slicers (long and thin) and picklers (short and prickly). Squash are grouped as summer and winter varieties. Summer squash — such as zucchini, pattypan, and crookneck — have tender skin and are best eaten soon after harvest. Winter squash — such as acorn, buttercup, and butternut — develop hard skins and dense flesh, making them good for storing through the fall and early winter.

Pumpkins range in dimension from apple-size to something resembling a small Volkswagen Beetle. Some are used for cooking; others are better for carving and ornament. For pies and soup, grow New England Pie, Baby Pam, or Small Sugar. For carving, Howden and Connecticut Field are among the standards. Grow Atlantic Giant or Big Max for the big-pumpkin contest at the county fair.

Finally, a few good melons include Earli-Dew and Burpee Hybrid muskmelon, as well as French Orange, a muskmelon/Charentais cross. *Charentais* are orange-fleshed French melons that resemble muskmelons. Cantaloupes, by the way, have smoother skins and smaller seed cavities than muskmelons, but taste pretty much the same. For something delicious and unusual, grow green-fleshed Passport cantaloupe. Try Crimson Sweet and yellow-fleshed Yellow Doll watermelon, or one of the new "personal size" varieties, such as Little Baby Flower and Mini Yellow, that weigh in at just 2 to 4 pounds.

✔ **Planting:** Sow these vegetables directly 1 to 2 weeks after your last frost date, when the soil is at least 60 degrees. In colder areas, start seedlings indoors 3 to 4 weeks before setting them outdoors to get a head start.

Even though many bush varieties are available, most squash-family plants need room to spread their vines, so space them according to seed-packet instructions.

✔ **Care:** These warm-weather crops need heat, water, and fertility to grow best. Amend the soil at planting with a layer of compost, and side-dress the plants with a complete fertilizer when they start vining. Keep the plants well watered. Protect all squash-family plants and fruits from frost.

Squash-family crops need bees to pollinate the flowers to get fruit. Plant bee-attracting flowers around the garden to ensure fruit pollination. If fruits form but rot and drop off before enlarging, it's probably due to poor pollination.

✔ **Harvesting:** Pick cucumbers when they are 4 to 6 inches long, before the seeds enlarge. Harvest summer squash when they're small and the flowers are still attached for best flavor and to keep the plants producing well. Harvest winter squash and pumpkins when the varieties turn the desired color and your thumbnail can't puncture the skin.

Harvest muskmelons when they slip off the vine easily when lifted. Watermelons are harvested when the skin color turns from shiny to dull and the spot where it rests on the ground turns from white to yellow. Also check the last *tendrils* (curlicues coming off the stems) before the fruit. When the tendril turns brown, it's harvest time.

✔ **Pests and diseases:** Squash-family vegetables have their own whole set of insects and diseases — many named after the plants they attack. The most prominent ones include cucumber beetles, which are yellow- and black-striped or spotted beetles that feed on young cucumbers, melons, and squash; squash vine borers, which attack mostly squash and pumpkins; and squash bugs. Turn to Chapter 8 for more detailed information on these bad guys.

Bacterial wilt disease attacks mostly cucumber and melons. The plants wilt during the day and are slow to recover even if they're well watered. Control this disease by planting resistant varieties and controlling cucumber beetles, which spread the disease.

Going beyond the ordinary

Looking for something different? Try some of these varieties in your vegetable garden:

✔ **Celeriac** (also called *celery root*), a gnarly, potato-like root vegetable that tastes like celery

✔ **Daikon radish,** a large white root vegetable with a mild radish flavor

✔ **Edamame,** soybeans that are harvested while green and eaten fresh

✔ **Florence fennel** (also called *finocchio*), whose basal leaves form a bulb with a refreshing anise flavor

✔ **Okra,** a mainstay in Southern cooking

✔ **Parsnip,** a mild-tasting root vegetable resembling white carrots

✔ **Tomatillo,** a tomato relative and an essential ingredient in traditional salsas

Chapter 14

Herbs for the Home and Garden

In This Chapter

▶ Growing and using the most common herbs

▶ Choosing herbs that attract helpful insects

Defining herbs is no easy feat when you consider that this group includes plants from every continent and climate — and the word *herbs* refers to everything from shrubs and trees to short-lived annuals and tough-as-nails perennials. Throughout history, herbs have served as food, medicine, fragrance, ornament, and even magical ingredients. In the days before refrigeration, people used strongly flavored chives, thyme, sage, rosemary, savory, basil, and mint to flavor meats. Aromatic herbs with scented flowers and leaves bring pleasant fragrance to homes today and still help protect woolen and linen fabrics from insect damage. Some medicines consist primarily of herbal preparations.

In this chapter, I focus on plants commonly grown to flavor foods, to add color and fragrance to the garden, and to make helpful companions for other crops.

Growing Herbs

How and where you choose to grow herbs is limited only by your imagination and, of course, by the needs and characteristics of the plants themselves. Most herb plants aren't too fussy about the soil they grow in as long as it's well drained. (If you're growing herbs simply for their ornamental flowers or foliage, give them fertile garden soil. Herbs grown for fragrance and flavor, however, are more pungent if they're grown in less fertile soil, so go easy on the fertilizer.)

Using herbs

Most herbs have fragrant or pungently flavored leaves or flowers that make them useful for cooking, crafts, natural remedies, potpourri, and more. Consider the following ways to use harvested herbs:

✔ **Food and drink:** Herbal teas offer alternatives to stronger brews, and no supper is complete without seasonings for soups and salads, meats, and vegetables.

✔ **Fragrance:** In the days before frequent bathing, central vacuum cleaners, and indoor plumbing, herbs played a large role in odor control. Today, *aromatherapy,* the art and science of affecting mood with scent, makes liberal use of dried herbs in little pillows and bowls of potpourri.

✔ **Crafts:** Herbs give color, structure, and fragrance to dried wreaths, arrangements, and other crafts. Some herbs lend their colors to fabrics and paints.

✔ **Medicine:** People have used herbs to treat every ailment known to mankind: headaches, depression, colds, general aches and pains, and so on. Check out *Herbal Remedies For Dummies,* by Christopher Hobbs (Wiley), for ways to use herbs as medicine. Laymen can safely use aromatic herbs to add zip or tranquilizing effects to ointments, massage oils, and baths.

Fitting herbs into your garden

You can fit herbs into your garden and landscape in myriad ways. Tuck herbs into your flower garden, plant them among your vegetables, or give them a special garden of their own. Take advantage of their flowers or leaves to add spark to container gardens and window boxes. Use creeping kinds between paving stones, or allow them to trail over retaining walls. Even if you're challenged for space, you can grow some herbs on a sunny windowsill as houseplants.

If you need a few ideas on how and where to grow herbs, here's a list for inspiration:

✔ **Herb garden:** Take a herbs-only approach and design an intricately patterned garden. A typical arrangement consists of a geometric border of tidy, compact plants such as basil or lavender surrounding groups of herbs with contrasting foliage colors and textures.

✔ **Ground cover:** Creeping herbs such as thyme can cover large areas quickly or fill the gaps between stones in a path. Allow them to trail over a wall to add color and soften the effect of the stone.

✔ **Vegetable garden:** Some herbs make natural companions for vegetable plants. Basil, for example, is said to improve tomatoes, whereas dill and cabbage complement each other.

✔ **Flower garden:** Many herbs have beautiful flowers or foliage that add color and texture to flower borders. As a bonus, some of these plants attract butterflies and provide food for their larva. Good additions to your flower garden include catnip, lavender, chamomile, borage, and oregano.

✔ **Container garden:** Treat them as ornamental plants or bring your culinary herbs closer to the kitchen by planting them in pots, tubs, or baskets. In cold climates, grow tender herbs such as rosemary and bay in pots that you can bring indoors for the winter. Be sure to give these Mediterranean-climate plants 14 to 16 hours of bright light year-round to keep them happy. Be sure to keep the soil moist but never soggy.

Watching for invaders

Some herbs have a very bad habit: They just don't know when to stop growing. These so-called *invasive herbs* travel in the following ways:

✔ **Seeds:** Some plants produce way more seeds than you need. Their little seedlings pop up everywhere, like weeds. Examples of prolific herbs include German chamomile, fennel, and garlic chives. Keep them in check by removing the flowers before they disperse seeds.

✔ **Roots:** With some herbs, such as comfrey and horseradish, your eradication efforts may lead to an even larger patch of the confounded plant. Any bit of root left in the soil may grow into a new plant. Introduce these unruly herbs to your garden with caution.

✔ **Rhizomes and stolons:** Some herbs take off cross-country, growing horizontal stems from their crowns that creep over or under the soil, forming new plants along the way. (*Rhizomes* grow under and *stolons* on top of the soil.) These plants are useful for covering large areas or filling gaps between paving stones, but rapidly become a nuisance in other situations. Tansy, mint, and artemisia can be particularly rampant; plant these herbs in containers or in gardens surrounded by 12-inch-deep barriers that prevent the roots from getting out. Pull up escapees as soon as they appear.

Encyclopedia of Herbs

Useful herbs number in the hundreds — at least. In this section, I highlight a few of the most commonly grown herbs. For information about more herbs, as well as in-depth discussions, pick up a copy of *Herb Gardening For Dummies,* by Karan Davis Cutler, Kathleen Fisher, and the National Gardening Association (Wiley).

Basil

Easily one of the most popular culinary herbs grown, basil *(ocimum basilicum)* is an annual that comes in more than 30 varieties, which include both ornamental and tasty forms. For plenty of pesto, grow sweet basil varieties such as Mammoth or Large Leaf in your vegetable garden. Or try varieties with unusual foliage, such as purple-leafed Dark Opal and Purple Ruffles or frilly Green Ruffles. To edge a garden or spice up a patio planter, grow compact, small-leafed varieties such as Spicy Globe and Green Globe. For an alternative taste sensation, grow lemon, anise, cinnamon, and Thai basil varieties.

- ✔ **Planting and care:** Sow seeds directly in the garden, or start indoors. Give basil moist, fertile, well-drained soil, and space plants about 1 foot apart in full sun. Water them in dry weather, and pinch off young flower buds to prevent bloom and encourage more leaves. Protect basil from frost, which will kill it.

- ✔ **Special uses:** Plant with tomatoes to discourage tomato hornworms. Use dried or fresh leaves to flavor food.

In recent years, a strain of fusarium disease has begun causing problems for basil growers. Choose at least one resistant variety, such as Nufar, for your herb patch.

Calendula

The beautiful flowers alone make planting calendula *(Calendula officinalis)* worthwhile. Add the fact that the flowers are edible and can be used in healing salves, and calendula becomes a must-have in the herb garden.

- ✔ **Planting and care:** Sow seeds directly in the garden in full sun, or start indoors. The plants can tolerate light frosts. If some flowers are allowed to form seeds, the plant will self-sow.

- ✔ **Special uses:** The yellow, gold, or orange flowers have a tangy and peppery taste; they can be used in dyes and added to salves, soaps, and lotions.

Caraway

Caraway *(Carum carvi),* a member of the carrot family, is a biennial that produces its aromatic seeds in its second growing season, although some plants may bloom the first year. The plants have fine, lacy foliage topped by umbels of tiny white flowers.

- ✔ **Planting and care:** Sow seeds directly in the garden in full sun, where they can remain for two growing seasons. In hot climates, give caraway partial shade. Seeds germinate slowly and have deep taproots, which bring minerals to the surface and loosen the soil. Plants grow 1 to 2 feet tall.

- ✔ **Special uses:** Add the leaves to salads or soups. Use the distinctively flavored seeds in breads, stews, and other foods. The flowers attract many beneficial insects.

Chamomile

Choose 2- to 3-foot-tall German chamomile *(Matricaria recutita)* or creeping, 9-inch Roman chamomile *(Chamaemelum nobile),* depending on your garden desires. The perennial Roman species is hardy through Zone 3 and thrives in cool, damp climates. German chamomile is an annual. Both plants have lacy, aromatic, apple-scented foliage and small, daisylike flowers.

- ✔ **Planting and care:** Sow seeds directly in the garden and keep moist until well established. Chamomile can tolerate some drought after that and appreciates full sun. Harvest the flowers when fully open, and dry them on screens in an airy place. Plants self-sow prolifically, so after you plant some, you'll have chamomile for a long time unless you remove all spent blooms before they develop seeds.

- ✔ **Special uses:** The dried flowers make a popular tea for relieving stress and heartburn. They're also used in many cosmetics and toiletries. Roman chamomile makes an excellent ground cover or mowed lawn in mild, moist climates similar to England or the Pacific Northwest.

Chives

Their grassy, onion-flavored foliage makes chives *(Allium schoenoprasum)* popular in the culinary arts, but this perennial plant makes a good 1-foot-tall addition to the ornamental landscape and vegetable garden, too. The dense tufts of lavender flowers bloom in early summer. A related species, garlic chives, grows about 2 feet tall and has starry white flowers in late summer to early fall. Both species self-sow freely.

- ✔ **Planting and care:** The best way to obtain chives is to divide a clump into groups of slender bulbs and plant in any well-drained garden soil. Chives prefer full sun but aren't fussy. If you sow from seed, cover the seeds lightly with soil, keep the soil moist, and be patient; the seeds may take 2 to 3 weeks to sprout. Keep weeds away to make harvesting easier. Harvest by shearing the stems to within a few inches of the ground.

✔ **Special uses:** The pungent foliage reportedly repels some injurious pests, especially around roses, tomatoes, carrots, grapes, and apples. Puree the leaves in a blender with water, strain, and use as a spray to prevent powdery mildew. The flowers attract beneficial insects. Use chives in cooking as you would onions, or serve fresh in salads, dips, and sauces.

Coriander and cilantro

This annual herb *(Coriandrum sativum)* is so versatile that it bears two names — cilantro for the leaves and coriander for the seeds. The flat, parsleylike leaves add pungency to Latin American and Asian dishes. The seeds play a major role in curry and other Middle Eastern fare. Ancient Mediterranean peoples prescribed cilantro and coriander for many medical ailments.

✔ **Planting and care:** Sow directly in fertile garden soil, where seeds will sprout in a couple of weeks. Plant every 2 to 3 weeks for continuous harvest, because the plants tend to set seed quickly (especially in hot weather) and stop producing new foliage. Harvest young tender leaves before plants send up flower stalks. Harvest seeds when the seed heads turn brown but before they scatter, and dry thoroughly before using for best flavor.

✔ **Special uses:** Use leaves and seeds in cooking. Plant near aphid-prone crops to help repel pests. The flowers also attract beneficial insects.

Dill

Dill *(Anethum graveolens)* is another member of the aromatic carrot family. The seeds are an essential ingredient in pickles, breads, and other savory dishes. The fine, threadlike foliage is rich in vitamins and flavor for fish, sauces, and dips. The tall, narrow plants of this annual herb grow 2 to 3 feet tall. Choose the variety Bouquet for seeds, or grow Dukat or 18-inch-tall Fernleaf if you want mainly leaves.

✔ **Planting and care:** Sow seeds directly in fertile, sunny garden soil. Barely cover the seeds and sow again every few weeks for continuous harvest. Protect from strong winds.

✔ **Special uses:** The flowers attract beneficial insects, and the foliage is a favorite of swallowtail butterfly larvae. It reputedly makes a good companion for cabbage crops and can be planted with low-growing lettuce and cucumbers. Use the seeds and leaves in cooking.

Herbs for companion planting

The idea of growing certain plants in close proximity for mutual benefit is well rooted in folklore and is gaining some ground in scientific circles. One way that plants help one another is by providing habitat for insects and other creatures that prey on damaging pests. Many herbs excel in this role because they have small, nectar-rich flowers and aromatic leaves. Herbs in the carrot family (especially dill, caraway, tansy, fennel, and parsley) attract the following beneficial insects:

- Lacewings
- Braconid wasps
- Aphid parasites
- Syrphid flies
- Spiders
- Mealybug and spider mite destroyers
- Trichogramma wasps
- Minute pirate bugs

Fennel

Useful in cooking and in the garden, 4- to 8-foot-tall fennel *(Foeniculum vulgare)* has a tropical look and resembles giant dill plants. Common fennel is hardy in Zones 6 through 11, but you can grow it as an annual in cooler climates. It self-sows and can become a nuisance weed. Try the bronze-red-leafed variety Purpureum as an ornamental plant. If you want to eat the root, look for the annual or biennial plant called finocchio or Florence fennel.

- **Planting and care:** Sow directly in fertile, sunny soil where you want it to grow. Its long taproot makes it difficult to transplant. Protect from strong wind.

- **Special uses:** You can use all parts of fennel, from the bulblike root to the leaves, stalks, and seeds. Harvest seeds when they turn brown; snip leaves and stems as needed, and use fresh or cooked lightly in soups and sauces. The flowers attract many beneficial insects.

Horseradish

Take care where you plant the tenacious perennial horseradish *(Armoracia rusticana)*; its pungent roots extend 2 feet into the soil, and the smallest piece can sprout into a new plant. The wavy, 1- to 3-foot-long leaves are attractive, however, and small white flowers add to the plant's appeal. It's hardy through Zone 5.

✔ **Planting and care:** Plant the roots in deep fertile soil about 1 foot apart and 2 inches deep in full sun. To keep horseradish from taking over your garden, plant it in a bottomless trash can sunk into the ground. Wait a year or so before harvesting the roots in the fall.

✔ **Special uses:** The roots are sharply pungent and valued for the zip they give sauces and tomato drinks. The young spring leaves are edible when they're cooked like spinach. Try a little horseradish to open your sinuses the next time you have a head cold. Some biodynamic farmers (see Chapter 2) believe that horseradish is beneficial in fruit orchards and around potatoes.

Lavender

One of the most recognized and popular scents for cosmetics, toiletries, and aromatherapy, lavender *(Lavandula)* also adds drama to your flower garden. Several species exist, all of which have needlelike foliage and spikes of purplish blue flowers. The English lavender varieties, such as purple Hidcote and Munstead, grow up to 24 inches high and are hardy through Zone 5. Pink-flowering varieties include Hidcote Pink and Miss Katherine. Other species are less hardy but equally appealing, including spike, French, and fringed lavenders.

✔ **Planting and care:** Start from stem cuttings, because seeds may not give you plants of uniform quality. Plant in compost-enriched, very well drained, even gravelly soil in full sun. Space plants 2 to 3 feet apart for a low hedge or mass planting. Prune in early spring to encourage bushy growth.

✔ **Special uses:** Harvest flowers as they begin to open, and dry them in bundles hung upside down in an airy place. The flowers attract bees and beneficial insects.

Mints

With 20 or so species and more than 1,000 varieties to choose from, you should find a mint *(Mentha)* to suit your taste. Peppermint and spearmint are the most popular, but fruit-flavored varieties also exist. Some plants have variegated foliage, including the pineapple mint Varieagata. Some mints, such as Corsican mint, creep along low to the ground; others grow 2 to 3 feet tall. Hardiness depends on the variety and species.

✔ **Planting and care:** Start new plants from stem cuttings of the varieties you want, to make sure that you get the flavor or scent you expect. Plant just below the soil surface and keep the soil moist until the plants begin to grow. Mints can be invasive, so contain them or plant them where you don't mind having a carpet of fragrant foliage.

✔ **Special uses:** Harvest the fresh leaves and add them to Middle Eastern dishes, soups, vegetables, and beverages. Mint flowers attract beneficial insects. Also, the fragrant plants reportedly repel some damaging insects and improve the health and flavor of nearby cabbages and tomatoes.

Oregano

Small fragrant leaves on sprawling 1- to 2-foot stems topped by loose spikes of white to pink flowers give oregano *(Origanum vulgare)* a casual appeal for planting in vegetable and flower gardens or trailing over a wall or basket. Many cooks prefer Greek oregano over the readily available common oregano. Before buying plants, pinch a leaf to test flavor and pungency. Some varieties, such as Aureum Crispum and Compactum, are more ornamental than edible. It's a hardy perennial in Zone 5 and warmer areas.

✔ **Planting and care:** Start new plants from stem cuttings to guarantee the best flavor. Seed-grown plants may lack their parents' pungent flavor. Any average, well-drained soil in full sun will do. Harvest leaves as needed, or cut the plant down to a few inches from the ground and hang the sprigs to dry.

✔ **Special uses:** The tiny flower clusters attract bees, butterflies, and other beneficial insects. The fresh and dried leaves add classic flavor to many Latin American and Mediterranean dishes. Some varieties look good in hanging baskets, patio containers, and flower gardens.

Parsley

A common garnish on restaurant plates, parsley *(Petroselinum crispum)* is probably the most recognized herb. The leaves contain loads of vitamins A and C, and help sweeten garlic breath. Although both varieties are edible, the flat-leafed variety has stronger flavor, whereas the curly-leafed kind is more commonly used as garnish.

The plants are biennial and hardy through Zone 5; they bloom only in their second year. The 1-foot-tall plants form tidy, bright green mounds of ornamental foliage. Plant in vegetable and flower gardens or in container gardens.

✔ **Planting and care:** Soak seeds overnight before sowing, and plant directly in the garden. If you start seeds indoors, plant them in *peat pots* (biodegradable compressed peat moss containers) so that you don't have to disturb their taproots when transplanting them later. Give the plants fertile garden soil and a cool, slightly shady spot in hot summer climates. Snip fresh leaves as needed, or cut the whole plant to a few inches high and dry the leaves on a screen.

✔ **Special uses:** Use for cooking, especially in Greek and Middle Eastern dishes. Parsley makes an attractive ornamental garden plant and serves as food for swallowtail butterfly larvae. The flowers attract beneficial insects.

Rosemary

Two types of this tender perennial evergreen shrub exist — upright and prostrate — and both are fragrant and edible. The short, needlelike foliage of Rosemary *(Rosmarinus officinalis)* gives off a heady, distinctive aroma when lightly bruised. Ornamental varieties include those with golden or variegated leaves, pink or bright blue flowers, and especially sprawling or upright forms.

✔ **Planting and care:** Start from rooted stem cuttings, and plant in well-drained garden soil. Rosemary doesn't tolerate soggy soil or complete drought. Although the herb is hardy only to Zone 8, you can grow rosemary in a greenhouse or indoors under strong light. Plant it in a pot at least 1 foot deep to accommodate its taproot, and maintain humidity by setting it over moist pebbles or misting the plant a few times a week.

✔ **Special uses:** As an ornamental, rosemary excels in the low shrub border or trailing over a low wall. Its aromatic foliage is said to repel flying insects from cabbages and other vegetables. Use fresh sprigs in meat stews; use dried rosemary for culinary use or to scent rooms and linens.

Sage

In Zone 5 and warmer areas, sage *(Salvia officinalis)* is a perennial that grows into a shrubby mound of fragrant leaves. It can grow up to 2 feet tall. The 2- to 3-inch-long leaves are fuzzy and oval, ranging in color from silver-green, purple, golden to mixed white, green, and pink, depending on the variety. Sage is equally at home in the herb garden and among the ornaments in a container or flower bed. In late spring, sage produces spikes of blue or white flowers.

Several sage species exist, varying in hardiness, pungency, and size. One of my favorites, pineapple sage, is winter-hardy only to Zone 8, but its soft-textured, pineapple-scented foliage and red flowers make a beautiful addition to my flower garden.

- ✔ **Planting and care:** It's easier to start sage from stem cuttings, but sage can grow slowly from seeds. Plant in organically rich, well-drained garden soil, and give it full sun. Avoid soggy soil. Prune to keep the growth compact.

- ✔ **Special uses:** The spiky flowers attract bees and other beneficial insects, and look great in the garden. Use sage to scent dresser drawers and to help prevent damaging clothing moths. Use the leaves, either fresh or dried, in poultry and meat dishes.

Stevia

The incredibly sweet leaves of Stevia *(Stevia rebaudiana)* can be used to sweeten a variety of foods and beverages.

- ✔ **Planting and care:** Hardy only to Zone 9, stevia is a tender perennial that you can grow as an annual or bring indoors in winter. The shrubby plants grow well in containers; you can snip off a leaf or two to chew on or drop into your tea.

- ✔ **Special uses:** To make stevia powder, remove the leaves; dry them in the sun; and grind them, using a mortar and pestle or an electric spice or coffee grinder. Use the powder to sweeten just about anything, but use it sparingly — it's very potent.

Sweet marjoram

A tender perennial shrub in Zone 9 and warmer areas and a relative to oregano, sweet marjoram *(Origanum majorana)* has to be grown as an annual. It tends to sprawl and is best confined in a container or planted in a herb garden.

- ✔ **Planting and care:** Start from seed in late spring indoors, or buy rooted cuttings to be sure that you get the plant that you expect. The plant prefers full sun and fertile garden soil. Remove the flowers to encourage more leaves. Harvest and dry the leaves for year-round culinary use.

- ✔ **Special uses:** The light-purple flower clusters attract many beneficial insects. The leaves taste similar to oregano and are used extensively in cooking, especially in vegetable and egg dishes.

Tarragon

A staple in French cooking, tarragon *(Artemisia dracunculus)* is used to flavor a variety of foods, especially chicken, fish, and egg dishes. French tarragon — the preferred variety for cooking — can be propagated only from cuttings and divisions. If you see tarragon seeds, they're likely Russian tarragon, a hardy but less flavorful plant.

✔ **Planting and care:** Plant tarragon in full sun and very well-drained soil, and water sparingly. Consider growing the herb in clay pots to ensure the excellent drainage it requires to thrive.

✔ **Special uses:** Use tarragon fresh or dried in just about any savory dish or sauce.

Thymes

Hundreds of thyme *(Thymus)* species and varieties are available, ranging from creeping 1-inch-high mats to 18-inch shrubs. All varieties have tiny oval leaves, in colors ranging from wooly gray to smooth green to golden to white-edged. Even the fragrance varies from very mild to pungent, and includes lemon, caraway, and coconut.

Creeping thyme makes a fragrant, attractive ground cover and excels between paving stones; shrubby types make useful low hedges. Clusters of tiny white, pink, or crimson flowers bloom in summer, sometimes covering the plants. The creeping thymes are the hardiest kind and survive in Zone 4.

✔ **Planting and care:** Start with rooted stem cuttings to guarantee the flavor and appearance of your thyme. Plant in organically enriched, well-drained soil in full sun. Divide the plants every few years, and keep them pruned to encourage dense growth.

✔ **Special uses:** The flowers attract bees and many beneficial insects. Much folklore exists on the use of thyme as a helpful companion plant for roses and vegetables. Use the herb between patio and walkway stones, or plant it as a ground cover to replace lawn in small areas. The trailing kinds look good in hanging baskets and planters. Harvest the leaves and young stems for cooking.

Chapter 15

Picking from the Berry Patch

. . . .

In This Chapter

▶ Planning where to plant

▶ Preparing the planting site

▶ Choosing the best fruits for your area

▶ Anticipating common pests and problems

. . . .

*F*ew plants give you more bang for your buck than berries. Homegrown raspberries, strawberries, blueberries, and grapes take little space and return months of mouthwatering fruit salads, pies, pancakes, and fresh-eating goodness. Although less commonly grown, elderberries, currants, and some other small fruits make excellent landscape specimens, and turn out fruit fit for delicious jellies and other homemade treats. Because berries are perishable and the soft fruits are difficult to package and ship, supermarket berries are expensive and often past their prime. Also, conventionally grown grapes, raspberries, and strawberries are some of the most heavily sprayed food crops, making growing your own even more attractive.

Some of these berries are easy to grow organically; others present a real challenge. Choosing disease-resistant varieties, using the pest- and disease-control methods described in Part III, and planting correctly go a long way toward producing healthful, pesticide-free berries.

Berry Patch Basics

Site selection and preparation are more critical for berries than for nearly any other food crop you may grow, because most of these plants stay in place for years. The varieties you choose, where you plant them, and how you prepare and maintain the soil determine whether your berry patch produces bumper crops or becomes a disappointing chore.

As you make decisions about where to plant your berry patch, keep the following requirements in mind:

- ✔ **Sun:** All fruits need at least six hours — preferably more — of full sun each day to produce large, flavorful crops.

- ✔ **Air circulation and drainage:** Moving air helps prevent disease organisms from settling on vulnerable fruits and leaves, so choose a slightly breezy site, if possible. High winds cause damage, however, so protect crops with a windbreak if necessary.

  Cold air settles at the bottom of slopes, where it may damage early-blooming flowers in the spring or ripening fruit in the fall. Plant your fruits on the slope of a hill instead of at the bottom.

- ✔ **Soil moisture and drainage:** With the exception of elderberries, all small fruits need well-drained soil. Soggy soil encourages root diseases, which are among the most serious problems for fruits. If your soil drains poorly, however, you can still grow fruits in raised beds. Make beds 6 to 10 inches high and 4 feet wide, and amend with plenty of organic matter.

- ✔ **Soil amendments and fertility:** Fruiting plants need fertile, moist, richly organic soil to produce the best crops. Improve the soil with several inches of compost or composted manure, and add any needed pH amendments and nutrients before planting. See Chapter 5 for more on soils and drainage.

- ✔ **Locally adapted varieties:** Some plant varieties grow better in particular situations than other varieties. Check with your local extension office or nurseries in your area for recommendations, or ask around at farmers' markets.

Plant your fruits close to the kitchen door, garage, or some other place that you visit daily. Frequent inspection helps you see potential pests and diseases before they become problems. Picking and maintenance feel like less of a chore, too, when the patch is just outside the door.

Weed control

Controlling weeds is more critical for small fruits than for nearly any other crop (except vegetables). Many fruits have shallow roots, which can't compete with more aggressive weeds for water and nutrients. Weeds also harbor insect pests that feed on your fruits. Perennial weeds often cause the most trouble because their roots persist from year to year and often sprout if even a small piece remains in the soil. Annual weeds come in the form of seeds blown by the wind or are carried by people, pets, birds, and rain.

Weeding a mature berry patch is a strenuous chore, because most of these plants have shallow roots that don't allow cultivation or that grow in such a way that hand-pulling each weed is the only solution. Weeding thorny brambles is an especially onerous job, so prevention is key. See Chapter 11 for information on controlling weeds.

Buying plants

It really pays to buy the best-quality plants that you can find. If you're fortunate enough to have a local nursery that grows its own fruit plants, by all means pay it a visit. Local nurseries usually offer the best varieties for your area and can give you valuable advice on growing them in your particular situation.

In many parts of the country, however, specialty mail-order nurseries are often the best sources of virus-free, disease-resistant fruits. For more tips on buying plants, turn to Chapter 12.

 A last piece of advice from someone who's been there and done that: Don't plant more than you have time to harvest and maintain. It's easy to get excited about all the promising fruits you can grow and end up buying more plants than you need. Luckily, small fruits freeze very well, but you still have to weed and pick them.

Guide to Small Fruits

Growing berries is one of my most rewarding gardening activities. The season begins with strawberries. Then raspberries, blueberries, elderberries, and grapes ripen in succession through the summer and early fall. Pick your own favorites from this chapter, and get growing!

Beautiful blueberry

I'd be hard pressed to name a shrub that I like better than blueberry (*Vaccinium* species). As an ornamental plant, it offers small white flowers in spring, glossy green leaves in summer, and spectacular crimson foliage in fall. As an edible fruit, it can't be beat for fresh eating, pies, pancakes, dessert sauce, and jam.

Blueberries grow in Zones 3 to 10, but the species and best varieties vary from one extreme to the other. Choose one of these three species to suit your climate:

- **Lowbush blueberry** *(V. angustifolium)* is the hardiest for Zones 3 to 6. These 8- to 18-inch-tall plants form spreading mats and produce small, intensely flavored berries. Grow them as ground-covering landscape plants in well-drained acidic soil, and enjoy the fruits as a bonus or leave them for wildlife. Prune only to remove dead, damaged, or diseased plants. Varieties include Northsky and Putte.

- **Highbush blueberry** *(V. corymbosum* and hybrids) can grow from Zones 4 to 10, but some varieties are better suited to either extreme. If you want plenty of large, flavorful, easy-to-pick fruit, choose highbush blueberries. Shrubs grow 2 to 6 feet tall and produce more fruit when you plant at least two different varieties. In the northern United States, try Bluecrop, Blueray, Earliblue, Northblue, Patriot, and Northland. In the South, plant Gulf Coast, Misty, O'Neill, and Reveille.

  Flower buds, which appear larger and rounder than leaf buds, form in the summer the year before the plants bloom and are most abundant on the 2- to 5-year-old woody stems, called *canes*. Prune in late winter to remove the oldest and most unproductive canes, leaving the most vigorous 15 to 18 canes.

- **Rabbiteye blueberry** *(V. ashei)* grows in the warmer Zones 7 through 9. Growing up to 10 feet tall, the varieties of this species have thicker-skinned berries. You need to plant two different but compatible varieties to get fruit. Good companions include Beckyblue and Bonitablue or Powderblue and Tifblue.

Blueberries belong to a group of plants that have very specific soil needs, including lots of decomposed organic matter and an acidic pH of 4.5 to 5.2. They grow where azaleas and rhododendrons naturally thrive, but you can also alter your soil with acidifying peat moss and sulfur to accommodate their needs. It takes at least 6 months to a year or more for amendments to significantly lower soil pH, so plan ahead, and test the soil before planting. See Chapter 5 for more on soil amendments and pH.

All blueberries have shallow roots and need moist, well-drained soil. Mix $1/2$ cubic foot of peat moss per plant into the soil at planting time. Cover the soil around the shrubs with organic mulch — such as pine needles, shredded oak leaves, or hardwood bark — to maintain the soil moisture and prevent weeds. Keep the soil moist throughout the growing season. Avoid deep cultivation, which can damage the shrubs' roots.

Blueberries have relatively few serious pests or diseases, but good sanitation practices are a must. Mummy berry fungus causes trouble in some areas, spreading from fallen fruit. You can prevent other fungus diseases by pruning, to encourage air circulation through the plants, and by keeping the foliage dry. Birds are the most serious pests; cover the plants completely with bird netting before the berries turn blue.

Ramblin' brambles

If you love fresh raspberries or blackberries, you'll be glad to know how easy they are to grow. These delicate and perishable fruits are expensive in the market, but you can plant your own small patch and produce enough for fresh eating and freezing, too.

When planning your patch of *brambles* (as these fruits are known), thoroughly follow the instructions in the "Berry Patch Basics" section earlier in this chapter. Pay special attention to air circulation and soil drainage: Raised beds work well with brambles; be sure to allow at least 8 feet between rows of plants. Taking weed-control precautions before you plant is also important, because most brambles sport hooked thorns, which make weeding the mature plants difficult, and shallow roots that are easily damaged by hoes.

Don't plant where other brambles or potatoes, tomatoes, or eggplants have grown in recent years due to risk of verticillium root disease infection. It's also best to eliminate nearby wild brambles, if possible, because they often spread disease.

Brambles range in growth habit from upright to sprawling. Some stand up on their own, but most need trellis supports to keep the fruiting canes off the ground. A typical arrangement consists of a T-shaped post and crosspiece at either end of the row, with taut wires or heavy twine running between them down the length of the row. Trailing varieties of blackberry can also be tied to a wire fence or another type of flat support.

Shoots called *canes* grow from either the roots or crown of the plant. Bramble canes are biennial, which means that plants flower on second-year canes, which subsequently die. Canes are called *primocanes* the first year they sprout and *floricanes* in their second year. Floricanes die after fruiting and should be pruned out. Most raspberries and blackberries produce fruit only on the floricanes, but some raspberry varieties — often referred to as *everbearing* — also produce on primocanes in the fall.

Depending on your preference and climate, you can choose among several bramble types and many different varieties for your garden.

Some diseases cause serious damage to raspberries and blackberries, leading to their decline and reduced fruiting. Root rot, verticillium wilt, and leaf rust are among the worst, but some varieties are less susceptible than others to disease. Whenever possible, choose a resistant variety.

Red raspberries

This delicate fruit grows best in cool climates, where plants will receive the 800 to 1,800 hours of chilling they need to produce fruit (see Chapter 16). Most varieties bear one crop per year; others produce two. Summer-bearing varieties produce fruit in the summer on floricanes. Everbearing types fruit in the summer on floricanes and again in the fall on new primocanes. Although most raspberries produce red berries, some varieties have yellow or purple fruit.

Prune summer-bearing raspberries twice a year. After summer fruiting, remove all the floricanes. In early spring, prune out winter-damaged and weak canes, leaving about three to four vigorous canes per square foot, or roughly 6 to 9 inches between canes. Cut these remaining canes back to about 3 to 4 feet high (see Figure 15-1). You can treat the everbearing types similarly or prune all the canes to the ground in late autumn or early spring. This severe pruning forfeits the summer crop but yields a bumper crop in autumn.

Summer-bearing red varieties include Latham, Boyne, Killarney, Milton, September, Canby (nearly thornless), and Nordic. Everbearing varieties include Heritage, Autumn Bliss, and Indian Summer. Yellow varieties include Fall Gold, Amber, and Honeyqueen. Purple varieties share red and black raspberry parentage and may resemble either one. Royalty is the most common variety.

Black and purple raspberries

Black raspberries, also called *black caps,* have a rich flavor and lack the core that characterizes blackberries. Plants grow new primocanes from the crown instead of from the roots; they're easier to contain within a row because they don't grow shoots several feet from the mother plant, as red raspberries do. Plant black raspberry plants 3 feet apart in raised hills.

To control their length and encourage *lateral branches* (side shoots) to form, prune 3 to 4 inches off the primocane tips when they reach 24 to 30 inches high in midsummer. The following spring, prune the lateral branches to about 6 to 10 inches long. At that time, also remove all but the strongest four to six canes. Black raspberry varieties include Black Hawk, Mac Black, Bristol, and Jewel.

Purple raspberries result from crosses between red and black raspberry varieties, but they are much less commonly grown. Their growth habit is similar to that of black raspberries, and the fruit is excellent for jams. Royalty is the most common variety.

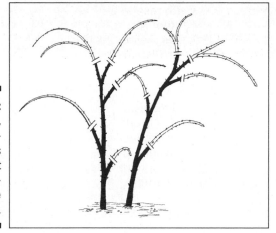

Figure 15-1:
In spring, prune raspberry canes to 3 or 4 feet to encourage more fruit.

Blackberries

Preferring hot southern summers, blackberries grow in Zones 6 and warmer, although some varieties make it into Zone 5 and warmer parts of Zone 4. Prune blackberries as described for summer-bearing raspberries, but leave the floricanes about 4 to 5 feet high.

Blackberries fall into two main categories: bush (or upright) and trailing. The trailing varieties make less appealing plants for most home gardeners because they require more trellising and maintenance, have more thorns than the uprights, and are less cold-hardy. Thornless blackberries are now available, including Arapaho, Black Satin, Chester, Navaho, Hull, and Triple Crown. Of the thorny upright varieties, Illini Hardy, Darrow, Lowden, and Ebony King are among the cold hardiest.

Keeping current with currants and gooseberries

A mainstay in European gardens and gaining popularity in North America, currants and gooseberries (*Ribes* species) make excellent jams, jellies, and dessert berries. The U.S. government at one time banned growing this group of ornamental and delicious fruits, because *Ribes* species contribute to a deadly white pine disease called white pine blister rust. Several states still restrict the sale and transport of *Ribes,* although disease-resistant varieties, which eliminate the problem, are now available.

Use currents and gooseberries as ornamental landscape shrubs. They bear attractive flowers and fruit, have maple-shaped leaves, and remain 3 to 4 feet high. Gooseberries do have thorns, however, so choose their planting locations carefully. Plant the plants 3 to 4 feet apart in fertile, well-drained, compost-enriched soil with a pH of 6 to 7. Full sun to light shade is best. Most plants in this group are hardy to Zone 3, but spring frost may damage the early flowers. In very cold regions, plant on the north side of a building or other location that warms slowly in the spring to delay bloom. Gooseberries' high chill requirement (see Chapter 16) makes them unsuitable for climates with warm or very short winters and hot summers.

The most commonly grown *Ribes* fall into two major groups:

- **Currants** don't have spines and bear ³/₈-inch fruit in clusters, called *strigs,* that look like miniature bunches of grapes. Red and white currants have a mild flavor, whereas black currants have a stronger taste. Disease-resistant red currants include Red Lake and Redstart. The most disease-resistant black currants are Consort and Crandall.

- **Gooseberries** have a spine at the base of each leaf. The fruit is larger than that of currants, varies in color from greenish white to red, and is borne singly or in small clusters. Popular varieties include Hinnonmaki Red, Invicta, and Poorman.

- **Jostaberries** have black currant and gooseberry parentage and have red or black fruits that are larger than currants. The plants are vigorous and generally pest-free.

Currants, gooseberries, and jostaberries can pollinate themselves and don't need another variety to produce fruit. Prune the shrubs in late winter, and remove only canes older than 3 years. Thin younger canes, if necessary, to prevent crowding.

Elegant elderberry

This underused shrub *(Sambucus canadensis)* is native to eastern North America. It has few serious pests or diseases, thrives in poorly drained soil, lives in Zones 3 to 9, and produces clusters of Vitamin C–rich fruit. If groomed to remove dead wood and wayward shoots, elderberry makes an attractive small landscape tree or large shrub, which grows up to 8 feet tall and 8 to 12 feet wide. Elderberries tend to send up new shoots from the roots and create thickets, but individual stems usually live for only a few years. Prune these stems out when they become unproductive.

Elderberries bloom in the late spring, producing 8- to 12-inch-wide, flat-topped clusters of flowers that nearly cover the plant. Elderflowers are used to make wine and a delicate liquor. You can also dip them in batter and fry them into fritters. The dark purple berries ripen in late summer. You can eat the berries raw, but they contain large seeds. I boil and strain the berries to collect the juice for jelly. Mixed with apple juice, they make a beautiful, clear, deep pink to wine-colored jelly. The St. Lawrence Nurseries (see Chapter 16) catalog suggests boiling a pint of juice with $2\frac{1}{2}$ cups of sugar and 10 whole cloves, and serving it over ice for stomach ailments and colds. I mix a similar concoction with sparkling water for a natural soft drink. Elderberry wine is another possibility, of course.

Plant elderberries in moist soil and full sun. For best fruiting, plant two different varieties or seedlings. Wild seedlings are adequate for my garden, but several good improved varieties exist, with larger and more numerous berries. These varieties include Kent, York, Nova, and Johns.

Going ape for grapes

Growing organic grapes (*Vitis* species) successfully depends on your climate, cultural strategies, and the varieties you choose. Arid climates provoke fewer diseases than humid climates. You can grow grapes nearly anywhere in Zones 3 through 10, and they tolerate a wide range of soil conditions; well-drained soil in the pH range of 5.5 to 7.0 is best. Grapes need full sun and very good air circulation to hamper diseases.

At least three grape species and countless varieties exist in North American gardens and vineyards. The European grape *(V. vinifera)* grows best in a Mediterranean climate, such as California and parts of the southwestern United States. In hotter, humid climates, many people grow muscadine grapes *(V. rotundifolia),* which thrive in Zones 7 through 9. The native North American species *(V. labrusca)* and its hybrids are the hardiest and best for most other regions of the country.

To sort out the complicated lineage, divide grapes into two broad categories: table grapes and wine or juice grapes. Table grapes have tender skins suitable for fresh eating and may contain seeds or be seedless. Wine and juice grapes may have tougher skins but plenty of sweet juice for liquid consumption or making into jelly. Ripe fruit colors range from green to pink and red to deep purplish black.

Before planting young grapes, prepare the soil thoroughly as described in the "Berry Patch Basics" section, earlier in this chapter. Install a sturdy trellis consisting of two or three heavy wires strung 24 inches apart on sturdy posts. Brace the end posts.

Several pruning and training systems exist, but the basic idea in all of them is to establish one or two main trunks per vine. Each trunk grows horizontal lateral branches, as described for kiwi (see the following section), which you attach to the wires. The flowers and fruit appear on wood that grows in the current year from the laterals that grew in the previous year. Starting in winter after the first growing season, begin the pruning and training as follows:

1. **In the first winter, choose two healthy, vigorous canes to keep, and remove the rest.**

   Prune these main trunks back to three or four buds each.

2. **The next summer, select the most vigorous shoot from each trunk, and remove competing shoots.**

   Train the shoots on a string until they reach the top wire; then pinch them to encourage lateral branching, as shown in Figure 15-2.

3. **In the second winter, remove all growth from the trunk and lateral branches.**

   Cut laterals back to ten buds. Let vines grow unpruned through the summer.

4. **In the third winter and subsequent years, choose the laterals for the current year, as well as replacement laterals for the next year.**

   Leave ten buds on the current-year laterals and two buds on the replacements. (Remember that grapes grow fruit on wood that grows in the current year from last season's laterals.) Prune off all other wood, removing as much 90 percent of the previous year's growth.

Prevalent diseases and pests include berry moth, mites, leafhoppers, and Japanese beetles, as well as Botrytis bunch rot, powdery mildew, and black rot. Some varieties are less sensitive to infection than other varieties.

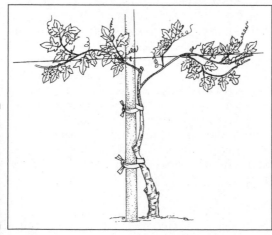

Figure 15-2:
Train grapes on a trellis, and prune to a main stem with lateral branches.

Grape varieties often grow best in specific regions of the country. Consult your local extension office or reputable nursery for recommendations. Also take a look at the "Surfing for small fruits" sidebar in this chapter.

Have a hardy kiwi, mate?

Unless you happen to live in Zone 8 or warmer, you can forget about growing the subtropical kiwis that appear in grocery stores. Luckily, if you live in a climate as cold as Zone 5 and even Zone 4, you can grow hardy kiwis. The hardy species, *Actinidia arguta,* produces very sweet, smooth-skinned, green fruit about the size of a large cherry, which ripens in late summer to early fall. You can eat these kiwis skin and all, and many people consider them more flavorful than the less hardy, store-bought kiwifruit. Male and female flowers occur on separate plants, so you need one male plant for every five female plants. The sweetly fragrant ornamental flowers smell like lily of the valley.

The hardy kiwi plant is a very vigorous vine that can grow 20 feet or more long and requires a strong trellis. A mature, properly pruned kiwi vine can produce more than 100 pounds of fruit per year. To make a trellis, set 4- to 6-inch diameter, 8- to 9-foot high posts at least 2 to 3 feet into the ground, and run heavy-gauge wire between them 6 feet off the ground. Train the vines up the posts and along the wire. Avoid planting where strong wind may damage the vines or blow down the trellis.

Space plants about 15 feet apart in full sun. Soil must have a pH around 6.5 and be well drained but moist, especially as new plants become established and while fruit develops. Root rot is common in overly wet soil. Mulch to suppress weeds and maintain soil moisture. Plants produce flowers and fruit on shoots that grow in the current spring.

Pruning is critical to control rampant growth and encourage maximum fruiting:

- **Summer pruning:** Establish one to four main trunks, using more in colder climates and fewer where cold damage is less likely. Train these trunks up the center post, and prune to 6-foot lengths when they reach the top to encourage them to sprout lateral shoots along the wires. These lateral shoots become the permanent arms from which fruiting wood will grow. In the summer, as the laterals branch, prune off 4 inches of new growth whenever the shoots reach 8 inches in length. The result should be a series of 4-inch sections of vine, called *spurs,* that will send out fruiting wood the following spring.

- **Winter pruning:** In late winter, remove fruiting wood older than three years, as well as very tangled or twisted vines. Shorten any vines that may reach the ground when growth resumes, but avoid cutting the spurs or arms.

Harvest the fruit in late summer when it softens and becomes sweet. (You may have to beat the squirrels to the harvest.) You can store kiwifruit in the refrigerator for a short time.

Sublime strawberries

Probably the most popular small fruits for the home garden, strawberries are also among the hardest to grow organically. Strawberries have many insect pests and diseases that damage plants and berries alike. Establishing your planting in well-drained, fertile soil and maintaining a weed-free patch are essential for success.

You can choose among three kinds of strawberries, depending on when you want fruit. Consult your local extension office or nurseries for the best varieties for your area. Also see the "Surfing for small fruits" sidebar in this chapter.

- **June-bearing** varieties produce one large crop of berries in late spring to early summer.

- **Everbearing** varieties produce two smaller crops: one in early summer and another in early fall.

- **Day-neutral** berries, the newest type, can produce fruit continuously throughout the growing season.

Strawberry planting and growing guide

Plant dormant, bare-root strawberry plants 18 to 24 inches apart in 3- to 6-inch-high, 3- to 4-foot-wide raised beds. Set the plants so that soil covers the roots but the crown remains above the soil, as shown in Figure 15-3. Keep the soil moist but not saturated. Pinch off all flowers until midsummer for the first season to encourage strong root and top growth.

The plants that you set out are called the *mother plants*. They send out runners that take root and develop new *daughter plants* in mid- to late summer. Space the daughter plants evenly around the mothers to give each plant plenty of space to grow. Daughter plants flower and fruit the year after they grow. In the second summer, you can remove the original mother plants to make room for new daughter plants. Another method is to rotary-till the sides of the bed in midsummer of the second or third year, leaving plants only in the 18- to 24-inch-wide center strip. Train new daughter plants into the tilled soil.

Plan to replace your strawberry planting every three to five years. Cover the planting with straw mulch after the ground freezes in cold-winter climates, and remove the mulch as the weather warms in spring.

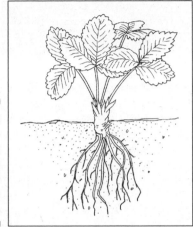

Figure 15-3:
Plant straw-
berry plants
so that the
crowns are
just above
the soil.

Diseases and insect pests that prey on strawberries

One of the most serious insect pests that affect strawberries is the tarnished plant bug, which can severely damage the developing fruit. These insects spend the winter in plant debris and live on weeds in and around your yard. Covering the strawberry plants in the fall with a floating row cover can offer some, but not complete, protection from the bugs in the following spring and early summer. Early-ripening varieties often suffer less damage than late-season berries.

The strawberry clipper or bud weevil is another significant pest in some areas. These insects fly into the planting from neighboring woodlots and hedgerows about the time that the flower buds swell. Adults destroy the developing buds by laying eggs in them. Many other insects, slugs, mites, and nematodes attack strawberry fruits and plants, reducing vigor and pro-duction, and introducing disease. Birds and ground squirrels also take their share.

Strawberries are subject to many fungal, bacterial, and viral diseases. Fungal infections include leaf spot, leaf scorch, leaf blight, powdery mildew, red stele, verticillium wilt, root rot, and several berry rots. Buy only virus-free plants from a reputable nursery, and avoid planting strawberries where tomatoes, eggplants, or potatoes previously grew to prevent wilt diseases. See Part III for more control strategies.

Surfing for small fruits

The Internet offers a wealth of information about any topic that you care to know about (and some topics that you don't), and small fruits are no exception. Government- and university-sponsored sites feature advice and instructions, as well as links to other related sites. Commercial mail-order nurseries sell their plants and offer online planting and care guides that help ensure your success. Here are a few of my favorites:

✔ **Tree Fruits: Organic Production Overview** (www.attra.org/attra-pub/fruitover.html): Funded by the U.S. government, Appropriate Technology Transfer for Rural Areas (ATTRA for short) has an excellent Web page with advice on establishing a small fruit patch for home use or commercial-size production. The site provides lots of good links and cultural instructions for specific crops, too.

✔ **Nourse Farms** (www.noursefarms.com): Nourse Farms offers a good assortment of small fruits and perennial vegetables. I drove by this large and well-established nursery frequently while attending college in western Massachusetts. You can also write to the company at 41 River Road, South Deerfield, MA 01373 or reach them by phone at 413-665-2658.

✔ **Raintree Nursery** (www.raintreenursery.com): Raintree Nursery specializes in fruits for the Pacific Northwest. You can also write to the company at 391 Butts Road, Morton, WA 98356 or call 360-496-6400.

✔ **Indiana Berry & Plant Co.** (www.indianaberry.com): Indiana Berry & Plant Co. offers a wide variety of small fruits as well as planting and care guides on its Web site. Write the company at 5218 W. 500 S., Huntingburg, IN 47542 or you can reach them by phone at 800-295-2226.

✔ **Edible Landscaping Online** (www.eat-it.com): Edible Landscaping offers in-depth care guides as well as many fruit and nut plants. Write the company at 361 Spirit Ridge Lane, Afton, VA 22920 or call 800-524-4156.

Chapter 16

Fruits and Nuts for Your Organic Orchard

· ·

In This Chapter

▶ Selecting tree size

▶ Cultivating fruits

▶ Growing nut trees in the landscape

▶ Choosing disease-resistant varieties

· ·

Freshly picked fruit from your own trees and shrubs is juicy joy — and easier to grow than you may think. Sure, some fruit and nut trees need more attention than many other plants, but the harvest is worth the effort. Many fruit varieties that you can grow at home taste far better than supermarket fruit. While better flavor is reason enough to grow your own fruit, if you're concerned about pesticides, you have another compelling reason: Cherries, peaches, apples, and apricots are among the 12 most pesticide-contaminated foods, according to the U.S. Food and Drug Administration.

Even if you have nothing more than a large patio planter, you can grow your own fruit; on a half-acre lot, you can plant an orchard large enough to provide fruit for yourself and half the neighborhood. As a bonus, most fruit trees and shrubs are ornamental, especially when they're blooming.

Anatomy of a Fruit Tree

Fruit and nut trees resemble other trees in most ways but differ in one important aspect: Unlike ornamental plants, fruit trees are grown primarily to produce food. To make these fruit factories more and more efficient, plant breeders continue to develop special techniques, such as reducing the size of the trees, to make trees produce at an earlier age and yield more fruit per acre. That's good news for home gardeners.

Size does matter

Trees are easier to harvest and maintain when all the branches are within arm's reach. Unfortunately, many fruit trees can grow up to 40 feet tall or even higher when left to their own devices. To keep them in bounds and to produce more high-quality fruit, most fruit varieties and many nuts are *grafted* onto the roots of smaller-growing varieties.

Some rootstocks influence the size that the tree will ultimately attain, although the mature size of the tree also depends on the standard height that's normal for the variety of fruit that's been grafted onto the rootstock. Dwarfing rootstocks are categorized by the amount of dwarfing they provide. Apple-tree sizes, for example, fall into several categories:

- **Standard-size** apple trees, grown on seedling or nondwarfing roots, may reach 25 feet.

- **Semidwarf** trees are about 75 percent of the standard height, or about 18 feet at maturity.

- **Dwarf trees** are about 50 percent as high as standard trees, or 12 feet tall.

- **Miniature trees** are only about 15 percent of the standard size. At a mere 4 feet in height, these trees are the best kind for growing in containers.

 As an organic home gardener, consider dwarf to semidwarf trees. It's easier to monitor and control pests when you can reach the top of the tree. On very small trees, you can even use a barrier fabric to help prevent insect infestations (see Chapter 8). You can also harvest fruit years sooner and pick the fruit more easily.

Sex and the single tree

Many fruit and nut species — such as apples, sweet cherries, European pears, Japanese plums, walnuts, pecans, and filberts — require cross-pollination to bear fruit. That means that you need two different but compatible varieties planted near each other so that the pollen of one species fertilizes the flowers of the other.

The trees must bloom at the same time for cross-pollination to occur, and some varieties are fussy about the trees with which they mix. Other fruit and nut species are *self-fruitful,* which means that they can pollinate their own flowers, but even those species often produce larger crops when they mix pollen with a friend. Reputable nurseries can tell you which varieties can pollinate each other. See the "Where to find fruits and nuts" sidebar, later in this chapter.

Chill out

Fruits and nuts have another peculiar requirement. Most need a certain number of hours below 45 degrees Fahrenheit — their *chill requirement* or *chill factor* — to produce lots of flowers and fruit. As you may guess, fruits (such as oranges) that grow mostly in warm climates have lower chilling requirements than some cold-climate fruits (like apples). The chill factor is not related to cold-hardiness, however. Even some frost-tender plants, such as fig trees, need some time below 45 degrees Fahrenheit to bear fruit properly. Table 16-1 lists the chill categories.

Look for specific varieties that match your climate. Some peach varieties need only 200 hours; others require more than 1,000.

Table 16-1	Chill Requirements	
Chill Factor	*Number of Hours below 45°F*	*Regions*
Low	Fewer than 400	Areas of California, southern Texas, and Florida
Moderate	Between 400 and 700	Gulf Coast, southeastern seaboard, and West Coast areas
High	More than 700 to 1,000	Most of the United States and Canada

Low winter temperatures and the timing of autumn and spring frosts play important roles in your selection of fruit species and varieties for your organic orchard. Local nurseries generally sell plants that are best suited to your local climate. Reputable mail-order nurseries and your local extension office can also steer you toward appropriate varieties.

Budding genius

Fruit trees grow different kinds of buds, and it helps to be able to recognize the various types. The *terminal bud* grows at the end of branches, and that's where new branches and twigs grow from each spring. When the terminal buds expand, they leave *bud scars,* which look like slightly raised rings around the twig. You can measure how much a tree has grown each year by looking at the distance between bud scars. *Leaf buds* appear along the twigs and expand into leaves. *Flower buds* are usually fatter than leaf buds and swell first in the spring. Some trees — such as most apple, pear, cherry, plum, and apricot trees — produce their fruit on *spurs,* which are short, modified twigs. Spurs usually live and produce flower buds for several years or longer before becoming unproductive. See Figure 16-1 for examples of these bud types.

The whys and wherefores of grafting

Tree nurseries slip a bud, called a *scion,* from a desirable fruit variety, such as Delicious apple or Bing cherry, under the bark of a dwarfing rootstock variety in early spring. The two grow together, and when the scion bud starts growing vigorously, the nursery prunes off the dwarfing rootstock's top growth to just above the bud. The place where the two parts meet is called the *bud union,* which usually shows up as a bulge, bend, or scar.

Plant breeders and tree nurseries graft fruit and nut trees for a variety of reasons:

✔ **Reproduce exact copies of desirable trees:** Nurseries can make as many trees as they need by grafting buds of a desirable variety onto uniform rootstocks.

✔ **Influence the mature size of the tree:** Reducing the tree size has many advantages, especially for home gardeners.

✔ **Encourage fruit bearing at an earlier age:** Some standard-size apple trees can take up to ten years to begin bearing fruit, whereas a dwarf bears fruit in two years.

✔ **Increase disease and pest resistance:** Some rootstocks resist soil-borne diseases and harmful pests better than others.

✔ **Adapt to different soils:** Some trees grow better in clay soils; others prefer loam.

✔ **Determine hardiness to particular climates:** Roots are among the most cold-sensitive parts of a tree. Some rootstocks increase the trees' hardiness to cold temperatures.

For the best-quality apples and pears, leave only one fruit on each spur, and pinch off the others in early summer. Spurs and flower buds develop best on limbs that are angled slightly above horizontal. Branches that grow upright and those that dangle below horizontal produce little, if any, fruit.

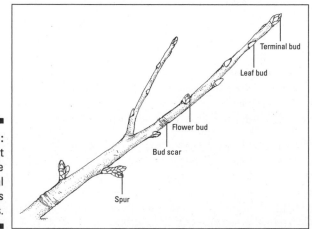

Figure 16-1:
Fruit and nut trees have several kinds of buds.

Terminal bud

Leaf bud

Flower bud

Bud scar

Spur

Cultural Exchange

Choosing the best kinds of fruit and nut plants for your climate is only one part of establishing a successful, low-maintenance organic orchard. You also have to plant your trees and shrubs where they can thrive, give them the fertile soil they need, prune them for health and maximum production, and plan your strategies for dealing with the inevitable pests and diseases.

Planting for success

All fruits need moisture-retentive but well-drained soil. (Flip to Chapter 5 for more on soil testing and drainage.) Soggy sites spell doom for these species. Adequate water is also critical, especially when the fruit is developing and expanding.

Professional fruit growers also consider air movement when they plan their orchard placement and layout. Air affects fruit and nut plants in several ways:

- **Wind:** Too much wind can keep pollinating insects, such as bees, from flying and pollinating the flowers at critical times. It also knocks fruit off the tree and can damage the branches. Plant a windbreak if necessary, or put the trees where a building shields them.

- **Frost pockets:** Cold air flows downhill and collects at the bottom of a slope. Trees that bloom in early spring are especially vulnerable to cold temperatures at that time, and the flowers may be severely damaged if they're planted where cold air collects. Plant fruit trees and shrubs on the slope instead of near the bottom, but avoid the windy top of a slope.

- **Circulation:** Constantly but lightly moving air helps prevent disease organisms from getting a foothold on your trees. Many fungus diseases that infect leaves need water and moisture to spread and grow, so keeping the leaves dry is important.

If you buy your plants locally, they usually are already growing in a container. If you order them from a mail-order nursery, however, they arrive in a *dormant* (nongrowing) state and *bare root* — without any soil around their roots. Be sure to plant bare-root trees and shrubs right away. Refer to Chapter 12 for information on how to plant container-grown and bare-root plants.

After planting, establish a wide ring of organic mulch around your trees to conserve soil moisture, prevent grass and weeds from competing with the tree roots, and reduce insect pests. See Chapter 11 for the lowdown on mulch and its benefits.

Because producing heavy crops of fruit stresses trees and shrubs, fruit- and nut-bearing species may need additional nutrients. See Chapter 5 for details on soil testing and Chapter 6 for more on fertilizers.

Pruning fruit trees

Producing bushels of high-quality fruit and developing a sturdy tree that can support the crop are the twin goals of pruning and training fruit trees. If you end up with an attractive landscape specimen too, that's a bonus! Although you use the same basic pruning techniques on all fruit trees, each kind of fruit tree has unique timing and methods for reaching your goals. For an introduction to basic pruning techniques and tools, flip to Chapter 19.

You need to prune fruit trees regularly for several reasons:

- **To remove dead, damaged, and diseased wood:** Do this before any other pruning and whenever necessary.

- **To control tree and shrub size:** Keep fruit down where you can harvest and care for it without a ladder.

- **To provide air circulation:** Circulation helps ward off pests and diseases. Crowded limbs invite fungus diseases and provide habitat for damaging insects.

- **To increase exposure to sunlight:** Fruit that's exposed to direct sunlight tastes better than fruit shaded by leaves and branches.

- **To increase the quality and quantity of fruit:** Branches trained to 60-degree angles where they meet the trunk develop the most flower buds. Spacing the limbs up and down and around the trunk provides the best conditions for the fruit to mature.

Professional fruit growers use several pruning and training methods, depending on the type of fruit they grow (see Figure 16-2):

- **Central leader:** Used mainly with apple, European pear and plum trees, large nut trees, and dwarf cultivars, this method yields trees with single, upright trunks, called *central leaders*. The main limbs should be spaced about 8 inches apart and extend in all directions around the trunk so that no limb is directly above another. To maximize sunlight penetration, prune the limbs so that those at the top of the tree are shorter than branches under them.

- **Modified central leader:** In this system, trees are trained to a single, upright central leader, with limbs evenly spaced until they reach a desired height — usually, 6 to 10 feet. At that point, you prune out the leader and maintain the tree at that height. All fruit trees can be trained to this form.

✔ **Open center (also called vase shape):** Peaches, nectarines, sour cherries, apricots, Asian pears, and Japanese plums produce easy-to-reach, high-quality fruit when the trees are pruned to this form. In this style, you select four or five well-placed main branches and then prune out the central leader. This method limits the height of the tree and creates a spreading crown.

Note: These styles apply mainly to temperate-climate fruit; tropical fruits, such as citrus, are trained differently.

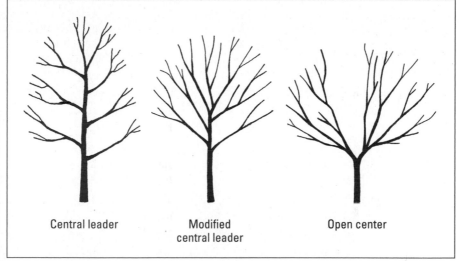

Figure 16-2:
From left to right: Central leader, modified central leader, and open center.

Central leader | Modified central leader | Open center

Choose young fruit trees with good structure to start with and shape them as they grow. Here's how to get your trees off to a good start:

✔ **At planting time:** Remove damaged and dead limbs, those less than 25 inches from the ground, and any with narrow crotch angles of less than 45 degrees. Leave branches with crotch angles between 45 and 80 degrees. If the tree has two shoots competing to be the leader, choose one and remove the other.

✔ **First winter:** In late winter, select three to four limbs to keep as main branches. They should be about 8 inches apart vertically, be well spaced around the trunk, and have approximately 60-degree angles at the trunk. Prune off all other limbs. Prune the remaining limbs back by one third of their length to encourage side branching. Prune the central leader to 24 to 30 inches above the uppermost limb for a central-leader-style tree. If you're pruning for an open center or vase shape, remove the central leader just above the top branch.

✔ **Second summer:** In midsummer, remove *water sprouts,* which grow upright from the branches, and *suckers,* which grow up from the base of the tree. In central-leader trees, choose the strongest, most upright leader; then remove the competing ones. Using the criteria mentioned for the first dormant season, choose the next tier of limbs, beginning about 15 to 18 inches above the top branch of the lower tier, and remove undesirable limbs. In open-center trees, remove competing, crowded, and upright shoots.

✔ **Second winter:** Remove undesirable limbs, competing leaders, water sprouts, and suckers, and prune the new growth of side branches back by one third. Use notched sticks called *spreaders* to spread the remaining limbs to 60-degree angles where they meet the trunk. Leave the spreaders in place until mid- to late summer. In open-center trees, prune new shoots by one third to *outward-facing buds* — buds that face away from the trunk — to encourage branching. Thin out crowded shoots by removing the weakest ones. See the "Where to find fruits and nuts" sidebar for sources of spreaders; many nurseries offer them.

✔ **Continuing care:** Continue to follow the directions for the second season year after year. To develop a modified central-leader tree, remove the central leader just above the uppermost branch you want to keep. Do this job in the summer to inhibit vigorous sprouting.

Preventing pests and diseases

Humans aren't the only beings who love fruit; insects, diseases, and other creatures appreciate these trees and shrubs too. Some insects damage the fruits; others concentrate their efforts on the foliage and wood. Insects take a toll, but you can control many of them without resorting to pesticides.

Sticky traps, baited either to resemble a ripe red apple or with hormones that the bugs find sexy, capture many codling moths, apple maggots, borers, and some scale and leaf-miner species. White and yellow plastic rectangles covered with sticky glue also attract several species of harmful insects. Horticultural oil sprays can control aphids, pear psyllas, mites, leaf miners, and caterpillars. Other insects can be trickier to deal with, but luckily, you can fool many pests with traps and barriers and, if necessary, well-timed organic pesticide sprays. See Chapter 8 for more information on organic controls and purchasing sources.

Plant breeders have developed many modern fruit varieties that resist or at least tolerate some of the most devastating diseases. And some old-time varieties are naturally resistant to certain pests. Learn what pests pose the biggest problems in your region and choose varieties that resist them.

Temperate-Climate Trees and Shrubs

Popular and easy to grow in U.S. Department of Agriculture Hardiness Zones 8 and northward, these fruits find their way into lunch boxes, fruit salads, and pies from coast to coast. All require some dedication to their cultural needs but richly reward your efforts.

Apples

Apples *(Malus sylvestris)* are among the most popular fruit trees to grow, but to harvest high-quality fruit, you must be prepared to regularly prune, feed, and deal with pests. Apples require cross-pollination; you can also use ornamental crabapples to pollinate apple trees. When choosing an apple-tree variety, consider these factors:

- **Ripening time:** Apples ripen from late summer through late autumn, so choose a variety that ripens its fruit before freezing temperatures in your area have a chance to damage the crop. Varieties also vary considerably in their chill requirements. Take a look at the "Where to find fruits and nuts" sidebar, later in this chapter, for sources of trees that are best suited for your area.

- **Size:** As trees increase in size, they become harder to prune and spray, so choose trees on semidwarf and dwarf rootstocks that reach only 8 to 12 feet tall. You can also use pruning techniques to control tree height. Prune apple trees in late winter, while they are dormant, and follow up in midsummer to remove overly vigorous sprouts.

- **Disease resistance:** This aspect is key when you're choosing apple varieties for organic orchards. Apple scab, cedar apple rust, powdery mildew, and fire blight devastate many common varieties, which makes them unsuitable for home orchards. Although the names of improved varieties may be unfamiliar, the fruit is just as flavorful. Some disease-resistant apple varieties worth seeking out, listed from those that ripen earliest (late summer) to latest (mid- to late autumn), include Redfree, Prima, Novamac, JonaFree, Priscilla, Freedom, Liberty, Nova Easygro, Enterprise, and GoldRush. Although you may not see these varieties in the supermarket, many farmers' markets and organic cooperatives offer the fruit in season, so you can do a taste test before you buy your own trees.

Apples have several serious pests that make them a challenge to grow organically. Plum curculio, apple maggot, and codling moths damage the developing fruits, frequently making them inedible. See Chapter 8 for more on these pests and how to control them.

European and Asian pears

Pears (*Pyrus* species) share many quirks and characteristics with apples, and they grow in similar climates. Like apples, pears are usually sold as grafted trees and require similar pruning and training. With their glossy dark green foliage, pears make especially good landscape specimens in addition to providing delicious fruit.

You can choose between European and Asian pears. They share most cultural attributes but differ in some other ways:

- **Pollination:** Most European pears require another variety planted within 50 feet for cross-pollination. Asian pears are mostly self-fruitful but produce heavier crops when cross-pollinated.

- **Shape:** European pear fruits have the traditional pear shape, with a wide bottom tapering to a narrower top. Most Asian pears resemble round apples.

- **Texture:** European pears have soft, melting flesh when ripe. Asian pears have crisp, applelike flesh.

Unfortunately, pears also share many diseases and insect pests with apples. Fire blight is its most devastating disease, and pear scab can render the trees and fruit unsightly. Avoid planting fire-blight-prone varieties, and control insect pests that spread the disease. Pear psylla, an insect that resembles a winged yellow-to-orange aphid, sucks the juice out of new foliage and excretes sticky droppings that support a black, sooty-looking fungus. You can control it with dormant spray oil and beneficial insects.

Fire-blight-resistant varieties of European pear, listed in order of ripening, include Harrow Delight, Harvest Queen, Starking Delicious, Moonglow, Stark Honeysweet, Magness, Seckel, and Harrow Sweet. The earliest varieties begin ripening in mid-August in Zone 5, with the latest finishing up in late September. Disease-resistant Asian varieties include Shinko, Shinseiki, Large Korean (also known as Dan Beh), Korean Giant, and Olympic.

Pears are best picked when they're still somewhat hard and allowed to ripen at room temperature or in the refrigerator. Fruit that overripens on the tree develops hard, gritty spots in the flesh and may turn brown and mushy near the core. Asian pears and late-season European pears keep for months in the refrigerator if they're picked just before ripeness.

Sweet and sour cherries

Cherries *(Prunus)* are glorious in their spring bloom; the fruit seems like a bonus. In Zone 5, cherries ripen from June into July, providing the first tree fruit of the season. Most cherries are red when ripe, but some sweet cherries are yellow. Cherries belong to the *Prunus* genus, along with peaches, almonds, and plums.

Although sweet and sour or tart cherries are similar in many respects, they differ in significant ways:

- **Pollination:** Sweet cherries need cross-pollination, except for the variety Stella, so you need two compatible varieties. Sour cherries, also called pie cherries, are self-pollinating. Sour cherries can pollinate sweet cherries but may not bloom at the same time. (The trees must bloom at the same time for the varieties to cross-pollinate.)

- **Hardiness:** Sweet-cherry trees grow reliably only in Zones 5 to 8, but some sour cherries thrive in Zone 4.

- **Culinary use:** Sweet cherries, common in supermarkets in early summer, are best when eaten fresh. Sour cherries make the best pies and jams, but you have to grow your own; markets rarely offer them. Some varieties are sweet enough to eat fresh, too.

The pests that plague apples, including plum curculio and apple maggot, also infest cherries, as do the cherry fruit fly and Oriental fruit moth. Birds will also take a portion of the crop, if not the whole thing, unless you cover the ripening fruit with a net. Birds tend to bother tart cherries less than sweet cherries, but better to be safe than sorry. The fruits of some varieties tend to crack in the rain as they ripen, but others resist this bad habit.

Of the diseases that affect all *Prunus* species, black knot fungus, bacterial canker, and leaf spot are the most serious. Practice good sanitation by raking up foliage and dropped fruit, and prune out any infected wood immediately.

For best flavor, let sweet and sour cherries ripen fully on the tree before picking, but keep them covered to prevent bird theft!

Montmorency is the most widely grown commercial sour cherry, but other varieties — such as Morello, Meteor, and Northstar — are good choices for home orchards. Good sweet-cherry varieties for homegrown fruit include Stella, Lapins, Glacier, Surefire, and Sunburst, which are self-pollinating. Bing, which is the most common commercial variety, is susceptible to canker and fruit splitting. Good varieties that require cross-pollination include Van and yellow cherries Emperor Francis, Stark Gold, and Rainier.

Peaches and nectarines

Peaches and nectarines *(Prunus persica)* are actually the same species, but peaches are fuzzy, and nectarines are smooth-skinned. They have the same diseases and pests as cherries but are worth growing for the juicy flavor and aroma that comes only from freshly picked, sun-ripened fruit. They are self-pollinating, so you need only one tree.

Geography and climate influence peach growing rather significantly. Diseases and pests that are prevalent in some parts of the United States cause little concern in other areas. Plum curculio, bacterial leaf spot, and fungus diseases, for example, present problems for peaches in the eastern United States, approximately from Fort Worth, Texas, to Fargo, North Dakota. Gardeners west of that region have an easier time growing peaches organically, except in the Pacific Northwest, where the damp climate encourages diseases. If you're in the eastern United States, vigilant housekeeping, pruning, and choosing a site that encourages air circulation, as well as using natural pesticides, can help you grow this problem-prone crop.

Peaches and nectarines grow reliably only in climates with mild winters and fairly dry summers, preferably Zones 6 to 9, although some varieties produce fruit in warmer parts of Zones 4 and 5. The hardiness of their overwintering flower buds is the limiting factor in cold-winter climates; several consecutive nights of –13 degrees Fahrenheit will kill them. Mild weather in winter or early spring followed by a return to freezing weather also spells disaster for their blooms. Plant breeders have developed varieties, such as Reliance and Veteran, that withstand temperatures as low as –25 degrees Fahrenheit, but they usually are less flavorful than peaches grown in warmer climates. If you want to try growing peaches in Zone 4 or 5, choose varieties with high chill requirements because they bloom later in the season.

Gardeners in Zones 9 and 10 can grow peaches successfully if they choose varieties with low chill requirements. Some varieties developed for Florida, for example, need only 150–400 hours below 45 degrees Fahrenheit to bear fruit.

Peaches and nectarines bloom on wood that grew in the previous year, so prune them in June after flowering. Maintain an open-centered form, and encourage lots of new growth each year. Maintain a vigilant pest- and disease-control program, too, because peach and nectarine trees are among the most susceptible to attack of all fruit trees. Peach leaf curl — a serious fungus disease — causes leaves and fruit to drop prematurely. Look for varieties that resist canker, brown rot, bacterial leaf spot, and pit splitting. Catalog or plant-tag descriptions usually tell you whether a variety is resistant to particular diseases.

Peach varieties that resist bacterial leaf spot include Harrow Diamond, Harrow Beauty, Delta, Southern Pearl, Desert Gold, Candor, Sweethaven, Redhaven, Reliance, Harbrite, Harken, and Veteran. Nectarine varieties include Sunraycer, Fantasia, RosePrincess, Mericrest, Hardired, and Harko.

European and Asian apricots

Members of the *Prunus* genus, European and Asian apricots enjoy the same mild climates and well-drained soils as peaches. Although plum curculio, codling moth, and brown rot can infest the fruits, the trees are more vigorous and resistant to disease than peaches. Prune apricot trees to a modified central leader or open-center form. If you can grow them in your climate, give apricots a try, because they have beautiful early-spring flowers followed by luscious fruit that supermarkets just can't match. Unfortunately, spring frosts damage the tender blooms in cold regions.

European apricots that you may see in your grocery's produce section grow on 10- to 30-foot trees that thrive in the warmer, drier parts of Zones 6 to 8. Trees grown in cool, humid climates produce less fruit, and it tends to be of poorer quality.

Choose varieties that are suitable for your specific climate. Local nurseries and your local extension office can make knowledgeable recommendations. Choose a freestone variety (discussed in the "Peaches and nectarines" section) if you want to dry the ripened fruits for storage. Good varieties include Harcot, Harglow, Hargrand, Harlayne, Puget Gold, Veecot, and Goldcot. For best flavor, allow the fruits to ripen on the tree before picking in July and early August.

Plums and prunes

Plums and prunes are among the most genetically complicated fruits in the *Prunus* group, because several species share the name *plum,* and all the various species commonly interbreed. The resulting fruits fall into several broad categories, including European, Japanese, and prune plums. They differ in important ways:

- **Japanese plums** are round, usually require cross-pollination to set fruit, and are pruned to an open-centered shape. They generally are hardy to Zone 6 and warmer parts of Zone 5, although some hybrids are hardier. Varieties include Shiro, Early Golden, Burbank, Redheart, Santa Rosa, Methley, and Beauty. Hybrids Elite, Superb, Tecumseh, Perfection, and Brookgold are hardy through Zone 4.

- **European plums** are oval, and most don't need a second variety for pollination. Train these trees to a modified leader form. Most varieties are hardy through Zone 5, and some produce fruit even in Zone 4. Varieties include Damson, Seneca, Verity, and Green Gage.

- **Prune plums** are European plums with drier flesh and a high sugar content that makes them suitable for drying. Common varieties include Stanley, French Prune, Fellenberg or Italian Prune, Valor, Earliblue, Sugar, and Mount Royal (which is hardy in Zone 4).

Japanese and European plums can't pollinate each other, so if your trees require cross-pollination, be sure to choose compatible varieties. Five to eight weeks after bloom, thin the fruits to hang 4 to 6 inches apart. Fruits ripen from July through September, starting with Japanese plums and ending with prune plums, depending on the variety.

Plant breeders have also crossed apricots with plums to create hybrids called apriums, plumcots, and pluots. These trees are hardy wherever European apricots grow, require cross-pollination, and otherwise have characteristics of both parents.

Where to find fruit and nut trees

Look to specialty catalogs for the widest assortment of fruit and nut varieties:

- Stark Bro's Nursery is one of the largest and oldest temperate-climate fruit nurseries in the United States and offers a comprehensive catalog. Phone 800-325-4180 or visit the Web site at www.starkbros.com.

- To purchase warm-climate fruits, try your local nurseries or, on the West Coast of the United States, contact Pacific Tree Farms at 4301 Lynwood Drive, Chula Vista, CA 91910, phone 905-468-7262.

- In the southeastern United States, try Garden of Delights at 14560 SW 14th St., Davie, FL 33325-4217. Phone 954-370-9004 or e-mail godelights@aol.com.

- If you live in Zones 3 to 5, contact St. Lawrence Nurseries at 325 State Highway 345, Potsdam, NY 13676. Phone 315-265-6739 or e-mail trees@sln.potsdam.ny.us for a catalog of cold-hardy fruits and nuts.

- In the Pacific Northwest, contact One Green World at 28696 South Cramer Rd., Molalla, OR 97038-8576. Phone 503-651-3005, fax 800-418-9983, or visit their Web site at www.onegreenworld.com. The company offers a variety of fruits and nuts.

- Another good nursery for the Pacific Northwest, Raintree Nursery, offers fruit and nut trees, as well as unusual fruits. Write to the company at 391 Butts Road, Morton, WA 98356; call 360-496-6400; fax 888-770-8358; or visit www.raintreenursery.com, which offers handy maps, charts, and detailed growing instructions.

Warm-Climate Fruit Trees

These trees grow where winter temperatures remain mild — generally in Zones 8 and warmer. Evergreen species, such as citrus, perish when the thermometer reaches or goes more than a few degrees below freezing, although some citrus varieties can grow in colder climes. Deciduous fruits like figs and persimmons are somewhat hardier, especially if you give them a favorable site. Gardeners in colder climates can grow some of these fruits successfully in containers, moving them to sheltered places in the winter or growing them as houseplants.

Citrus

This large tropical and subtropical group covers a wide range of juicy fruits from tiny kumquats to huge pummelos, which require almost frost-free climates to produce fruit (most can take 25–28 degrees Fahrenheit for several hours) and hot summers to help ripen and sweeten the fruit. These trees need temperatures between 70–90 degrees Fahrenheit for best growth. In the United States, the citrus-growing region is limited to Florida, coastal areas of the Gulf Coast states, and parts of Arizona and California.

Citrus trees have evergreen foliage, and most have thorny limbs. Trees usually are grafted (see the "Size does matter" section earlier in this chapter). Most species bloom in early spring and don't require cross-pollination. Fruit ripens from autumn to spring, but some everbearing trees produce fruit year-round. Allow fruit to ripen on the tree for best flavor. Here's a rundown of some popular citrus fruits:

- **Grapefruits:** Grown primarily in Florida and southern Texas, the trees reach 30 feet in height. Varieties include seeded and seedless types, and those with red, pink, or white flesh.

- **Kumquats:** A bit hardier and smaller than most citrus trees, kumquats can tolerate temperatures as low as 18–20 degrees Fahrenheit and also make good houseplants. You can eat the small fruits whole — rind and all.

- **Lemons and limes:** Among the most cold-sensitive citrus, this group grows best in frost-free climates. Some varieties do well as houseplants, producing the sour fruits indoors.

- **Mandarins:** Members of this large group have somewhat flattened shapes and loose, easy-to-peel skins. Varieties include tangerines, clementines, and tangelos. The Calamondin variety makes a good houseplant or container shrub, and produces loads of small fruit with edible rinds. Most mandarin varieties need Zone 9 and warmer, although Calamondin and Satsuma varieties tolerate temperatures down to 20 degrees Fahrenheit.

✔ **Oranges:** You can choose among many varieties, which vary in ease of peeling, sweetness, number of seeds, hardiness, quality of juice, color, and time of ripening. Although most types ripen during December and January, some are ready to pick in November; others, such as juicy Valencia varieties, don't ripen until late winter to spring. Navel oranges are among the hardiest varieties.

Annual pruning isn't necessary for citrus trees, which is a good thing, because most of these trees sport long, sharp thorns. They require pruning mostly just to keep the centers of the trees open to light and air and to remove dead branches. If trees get too big to pick easily, you can cut back the limbs with thinning cuts (see Chapter 19) every year or two. Wait to prune frost-nipped trees until new growth shows the extent of damage. To prevent sunburn after pruning, paint exposed branches that were previously shaded by foliage with whitewash made from a 1:1 mix of water and a white water-based paint.

Citrus demands moist but well-drained soil and regular applications of nitrogen fertilizer beginning in January and ending in late summer. Adequate water is especially necessary when the trees are actively growing and developing fruit. Pests and diseases infrequently cause problems except when trees are stressed from drought or other weather-related factors. Scale, mites, thrips, and whiteflies may infest these trees, in addition to cankers that infect the wood. You can easily control most pests with fine oil spray, as described in Chapter 8.

Figs

These attractive trees have smooth, gray bark and large, lobed, tropical-looking leaves. Figs *(Ficus carica)* can take winter cold down to 15 degrees Fahrenheit, but freezing temperatures kill the upper branches and even the trunk of the tree. When this happens, the tree sprouts up from its roots and forms a shrub with several stems. Following such a freeze, the plants may not produce fruit in the following season, depending on the variety.

Figs grow best in subtropical climates with mild winters and long, hot summers to ripen their fruit. They need well-drained soil.

Figs make good container specimens for climates where they can't survive outdoors year-round. Move the containers into a cool, protected location where temperatures remain above freezing. Bring the plants into a warm, sunny location in early spring when the buds begin to swell.

Figs typically ripen two crops per year in warm climates. Leave the fruit on the trees to fully ripen before picking, but protect them from hungry birds. Prune to encourage new shoots, prevent branch crowding, and remove dead wood. Encourage the plant to form three to five main stems. If you prune when the trees are dormant, you'll decrease or eliminate the first crop but increase the second crop of the year.

Fig trees have no serious pests except for fruit flies and ants, which attack the fruit in some climates. In some areas, the trees are prone to fig rust. (See Chapter 9 for more on disease control.) Brown Turkey, Celeste, Magnolia, and Mission are common varieties.

Persimmon

This lovely landscape tree grows up to 25 feet tall and wide, with bright yellow, red, and orange fall foliage and gracefully drooping branches. Its orange fruit dangles from the ends of the limbs as they ripen. Although this tree can withstand winter temperatures to 0 degrees Fahrenheit, in colder regions it tends to break dormancy and begin growing before the cold weather has fully departed.

Plant persimmons in well-drained, acidic soil, but keep the soil moist, especially during the summer, when the tree is carrying fruit. Prune only to establish a modified central-leader branching structure of young trees and to remove dead and damaged limbs from mature trees.

Persimmons have few serious pests or diseases, although fungus disease can affect the fruit late in the season, and trees are susceptible to wilt disease in some areas. Control scale insects with dormant oil spray in late winter. The trees need little pruning.

Oriental persimmon *(Diospyros kaki)* fruit falls into two categories: astringent and nonastringent. The fruit of the astringent varieties is eaten when the flesh is soft and almost jellylike, whereas nonastringent varieties can be eaten when firm. Some varieties have seeds; others are seedless. The best astringent varieties include Saijo, Tanenashi, and Yomato Hyakume. Good nonastringent varieties include Fuyu, Hanagosho, and Hana Fuyu.

Female trees don't need male trees to set fruit and, in fact, produce seedy fruit with dark streaks in the flesh when pollinated. Harvest in autumn when the fruit feels slightly soft. Protect from birds.

The common persimmon *(Diospyros virginiana),* which is native to the United States, grows vigorously from Zones 4 to 9, and spreads easily from seeds eaten by birds and animals. The trees tend to form thickets of suckers. Fruits measure 1 to 2 inches across. Some varieties with larger fruit exist.

Oh, Nuts!

Plant these ornamental or shade trees, and enjoy the nut harvest as an added treat. Most nut trees need little care but can be messy when the fruit and foliage drop. Plant the large-nut species, such as walnuts and pecans, where you can enjoy their beauty without worrying about falling nuts. Use smaller species, such as filberts, as hedges or small landscape trees. Most nut trees and shrubs require cross-pollination, which means you need two compatible varieties to produce nuts.

Filberts

Also known as hazelnuts (*Corylus* species), these delicious nuts grow on ornamental 20-foot-high trees or large shrubs in Zones 5 to 8. Several species exist, but the one most commonly grown is the European filbert *(Corylus avellana)*. Native North American species *(C. americana)* have smaller nuts that make excellent wildlife food but can be harvested as well. European filberts like moist, well-drained soil and climates in which late-spring frosts don't damage their flower buds, but native species tolerate a wider range of conditions from Georgia into Canada. Commercially, European filberts grow best in the coastal valleys of the Pacific Northwest, where summers are cool and winters mild.

Filberts require cross-pollination with another filbert variety to set fruit, which is ready to harvest in late summer. Variety pairs that can pollinate each other include Barcelona with either Daviana or Casina and Royal with Hall's Giant. Prune and train to a central-leader tree or maintain as a shrub. Collect the nuts as they fall from the trees; dry them in the sun until the kernels snap when bitten; and store them in a cool, dry place.

Squirrels and nut-eating birds are the most serious pests. Eastern filbert blight, however, is a devastating disease that has no known cure. The native North American species is less affected than the European filbert.

Almonds

Almonds *(Prunus amygdalus)* are related to peaches, plums, and apricots, and require similar growing conditions. Although the trees are hardy to Zone 6, they have a chilling requirement of only 300 to 500 hours (see the "Chill out" section, earlier in this chapter), which results in early-spring flowering. Warm spring weather followed by a cold snap ruins their lovely pink flowers and damages their developing fruits. Warm, dry summers in Zones 6 to 9 ensure a good harvest of the sweet oval nuts.

Trees range in height from 10 to 40 feet, depending on the rootstock and variety. They require cross-pollination to set fruit except for the varieties All-in-One and Garden Prince.

Pests and diseases are the same as for peaches. Train trees to an open-center shape, and remove limbs that become unfruitful. Almonds fruit on spurs up to 5 years old. Harvest the nuts in early to midautumn by shaking or knocking them from the tree when the hulls begin to split. Let them sun-dry for a day or two and then store them in a cool, dry place.

Pecans

Pecans *(Carya illinoensis)* grow best in peach country in Zones 6 to 9, but they need at least 140 to 200 or more frost-free days to develop their fruit, depending on the variety. Although these trees may live in cool climates, they may not produce fruit unless temperatures remain in the 75–85 degrees Fahrenheit range. High humidity encourages disease and other problems. They can serve as 60- to 100-foot shade trees in large home landscapes, although the dropping fruits can make quite a mess on the lawn.

Choose varieties that grow well in your climate and look for varieties with thin nuts that are easy to shell. Pecans are grouped according to growing conditions:

- ✔ **Warm, humid climates:** Look for scab-resistant varieties that tolerate humidity. Varieties include Stuart, Candy, Chickasaw, and Choctaw.

- ✔ **Cold-winter climates:** Choose pecans that can mature their nuts within the shorter growing season, such as Colby, Starking Hardy Giant, and Fritz.

- ✔ **Arid climates:** These varieties — including Cheyenne, Sioux, and Western Schley — are often susceptible to scab disease but grow in more alkaline soil.

Pecans require cross-pollination and adequate water to set good crops. Keep the soil moist during the growing and fruiting season. Train the young trees to a modified central-leader form, and prune older trees to remove dead or undesirable limbs.

Walnuts

These stately 50- to 150-foot shade trees grow from Zones 4 to 9, depending on the species, variety, and origin of the seedling. They enjoy fertile, deep soils with adequate moisture and require cross-pollination to produce good fruit. English and black walnuts are the two most commonly available types:

- **English walnuts** *(Juglans regia)* grow primarily in Zones 5 to 9 and have thin shells. They are susceptible to walnut blight on early-spring foliage, especially in cool, damp climates. Codling moths and walnut husk flies damage developing young nuts. To ensure high-quality nuts, choose grafted varieties such as Lake, Stark Champion, Hartley, and Franquette.

- **Black walnuts** *(J. nigra)* are native North American trees that grow as far north as Zone 4. They have hard shells and intensely flavored nuts. The lumber from these huge trees is valuable for fine woodworking. Choose locally adapted trees to ensure their hardiness in your area. Although black walnuts are often grown from seed, cultivated varieties include Thomas and Ohio. Black-walnut roots produce a chemical that inhibits the growth of many other trees and plants. Flower and vegetable gardens may not grow readily within the root zone of these trees.

You may have to fight off the squirrels, but collect the nuts as they fall, and remove the husks as soon as possible to hasten drying. The hulls contain a yellow-orange dye that readily stains everything they touch, so take care when handling them.

Chapter 17

Say It with Flowers

Trees and shrubs give your landscape structure, and vegetables and fruits put food on the table, but flowers are pure fun. You plant them to bring your landscape to life — to add color, vibrancy, drama, and romance. Daffodils, tulips, and other spring bulbs cheerfully greet the end of winter, whereas annual and perennial flowering plants put on a constantly changing and colorful show from one end of the growing season to the other.

Flowers are among the easiest crops to grow organically. Yes, insects and diseases do bother some of them, but you have many control strategies to choose among. Keeping them well fed isn't hard, either. This chapter covers all the basics you need to grow happy flowers almost year-round.

Mixing It Up with Flowers: The Basics

Flowers are diverse, resilient, and compatible with one another. You can mix them up any way you like, and as long as you give them their basic food, soil, water, and sun requirements, you can reasonably expect loads of blooms or attractive foliage. Even if a plant dies or gets eaten by bugs, it usually costs little to replace. In the case of annuals, which live only for the summer anyway, you can always try again next year.

Promoting diversity in any garden and landscape is a crucial part of organic gardening, and nowhere is it easier than in the flower garden. Except for large formal plantings or commercial-cut flower fields, most gardeners grow only a few plants of each flower species or variety and tend to mix them up in their gardens. Here are a few good reasons to continue that practice:

✔ **Beneficial insects** and other organisms, which fight harmful pests and diseases, thrive in diverse environments.

✔ **Season-long color** is easier to manage when you plant perennials, annuals, and bulbs that bloom at different times throughout the spring, summer, and fall. You can mix and match color schemes, too.

✔ **You can save garden space** by planting ornamental vegetables and herbs in your flower beds or by planting flowers in your vegetable or herb garden. You can plant bulbs right under the root zones of annuals and perennials to extend the season of color.

✔ **You can fool pests** by planting only a few plants of each species in spots around the garden or landscape. The critters may find some — but not all — of your zinnias or lilies!

Before you fill out the catalog order form or head out to the garden center to buy every flower that tickles your fancy, take time to plan your garden for success and prepare your soil, as the following sections explain. (For more info on garden planning and soil preparation, go to Chapters 3 and 5, respectively.)

Designing for year-round beauty

Flowers come in a rainbow of colors and a vast array of shapes and sizes. To me, mixing and matching them with creative flair is the best part of gardening. As you're planning your garden, choose plants to provide color and texture in all four seasons. Spring-flowering bulbs start off the season, followed by summer's bountiful blooms. Fall brings mums and asters, as well as colorful foliage, and winter snow decorates ornamental grasses and the seed heads of late bloomers.

When you design your flower garden, whether you choose annuals, perennials, bulbs, or combinations of each, keep in mind that plants have a greater impact when you plant them in groups of the same kind. A single petunia looks lost in a 5-x-20-foot border, for example, but six petunias of the same color make a bold statement. The same goes for perennials; always plant at least three and preferably five or more of each kind, especially the smaller varieties. With bulbs, I consider a dozen the bare minimum for tulips and daffodils and two dozen for crocus and small bulbs. Plant in circular or free-form groups, and avoid rigid rows.

Annuals complete their life cycle in a single year, whereas *perennials* grow from one year to the next, usually sprouting from their overwintering roots. *Bulbs* are perennial plants that store food in special swollen stems or roots.

Preparing your soil

Annual flowers grow rapidly from seedling to mature flowering plant in just a few short weeks, so they need plenty of good nutrition. Perennials and bulbs, too, need to put down roots and develop leafy tops to make food for their roots, which live from one year to the next. Adequate soil fertility, moisture, and organic matter keep your flowers growing robustly, producing more and larger blooms, and fending off pests and diseases.

When you're done preparing your soil, make a list of plant combinations that suit your site; then boldly go forth to make your selections. For information on choosing the healthiest specimens and proper planting techniques, refer to Chapter 12.

Caring for your flower garden

Consistent maintenance throughout the growing season guarantees plenty of flowers and lush, healthy plants. Perennials and bulbs, which live for more than a year, are better prepared for winter, too, when they've had adequate nutrition and water during the summer and fall.

Keeping your garden looking good and growing strong doesn't have to be a lengthy chore if you take a few minutes each day or on the weekend. Here's what you can do to keep your garden looking its best:

- **Deadhead:** Removing spent flowers — a practice called *deadheading* — before they go to seed keeps annuals and some perennials blooming longer. Snip or pinch the dead flower off, making the cut just above a bud or a leaf.

- **Pinch:** Flowers that get tall and floppy, especially perennial asters and chrysanthemums, stay more compact if you pinch back their early-summer stems to encourage them to grow shorter and more numerous shoots. When the plants reach 1 foot high in spring, snip off the top 3 to 4 inches. Repeat once more in midsummer, but not after you see flower buds forming.

- **Support:** Some tall, floppy flowers, such as delphiniums and peonies, need a little help to stay upright. Use bamboo stakes to tie up individual delphinium or lily stalks. Surround peony clumps with purchased circular wire or homemade stake-and-twine supports. I often use branches left over from tree and shrub pruning to support plants, too.

- **Scout for problems:** As you walk through the garden, keep a sharp eye out for anything unusual, such as holes in flowers or leaves, wilting, insects, or off-color foliage. Catch a problem early, and you have a better chance of solving it without taking drastic action.

✔ **Fertilize:** Plants need plenty of fuel to keep pumping out the flowers. Supplement your fertile soil with composted manure in the spring, and feed again in midsummer with a mild complete fertilizer, such as fish emulsion.

✔ **Water:** If Mother Nature provides regular, gentle rainfall from spring through fall, you've got it made. Otherwise, you may have to supplement. Dig into the top 6 to 8 inches of soil, and if it's dry, irrigate your garden until the water reaches an 8-inch depth. Shallow watering that wets only the top few inches encourages roots to grow close to the surface, where they're more vulnerable to drought.

✔ **Weed:** No, weeding isn't the most fun, but it's necessary. Pull up or hoe small weeds as soon as they appear, disturbing the soil as little as possible. Try corn gluten meal (see Chapter 6) as a fertilizer in established beds because it also prevents weed seeds from sprouting. Replace or add more mulch as needed to smother weeds, but keep the mulch an inch or two away from plant stems.

If you grow flowers in gardens surrounded by lawn, as I do, you face the additional chore of edging. *Edging* means keeping the lawn and the flowers separated by a barrier. I use a half-moon edging tool to cut away a slice of lawn around the entire perimeter of the garden in the spring and again in midsummer. To use the tool, push the blade straight down into the turf about 4 to 6 inches, and pull the handle back toward yourself to pop out the wedge. Other edging options include flexible plastic edging (available at garden centers) that you install around the garden or bricks, landscape timber, or stones. If you use these materials, bury them so that they're flush with the ground, which makes mowing easier.

Annual Events

Annual plants live short but spectacular lives because they have to accomplish their entire life's purpose — perpetuating the species — in only one growing season. Most annuals bloom nonstop from spring to autumn or until they succeed in setting seed. The secret to keeping annuals blooming all summer is preventing the plants from forming seeds by deadheading (see "Caring for your flower garden," earlier in this chapter). Some plants that you may consider to be annuals — such as *Vinca rosea,* ivy geraniums, and begonias — actually are perennials in nonfreezing climates. Count yourself lucky if you can enjoy these plants year-round.

Use versatile annuals anywhere you want nonstop color. Plant them in mixed gardens with perennials to provide constant bloom, in the cut-flower garden for bouquets, or in hanging baskets and patio planters for portable color. You can also dedicate a garden just to them. The beauty of annuals is that you can change the garden completely from one year to the next to suit your current taste and whim.

Hundreds of annual flowering plants are available in every shape, form, color, and size imaginable, and it's beyond the scope of this book to describe them all. I've divided a few of the most popular annuals into categories to help you find the best ones for each landscape use. Consult the label that comes with each particular plant for spacing and cultural requirements.

Some annuals, especially those with large seeds, are easy to start yourself from seed, either right in the garden or in the house before transplanting. Refer to Chapter 12 for information on starting from seed. The easiest flowers to grow from seed include calendula, cosmos, marigold, zinnia, aster, nasturtium, morning glory, sunflower, and sweet pea. Plants with tiny seeds — such as begonia, petunia, and impatiens — are tough to start or need several months of pampering before they're ready for the garden.

Bedding plants for mass planting

Gardens devoted to just annuals make a big impact along streets, sidewalks, and other places where the mass of color is more important than the individual plants. Look for plants that grow fairly low (usually up to a foot high) and that bloom for at least two to three months with little maintenance. Bright red, yellow, orange, and white work best in plantings viewed from a distance; cool blue and purple are better for close-range viewing. To find the number of plants you need to fill a 100-square-foot garden (10 feet x 10 feet), consult Table 17-1.

Table 17-1		Plants Needed to Fill 100 Square Feet
Space between Plants		**Number of Plants**
Inches	**Centimeters**	
6	15	400
9	23	178
12	30	100
18	46	45
24	61	25

Popular bedding plants include ageratum, calendula, celosia, coleus, coreopsis, dahlia, dusty miller, impatiens, marigold, nasturtium, nicotiana, pansy, petunia, salvia, snapdragon, sweet alyssum, verbena, *Vinca rosea,* and wax begonia.

Cutting flowers for bouquets

Plants that produce long stems for cutting, as well as colorful or fragrant flowers, are tops in my garden. Many of these plants mix well in a perennial border, or you can devote a row in your vegetable garden to them. If you have space and a passion for bouquets, give them a garden of their own. Don't forget to add some *everlasting* flowers, such as statice and strawflower, which have papery petals that remain colorful for months or even years when dried. Use them for making dried bouquets and craft projects.

For the freshest and longest-lasting bouquets, cut the flowers in the morning before the sun heats up, and plunge the stems right into a bucket of water. Use a sharp knife or scissors to cut stems at a 45-degree angle, and choose stems with only partially opened buds. Strip the leaves from the submerged parts of the stems. Use clean vases and change the water daily, adding a floral preservative or two to three drops of bleach per quart.

Great annuals for cutting include aster, baby's breath, calendula, campanula, cosmos, sweet William, gloriosa daisy, larkspur, lisianthus, pincushion flower (scabiosa), salpiglossis, salvia, snapdragon, stock, sweet pea, sunflower, and zinnia. For dried-flower bouquets, try strawflower, statice, cornflower, salvia, celosia, ageratum, globe amaranth, larkspur, baby's breath, and love-in-a-mist. Cut them before the flowers open fully; bundle the stems with a rubber band; and hang them to dry in a cool, dry, airy place away from the sun.

Foliage fillers

Flowers usually take center stage, but you need supporting players too. Plants with attractive foliage provide a soothing foil for their more flamboyant companions, although some plants have foliage that's colorful enough to stand alone. Popular favorites include dusty miller, coleus, Kochia (or firebush), Persian shield, nasturtium Alaska, ornamental cabbage and kale, amaranthus, and polka dot plant.

Best for baskets and containers

These plants stay small enough to live in confinement all summer without complaint. In containers, you can plant everything closer together than usual, but the limited soil space means that the plants need more attention (watering, fertilizing, and pruning) than other landscape and garden plants do.

TIP

Although it's tempting to use your own garden soil to fill containers, consider a pasteurized, lightweight alternative instead. When you put garden soil into a container, it loses its loose, well-aerated structure and becomes too compact for healthy root growth. In most cases, a soilless mix is best. I usually add up to 25 percent pasteurized topsoil or composted manure to the mix, as well as some water-retaining gel crystals, which help the soil hold more moisture.

For the best design effect, combine trailing, upright, and low-growing plants in each container. Good trailing plants include browallia, creeping zinnia, lobelia, nasturtium, nierembergia, petunia, scaevola, sweet alyssum, and verbena. Choose bedding plants to fill in most of the container. Consider adding a trellis to larger containers to hold an annual vine, such as canary creeper, morning glory, or thunbergia.

Perennial Favorites

Perennial plants, by definition, live from year to year, but *herbaceous perennials* actually die to the ground in the fall and sprout from their roots again in the spring. Happy perennials increase in size and bloom potential with each growing season that passes. Unlike with annual flowers, however, your U.S. Department of Agriculture Hardiness Zone and American Horticultural Society (AHS) Heat Zone make a difference in your garden's success (see Chapter 3). Use the information as a guide when buying plants.

Popular myth claims that perennial gardening is low-maintenance compared with other types of gardening — you know, plant it once and forget about it. That's simply not true, as any experienced perennial gardener quickly points out. Although many plants live for a long time, they also require regular maintenance. See "Caring for your flower garden," earlier in this chapter, to see what your perennials need to flourish.

Making more perennials

One of the best features of perennials is that you can start with one plant and divide it into more plants as it grows. This trick doesn't work with all perennials, however, especially those with taproots that grow straight down, deep into the soil. The best plants for dividing form clumps of stems and have fibrous roots. Easy plants to divide include daylilies, hosta, bee balm (*Monarda* species), Siberian iris, ornamental grasses, and almost anything else that creeps over the ground, rooting as it grows.

The best time to divide perennials depends partly on their season of flowering and your climate. I find it easier to divide mid- to late-summer-flowering plants, such as asters, in the spring as soon as they start growing. Spring and early-summer bloomers, such as peonies and iris, recover better if they're divided later in the summer. A few, such as daylilies and Siberian iris, can be divided any time you have a shovel handy.

Here's the basic method for dividing perennials with fibrous roots:

1. **Soak the soil to make digging easier.**

   Water the day before, if possible, so that the soil isn't still muddy.

2. **Cut down some or all of the stems to within 6 inches of the ground unless you're dividing newly sprouted plants in the spring.**

   The roots won't be able to support big leafy tops until they recover fully.

3. **Dig up the whole clump, and drag it onto a tarp.**

   Check it over, looking for groups of rooted stems that could form new, self-supporting plants. Blast the clump with spray from the hose to wash away soil that obscures the crown, or soak the whole clump to make root separation easier.

4. **Pry, tease, cut, or pull apart the clump.**

   Some perennials come apart easily; others may require a sharp knife or other drastic measures. For large tough grasses, Siberian irises, and daylilies, push two garden forks into the clump back to back, and pry the handles apart to divide the clump in two, as shown in Figure 17-1. Repeat as needed to reduce the clump to manageable pieces.

5. **Discard dead and less vigorous pieces.**

6. **Replant the pieces as soon as possible.**

   See Chapter 12 for planting advice.

Some perennial plants, such as bearded iris, get bare spots in their centers as they expand outward, so they need dividing to keep them vigorous. Bearded irises need slightly different treatment during division. After the plants finish blooming, proceed with Steps 1 through 3. Then choose the fattest sections of fleshy roots, called *rhizomes,* with the most vigorous fans of foliage and roots. Using a sharp knife, cut the rhizomes apart into one- or two-fan sections, as shown in Figure 17-2. Discard woody and insect-damaged pieces as well as the oldest parts. (The newest rhizomes are firm and grow at the outer edges of the clump.) Plant immediately in fertile soil, draping the roots over a ridge of soil so that the top of the rhizome is just at the soil surface when watered.

Figure 17-1:
Using garden forks to divide perennial clumps.

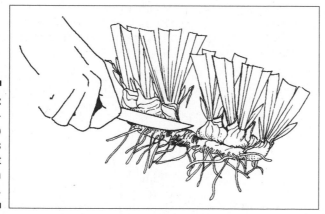

Figure 17-2:
Cut iris rhizomes into sections with at least one fan each.

Using popular perennials

You have hundreds, if not thousands, of perennial plants to choose among. Instead of trying to memorize all those plants, think of them in groups. You can divide them into groups based on garden placement, cultural requirements, flower color, season of bloom, use, or any number of other criteria. For more information on gardening with perennials, look for *Perennials For Dummies,* by Marcia Tatroe and the Editors of the National Gardening Association (Wiley). I've chosen the following categories with organic gardeners in mind:

- **Butterfly- and bee-attracting plants:** Butterflies and moths glide from flower to flower looking for energy-rich nectar. Some of their favorites include butterfly weed, aster, butterfly bush, *Centaurea,* purple and orange coneflowers, Joe-pye weed, *Penstemon,* goldenrod, verbena, salvia, and bee balm.

- **Shade-loving perennials:** Shade is a relative concept, ranging from dense to dappled. Most of these perennials prefer a few hours of direct sunlight each day but can survive in all but the deepest shade. For your shady nook, try hosta, forget-me-not, pachysandra, lungwort, meadowrue, foamflower, myrtle, coral bells, lily-of-the-valley, foxglove, *Bergenia,* wild ginger, and Solomon's seal.

- **Deer-resistant perennials:** Although it seems that deer will eat anything, it's really not true. Plants with strong scent or flavor repel them, as do some toxic plants. Resistant plants include alliums, artemesia, black-eyed Susan, lupine, catmint, delphinium, hellebore, tansy, and yarrow.

- **Hard-to-kill perennials:** If you're just starting or need low-maintenance plants, give these tough customers a try. Perennials that can survive in well-drained soil almost anywhere include yarrow, *Artemesia,* tickseed (*Coreopsis* species), *Euphorbia,* blanket flower, *Heliopsis,* catmint, Oriental poppy, sedum, and feverfew. If your soil tends to run on the damp side, try Siberian iris, daylily, bee balm, and mint.

- **Foliage friends:** Flowers aren't everything, and these lovely leafed perennials prove it. Although some of these also have nice blooms, for fabulous foliage try hosta, dead nettle (*Lamium*), lungwort (*Pulmonaria*), coral bells, astilbe, peony, thyme, sage, liriope, amsonia, artemesia, ginger (*Asarum* species), *Bergenia,* crane's bill geranium, ornamental grasses, and many others.

Perennials work well in containers, too. See "Annual Events," earlier in this chapter, for ideas on how to use them in patio planters and baskets.

Blooming Bulbs

Some plants form swollen underground roots or stems, which people tend to lump together and refer to as *bulbs.* Not all these fleshy appendages are the same, however, and the differences affect how you plant and use them, as explained in "This side up: Putting down roots," later in this chapter.

True bulbs — including onions, lilies, tulips, and daffodils — have pointed tops and flat bottoms called *basal plates,* from which roots grow. If you cut one open, you see that a bulb consists of rings or layers with developing leaves, flowers, or stems in the center. The bulb itself lives from year to year and develops new daughter bulbs from its base.

Other bulblike plants form corms, tubers, or rhizomes. *Corms* — such as crocus, colchicum, crocosmia, and gladiola — resemble bulbs, but their flesh isn't layered when it's cut open. Each corm lives for a single year, but it produces *offsets* or new corms around its basal plate. *Tubers* — such as potatoes, caladiums, and tuberous begonias — don't have a basal plate and sprout from several *eyes,* or growing points. They just grow larger and form more eyes each year but don't produce offsets. *Rhizomes,* such as bearded iris and canna, are simply swollen, creeping stems. They grow from the tip, which may branch and root, forming new plants.

To simplify bulbs and bulblike plants, I've divided them into two broad groups:

- ✔ **Spring-blooming bulbs** include tulips, narcissus (daffodils), crocus, fritillaria, snowdrops, winter aconite, hyacinths, bluebells, and glory of the snow (*Chionodoxa* species). These bulbs survive in the ground in cold-winter climates and bloom when the soil warms in the spring. Plant them in early autumn to allow them time to root before winter.

- ✔ **Summer-blooming bulbs** include lilies, alliums, canna, caladium, dahlia, gladiola, tuberous begonia, crocosmia, and amaryllis. Many of these bulbs are frost-tender; dig them up at the end of the growing season and store them in a nonfreezing place. Many species and varieties of lilies and alliums, however, are perfectly winter-hardy throughout most USDA hardiness zones. Plant tender bulbs in the spring and hardy ones in the fall.

When you shop for bulbs, look for firm, heavy, unblemished specimens. Avoid those with gouges or signs of withering, softness, or decay. Bulbs vary enormously in size from one species and variety to the next. In general, you want to buy *top-size* bulbs, which usually are the largest bulbs available for the particular variety. *Landscape-size* bulbs are smaller, and produce fewer stems and smaller blooms.

After you get your bulbs home, plant them as soon as possible. If you must store them — even briefly — keep them dry and cool (50°F to 65°F). Don't store them with apples or other fruit, however, because ripening fruit gives off ethylene gas, which is deadly to dormant flower buds inside the bulbs.

This side up: Putting down roots

Bulbs appreciate the same loose, fertile, well-drained garden soil that your other plants enjoy. If you're planting bulbs in an existing, well-maintained garden, you need only add a bit of fertilizer to the hole at planting time; otherwise, turn back to Chapter 5 for more on soil preparation. Slow-release, complete, granular fertilizer works best at planting time. Mix it into the soil at the bottom of the hole, covering it with a thin layer of unamended soil before setting in the bulbs.

Contrary to tradition, bonemeal is not the best fertilizer choice for bulbs. It attracts skunks and other scavengers willing to dig up a tasty meal. If the bonemeal is well mixed in small quantities with composted manure and other nutrient-rich fertilizers, however, your garden is less likely to have nocturnal visitors.

How deeply you plant your bulbs depends on whether you have true bulbs, corms, tubers, or rhizomes. Each is handled a little differently:

- **True bulbs and corms:** As a general rule, plant them so that the top is buried twice as deep as the bulb is tall. A daffodil that measures 2 inches from base to tip, for example, needs a hole 6 inches deep so that 4 inches of soil covers the top of the bulb. Bulb companies always provide handy charts, too, with specific instructions for each type of bulb. Depending on your soil type, you can vary the planting depth a bit. Set bulbs 1 or 2 inches deeper in sandy soil and 1 to 3 inches more shallowly in heavy clay. Gardeners in warm-winter climates who want to grow daffodils can plant the bulbs twice as deeply as northern gardeners do.

- **Tubers and rhizomes:** These bulbs get special planting treatment because they prefer to grow closer to the soil surface. Tuberous begonias and cyclamen, for example, need only 1-inch depth, whereas gladiolas and cannas prefer 2 to 3 inches of soil over them. Plant bearded iris rhizomes so that the tops of the rhizomes are just barely exposed after you water the planting site.

Determining which end goes down and which points up is easy for bulbs with a pointed top or roots clinging to the bottom. But what do you do with shriveled, featureless anemone tubers? If you can't tell which side is up, plant the bulbs on their sides; the plants will figure things out.

Finding the best bulb source

You can buy bulbs from so many sources that it's downright confusing to know where to get the best value and quality. Here's my take on the choices:

✔ **Mail-order bulb suppliers** have selling down to an exact science. Most catalogs offer a hefty discount if you order early, which results in big savings. Specialty bulb suppliers also carry the widest assortment, including rare, unusual, and hard-to-find bulbs as well as the most popular varieties.

Avoid catalogs that give inadequate information or offer prices significantly lower than similar catalogs. They may be offering smaller bulbs that produce smaller and fewer flowers.

✔ **Garden centers** usually start selling bulbs shortly after the bulb farmers harvest them, which is the right time to plant them in your garden. When the bins of bulbs appear in the stores, they're as tempting to a gardener as candy to a chocoholic! Go ahead and indulge, but keep a few tips in mind: Boxes of loose bulbs may get mixed up (think of playing children), the selection is relatively limited, and the bulbs are often smaller than those available from specialty catalogs. On the other hand, you usually can inspect the bulbs before you buy. Bulbs stored in sunny windows or hot corners may not grow as well as those stored at cooler (50°F to 65°F) temperatures.

Planting methods vary depending on whether you're putting in a handful of bulbs or planting dozens. The most efficient system is to dig a hole large enough to accommodate a group of bulbs. I dig the hole to the proper depth, amend the soil (see Chapter 5), space the bulbs around the hole, backfill, and water. Bulbs grow best in the loosened soil. I find those little bulb planters that look like open-ended tin cans with handles to be useless. You can't amend the soil effectively, planting takes longer, and the soil around the sides of the hole remains compact.

Protecting your assets

Bulb-producing plants need leaves to make food and keep their bulbs fat and happy during their dormant season. Although yellowing leaves look unsightly after the flowers bloom, leave the foliage alone (and resist the urge to braid it) until it naturally withers away. If you cut the blooms of lilies, gladiolas, and other leafy stemmed plants, leave as much foliage behind as you can. Bulbs robbed of their food source will produce fewer — if any — blooms in subsequent years.

In climates where the ground freezes, gardeners must dig up and store tender tropical bulbs, corms, tubers, and rhizomes for the winter. (Tulips, daffodils, lilies, and other hardy bulbs can remain in the ground.) You can keep cannas, dahlias, tuberous begonias, and other tubers and bulbs from one year to the next by putting them in a cool, nonfreezing place. Dig up the bulbs after the leaves die back, brush off loose soil, and trim off the leaves and stems. After letting them dry for a few days in a nonfreezing place, brush off more soil, and place the bulbs in dry wood shavings or peat moss in a cardboard box. Don't let the pieces touch each other. Cover with more shavings or moss, and store in a cool, dry place until spring.

Gladiola and similar corms are even easier to store. After brushing off the soil, place them in a mesh bag (like the ones that onions come in), and hang the bag in a cool (35°F to 41°F) place where mice can't reach it.

Bulb-munching rodents and deer can take a bite out of your bulb garden, but you can take preventive action. My favorite method is to plant bulbs that these animals won't eat, such as narcissus, fritillarias, snowflakes (*Leucojum* species), and snowdrops (*Galanthus* species). The bulbs are toxic and may give some protection to surrounding nontoxic species. Animals seem to stay away from alliums, too.

If you want to succeed with tulips, crocus, lilies, and other tempting morsels, plant your bulbs in a wire cage (see Figure 17-3) that excludes the trouble-some animals. Bend hardware cloth into a shallow cage, and bury it at the appropriate depth to keep out voles and mice. For the top, choose a wire opening large enough to allow the shoots to grow through. Use chicken wire for woodchucks and other large diggers.

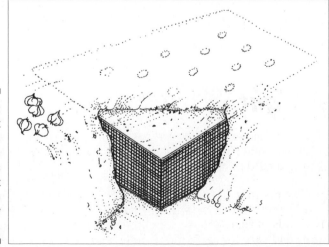

Figure 17-3:
Plant bulbs in wire mesh baskets to protect them from hungry rodents.

Chapter 18

Run for the Roses

Roses have an undeserved reputation as temperamental, demanding, pest-prone plants. That's why you may have assumed that to grow roses successfully, you have to use toxic pesticides. Yet the keys to growing roses organically are really quite simple:

✔ Choose varieties of roses that grow best in your region.

✔ Get the plants off to a strong start by carefully selecting disease and pest-resistant plants and planting them properly.

✔ Catch and treat pest problems early.

Fortunately, you can find the details on performing all these tasks successfully in this chapter.

Making the Right Choice

Over the years, rose fanciers have developed many categories of roses, such as hybrid tea and antique roses. Although they share the name *rose,* each has unique features and garden merit.

I prefer to grow plants that don't need lots of extra care, and you probably do, too. So to help you choose the easiest roses for your garden, I've compressed all the kinds of roses into two groups, based on how easy or hard they are to grow and care for: show roses and garden roses.

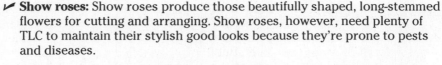

✔ **Show roses:** Show roses produce those beautifully shaped, long-stemmed flowers for cutting and arranging. Show roses, however, need plenty of TLC to maintain their stylish good looks because they're prone to pests and diseases.

Those classic long-stemmed roses — the kind that made roses so popular in the first place — attract the most insects and dastardly rose diseases. You may decide to throw good sense to the wind and plant one of these varieties despite my good advice to the contrary. Many disease-prone roses are among the most popular and readily available varieties at some garden centers; your choices include Climbing America, Apricot Nectar, Chrysler Imperial, Don Juan, Double Delight, Fragrant Cloud, Mister Lincoln, Queen Elizabeth, Pristine, and New Dawn. Nevertheless, you can try to grow them organically — that is, with an ecological perspective. Also, if you're planting new roses, keep in mind that many varieties are both beautiful *and* disease-resistant.

✔ **Garden roses:** Garden roses are easy to grow. They're more like other flowering shrubs — laid back and easygoing. They add lots of color and fragrance to the garden without too much fuss but aren't really grown for their dramatic bouquet potential.

If you'd like to know more about all the kinds and varieties of roses, I highly recommend *Roses For Dummies,* 2nd Edition, by Lance Walheim and the National Gardening Association (Wiley). It's one of the most complete and up-to-date guides available, not to mention the most fun.

Choosing disease-resistant roses

If you're starting a new rose garden or wanting to replace your pest-prone varieties, try garden roses, because many of them are among the most trouble-free plants you can own. Some of my favorite disease-resistant garden roses are pink-flowered Baby Blanket, Bonica, Carefree Delight, Carefree Wonder, Cécile Brunner, Flower Carpet Pink, Lady of the Dawn, Pink Meidiland, Simplicity, and The Fairy; and red-flowered Kardinal, Red Meidiland, and Red Ribbons. Good white roses include Alba Meidiland, Bolero, Fabulous, Moon Dance, and Sea Foam. Also try orange Livin' Easy and Ralph's Creeper, yellow Julia Child, and lilac-pink Lavender Dream. Finally, all the roses in the Knock Out series are exceptionally resistant to common rose diseases.

Picking winter survivors

Depending on where you live, you must consider hardiness (the rose's ability to survive cold winter temperatures; see Chapter 3). Hardy roses stay healthier because they aren't struggling for survival when spring warmth — and pests — return. Gardeners in warm climates, where temperatures rarely drop below 15 degrees Fahrenheit, don't have to worry whether their roses will survive the winter. But if you live in colder places, you may have greater success if you stick with the roses that can put up with frosty weather.

If you live in U.S. Department of Agriculture Zone 5 or colder, you can still grow most any kind of rose, but your plants will need winter protection, as described in "Preparing Roses for Winter," later in this chapter. Unless you really must have a particular rose variety regardless of its hardiness, I advise you to stick to the hardier roses.

Cold-hardy stalwarts that show good disease resistance include Autumn Sunset, Blanc Double de Coubert, Bonica, Carefree Beauty, Carefree Wonder, John Cabot, The Fairy, and William Baffin. Bred in Canada, roses in the Explorer series are very cold-hardy, as are rugosa and moss roses.

Buying Roses

Everybody sells roses — from grocery stores to hardware stores to mail-order nurseries. Impulsively grabbing a $4 rose with a pretty picture on the wrapper and dropping it into your cart, however, won't guarantee you the best value. You've heard it before: You get what you pay for.

Different nurseries often sell exactly the same rose varieties, but the difference is in how they handle the plants. Buy from stores that take good care of their roses. Don't buy plants that have shriveled canes, wilted leaves, or dusty dry packing material around their bare roots.

Mail-order nurseries can also provide a good selection of high-quality plants. Most guarantee their plants to grow and bloom, given normal care. (Look for catalogs that list the recommended winter-hardiness zones, too, if you live where winters get frigid.)

You can buy roses in two forms: potted and bare root. *Bare-root* plants are dormant and have no soil around their roots. Stores usually have large bins full of bare-root roses in plastic-wrapped packages at the start of the growing season. Mail-order nurseries also sell bare-root plants because they cost less to ship than potted plants and survive transport more easily. Bare-root roses grow vigorously after planting as long as they remain cool and moist before you buy them.

Both bare-root and potted roses are graded to ensure quality, with Grade 1 indicating the highest quality.

Members of local garden clubs and rose societies are always good sources of specific information regarding varieties of roses that do well in your area. Local rose growers are happy to share their knowledge about varieties that grow best where you live and garden. The American Rose Society also offers a list of where to buy roses, plus lots of other information. Visit its Web site at www.ars.org. The other rose organization you'll hear about is All-America Rose Selections, a not-for-profit organization that evaluates new roses under actual garden conditions and then selects and recommends superior varieties to the rose-buying public. You can find out more about AARS and its recommendations at www.rose.org.

Planting Roses

Nearly all roses are made of two parts grafted together. The top part, called the *scion,* is the desirable flowering rose. The *rootstock,* on the bottom, adds hardiness and tolerance to a wide range of soil types. Where the two parts meet is called the *bud union,* shown in Figure 18-1.

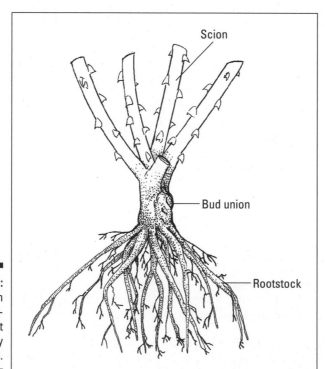

Scion

Bud union

Rootstock

Figure 18-1:
The scion and root-stock join at the knobby bud union.

Growing beautiful roses begins with putting them in the right place and planting them properly. The following sections show you how to get your new roses off to the best possible start.

Picking an ideal time and place

Roses establish faster, and resist pests and diseases better, when you plant them in an ideal location. Roses require at least six hours of direct sunlight each day for good flowering and growth. An eastern exposure, which receives morning sun, is ideal. Choose a planting location away from shady buildings or trees, and avoid trees and shrubs with roots that will compete with the roses for moisture and nutrients.

Make sure that the site is open to allow the summer breezes to blow through; good ventilation helps keep leaf diseases to a minimum. Also choose a location from which water drains promptly. Roses don't grow well where soil stays wet or where water puddles on the surface.

You can plant roses any time from early spring to early fall, but the best planting time depends on where you live and how your plants are packaged. Plant bare-root roses in early to midspring, before the new shoots start to develop and before daytime temperatures rise above 70 degrees Fahrenheit — usually late March to early April in the middle latitudes of North America. You can plant container roses any time from spring to early fall, after danger of spring frost and a month or so before danger of fall frost.

Preparing the planting site

Roses thrive in loamy, well-drained garden soil with a pH of 5.5 to 7.0 (see Chapter 5). Begin with a soil test to determine pH and nutrient levels so that you can make corrections, if necessary, while you prepare the soil.

Most soils, whether clay or sandy, benefit from the addition of organic matter, which improves drainage, aeration, and nutrient-holding capacity. Spread a 2- to 4-inch layer of organic matter — such as compost, rotted manure, shredded leaves, or finely ground potting bark — on the soil surface, and work it into the top 8 inches of soil.

To prepare your planting site, follow these steps:

1. **Dig out enough soil to form a hole approximately 15 inches deep and at least 18 inches, but preferably 36 inches, wide.**

   It's important to improve the soil in the entire future root zone.

2. **Mix 3 to 6 shovelfuls of your chosen organic matter with the soil removed from the hole.**

3. **Add to that mixture about 10 cups of fertilizer made of a half-and-half mixture of alfalfa and cottonseed meals, and mix thoroughly.**

   This substance becomes the backfill soil for the new plant.

Plant spacing varies according to the growth habit of the rose plant. Plants that grow too close together are tall and spindly, and produce only a few small flowers. For a guide to plant spacing by rose type, see Table 18-1. The plant description in the catalog or on the plant tag should tell you what type of rose you have and also recommend the proper spacing.

Table 18-1	Rose Plant Spacing
Type of Rose	*Spacing*
Hybrid tea	30 inches
Grandiflora	36 inches
Floribunda	24 inches
Climbing roses	8 to 12 feet
Shrub roses	4 to 5 feet
Ground-cover roses	36 inches
Miniature roses	12 inches

Planting a bare-root rose

Plant bare-root roses as soon as possible after purchasing or receiving them through the mail. Unwrap plants from the packaging and soak the root system in a bucket of tepid water for about an hour before planting. If you must delay planting for a few days, keep the plants moist and in a cool, dark location, or place them in a temporary soil trench in a shaded location.

Don't store rose plants with any ripening fruit, such as in a refrigerator or root cellar, because the fruit gives off ethylene, which harms growing plants.

Follow these steps to plant your bare-root rose:

1. **Prune out any damaged or dead roots and stems before planting.**

   Refer to Chapter 12 for general information on bare-root plants.

2. **Make sure that your planting hole is twice as wide as your plant's root spread; then loosen the soil in the bottom of the hole, and make a cone of soil.**

   Use the prepared backfill soil discussed in "Preparing the planting site," earlier in this chapter.

3. **Set the plant on top of this cone, spreading out the roots, and then check its *planting height* — the place where the knobby bud union (refer to Figure 18-1) is relative to the ground at the top of the hole.**

   In most parts of the country, adjust the height of the cone until the bud union is just above the level of the surrounding soil, as shown in Figure 18-2. In cold-winter climates (USDA Zones 3 to 5), set the bud union 3 to 6 inches belowground to help protect it from freezing.

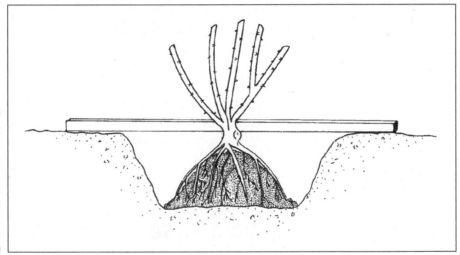

Figure 18-2: Place the roots over a cone of soil, and adjust the depth of the bud union.

4. **When the rose is properly positioned, begin filling the planting hole with the prepared backfill.**

5. **Work the backfill around each root with your hands, and when you're about halfway done, add water to the hole to settle and moisten the soil around the roots. After the water drains away, finish backfilling.**

   If you live where irrigation is a necessity, build a water-retaining ring of soil around the outside edge of the planting hole, and water again (refer to Chapter 12 for building a shallow basin around a plant).

6. **After the plant is set, mound the canes with an additional 4 to 6 inches of soil or mulch to prevent the canes from drying out before roots start growing (see Figure 18-3).**

   When the new shoots appear and the danger of frost is past, remove this soil slowly, over a week's time.

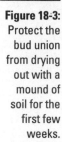

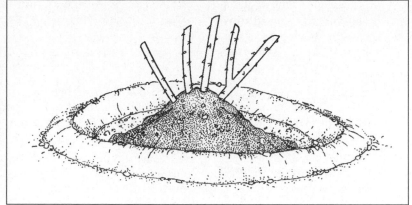

Planting a container-grown rose

Keep container-grown plants watered and in a sunny location until they can be planted in the garden. Make sure that the soil in the pot is moist but not sopping wet at planting time to make handling the plant easier. Prune out any damaged, dead, or broken stems before planting. Refer to Chapter 12 for details on planting container-grown plants.

Cultivating Roses

Roses need plenty of nutrients and regular watering to grow vigorously and flower profusely. You don't need synthetic chemical rose fertilizers, though; many organic options are available.

Fertilizing

Organic fertilizers — such as fish emulsion, compost, and aged manure — not only contribute nutrients to soils but also provide organic matter that has positive, long-term benefits on soil health. Compared with chemical fertilizers, organic fertilizers also release their nutrients more slowly over a longer period and feed the beneficial soil microorganisms. Therefore, don't expect fast results when you first apply the fertilizer.

My favorite organic fertilizer for roses is a half-and-half mix of alfalfa and cottonseed meals. Use about ten cups per plant every ten weeks through the growing season, mixing it lightly into the top inch or two of soil.

You can save a lot of money if you shop for organic fertilizers like alfalfa and cottonseed meal at feed stores rather than at garden centers. Animal-feed dealers sell much greater quantities of these materials compared with garden centers, so they can offer them at a much lower price per pound. If you can't find the selection of organic fertilizers you like, check with Peaceful Valley Farm & Garden Supply at www.groworganic.com or Gardener's Supply Company at www.gardeners.com.

Apply fertilizer when new spring growth is well established and all danger of frost has passed. Make a second application four to six weeks after the first application, or monthly at lower rates if plants show evidence of mineral deficiencies, such as yellowing of leaves from lack of nitrogen.

Don't apply any type of nitrogen fertilizer within six weeks of the expected first frost in fall. When applied late in the season, nitrogen may stimulate fresh growth and delay hardening of the wood before winter.

Watering

How much and how often you need to water roses depends on several conditions, including the type and age of the rose, the soil, where you live, and the weather. But if you're looking for a rule to remember, figure that a mature rosebush needs about 1 inch of water per week applied over its root zone. Water enough to soak the entire root zone; then wait until the soil is dry 2 or 3 inches down to water again. You can check the water penetration in the soil by digging out a shovel-length wedge of soil, but try not to damage the plant roots in the process.

Drip irrigation is particularly useful for organic and conservation-minded gardeners because it delivers the water to the root zone under the rosebush without waste. Additional benefits include fewer weeds to contend with and dry foliage, which reduces the incidence of many diseases. See Chapter 11 for more ways to prevent and control weeds.

Pruning Roses

Although some kinds of roses don't absolutely require pruning to remain in good health, most do. Pruning improves the plant's health by letting more air and light reach all the leaves and stems, which discourages some insects and diseases. Left unpruned, some roses become a tangled mess of barbed, disease-prone canes. Reaching into such a thorny thicket to weed and prune takes nerves of steel and heavy leather gloves! Some vigorous roses just don't know where to stop, and you need to prune them to keep their stems within bounds.

Well-pruned roses give you more bang for your buck because you remove the weak and unproductive shoots and the spent flowers that divert the plant's energy from making new flowers. Show roses — the kind with the long stems and big, luscious blooms — respond especially well to pruning by growing even bigger flowers with longer stems. Garden roses that produce clusters of flowers bloom more prolifically when you keep them groomed. (For more information about show and garden roses, refer to "Making the Right Choice," earlier in this chapter.)

Making the cut

Use only sharp, clean tools to prune roses. Dull blades crush stems and tear or fray the edges of the cut, making it easier for diseases to gain a foothold. Also, disinfect your tools between plants to prevent the accidental spread of disease. Just give the blades a wipe with a cloth dampened in isopropyl rubbing alcohol.

Bypass hand pruners are the tools I use most frequently, because they snip everything from dead flowers to canes up to ½-inch thick. Loppers take care of canes up to 1-inch thick, and the long handles allow me to reach into a prickly tangle without endangering my arms. If you're dealing with a big old rosebush with large dead canes, use a fine-toothed pruning saw.

Your three primary pruning goals are

✔ To remove weak, dead, and undesirable canes

✔ To open the center of the bush to air and light

✔ To remove old flowers

If you don't know where to start, remove the dead wood first, cutting back to healthy tissue. Living wood is beige or white. If you see dark brown tissue in the stem, cut back a little farther.

Most people start getting cold feet when cutting into living wood. Following a few simple rules and keeping your goals in mind should alleviate your fears:

✔ **Prune most roses right after they bloom.** Cut the flowers off just above a healthy five-leaflet leaf, as shown in Figure 18-4. Cut farther down the stem to encourage stockier growth or to shorten overlong canes.

✔ **Make cuts at a 45- to 60-degree angle about ¼ inch above a bud.** The angle and proximity to a bud are important because the cut heals more quickly and sheds water away from the bud (see Figure 18-5).

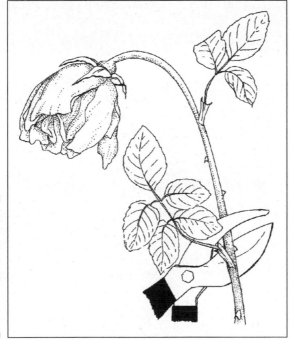

Figure 18-4:
Remove dead flowers by cutting just above a healthy five-leaflet leaf.

Figure 18-5:
Prune ¼ inch above a bud, and cut at a 45- to 60-degree angle.

✔ **Cut to a bud that points away from the center of the bush.** Imagine a V or vase shape with the center of the bush mostly free of stems and branches.

As you prune, keep in mind that buds grow in the direction in which they point.

✔ **Remove suckers that grow from the rootstock.** Most roses consist of a scion of a desirable flowering variety grafted onto a rootstock of a more vigorous type of rose. Suckers often arise from this rootstock, and because they are more vigorous than the scion variety on top, they eventually crowd out the flowering rose. It's easy to distinguish sucker growth, because the leaves and flowers look very different. Cut or pull them off below the soil line.

Pruning climbing roses

Roses with very long canes, called *climbing roses* (which I consider to be garden-type roses), offer a special challenge to rose growers because they have two different kinds of shoots: the main structural canes and the flowering shoots, called *laterals,* that grow from them. For the first two or three years after planting, allow the structural canes to grow with abandon, removing only dead or damaged canes. Tie them to a trellis or other support as desired.

Some climbing roses bloom just once, in the spring. The time to prune them is right after flowering, as you would for other garden roses.

Another kind of climbing rose, called *everblooming,* blooms throughout the summer, and these roses need a different pruning strategy. Tie their structural canes at a nearly horizontal angle to encourage them to sprout flowering lateral branches. In the winter or early spring, when the plant is dormant, prune these laterals back to about two to three buds above the structural canes. These buds will grow vigorously and produce flowers. After blooming, remove the flowers as you would for other roses.

Preparing Roses for Winter

If you live where winter temperatures rarely dip much below 15 degrees Fahrenheit — USDA Zones 9 through 11 — you can skip this section. Just about any rose can handle typical winters in these zones without any special attention.

Zones 6 through 8 are transition zones for winter-hardiness. If you live in one of these areas, you can grow most any kind of rose, but the more tender ones may be damaged by some winters. Often, it's not the absolute cold that does them in, but the wide temperature swings from cold to warm and back to cold again. That's why gardeners in these zones are likely to take measures to protect their favorite plants.

If you live in Zone 5 or colder, expect the harshest winter cold and winds, and protect all but the hardiest of roses.

The bud union is the most cold-sensitive part of most rose plants. Covering the bud union with soil protects it from the cold. To prepare the bud union for winter, follow these steps:

1. **Tie all the canes together to keep them from being windblown and loosening the soil around the base of the bush, or shorten the canes to reduce the effect of winds.**

   Don't cut the canes to soil level, though, because you want the buds near the bottom of the canes to sprout into new canes in the spring.

2. **Mound soil 8 to 10 inches high around the base of canes after the first hard frost but while you can still work the soil.**

   Bring soil from another part of the garden for mounding, because you may injure roots if you remove soil from around the rose plant or bed. Avoid using clay or heavy soils to build these mounds, because they hold too much moisture.

3. **Pile hay, straw, horse manure, leaves, or similar loose material over the mounded canes.**

   To prevent invasion by mice, wait until after the ground has frozen in late fall — around Thanksgiving in northern areas. Hold the material in place by covering it with some soil. These materials help keep the soil temperature constant. For additional protection, place twiggy branches or evergreen boughs over the top of the bushes. (I use limbs from my Christmas tree.) These branches help accumulate snow between the bushes, which may help reduce injury to the roots while still allowing some air circulation.

You can also make or buy cylinders, such as styrofoam cones, to place around your rosebushes, but these devices work only for small plants. Set the cylinders in place after two hard frosts have occurred — usually, after Thanksgiving. If you use an open-top cylinder, tie the rose plant's canes together; put the cylinder in place; cut the canes even with the cylinder's top; and then fill the cylinder with dry organic matter, such as leaves or straw. (Don't use peat moss.) Cover the top with polyethylene film to keep the insulation material dry, and anchor it in place to keep it from blowing over. Check the plants occasionally in winter for rodent, wind, and other damage.

Remove protective materials in spring as soon as the danger of hard frost passes but before new growth appears. Carefully remove the soil mounded around the bases of plants to avoid breaking off any shoots that may have started to grow. Never uncover the bushes in spring before the ground has thawed, because the tops may start to grow before the roots can provide water.

The most important thing you can do to help prevent winter injury is to keep your roses healthy during the growing season. Roses that were free of disease and properly nourished during the summer are less likely to suffer damage come winter.

Solving Common Rose Troubles

Choosing disease-resistant roses in the first place eliminates many common problems, but many of the most popular roses need intervention to keep them healthy. Show roses regularly fall prey to the common diseases, especially in climates with humid growing seasons. If you're in a low-humidity region where summer rainfall is rare, you have the best chance of growing disease-free show roses without fungicides.

Rose diseases

Diseases that damage leaves look unsightly and prevent plants from making enough food to flower and grow robustly. The two most common rose diseases throughout most of the United States are black spot and powdery mildew. My observation from years of growing and watching roses is that the favorite show roses — dark red and richly scented — are more prone to powdery mildew than others. Similarly, roses with yellow flowers or yellow-flowered ancestors are also somewhat more subject to disease. Other common rose diseases include downy mildew, rust disease, and rose mosaic virus. You can find out more about plant diseases and control methods in Chapter 9.

Insect pests

Many insect pests feed on roses, but few cause really devastating harm. Vigilance and applying a strong blast of water or handpicking take care of most pests, such as common aphids, Japanese beetles, rose slugs, rose curculios, and caterpillars. Other common pests include spider mites, scale insects, and thrips. You can read more about insect pests and how to control them in Chapter 8.

Recognize the difference between your rose-garden friends and the pests. Don't assume that any insect you spot in the garden is the perpetrator of some damage. Nothing could be further from the truth. Most of the insects you see in your garden are harmless; only a few cause damage. Some actually help!

Chapter 19

Managing Landscape Trees and Shrubs

Trees and shrubs lend structure to the landscape; they form the framework around which you plan your flower and vegetable gardens. As these long-lived plants mature, they become like old friends. Losing one to accident or disease leaves a hole in your landscape — a gap in the hedge. Taking care of these irreplaceable assets and using them to your best advantage starts with choosing the right plants in the first place, planting them correctly, and caring for them to keep them thriving.

Planning for Low Maintenance

I like to have a map in hand when I set out into unfamiliar territory. Knowing the lay of the land — what to expect around the next bend in the road — saves me missteps, as well as valuable time and energy. Using a map of your yard works the same way when you're choosing the best trees and shrubs. Miss a turn, and you may not get where you intended to go. In Chapter 3, I talk about how to assess your growing conditions. That chapter is a good reference as you browse through this one.

Putting everything in its place

When they're happy, trees and shrubs live for a long time and suffer few problems. Even before you begin shopping for these long-term landscape investments, assess the conditions of your planting site and use this assessment to narrow the list of potential plants to those that thrive in your particular situation.

One aspect that many people fail to consider when placing trees and shrubs in their landscapes is the plants' mature size. Most of these woody plants grow so slowly that it's easy to forget that the spindly twig you planted by the mailbox will grow wide enough to divert traffic within a few years. Play it safe by spacing trees where they can grow to full size without overhanging buildings and roads, growing into utility wires, or crowding the house. Choose shrubs that won't cover the windows or sidewalk. If the space between your small, newly planted shrubs looks too bleak and barren, plant some colorful annual or perennial flowers in the gaps until the shrubs fill in.

Avoiding troublemakers

Buying trees is like entering into any other long-term relationship: The characteristics that attracted you in the first place may lose their appeal in time if the bad habits outweigh the good ones. When you choose trees and shrubs for your landscape, consider the attributes that you want your plants to have. It's easy to focus on color, texture, shape, and flowers, but keep other factors in mind too. If you want a shade tree to plant in the lawn, look for deeply rooted, long-lived species. No time for raking? Stay away from trees that drop copious twigs and leaves. Following are some notorious troublemakers:

- **Invasive roots** wreak havoc in septic fields and often grow close to the soil surface, making lawn mowing difficult. Trees to avoid in lawns include red and silver maples, box elders, birches, beeches, *Ficus* species, poplars, and willows.

- **Weak-wooded trees** frequently break under ice and wind stress, causing property damage. Home wreckers include red and silver maples, box elders, horse chestnuts, *Catalpa* species, *Eucalyptus* species, poplars, and willows.

- **Messy trees** drop leaves, sap, fruits, nuts, and twigs frequently, adding to yard maintenance. Species to avoid include box elders, oaks, walnuts and other nut-bearing trees, *Catalpa* species, sweetgums, pines, magnolias, and plane trees and sycamores.

If you space them to allow some of these troublesome trees to grow without endangering or inconveniencing you, by all means plant them. They do have some endearing traits. But it pays to be forewarned. Find out as much as you can about a species before you buy, and choose varieties that offer disease resistance, if available. I mention disease-resistant varieties in the plant descriptions in this chapter.

Planting for Success

How you plant your tree or shrub may determine whether it thrives, merely survives, or dies. Not long ago, a neighbor asked me to look at a young crabapple tree that he planted several years earlier. It wasn't growing well and looked a little sadder each year. After digging around the trunk a bit, I discovered that he had planted it about 6 inches too deep — the tree was suffocating! We replanted that tree, and now it's blooming reliably every spring. Those 6 inches seem like such a small thing, yet they meant life or death for that tree. Read the following sections to get your plants off to the best possible start.

There is a season . . .

The best time of year to plant trees and shrubs depends mostly on your climate and the type of plant you're installing. Newly transplanted trees and shrubs have small root systems that need time to grow before they can support lots of leafy twigs and flowers. Identify your climate to find the best planting times for your trees and shrubs:

- ✔ **Cool, rainy winters:** Plant in autumn at the beginning of the rainy season to take advantage of the natural moisture.

- ✔ **Freezing, snowy winters:** Plant in early spring as soon as the ground thaws or in late summer to early autumn. Roots continue to grow until the ground temperature approaches 40 degrees Fahrenheit.

- ✔ **Warm year-round:** Plant at the beginning of the coolest, wettest season.

Deciduous and evergreen plants have somewhat different needs in the months following transplanting, which can affect the best time to plant in your area:

- ✔ **Deciduous:** Plant when the trees have an opportunity to grow roots without the added stress of leaves — usually, early autumn to spring.

- ✔ **Evergreen:** These plants lose water through their leaves year-round but can't take up water through their roots when the ground is frozen. Avoid planting just before winter in cold climates.

Nurseries sell woody plants in three ways: in containers, bare root, and balled and burlapped. Consult Chapter 12 for details on planting trees in these different forms.

Picking out healthy plants

My mantra throughout this book is prevention, prevention, prevention. One of the first steps to low-maintenance, problem-free trees and shrubs is picking out healthy specimens. Refer to Chapter 12 for tips on choosing healthy plants in general. Here are a few tips specific to trees:

- ✔ **Mechanical damage:** A few broken twigs usually aren't reasons to reject a plant, but avoid those with gashes on the trunk and main limbs, as well as any with torn limbs. Balled and burlapped (B&B) plants should have a solid, unbroken root ball, which indicates intact roots.

- ✔ **Branch and trunk structure:** Look for trees with straight, evenly tapered trunks and evenly distributed limbs. Unless the tree is supposed to have several trunks or large main branches, such as ornamental cherries and crabapples, choose trees with a single main trunk that doesn't fork. Avoid trees with crowded or lopsided branches. Trees (such as birches) that are sold in clumps should have similar-size trunks that don't rub against one another; the trees will become larger and more crowded as they grow. Figure 19-1 compares trees with good and poor structure.

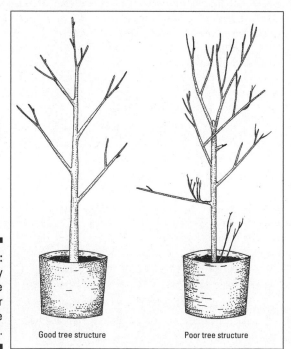

Figure 19-1:
Healthy
structure
(left); poor
structure
(right).

Good tree structure   Poor tree structure

Shrubs vary considerably from species to species; desirable structure in one may be undesirable in another. In general, choose shrubs with symmetrical branches that don't rub against one another. Avoid shrubs with roots growing on the surface or out of the drainage holes of their pots.

Long-Term Care for Landscape Trees and Shrubs

Established trees and shrubs need less attention than just about any other landscape plants. Except in unusual circumstances, they rarely need watering. They need little fertilizer. All they ask for are observation for potential problems and occasional pruning to keep them healthy and respectable-looking.

Fertilizing follies

Unless your soil is unusually infertile or you want your trees to grow extra fast, you don't need to fertilize them regularly. If you do choose to fertilize, don't apply more than 1 pound of nitrogen per 1,000 square feet per year. (Never add it to the hole at planting time, however.) You can apply organic granular fertilizer or spread composed manure over the root zone. The *root zone,* where the roots grow, usually is at least twice as wide as the branch spread. If the branches measure 10 feet from trunk to tips, figure that the roots stretch about 20 feet. To calculate the square feet in the root zone, use this formula: $3.14 \times$ (root radius) $\times$ (root radius). In this case, $3.14 \times 20 \times 20 = 1{,}256$ square feet. See Chapter 6 for more on using organic fertilizers.

Pruning 101

You need a good reason to prune a twig or remove a limb from a tree or shrub; every time you cut into a plant, you open a wound that's vulnerable to disease. Having a goal in mind helps guide you toward making the right cuts and minimizes the size and number of cuts you need to make. Common reasons to prune include the following:

✔ **Removing dead, damaged, and diseased wood:** Prune any time you see these three Ds to prevent the damage or disease from spreading. If the trunk or major limbs are affected, call an arborist for help.

✔ **Establishing healthy structure:** Removing poorly placed, crowded limbs when they're small prevents major pruning cuts down the road. Limbs that rub against one another, emerge too close together from the trunk, or have very narrow crotch angles where the limb meets the trunk are all candidates for removal.

✔ **Controlling growth:** Part of your annual yard maintenance includes shaping shrubs that grow out of bounds, removing old and unproductive shoots, and trimming limbs that get in the way.

✔ **Increasing flowers:** Fruiting and ornamental flowering trees and shrubs produce more flowers and better-quality fruit when pruned properly. As a rule, prune spring-flowering shrubs right after they finish blooming. Prune summer-blooming shrubs and most trees when they're dormant in the winter.

The tools you need to do a good pruning job include hand pruners for cuts up to ¾ inch in diameter, and loppers for cuts between ¾ inch and 1½ inches in diameter or for limbs that are just out of arm's reach. Use a pruning saw with a curved 8- to 12-inch blade for larger cuts. To prevent the spread of disease, always clean your tool blades with isopropyl alcohol between prunings of trees and shrubs. Don't coat the wounds with paint, tar, or any other material; it actually slows the healing process.

If the pruning job is too high to reach from the ground, use a pole pruner with a telescoping handle, or call a professional. *Never* climb a tree when using power equipment (such as a chain saw), and never cut limbs near utility wires.

You need to know only two basic pruning cuts to maintain your trees, shrubs, and flowering plants: thinning and heading.

✔ **Thinning cut:** A *thinning cut* removes a branch back to its origin, as shown on the left in Figure 19-2. Use thinning cuts to maintain plants' natural appearance while decreasing their height, width, or branching density.

✔ **Heading cut:** A *heading cut,* shown on the right in Figure 19-2, removes shoots or branches back to buds. Plants usually respond to heading cuts by sprouting new shoots near the pruning site, resulting in denser growth. *Deadheading,* a technique used to remove spent flowers, helps increase future flowering. Pinch or prune off the flowers to a point just above healthy-looking buds.

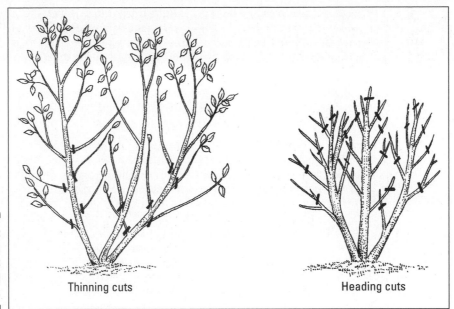

Figure 19-2:
Thinning
cuts (left);
heading
cuts (right).

Thinning cuts

Heading cuts

When you make a thinning cut, it's really important to cut at the right place. If you look closely where a branch joins the trunk or a larger limb, you should see a series of raised ridges, called the *branch collar*. That's where the scar tissue begins to form when the limb dies or is removed. Make your cut just outside that collar without leaving a stub. Stubs invite infection that may lead to the death of the tree. Never cut a limb flush with the trunk, either. And always support the limb you're removing to avoid tearing the bark on the trunk.

Choosing the Perfect Trees and Shrubs

When you choose new trees and shrubs, think about what you want these plants to do in your landscape. Do you need shade or shelter from the wind? Does a corner of the yard need a spark of color? Consider all the seasons of the year when you make your decision; the best shrubs and trees have practical or decorative value in several seasons, not just one. A Japanese maple, for example, may have ornamental leaves in spring and summer, colorful fall foliage, and interesting branching patterns and bark in the winter. I've chosen some of the best and most versatile landscape trees and shrubs for this section.

If you want to know more about flowering and shade trees, shrubs, and conifers, and how to care for them, pick up a copy of *Trees & Shrubs For Dummies* (Wiley). The book also lists many of the most attractive and disease- and pest-resistant varieties of each tree and shrub.

Shade trees

Shade trees frame the landscape, cool the space around them, and provide a backdrop for colorful flowering trees and shrubs. Most of these trees grow too tall for you to treat for pests or diseases, so if you're planting new trees, your best bet is to choose species that suffer few problems in the first place. If you already have large shade trees with chronic pests, or if you suspect disease, call an arborist who can diagnose the trouble and offer advice and treatment.

✔ **Maple (*Acer* species):** A large and diverse group of valuable landscape trees, maples range in mature size from 20 to 100 feet, depending on species. The larger species serve as shade trees; smaller ones make good specimens and street trees. Many maples are renowned for their brilliant autumn foliage; some also have attractive bark.

Maples that grow 25 to 30 feet high include trident *(A. buergeranum)*, hedge *(A. campestre)*, fullmoon *(A. japonicum)*, Japanese *(A. palmatum)*, Amur *(A. tataricum)*, and Shantung *(A. truncatum)*. All have yellow, orange, or crimson fall foliage. Larger species for shade include paperbark *(A. griseum)*, red *(A. rubrum;* note this tree's bad habits in "Avoiding trouble-makers," earlier in this chapter), and sugar *(A. saccharum)* maples.

Most maples prefer well-drained, fertile soil and regular moisture. Some maples, including hedge and trident, tolerate drier and less fertile soil, such as occurs near roads. For damp soil, try red or Amur maples. Prune only to remove dead, damaged, or diseased limbs, or any that rub or hang over buildings. Prune in early summer, avoiding late winter through spring, when pruning cuts will bleed sap profusely.

Leaf spots, cankers, caterpillars, borers, leafhoppers, and scale insects injure maples, especially those growing in stressed conditions or in unsuitable soils. Some species are also more prone to insects, disease, and structural damage than others, including box elder *(A. negundo)*, silver *(A. saccharinum)*, and sycamore *(A. pseudoplatanus)* maples. In hot, dry climates, look for brown leaf edges that signal leaf scorch. Give additional water to moisten the soil to a depth of at least 12 inches.

✔ **Birch (*Betula* species):** When you think of birches, you likely picture a clump of white-barked trees. Not all birches have white bark, however. Many actually make better landscape specimens, especially for organic gardeners, because they resist the most common and devastating pest — the bronze birch borer — and tolerate a wider range of growing conditions.

Birches cast light shade, making them good choices for cooling a shady seat. Most birches thrive in moist, well-drained, acidic soils, but try gray birch in drier situations and river birch in damp soil. Prune birches in late spring to early summer after the leaves have fully emerged. If pruned too early or late in the season, they bleed sap excessively. Avoid disturbing the soil around their shallow roots.

Birches are subject to attack from many insects and several diseases, including leaf miners, canker, and leaf diseases. The bronze birch borer decimates the white-barked birches, especially the European white birch throughout the eastern and midwestern United States, targeting stressed trees and older specimens first. The first symptoms of infestation are dead branches near the top of the tree.

Choose species that resist the bronze birch borer, such as Asian white (*B. platyphylla japonica*), gray (*B. populifolia*), and river (*B. nigra*) birches. If the pest is not a problem in your area, try white-barked paper (*B. papyrifera*) and European white (*B. pendula*) birches. All these birches are hardy in Zones 3 to 6 except Asian white birch, which grows north to Zone 4, and river birch, which grows south to Zone 9.

✔ **Hackberry (*Celtis* species):** These native North American species thrive in adverse conditions, tolerating wet to dry soil and urban to open prairie situations. They grow 40 to 60 feet tall and form an elmlike silhouette. Common hackberry (*C. occidentalis*) grows in Zones 3 to 9, tolerates midwestern wind and dry soil, and has wildlife-attracting berries. Sugar hackberry (*C. laevigata*) grows in Zones 5 to 9, prefers low wet areas, has smooth gray bark, and resists some common hackberry diseases.

Common hackberry is prone to a disfiguring disease called witches' broom that makes the twigs grow abnormally. The cultivar Prairie Pride resists the disease. Other problems include leaf spots and galls. Mourning cloak butterfly larvae enjoy its foliage.

✔ **Ginkgo (*Gingko biloba*):** Growing 50 to 80 feet tall and 30 to 40 feet wide, ginkgo is best suited to large yards. Young trees have a pyramid shape, but older trees become widely spreading. Varieties also differ significantly in width and shape. Ginkgo's pollution tolerance and neat habits make it attractive for planting along streets, in parks, and in other urban and suburban areas.

Not fussy about soil, the gingko thrives in Zones 4 to 8. It needs little care and has no significant pests or diseases. Choose a male cultivar such as Autumn Gold, Fairmount, or Princeton Sentry to avoid the unpleasant-smelling fruits that drop from female trees.

✔ **Katsura *(Cercidiphyllum japonicus):*** This tree has so many good things going for it that's it hard to go wrong by choosing it for your yard — as long as you have the space to accommodate it. It grows 40 to 60 feet high and spreads just as wide from several branched trunks. The nearly round leaves are attractive from spring to their final fall blaze of apricot-orange.

Katsura prefers moist, slightly acidic, well-drained, fertile soil and full sun. Keep the soil moist but not saturated for the first few years after transplanting. Mulch to hold soil moisture. The species has no significant pests or diseases. For something different, look for the cultivar Pendula, which grows cascading limbs that reach 15 to 25 feet high with a wider spread.

✔ **Oak (*Quercus* species):** The queen of trees, oaks suggest majesty wherever they grow. Oak species fall into three broad categories:

- **White oaks** have leaves with rounded lobes and grow 80 feet high — too large for most home landscapes.

- **Red oaks** have leaves with pointed lobes and make better landscape specimens.

- **Narrow-leafed oaks** don't have lobed leaves, and many are suitable for home landscapes.

Plant dormant, balled and burlapped, or container-grown specimens in well-drained soil. Pin oak *(Q. palustris)* and swamp white oak *(Q. bicolor)* can grow in wet soils. Preferred soil pH varies widely. Pin oak is especially sensitive to high pH soils, and the leaves will turn yellow if the soil isn't acidic.

Oaks suffer from many insect pests that eat their leaves — including gypsy moths, oak moths, mites, and borers — plus various fungus diseases. Few pests prove fatal to otherwise-healthy trees.

Other shade trees to consider are ash *(Fraxinus* spp.), beech *(Fagus* spp.), black gum *(Nyssa sylvatica),* Chinese pistache *(Pistacia chinensis),* hickory *(Carya* spp.), Japanese zelkova *(Zelkova serrata),* Kentucky coffeetree *(Gymnocladus dioicus),* lacebark elm *(Ulmus parvifolia),* linden *(Tilia* spp.), and yellowwood *(Cladrastis kentukea).*

Flowering and ornamental trees

Flowering trees give your yard a colorful exclamation point whenever they bloom. The anticipation of cherry or crabapple blossoms marks the changing of the seasons, often highlighting the start of the gardening season.

- **Serviceberry (*Amelanchier* species):** These trees grow about 20 feet high in Zones 3 to 7 and often form multiple-trunked trees with silvery bark. In spring, they produce clouds of white flowers, which ripen to delicious deep red to black fruits similar to blueberries by early summer. Their glossy, deep green, oval foliage turns brilliant yellow to orange in the fall. They have a few diseases, such as leaf spots and rust, and though insects pester them, no pests are serious. Plant in moist, acidic soils.

- **Redbud (*Cercis canadensis*):** Although hardy in Zones 5 to 9, individual trees may have a much narrower range, depending on where their fore-bearers grew. If possible, choose trees from a similar climate to your own. Trees grow up to 25 feet tall and tend to form wide-spreading, multiple-trunked canopies. Leaves are heart-shaped and follow the pink early-spring flowers. Plant in moist, well-drained soil and full sun to light shade. Canker disease is the only serious problem; prune infected limbs.

  Varieties with unusual foliage include Forest Pansy, which grows in Zones 6 to 9 and has dark purple new leaves that mature to deep burgundy; and Silver Cloud, which has creamy-white, variegated leaves. Other varieties have flower colors ranging from white to reddish purple.

- **Dogwood (*Cornus* species):** Distinctive horizontal branching, clouds of spring flowers, and fiery autumn foliage make this group of landscape trees well loved. The most commonly planted species is flowering dogwood (*C. florida*), which is hardy in Zones 5 to 9.

  Many good varieties exist, including Cherokee Princess, which is very cold-hardy and disease-resistant. Another underappreciated species is kousa dogwood (*C. kousa*), which grows in similar conditions but stays smaller and blooms later than flowering dogwood, and is more resistant to anthracnose disease.

  Plant dogwoods in well-drained, moist, humus-rich soil. In hot climates, give midday shade. Canker, twig blights, anthracnose, and wood-boring insects frequently damage these trees. Prune out diseased wood when you see it. Dogwood is also prone to rot diseases if the bark is damaged — take care with the mower and string trimmer!

✔ **Hawthorn (*Crataegus* species):** This group of trees tolerates urban pollution and poor, dry soil; in return, it offers clouds of spring bloom, followed by crabapplelike fruits. Most have thorny branches and grow in Zones 4 to 7 or 8. Fire blight, leaf rust, blights and spots, apple scab, leaf miners, and aphids plague hawthorns. A few varieties — such as green hawthorn *(C. viridis)*, Lavalle hawthorn *(C. x lavellei)*, and English hawthorn Crimson Cloud *(C. laevigata)* — are more resistant to leaf diseases.

✔ **Magnolia (*Magnolia* species):** Ranging in size from shrubs to magnificent trees, magnolias include both evergreen and deciduous species. Some grow only in warmer climates from Zones 6 to 9; others tolerate Zone 5 and even Zone 4. Magnolias prefer moist, well-drained, slightly acidic soil with plenty of organic matter and full sun to light shade. Protect the shallow roots from drought and weed competition with a layer of organic mulch. Prune only to shape the tree and remove undesirable limbs. Magnolias as a group suffer from few pests or diseases except for saucer magnolia *(M. x soulangiana)*, which is prone to several leaf diseases.

For shrub to small tree-size magnolias, look for lily magnolia *(M. liliiflora)*; any of the Kosar-DeVos hybrids, such as Ann or Betty; sweetbay *(M. virginiana)*; and star magnolia *(M. stellata)*. Species that grow up to 30 feet tall include Yulan *(M. denudata)*, Loebner *(M. x loebneri)*, and many hybrids.

✔ **Flowering crabapple (*Malus* species):** One of the most widely grown flowering trees in Zones 4 to 7 for home and public landscapes, flowering crabapples have a lot to offer. Spring bloom, persistent and colorful fruit, and attractive branching and bark make them justifiably popular. Hundreds of varieties are available, and many of the newest ones have built-in disease resistance. Plant in nearly any well-drained, moderately fertile soil and full sun. Prevent weed and grass competition with organic mulch. Prune while dormant, in late winter to early spring.

Choose the best varieties by first looking at disease resistance. Crabapples suffer from many serious diseases, including leaf scab, cedar-apple rust, powdery mildew, and fire blight. Expect aphids, mites, caterpillars, rodents, and deer to take a bite too.

After selecting disease-resistant cultivars, select for flower color (white to deep pink), height and growth shape (column to wide and low), leaf color (green to reddish), and fruit size and color (red to yellow).

✔ **Stewartia (*Stewartia* species):** If you have moist, well-drained, acidic soil, consider stewartia for its flaky, mottled bark; late-summer bloom; and striking fall foliage. Trees stay 20 to 40 feet tall, making them ideal for most home landscapes. They suffer from few pests or diseases and need little pruning.

Other small, ornamental trees include white fringetree *(Chionanthus virginicus)*, goldenrain tree *(Koelreuteria paniculata)*, purple-leaf plum *(Prunus cerasifera)*, red buckeye *(Aesculus pavia)*, sassafras *(Sassafras albidum)*, and silverbell *(Halesia carolina)*.

Flowering and ornamental shrubs

The seasonal stars of the show, flowering shrubs light up the landscape with drifts and spots of bloom. The best shrubs, however, offer more than a week or two of flowers; attractive foliage, stems, and colorful berries can carry the show through the rest of the year.

- **Summersweet *(Clethra alnifoli):*** This North American native offers spikes of fragrant, white to pink, late-summer flowers that attract butterflies and many other pollinating insects. It grows 6 to 10 feet tall and wide, but the award-winning cultivar Hummingbird grows only 36 inches high. It grows in Zones 4 to 9 and prefers moist, acidic soil and part shade to full sun but tolerates less hospitable seashore conditions. It has few pests except for mites in overly dry sites. Prune to maintain shape and to remove spent flowers.

- **Cotoneaster *(Cotoneaster* species):** Deciduous members of this group have small leaves; attractive fruits; and distinctive, herringbone-patterned branches. Some, such as spreading cotoneaster *(C. divaricatus)*, grow upright to 5 or 6 feet, but most species remain under 3 feet tall. Creeping *(C. adpressus)*, cranberry *(C. apiculatus)*, and rockspray cotoneaster *(C. horizontalis)* spread up 6 feet wide, making them useful as ground covers.

  Plant cotoneasters in nearly any well-drained soil, including sandy, heavy clay, drought-prone, salty, and high- or low-pH soil. Prune to shape or remove damaged limbs. Pest and disease problems include fire blight, leaf spots, canker, and spider mites.

- **Forsythia *(Forsythia* species):** Cheerful, yellow, bell-shaped flowers welcome spring, but the shrubs frequently become straggly and over-grown unless pruned regularly. Prune after flowering in the spring, choosing one-fourth of the oldest stems and cutting them right to the ground. To ensure consistent flowering in the most northern parts of its Zone 4 to 8 range, choose hardy varieties, including Northern Sun, Northern Gold, and Meadowlark. Plant in nearly any soil in full sun. Although several species of insects attack forsythia, none is serious. Prune out twigs that die back.

✔ **Hydrangea (*Hydrangea* species):** Popular for its huge balls of white, pink, and blue flowers, this group of shrubs grows in nearly any soil and sun conditions. Most varieties prefer some midday shade in hot climates, however. As a rule, hydrangeas are tough as nails, although some are prone to powdery mildew in humid climates, and aphids, mites, and scale can cause some damage. Prune smooth hydrangea *(H. arborescens)* and panicle or PeeGee hydrangea *(H. paniculata)* in late winter or spring because they bloom on new growth. Bigleaf or French hydrangea *(H. macrophylla)* and oakleaf hydrangea *(H. quercifolia),* however, bloom on last year's wood, so prune them right after they bloom in the summer, and avoid spring pruning.

✔ **Holly (*Ilex* species):** This huge group of mostly evergreen trees and shrubs includes everything from the classic English holly *(I. aquifolium)* to the less-well-known inkberry *(I. glabra)* and hundreds of species and varieties in between. Hardiness ranges from inkberry's span of Zones 4 to 9 to the tender Chinese holly *(I. cornuta),* which prefers Zones 7 to 9. Most hollies produce large crops of attractive, persistent berries, but most species bear male and female flowers on separate plants. Plant at least one of each species if you want berries, and look at the plant names for clues about the sex of the shrub. Blue Boy and Blue Girl make good companions, as do China Boy and China Girl.

Hollies in general enjoy moist, well-drained soil and full sun, although Chinese holly withstands drought and flooding with aplomb. In windy areas and climates where the soil freezes, protect the foliage from drying out by covering with burlap or other windbreak material. Hollies suffer from many pests and diseases, including scales, spider mites, nematodes, leaf miners, and various bugs and caterpillars, as well as mildew and leaf spots. The most problem-free species include Yaupon *(I. vomitoria),* inkberry, and the Foster hybrids.

Winterberry *(I. Verticillata),* one of my favorite hollies, grows in Zones 3 to 9. It loses its leaves in winter but retains the characteristic masses of red berries. Winterberry has few pests or disease problems.

✔ **Spirea (*Spirea* species):** These easygoing shrubs are useful for informal hedges, foundation plantings, and mixed shrub borders. Most have flat clusters of little white to pink flowers; some, such as Magic Carpet and Goldflame, even offer three seasons of interest with their brilliant yellow foliage, floral display, and autumn color. Plant in any well-drained soil, and give them full sun and regular watering in dry spells.

Spireas come under attack from many pests and diseases, but these attacks rarely prove to be fatal. After flowering, cut the weakest or oldest one-fourth of the shoots to the ground each year to keep shrubs vigorous and tidy.

✔ **Lilac (*Syringa* species):** If you give your lilac moist, fertile soil and full sun, and prune it to remove spent flowers and weak growth, you can expect it to live for many years. Varieties now exist that can grow in any zone from 3 to 9. Major problems include lilac borer, scale insects, lilac blight, and powdery mildew. The common lilac *(S. vulgaris)* offers the widest range of flower colors, from white to pink and blue to deep purple. Some varieties have double flowers or extra fragrance. Meyer lilac *(S. meyeri)* and Manchurian lilac *(S. patula)* Miss Kim stay smaller than the common species. Japanese tree lilac *(S. reticulata)* grows 20 to 30 feet tall and has white blooms in June.

✔ **Viburnum (*Viburnum* species):** This diverse group shares the attribute of profuse flowering; some, such as Korean spice viburnum *(V. carlesii)* and fragrant viburnum *(V. x carlcephalum),* have intoxicatingly fragrant flowers. Many also produce attractive berries, although with some species, such as Korean spice viburnum, you have to plant both male and female shrubs. Birds appreciate some native species for food. Most of these shrubs grow in any well-drained but moisture-retentive soil. Some prefer acidic soil; others are less fussy. Full sun to part shade suits them fine, depending on the species and climate.

Species that grow in dry soils include wayfaring tree *(V. lantana),* arrow-wood viburnum *(V. dentatum),* and blackhaw viburnum *(V. prunifolium).* Few pests or diseases cause serious damage.

Other shrubs to consider include azaleas and rhododendrons *(Rhododendron* spp.species), mountain laurel *(Kalmia latifolia),* red-osier dogwood *(Cornus sericea),* and Virginia sweetspire *(Itea virginica).*

Conifers

Needle- and cone-bearing trees and shrubs, called *conifers,* provide the backdrop for more colorful garden elements and serve as hedges, screens, and windbreaks. Their imposing size and stiff formality make many evergreen trees difficult to integrate into small home landscapes. Think twice before planting a potentially 50-foot-tall Colorado blue spruce in your front yard! In larger settings, where the trees can attain full size, evergreen trees add grandeur and provide refuge for wildlife.

Shrub-size conifers are invaluable for the year-round color and texture they add to the landscape. Some creep over the ground and drape over walls; others grow into neat cones, pyramids, and rounded cushions. Foliage colors range from gold through a wide range of greens to silver and even purplish. Some plants appear fuzzy and soft; others are stiff and bristly.

Although you can shape many conifers into geometric and fanciful forms, most don't require pruning at all except to remove dead, diseased, or damaged limbs and undesirable growth that detracts from the plant's appearance. In fact, pine, spruce, and fir trees that grow in *whorls* (with layers of branches around the trunk) will not sprout new limbs in response to pruning. To control their growth, pinch or prune their new, soft growth in late spring before it hardens, cutting into only the new tissue. Arborvitae, false cypress, cypress, juniper, and yew plants with random branching can tolerate more pruning, however, and usually will sprout new limbs to replace the ones that you remove. Conifers that usually grow into a pyramid shape with one central trunk sometimes develop additional *leaders* (competing main trunks) at the top of the tree. Remove all but one leader to retain the tree shape.

As a group, conifers suffer from their share of pests and diseases. The most troublesome pests include spruce budworm, bagworms, and various caterpillars. Bacterial and fungal diseases cause blights, cankers, and root rots. See Part III for more information about these pests and diseases. The best defense against disease is to plant your trees and shrubs in the soil and sun conditions they prefer, and keep them growing strong. Protect evergreens from drying winter winds wherever the ground freezes.

✔ **Fir (*Abies* species):** Imagine the perfect Christmas tree, and you probably picture a fir. Firs have short, bristly needles and a pyramid shape. Although popular for home landscapes, balsam *(A. balsamea),* white or concolor *(A. concolor),* and frasier *(A. fraseri)* firs grow 30 to more than 40 feet tall and spread 25 feet or more at their bases when mature. Use as windbreaks, or plant as groups in large areas. Firs prefer cool, moist, acidic soils and don't readily tolerate dry, alkaline soil. They require no pruning except to remove damaged limbs. Insect pests include spruce budworms, bagworms, spider mites, and scales. Diseases include leaf and twig blights and rust fungus.

✔ **Cypress and false cypress (*Cupressocyparis* and *Chamaecyparis* species):** These two closely related groups share many features but differ in their preferred growing conditions. False cypress *(Chamaecyparis)* prefers cool, moist, humid conditions; cypress *(Cupressocyparis)* enjoys the heat and drier soil found in more arid climates. The hybrid between the two groups, Leyland cypress, tolerates a wider range of soils and climates than either of its parents. Cypresses have flat, scalelike foliage that's compressed against the twigs, giving the branches stringy or fanlike textures.

Hundreds of varieties are available, including low-growing shrubs to stately trees. Leyland cypress is used widely for hedges because it grows up to 3 feet per year and tolerates salt spray and any soil except poorly drained. Hinoki *(C. obtusa)* and threadleaf *(C. pisifera)* false cypresses have many popular varieties used in home and commercial landscapes. Cypresses require no pruning except to shape the plant or remove damaged limbs. Bagworms are the only troublesome pests. Twig blight occurs in some areas but isn't prevalent.

✔ **Juniper (*Juniperus* species):** Versatile and tough as nails, junipers are justifiably among the most popular landscape shrubs. They tolerate poor, dry soil, as well as urban and roadside conditions; they come in a seemingly infinite number of shapes, sizes, colors, and textures. Depending on the species and variety, you can find a juniper to grow in any climate from coastal Florida to the Canadian plains. Ground-hugging forms make excellent carpets for slopes and lawn substitutes. Taller varieties serve as shrubs for hedges and planting around buildings.

In cold-winter Zone 3 or 4, and warmer, look for Chinese (*J. chinensis, J. x media),* creeping *(J. horizontalis),* savin *(J. sabina),* and Rocky Mountain *(J. scopulorum)* juniper varieties. Shore juniper *(J. conferta)* enjoys the heat in Zones 6 to 9 and tolerates coastal conditions.

Junipers can suffer from several insect pests and diseases, including bagworms, scales, webworms, borers, twig blight, and cedar-apple rust. Creeping juniper is more disease-prone than others, but savin juniper varieties Calgary Carpet, Arcadia, Scandia, Blue Danube, and Broadmoor resist juniper blight. In wet, poorly drained soils, junipers are prone to root rot.

✔ **Spruce (*Picea* species):** Give spruce trees plenty of room if you plant them in your landscape, because they tend to spread widely at the base as they mature, often measuring 20 feet or more across at the ground. Most spruce have a stiff, formal pyramid shape, which looks best in large landscapes or when the trees grow in groups. Use for windbreaks or large screens.

A few dwarf varieties are available; they grow into small mounds or weeping specimens suitable for planting in home landscapes. For dwarf varieties, look for Norway *(Picea abies),* Little Gem, Pumila, Nidiformis, or Bird's Nest Spruce; black *(P. mariana)* Nana; or white spruce *(P. glauca)* Conica, also known as Dwarf Alberta Spruce.

Spruces prefer cool climates and well-drained but moderately moist soil. Avoid planting them in dry soil and polluted urban locations. They often suffer from aphids, spruce budworms, bagworms, and other pests, as well as canker and twig blight.

✔ **Pine (*Pinus* species):** Most pines grow into large, picturesque trees up to 100 feet tall, but a few dwarf varieties stay small enough to serve in home landscapes. For small pines, seek out Japanese red pine *(Pinus densiflora)* Umbraculifera, Japanese white pine *(P. parviflora)* Glauca, Japanese black pine *(P. thunbergii),* and mugo pine *(P. mugo).*

Pines have long needles that give them a softer texture than most other conifers. The needles occur in bundles of two, three, or five. Pines with the same number of needles in a bundle often have other common characteristics, such as growth habits and cultural requirements. *Two-needled pines,* such as Scotch pine *(P. sylvestris),* for example, tolerate drier soil and more heat than the *five-needled species,* such as white pine *(P. strobus).*

Pines don't tolerate air pollution or road-salt spray. Common diseases and pests include white pine blister rust, spruce budworms, and white pine weevils.

✔ **Yew (*Taxus* species):** Yews, among the most widely grown conifers for hedges and shearing into fanciful shapes, respond to pruning by sprouting ever-denser growth. Keep in mind that most yews will grow into 30- to 60-foot trees if allowed to do so. They grow best in well-drained, fertile, moist soil and full sun to part shade, and may need protection from the winter wind in cold climates.

In hot, muggy climates, look for the variety Tauntonii, which tolerates the summer heat better than most other yews. Pests include deer, weevils, and mealybugs, as well as blights and root rot.

✔ **Arborvitae and white cedar (*Thuja* and *Platycladus* species):** These tough trees and shrubs grow in a wide range of soils and climates, from soggy to well drained, in Zones 3 to 11. They need full sun to grow lush and full. Few pests or diseases cause them serious trouble, although bagworms, spider mites, blight, and canker can show up when plants are stressed. Protect them from road-salt spray and drying winter winds.

As trees, arborvitae grow up to 50 feet high, but many varieties stay shrub-sized and come in many shapes, including globe, cone, column, pyramid, and weeping. Some have yellowish foliage; others have deep green foliage. Choose a variety that matches your climate, soil, and specific landscape needs. Arborvitae make a classic tall hedge without shearing, and smaller varieties are suitable for planting around buildings.

Chapter 20

Caring for Your Organic Lawn

. . . .

. . . .

Many people think that to have an attractive lawn, they have to douse it with herbicides, insecticides, and fungicides. That, of course, is a fallacy. It's possible — and even easy — to grow a great-looking lawn organically. An organic lawn-care program requires an attitude adjustment, however. The secret is to think of your lawn as a mixed garden of grass and other compatible, low-growing plants that tolerate mowing.

As in any other kind of gardening, your success depends on how well you lay the groundwork by preparing the soil, choosing the right grass varieties, and giving the plants what they need. This chapter explains what you need to know about your lawn's growth habits, fertilizer needs, and pests and diseases.

Getting Down to Grassroots

If you dig out a wedge of turf and soil and look at it, you'll see several layers. At the top is the mostly flat grass blade, which should be bright green. That's the part of the plant that you mow every week. At the next-lower level, you see rounder grass stems and then the *crown,* where the roots meet the stems. The new grass growth emerges at the ground-hugging plant crown. Under the soil, you'll find miles of roots for each grass plant. The root length is directly proportional to the plant health: The longer the roots, the healthier the plant. Grass plants come in two basic forms: clump-forming and creeping.

✔ **Creeping:** With *creeping* or sod-forming grasses, such as Kentucky bluegrass or Bermuda grass, horizontal stems called *stolons* and *rhizomes* grow out of the crown, take root, and form new plants. Stolons grow on top of the soil; rhizomes grow underground, as shown in Figure 20-1.

✔ **Clump-forming:** *Clump-forming* or noncreeping grasses, such as chewings fescue and hard fescue, don't spread by stolons or rhizomes. If allowed to grow without mowing, these and other grasses send up a tall flowering stalk that may produce seed.

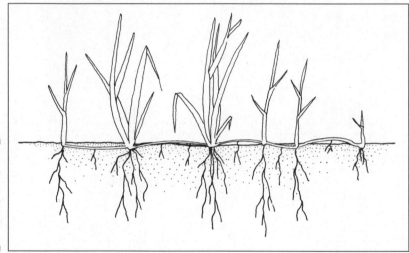

Figure 20-1: Many grass types spread by stolons and rhizomes.

Choosing the Right Grass

Organic lawn care gets a lot easier if you grow the right grass for your climate, sun, and soil conditions. You can find grasses that thrive under nearly every combination of lawn conditions. Finding the right grass variety for your lawn is easier than ever because plant breeders have worked hard to produce grasses that thrive under different conditions.

One particular variety can't do it all. For that reason, most grass seed and turf is sold as combinations of grasses that complement one another. The labels on grass seed packages list the percentage of each seed by weight, as well as other information such as what percentage of weed seed and inert matter the package contains and when the seed was tested for germination. The most important things to look for are improved varieties, current-year test date, and weed content of less than 1 percent.

Cool-season and warm-season grasses

Turfgrass species (grasses that are used for lawns) are classified as either cool season or warm season. The *cool-season grasses* grow best north of the so-called *bluegrass line* — an imaginary border that stretches from the middle of North Carolina through the centers of Arkansas and New Mexico into Southern California. The *warm-season grasses* grow best south of that line.

Too cool, man

Cool-season grasses prefer moist, cold-winter climates with mild summers. These grasses grow most actively in the cool spring and fall months; they may turn brown and become dormant during extended hot, dry periods in summer. Although traditionally grown north of the bluegrass line, cool-season grasses also grow well at higher elevations and in other, cooler microclimates south of the bluegrass line. (Jump to Chapter 3 for information about microclimates.) Trying to grow cool-season grasses outside their preferred climate, however, adds up to more maintenance and trouble. These species need frequent watering in arid climates and are prone to disease and insect attack in hot-summer spots. The main grass species that grow in the north include the following:

- **Kentucky bluegrass** is known for its cold-hardiness, fine-textured blades, and rich green color.
- **Perennial ryegrass** is tough enough to be used on athletic fields.
- **Tall fescue** is a good low-maintenance grass that can be allowed to grow tall.
- **Chewings fescue** grows well in light shade and tolerates cold and drought.
- **Hard fescue** is a low-maintenance species good for the far North.
- **Red fescue** (also known as *creeping fescue*) withstands shade and drought well.
- **Bent grass** is the very fine-textured (and very fussy) grass used mainly on golf putting greens.

Some like it hot

Warm-season grasses thrive where winters are mild and summer temperatures stay above 85 degrees Fahrenheit for months on end. Most don't appreciate freezing weather and respond by turning brown. They grow vigorously, especially during the summer. Warm-season grass species for the South include the following:

- ✔ **Bahia grass** makes a thick, drought-tolerant lawn in the Gulf Coast states.

- ✔ **Bermuda grass** is the workhorse grass of the South. It grows fast and can withstand hot, dry weather.

- ✔ **Centipede grass** is called lazy man's grass because it needs less mowing and water than other grasses do.

- ✔ **Carpet grass** has thick, coarse blades, but it grows well in the coastal plain region.

- ✔ **St. Augustine grass** may be the most attractive of all warm-season grasses, but it does require frequent watering and feeding to stay that way.

- ✔ **Zoysia grass** withstands more shade than most warm-season southern grasses but is slow to establish.

Regional preferences

Because climates vary in many ways other than temperature, it helps to divide the United States into nine turf-growing zones, as shown in Figure 20-2. Each zone has specific grass species best suited to grow in its climate.

- ✔ **Zone 1 (the coastal West)** is characterized by dry summers and cool, wet winters. Grow cool-season grasses such as Kentucky bluegrass, tall fescue, fine fescue, and perennial ryegrass.

- ✔ **Zone 2 (the western transitional zone)** has long dry summers and moderate winters. You can grow either warm- or cool-season grasses here. Hybrid Bermuda grass is popular for the summer. For winter color, sow seeds of a cool-season grass, such as ryegrass or tall fescue, over your warm-season grass lawn when it starts to turn brown or yellow in the fall.

- ✔ **Zone 3 (the arid Southwest)** has long, hot, dry summers and dry winters. Plant Bermuda grass or zoysia grass for summer in low-elevation areas and overseed with ryegrass or fescue for winter color. In high elevations, plant drought-resistant buffalo grass.

- ✔ **Zone 4 (the Great Plains)** has two native turfgrasses: buffalo grass and blue grama grass. Plant them for a low-maintenance lawn. Use Bermuda grass or zoysia grass in the southern region, and use northern grasses, such as Kentucky bluegrass or perennial ryegrass, in the northern region.

✓ **Zone 5 (the Midwest)** offers moist, humid summers and cold winters. Any cool-season grasses will grow here, such as Kentucky bluegrass, perennial ryegrass, and any of the fescues. Warm-season zoysia grass may be grown in the southernmost areas.

✓ **Zone 6 (the Northeast)** has a climate similar to the Midwest, except with cooler summers and longer winters. Grow the same types of grasses — all cool-season species, especially Kentucky bluegrass and perennial ryegrass.

✓ **Zone 7 (the eastern transitional zone)** is an area where both warm-season grasses such as Bermuda grass and cool-season grasses such as Kentucky bluegrass grow.

✓ **Zone 8 (the central Southeast)** has a warm, humid, and wet climate year-round. Although the cool-season grass tall fescue may be grown in high-elevation areas, this is primarily warm-season country, best suited for Bermuda grass, zoysia grass, and centipede grass.

✓ **Zone 9 (the Gulf Coast)** is even warmer and wetter than the central Southeast. Along with Bermuda grass and zoysia grass, you can grow centipede grass, Bahia grass, and St. Augustine grass here.

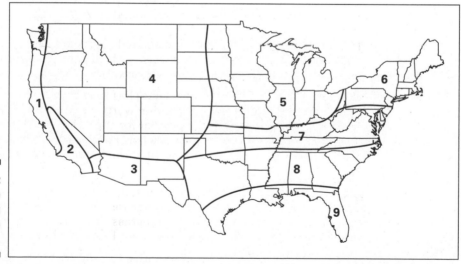

Figure 20-2:
The nine turf-growing zones in the U.S.

Best grass for trouble spots

Anybody can grow a lawn when conditions are perfect. But when they're not so great, you can stack the odds in your favor by choosing grasses that have been proven to succeed under less-than-optimal conditions. Table 20-1 lists some of these varieties.

Table 20-1	Grasses for Trouble Spots	
Condition	*Cool-Season Grasses*	*Warm-Season Grasses*
Shade	Rough bluegrass, fine fescue, tall fescue	St. Augustine grass, centipede grass, Bahia grass
Drought	Tall fescue, perennial ryegrass, fine fescue	Bermuda grass, zoysia grass, Bahia grass
Heat	Perennial ryegrass, tall fescue, fine fescue, Kentucky bluegrass	Bermuda grass, centipede grass, zoysia grass, St. Augustine grass
Cold	Kentucky bluegrass, Canada bluegrass, fine fescue, creeping bent grass	Bermuda grass, zoysia grass, hybrid St. Augustine grass

Researchers recently discovered that some grass species show increased resistance to insect and disease attack, and also need less water and fertilizer, when the grass plants are colonized by beneficial fungi called *endophytes*. So-called endophyte-enhanced lawn seed mixes are now available for home lawns. You can't see the fungi on the lawn; they're inside the grass plant. Also look for grass mixes described as dwarf or semidwarf. These grasses grow more slowly than regular grasses, so they need less water, less fertilizer, and less-frequent mowing.

Endophyte-enhanced seed is only for lawns; it's toxic to livestock and horses, and should not be used in pastures.

Preparing the Soil

When you're planting a new lawn, you have only one chance to get it right. After you plant the grass, you can't easily improve the soil or add amendments, as you can with your vegetable gardens. Here are things you need to do to prepare your soil:

✔ **Test for pH.** The soil should be neutral to slightly acidic; pH 6 to 7 is best. Add enough lime or sulfur to bring the pH to the proper level.

✔ **Add organic matter.** Spread a 1-inch layer of compost, and till it in to a depth of 6 inches.

✔ **Correct any potential drainage problems.** Install drain tiles if necessary. Wet spots attract disease.

✔ **Remove every single weed root.** Allow the prepared soil to rest for a week or two, to allow weeds and weed seeds to sprout; then use a hoe to slice them off just under the soil.

✔ **Rake the soil smooth and level.** Hollows, ruts, and dips cause uneven turf growth, and result in wet or dry patches that encourage disease and attract insect pests.

For more about improving your soil, changing pH, and adding organic matter and other amendments, flip to Chapter 5.

Planting the Lawn

Whether you're planting seed or laying sod, do it during the prime grass-growing time for your area if at all possible. In the northern United States, late summer or early spring is best. In the South, the best time is late spring or late summer. As a rule, it's okay to plant any time when you can count on about a month of temperate and moist weather to follow. That should give your grass enough time to get off to a good start.

If you need a lawn in a hurry, but it's the wrong time to plant, sow a temporary crop of annual ryegrass. The turf comes up fast. While it won't survive a freezing winter, it can help prevent erosion and discourage weed seeds from sprouting until you can replace it with a permanent lawn.

Going for sod

Most people assume that starting a lawn from sod is easier, faster, and more reliable than seeding. Well, at least one of those assumptions is true: It's faster. With sod, you can have a great-looking lawn in one day. But *sodding* (installing sod) requires just as much soil preparation work as seeding and even *more* aftercare. On the other hand, if you plant sod properly and nurse it through its establishment period, your lawn will start out entirely free of undesirable weedy plants, such as dandelions and thistle.

Installing sod

When it comes to installing sod, follow these two important rules for best results: Get the soil thoroughly moist and work quickly. It's also a good idea to get the ground as level as possible and make sure that the soil is good to go before the sod arrives. You don't want to let it sit and dry out in a heap.

If for some reason you can't install the sod immediately, store it in a cool area out of the sun and cover it lightly with a tarp to keep it moist until you can install it. Mist it with water, if necessary, but don't soak it. Wet sod is heavy to work with and may fall apart.

To lay the sod, start at a straight edge, such as a driveway or sidewalk. Lay the sod pieces end to end, making sure that they butt up against each other tightly, with no bare soil showing. When you finish one row, offset the beginning of the next row so that the starting ends of each row are staggered instead of in a line.

Caring for your sod

Even after the entire area has been covered, your job is far from over. Aftercare is critical for success. Follow these steps:

1. **Roll the entire area with a lawn roller to make sure that the sod is in good contact with the soil beneath it.**

   You can rent a roller from any tool-rental agency.

2. **Spread a small amount of topsoil over the sod, and work it into the cracks between strips with a broom.**

3. **Water — and keep watering!**

   The sod needs pampering until the roots dig deep into the soil to forage for their own water. Don't let the sod dry out for four weeks.

4. **Mow the grass when it starts growing vigorously.**

Creating a lawn from seed

If you start your lawn with seed, weeds can and will sprout along with the grass. That's the major disadvantage of seed versus sod. But you have many more improved varieties of seed to choose among. Choosing seed also allows you to add the seeds of other desirable lawn plants, such as clover and white yarrow. Seed is much less expensive than sod, too.

How much seed do you need? That depends on the type of grass you're planting. Use the number on the box to figure how much you need, and buy about one-quarter more than you think you need.

Prepare the soil as described in "Preparing the Soil," earlier in this chapter, and then go over it one more time with a rake to remove all rocks and make the surface as level as possible. Water the area thoroughly.

You can sow the seed with a broadcast or drop spreader. A *broadcast spreader* spins the seeds out in a wide pattern. A *drop spreader* places the seeds in a band between the wheels. If the lawn area is small, you can also sow the seed by hand. No matter how you do it, be careful to get uniform coverage. Here's how:

1. **Divide the seed into two equal lots.**

   If you need to spread 20 pounds of seed, for example, divide the seed into two 10-pound applications.

2. **Adjust your spreader to deliver seed at half the rate recommended on the seed package.**

3. **Sow the first half of the seed across the lawn in rows.**

4. **Sow the second half of the seed in rows at right angles to the first until the whole lawn has been covered.**

5. **Rake very lightly to mix seeds into the top ⅛ to ¼ inch of soil.**

6. **Roll with a water-filled lawn roller.**

To speed germination, mulch the area with organic materials, such as finely shredded compost or dried manure, topsoil, finely chopped straw, or even a thin layer of sawdust. Apply it no more than ¼ inch thick and as evenly as possible. Avoid hay, which contains weed seeds.

Letting the tender grass seedlings dry out will kill them. For complete germination, you must keep the top layer of soil constantly moist. Soak the soil to a 6-inch depth after sowing; then lightly sprinkle by hand or with a sprinkler as often as three to four times daily until the young grass is established.

Allow the young grass to reach its maximum recommended height before mowing. Read "There's more to mowing," later in this chapter, to find the best mowing height for your lawn grass.

Maintaining an Organic Lawn

Maintaining turf without chemicals requires that you understand a little bit about the habits of grass and the problems that plague it. Fortunately, proper mowing, watering, fertilizing, and aerating can go a long way toward preventing pest problems, especially diseases.

There's more to mowing

The lawn mower is your most important turf-maintenance tool. Mowing not only cuts the grass down to size, but done properly, it also helps grass grow thicker. It can reduce the weed population, too, and even feed the turf.

Every type of grass has its own preferred height. Table 20-2 lists how high to set your mower blades. For best results, mow when the grass is no more than 50 percent taller than its optimal height (see Figure 20-3). If your grass should grow to 3 inches, for example, mow it when it reaches 4½ inches tall. In general, mow at the bottom end of the range when the grass is actively growing and at the top end of the range during times of stress or slow growth.

Table 20-2	Best Mowing Heights		
Cool-Season Grasses		*Warm-Season Grasses*	
Bent grass	¼ to ¾ inch	Bahia grass	2 to 3 inches
Chewings fescue	1 to 2 inches	Bermuda grass	½ to 1 inch
Hard fescue	1 to 2 inches	Blue grama grass	2 to 3 inches
Kentucky bluegrass	2 to 3 inches	Buffalo grass	2 to 3 inches
Perennial ryegrass	1½ to 2½ inches	Carpet grass	1 to 2 inches
Red fescue	1½ to 2 inches	Centipede grass	1 to 2 inches
Sheep fescue	2 to 4 inches	St. Augustine grass	1 to 3 inches
Tall fescue	2½ to 3 inches	Zoysia grass	½ to 1 inch

Here's how to get the best cut from your mower:

- Make sure the blade is sharp (sharpen it at least twice per season).
- Vary the mowing direction once a month to avoid soil compaction.
- Don't mow when the grass is wet.
- Overlap by about one-third of the width of the mower deck with each pass.
- Clean the grass off the mower after each mowing.

One of the best things to happen to the organic lawn is the *mulching mower,* which pulverizes grass clippings into smaller pieces than a conventional mower does. Grass clippings are probably the best fertilizer your lawn can get because they provide free and natural nitrogen. When chopped into little bits, the clippings begin to break down into useful nitrogen almost as soon as they hit the ground.

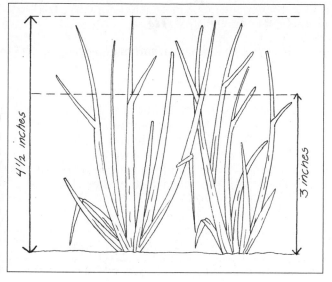

Figure 20-3:
Mow when grass reaches 50 percent taller than the recommended height.

4½ inches

3 inches

Watering

People spend a lot of time, effort, and money keeping their lawns watered. In many parts of the country, that effort is wasted, because the lawn can survive the summer without any supplemental water. To withstand periods of drought, many types of turfgrass enter dormancy. They stop growing and turn brown. But when the rains return, the grass springs back to life. Sometimes, raising an organic lawn means putting up with an unattractive lawn for a while instead of using precious water resources. If and when you do irrigate your lawn, you must water deeply and slowly. Follow these tips:

✔ **Water long enough to moisten the soil to a depth of 6 to 12 inches.** The amount of time it takes to achieve this goal depends not only on the sprinkler, but also on the type of soil under the lawn.

Standing out on the front lawn in the evening with a hose in hand does more harm than good. You'd have to stand out there for hours and hours to apply an adequate amount of water. Plus shallow sprinkling makes the roots lazy; if they get a little bit of water regularly, they become conditioned to staying near the surface of the soil. If you stop watering, your lawn will die of drought because the roots haven't grown deep enough to forage for their own water.

✔ **Apply water slowly enough so that it doesn't puddle or run off your lawn.** Look for a sprinkler with a low flow rate of less than ¼ inch of water per hour, especially if you have clay soil. On such heavy soil, you may need to cycle your watering by turning the water on for 15 minutes, off for 15 minutes, on again, and so on.

In general, high-quality oscillating and impulse sprinklers offer the most uniform coverage and cover the most ground.

The best time of day to water your lawn is early morning, which features cooler temperatures. You'll lose less water to evaporation than at midday, and the grass blades will dry quickly, minimizing disease problems.

Feeding the lawn

Grass needs more nitrogen than any other nutrient for strong growth, and because it grows almost continuously, it needs a constant supply. Grass clippings themselves provide some natural fertilizer, but you can use several other organic materials to feed your lawn as well.

Natural fertilizers contain nitrogen that doesn't dissolve readily in water but needs a little help from soil microorganisms to become available for plants. That's good. It means that the nitrogen is released slowly, and consequently, the lawn grows slowly and steadily. Synthetic chemical lawn fertilizers, on the other hand, tend to release lots of nitrogen all at once, which makes the lawn grow fast at first, adding to your mowing chores. Also, chemical lawn fertilizers are among the largest sources of water pollution in the country.

Figuring out how much fertilizer you need

Your lawn probably needs less nitrogen than you think. You can figure out how much nitrogen to apply by using the following steps:

1. **Find the amount of actual nitrogen required by the type of grass in your lawn.**

   Cool-season fescues need 1 to 3 pounds of nitrogen per year per 1,000 square feet. Kentucky bluegrass and perennial ryegrass need 2 to 3 pounds, and bent grasses prefer 2 to 6 pounds. Warm-season blue grama and buffalo grasses need only ½ to 1 pound of nitrogen; Bermuda and carpet grasses need 1 to 3 pounds; Bahia, centipede, and zoysia grasses need 2 to 3 pounds; and St. Augustine grass needs 3 to 6 pounds.

   If you don't know the predominant type of grass in your lawn, dig up a sample and take it to your local extension office or a full-service nursery for identification. Or start with 1 pound of actual nitrogen per 1,000 square feet twice a year; that's a safe maintenance dose.

2. **Find the percentage of actual nitrogen in the fertilizer you want to use.**

   See Chapter 6 for naturally nitrogen-rich fertilizers and the percentage of nitrogen they contain.

3. **Plug those numbers into the following formula to determine exactly how much material you need to feed your lawn:**

Pounds of nitrogen that grass requires per year ÷ percentage of nitrogen in the fertilizer = pounds of fertilizer required per year per 1,000 square feet.

Kentucky bluegrass, for example, requires 2 pounds of actual nitrogen per year, per 1,000 square feet. A bag of 10-6-4 organic lawn fertilizer contains 10 percent actual nitrogen, and 2 divided by .10 (10 percent converted to decimal) equals 20. So 1,000 square feet of Kentucky bluegrass would require 20 pounds of 10-6-4 fertilizer per year.

4. **Divide the pounds of fertilizer required per year by the number of applications you plan to make.**

   If you plan to fertilize your lawn twice, for example, divide the answer you get in Step 3 by 2 to find the amount you need for each application.

Just by leaving the grass clippings on the lawn to decompose, you're adding the equivalent of about 1 pound of nitrogen per 1,000 square feet. Consider this fact in your fertilizer calculations.

Many homeowners think of their property in terms of acres rather than square feet. A ¼-acre lot is roughly 10,000 square feet. Subtract the square footage of nonlawn areas to get the approximate size of your lawn.

Knowing when to feed

Most folks go into a lawn-feeding frenzy at the first sign of spring, but for most of the country, that's not the best time to feed the grass. It's better to fertilize in autumn in cold climates. That practice helps the grass grow strong and packs away some nutrients for the following year. In warmer climates, the best time to feed is late spring, after the grass breaks out of dormancy and begins to grow again. Warm-season grasses need regular feeding to survive the stressful summer months. Cold-season grasses usually can get by with just one or two feedings per year.

If you want to green up your lawn quickly and naturally, use a hose-end sprayer to apply liquid seaweed. The iron in the seaweed encourages a rich green color.

Thinking about thatch

As grass plant parts die, they can form a tangled mat of undecomposed or partially decomposed organic matter on the surface of the soil called *thatch*. A little thatch is a good thing. If it's less than ¼ to ½ inch thick, thatch helps cool and cushion the soil, as well as conserve moisture. Thick thatch may cause problems, however. A layer more than ½ inch thick keeps water and nutrients from reaching the soil and provides a cozy home for turf-destroying insects and diseases.

If thatch builds up on your lawn, remove it, or *dethatch* the lawn. For small areas, you can use a thatch rake (sometimes called a *cavex rake*) to scratch the thatch from the soil. This job is backbreaking work, however, so try it only on small lawns. For large areas, rent a *dethatcher* (also called a *vertical mower*). This gasoline-powered device cuts the thatch and lifts it to the surface, where you can easily rake it up.

Loosening the soil

The soil under a lawn takes a lot of abuse. You walk and run over it, stand on it, run a heavy mower over it regularly, and sometimes even drive over it. The result is compaction that slows the growth of the grass. With you can't turn and condition the soil every year for a lawn, there is a specialized way to cure lawn compaction and invigorate the soil: aeration.

Aeration is simply the process of creating holes in the turf. Done right, it removes cores of compacted soil, leaving room for air, water, and nutrients to penetrate. On small lawns, you can aerate by hand. For less than $20, you can buy a hand aerator that uses foot power to remove cores of soil. For large lawns, you can rent a power aerator from the local tool-rental shop. Steer it over the lawn like a lawn mower as it jams its tines into the turf, removing cores of soil in the process.

With either implement, the next step is to break up the cores and leave them on the surface of the lawn to decompose — or, if you find the waste too unsightly, rake it up and toss it into the compost heap. If you use your lawn heavily, aerate once a year, just like they do down at the ball field.

Top-dressing

Most lawn owners neglect one very important organic lawn-care practice: *top-dressing,* which is simply spreading a thin layer of organic matter over the lawn. No, it's not fertilizing per se, but it does improve the soil and can provide nutrients depending on the material used. Top-dressing is vital because you don't dig up the lawn every year; the only way to improve the soil is from the top down.

Top-dressing is a simple process. In autumn, spread a very thin (about ¼ inch deep) layer of organic matter over the lawn. Use topsoil, shredded compost, or any other organic matter. The material works its way down through the sod, with the help of earthworms and other critters, to improve the texture of the soil. You can make the process even more effective by aerating the turf first (refer to "Loosening the soil," earlier in this chapter).

Weeding

The best way to defeat weeds is to grow a healthy, thick sod. Fertilizing, watering, and mowing properly all make the grass thicker, which makes it tougher for weeds to get a foothold. In fact, correct mowing alone can help control certain types of weeds. University experiments show that mowing a bluegrass lawn at a height of 2 inches helps reduce the amount of crabgrass in a lawn significantly. Mowing your lawn higher helps the grass outcompete low-growing weeds, such as crabgrass and creeping Charlie.

You can also use old-fashioned elbow grease. When you find weeds in your lawn, pull 'em or chop them out. Long-handled specialty weeding tools for the lawn, such as the Houn Dog Weeder and the Speedy Weeder, make a surprisingly fast and easy job of pulling dandelions, plantain, and other lawn weeds.

Recently, some natural herbicides have become available that give organic-lawn owners a lucky break. Corn gluten meal is a highly effective natural turf herbicide. It works as a pre-emergent to kill sprouting plantain, creeping bent grass, dandelion, and many other weed seeds. Apply 25 pounds per 1,250 square feet in spring before weeds begin to sprout. Don't apply it to newly seeded lawns, however. Corn gluten meal also contains about 10 percent nitrogen, so it serves double duty on the lawn. For already growing weeds, you can also try Sharpshooter, a broad-spectrum, soap-based organic herbicide that kills all vegetation on contact. Use it with caution, because it kills grass as well as weeds. For more on weeds and weeding, turn to Chapter 11.

 Perhaps the best way to deal with weeds is to change your definition of them. Take clover, for example. Just because clover isn't a grass plant doesn't mean that it doesn't belong in the lawn. Clover stays green through tough weather, recovers nicely from mowing, and is soft and cushiony. Also, unlike grass, it increases the fertility of the soil by taking nitrogen from the air and making it available to plant roots in the soil. Other so-called weeds, such as yarrow and Roman chamomile, attract beneficial insects.

Managing pests

Although a long list of insects may chow down on grass, only a few pests really do serious damage to turfgrass, and organic treatments exist for all of them. The most notorious and damaging turf pest is the grub, which is an immature beetle that lives in the soil. Grubs, especially the larvae of Japanese beetles, can do a number on turf. They feast on grass roots and kill the plants in the process. Pull up a patch of sod, and if you see a dozen grubs per square foot, it's time to take action. Here are two biological controls for grubs:

✔ **Milky spore disease:** This bacteria species infects and kills grubs. Apply at a rate of 4 ounces per 1,000 square feet any time the grubs are active. It works best in areas where the soil temperature remains above 70 degrees Fahrenheit for several months a year.

✔ **Beneficial nematodes:** Spray these microscopic worms onto the soil, and they begin killing grubs within 48 hours and continue their grub-killing duty for months. In the process, they also eliminate cutworms and armyworms. Flip to Chapter 8 for more on milky spore disease, beneficial nematodes, and other safe pest controls.

Intensive turfgrass breeding has yielded several new varieties of grass that actually resist damage from greenbugs, armyworms, billbugs, cutworms, and sob webworms. Look for the tall-fescue variety Apache and several perennial varieties, including Premier, All Star, Cowboy, Prelude, Sunrise, Pennant, Citation II, and Repell. Also look for endophyte-enhanced lawn seed mixes that minimize insect damage (refer to "Best grass for trouble spots," earlier in this chapter).

Switching to Lawn Alternatives

Lawns just don't belong in some places, and trying to grow grass where it won't thrive is just going to cause heartache. Grass doesn't like shade. It doesn't like wet roots. Sometimes it can't stand too much foot traffic. It doesn't like hard and dry soil. In situations like these, you may do better to find a substitute for turfgrass that enjoys the conditions you have.

Using low-maintenance grass

If you really want a lawn, but your conditions just don't suit most turfgrasses, consider a tough-as-nails native grass instead. Two native grasses — buffalo grass and blue grama grass — work well in hot, dry conditions with little maintenance. You can mow and maintain them as a lawn or let them grow as meadow grasses.

✔ **Buffalo grass** is a Plains native and as such has adapted to survive with very little water. It makes an attractive fine-textured lawn when watered and mowed; it's also an ornamental prairie grass when it's allowed to go dormant during periods of low rainfall. For the best-looking lawn, mow it high — 2 to 3 inches high — to discourage weeds. Despite its tolerance to heat, sun, and hard dry soil, buffalo grass doesn't like shade or sandy, wet soils.

> ✔ **Blue grama grass** is another North American native. This bunch-type grass forms a dense sod of fine-bladed grass. During drought, it goes dormant and turns brown. It requires little fertilizer, no watering, and only infrequent mowing while surviving extreme heat and cold.

Growing ground covers

When you're trying to fill a shady spot where grass won't grow or reducing the size of your lawn, you're likely to look for ground covers. By their very nature, ground covers are low-growing plants that spread rapidly to colonize large expanses. Good ground-cover options include partridgeberry *(Mitchella repens),* wild ginger *(Asarum canadense),* Allegheny spurge *(Pachysandra procumbens),* and creeping phlox *(Phlox stolonifera).* Many taller perennials would make fine shade garden plants; see Chapter 17 for ideas.

Some of the fastest-growing ground covers can quickly become troublesome, invasive plants. Ajuga, lily of the valley, pachysandra, periwinkle, and (to a lesser extent) liriope are common, readily available, shade-tolerant ground covers that are also notoriously invasive.

Sun-loving, noninvasive ground covers include *Phlox subulata,* three-toothed cinquefoil *(Sibbaldiopsis tridentata,* formerly *Potentilla tridentata),* and golden-star or green-and-gold *(Chrysogonum virginianum).*

Making a meadow

Meadows and prairies sound too good to be true, and in a way, they are. Despite the common belief that making a meadow involves little more than sowing some seeds and allowing nature to take its course, meadows require more work than that. It's true that after it's established, a meadow or prairie takes less time and labor than a lawn or a flower bed. But getting a meadow started takes just as much preparation and labor as establishing a lawn.

You can plant a meadow or prairie in either of two simple ways. If you start with bare ground, follow this procedure:

1. **Prepare the area as you would for a lawn.**

   Rotary-till the top few inches of soil and rake it smooth, removing as many weed roots, stolons, and tubers as possible.

2. **Sow a low-maintenance, clump-forming grass, such as sheep fescue, in cold climates or buffalo grass in warmer areas.**

Avoid grasses that spread by runners or stolons. Sow it at one-half the recommended rate.

3. **Plant transplants or sow wildflower seed at random spots, about 2 or 3 feet apart, throughout the area.**

   Keep those spots grass free until the wildflower plants are established.

A less labor-intensive way to establish a meadow is to plant in existing turf. Remove patches of turf throughout the lawn, and replace it with wildflower plants or seeds. Gradually remove more and more of the lawn each year.

Table 20-3 list good meadow grasses and prairie plants for the different regions of the United States.

Table 20-3	Meadow Grasses and Prairie Plants
Eastern and Midwestern U.S.	*Plain and Western States*
Purple coneflower (*Echinacea purpurea*)	Pale lobelia (*Lobelia spicata*)
Queen of the prairie (*Filipendula rubra*)	Boneset (*Eupatorium perfoliatum*)
Butterfly weed (*Asclepias tuberosa*)	Prairie coreopsis (*Coreopsia palmata*)
Meadowsweet (*Spirea latifolia*)	Pale purple coneflower (*Echinacea pallida*)
Bee balm (*Monarda didyma*)	Big bluestem grass (*Andropogon Gerardii*)
	Prairie dropseed (*Sporobolus heterolepsis*)
	Flowering spurge (*Euphorbia corollaata*)
	Prairie smoke (*Geum trifloorum*)

Part V
The Part of Tens

The 5th Wave   By Rich Tennant

"That should do it."

In this part . . .

If you like lists as much as I do, welcome to Part V. It's also a good place to get started if you want to be an organic gardener but really don't know what to do first. This part sums up the major principles and techniques of organic gardening in a few short pages and offers ideas for making your home and landscape more eco-friendly.

Chapter 21

Ten Best Organic Gardening Practices

In This Chapter
▶ Combining the best strategies
▶ Beating the pests naturally
▶ Promoting plant health

The most successful organic gardeners use a combination of strategies to grow healthy food and ornamental plants. They monitor and increase soil fertility, observe and emulate nature, and make planting decisions based on the needs of the plants and opportunities of the site. Organic gardeners see their gardens as small parts of the larger natural world and understand that their gardening practices have an impact that goes far beyond the borders of their yards. If you're just getting started, though, all these practices can seem daunting — even discouraging. Keep in mind that gardening is a process, and take it one step at a time. Add the ten practices in this chapter one at a time, and you'll be gardening organically before you know it.

Enrich Your Soil

Plant health starts with the soil, so it makes sense to put this organic gardening practice at the top of the list. Get your soil right, and many other potential problems are apt to be less troublesome.

Soil is composed of various sizes and shapes of mineral particles, which give it texture. You can't do much to alter your soil's texture except bring in loads of sand or topsoil, but you can change the other soil components: organic matter, air, water, and soil organisms. Organic matter, which decomposes into humus, increases soil's ability to hold moisture and drain efficiently, feeds the beneficial soil organisms, and adds important plant nutrients. You can increase the amount of organic matter in your soil by adding compost and using plant-based mulches, such as shredded leaves, bark, and straw. Make your own compost, as described in Chapter 5, or buy it in bags or bulk from a local nursery.

You can improve the ratio of air and water in your soil, too, by avoiding excessive tilling, compacting the soil as little as possible, and adding organic matter.

Mulch Early, Mulch Often

Weeds flourish on open ground, but mulch can slow them — or even stop them in their tracks. Surround your garden and landscape plants with bark, pine needles, grass clippings, shredded leaves, straw, and other organic materials to shade the ground and keep weeds from sprouting. Use landscape fabric or newspaper in paths and around trees and shrubs, covering them with loose mulch materials.

Grow living mulches, too: Sow cover crops in empty vegetable garden beds and over the whole garden at the end of the growing season to crowd out weeds. Find out more about mulches and cover crops in Chapter 11.

Choose Healthy and Disease-Resistant Plants

Your plants won't get sick if they're immune to or at least tolerant of the nastiest diseases. Plant breeders work long and hard to develop varieties of your favorite fruits, vegetables, flowers, and landscape plants that fight off devastating diseases. Read catalog descriptions and plant tags to find resistant plants whenever possible. It also pays to buy and plant only healthy plants. Take time to find the healthiest specimens, as I describe in Chapter 12. Don't bring home any insect-infested plants, either. If you have any doubts about a plant's health, quarantine a new plant in a separate area before adding it to your landscape or garden.

Put Plants in the Right Place

Struggling plants attract diseases and insects, but thriving plants fight them off. Give your plants the soil, sun, and moisture conditions they prefer to keep them healthy and thriving. Consider native plants that naturally grow in your region or in a similar climate. If you have an established garden, replace the unhappy campers with plants that have a can-do attitude. Use the observation and planning steps in Chapter 3 to inventory what your yard has to offer; then find plants with needs that match.

Use Organic, Slow-Release Fertilizers

Many synthetic fertilizers contain highly soluble nutrients that force plants into quick, lush growth. Although this growth may seem like a good thing, it's not; succulent growth is very attractive to insect and disease pests. Also, any fertilizer that isn't taken up immediately by plants may run off and pollute waterways. Most organic fertilizers are the slow-release kind. The nutrients are bound up in large molecules and are released slowly through the action of microorganisms. Plants receive a slow, steady diet of nutrients, and the risk of runoff is minimized. See Chapter 6 for full details on fertilizers.

Encourage Beneficial Organisms

Each harmful insect has a predator or parasite that attacks it, making your work easier. You can cheer these helpmates by planting flowers and other plants that they're attracted to and by avoiding the use of pesticides. Other garden visitors — including birds, bats, and toads — can also help you in your pest control efforts, so welcome them into your landscape.

Many crops require pollination by visiting insects, and unfortunately, the populations of many native pollinating insects are in decline. Invite these important garden denizens by providing food and shelter, in addition to avoiding pesticides. Chapter 7 gives you more information on beneficial creatures versus pests.

Practice Integrated Pest Management

Integrated pest management (IPM for short) is the practice of looking at all the costs and options before deciding on a course of pest treatment. Instead of merely eradicating pests, you manage them. In practicing IPM, you do the following:

- **Monitor the weather carefully.** The appearance of many insects and diseases is tied closely to the temperature, humidity, and time of the year.

- **Monitor pests.** It doesn't make sense to treat for pests unless they're causing serious damage. A few pests may be insignificant and tolerable in the big picture.

✔ **Keep everything clean.** Practice good cultural techniques: Rotate crops from one part of the garden to another, destroy harmful weeds, and clean up infested plant debris.

✔ **Use the least invasive and least toxic control methods first.** Start with nontoxic controls, such as dislodging insects with a strong blast of water.

Control Pests with Traps and Barriers

Sometimes, protecting your crops from insects is as easy as throwing a fabric row cover over them. If the cabbage moths can't reach your broccoli to lay their eggs, for example, you won't find caterpillars in your vegetables. A strip of newspaper wrapped around the tender stem of a seedling can prevent a cutworm from chewing through it. You can foil many common pests with specially colored, sticky-coated traps. See Chapter 8 for more ideas.

You can also use insects' own attractants against them. *Pheromones,* which are scents secreted by insects to attract a mate, are among the most powerful tools in your pest control kit. Pheromone baits combined with traps are the downfall of millions of Japanese beetles and other pests every year. These baits attract only the pests you want to eradicate, so they're safe to use around beneficial insects.

Avoid the Most Toxic Pesticides

Commonly available synthetic pesticides are some of the most toxic materials used by homeowners. Fortunately, gardeners who choose or need to use some pesticides have organic alternatives to synthetic chemicals. Even organic pesticides, however, such as pyrethrum and neem, can harm beneficial organisms. Always follow the label directions precisely if you choose to use pesticides, and use them as a last resort. See Chapters 7 and 8 for more information on managing pests without pesticide sprays.

Promote Diversity

Natural plant populations contain many species scattered over a large area, making them less vulnerable to insect and pest eradication. Use the same concepts in your garden by mixing crops within a row and avoiding large patches of the same variety. Instead of planting a long hedge made up of a dozen or more specimens of the same species of shrub, for example, consider designing a mixed border that includes a variety of evergreens and perhaps some flowering and fruiting small trees and shrubs.

Chapter 22

Ten Ways to be Eco-Friendly

In This Chapter

▶ Let it be

▶ Observe the three Rs: Reduce, reuse, recycle

▶ Plan and plant for the future

*B*eing eco-friendly means more than simply not spraying chemicals. You can minimize your ecological footprint, both in what you do and in what you don't do. Here are some ways to conserve resources, reuse and recycle, and minimize the environmental effect of activities in your home and landscape.

Don't Be a Perfectionist

Seeking perfection — unblemished red apples, long straight stems topped by curvaceous rosebuds, or a lawn with nary a dandelion in sight — is tempting. Usually, though, that perfection just isn't worth the effort and the resources required. If you tend to be a perfectionist, consider a change of perspective. I find perfection in many things, such as a balanced ecosystem of plants, insects, and microorganisms that benefit one another. I find it in a lesson learned from experience. I find it in the satisfaction of knowing that I did my best.

If you must have perfection in your garden, choose one thing and nurture it well, but let the rest be what it will. My own obsession is a neatly tended patch of blueberry bushes. Visitors find weeds in my lawn and gardens, but not in the blueberries!

Reduce, Reuse, and Recycle

Before you buy a product, consider its useful life and what will happen to it when you're through with it. Is it something that will last a long time? Can you reuse or at least recycle it? Reducing the number of throwaway products is an important part of an eco-friendly lifestyle. Similarly, look for products with minimal or at least recyclable packaging.

Before you throw anything away, consider whether it could be of use to someone else. Used plastic pots, for example, may be trash to you, but organizers of a local school garden may welcome them.

Compost Kitchen Scraps and Yard Debris

Layer kitchen scraps with lawn clippings, chopped dry leaves, shredded twigs and plant stalks, and other landscape and garden debris to make rich compost. Composting recycles the nutrients contained in organic materials. My family keeps a small plastic bucket with a lid right in the kitchen sink, and that bucket is where all our eggshells, teabags, fruit and vegetable scraps, and inedible leftovers go. When it's full, my uncomplaining spouse carries it out to spread in the compost bin. (I love that man.) Our composting habit keeps our trash can smelling better, makes the earthworms happy, and keeps our dog from getting fat. Flip to Chapter 5 for details on how to make your own compost pile.

Reduce (Or Eliminate) Your Lawn

Reducing or eliminating your lawn is a great way to cut your water bill, especially if you live where less than 30 inches of rain falls during the growing season. (Spread out evenly over the span of a growing season, 30 inches of rain equals about 1 inch of water a week — the amount of water that lawns need to grow well.) Even if you live where water is plentiful, making your lawn smaller makes ecological sense.

In the many parts of the western United States, water is diverted from distant rivers and springs so that city residents can have plenty of water. Although much of the diverted water is necessary for city survival, using it on lawns is a questionable practice at best. Moving water from where it's plentiful to where it isn't takes energy. Many gardeners worry about the fumes that lawn mowers make, and that concern is a valid one. But power plants also spew out fumes as they create electricity for the water pumps that move the water through the pipes over the mountains and across the deserts to the lawn sprinklers.

If you must have a lawn, make it smaller. Think of it as an appetizer instead of the main course. Plant drought-tolerant grasses, and use the water-saving tips in Chapter 20.

Plant a Tree

The list of reasons why trees are good for the environment is long, and you've probably heard many of the them before: wildlife habitat, shade, erosion control, increased property value, wind protection, and carbon dioxide trapping, to name a few. Trees are also beautiful in their own right. To plant a tree is to plan for the future — your children's future, your neighborhood's future, your planet's future. Check out Chapter 19 for information about good trees and how to plant them.

Choose Human-Powered Equipment

Whenever possible, choose tools powered by old-fashioned elbow grease. Think rakes and brooms instead of leaf blowers, for example. Although electric- and battery-powered equipment creates less on-site pollution than gasoline-powered tools, keep in mind that the electricity they use has to be generated somewhere, invariably causing some degree of pollution — just not in your backyard. If you have a small lawn, consider a new, high-quality version of the traditional reel mower. This type of mower is quiet and easy to push.

Minimize All Forms of Pollution

The fumes from your two-stroke, oil-burning, gas-powered string trimmer — and the loud noise it makes — are obvious sources of air and noise pollution. Keep your eyes out for more subtle types, too. Evaluate your landscape lighting, and eliminate unnecessary lights to decrease light pollution, for example. Consider quiet, solar-powered pumps for fountains.

Teach Your Children Well

Helping children discover the pleasures of gardening and connecting with the natural world ensures that future generations will become eco-friendly, too. Start small by sprouting seeds together or talking about the plants you see on a walk. Name the vegetables and fruits in the supermarket, and talk about where and how they grow. For more great ideas about gardening with children at home and in schools, visit the National Gardening Association's Kidsgardening Web site at www.kidsgardening.com.

Become a Locavore

Most of us can't grow all our own food, but we can strive to eat locally produced foods harvested at their peak of flavor and nutrition. Support local farmers by buying direct from the farm and at local farmers' markets. Or join a CSA (Community Supported Agriculture) organization, which is essentially a subscription for locally produced foods. You pay a certain amount to the farmer up front, usually in early spring, and then receive weekly deliveries of produce, flowers, fruit, eggs, or other farm products.

Many small farms are organic; those that aren't usually use ecologically sound practices. Ask the farmers, and they'll be happy to tell you about their farming philosophy and techniques. For products that can't be grown locally, such as coffee and chocolate, look for organic options. Also, some companies sell products described as "fair trade" or "sustainably grown" that benefit both the environment and family farmers in their native countries.

Consider the Seventh Generation

According to The Great Law of the Iroquois, "In every deliberation we must consider the impact on the seventh generation." By looking at all your decisions through this lens, you'll choose activities and products that have a minimum negative effect on the environment. After all, don't you want your great-great-great-great-great-grandchildren to inherit a vibrant, ecologically diverse Earth that is able to sustain them and their progeny? Maintaining your gardens and landscape by using organic techniques is one step toward this goal.

Index

• D •

• M •

• N •

• O •

• Z •

BUSINESS, CAREERS & PERSONAL FINANCE

counting For Dummies, 4th Edition*
8-0-470-24600-9

ookkeeping Workbook For Dummies†
8-0-470-16983-4

ommodities For Dummies
8-0-470-04928-0

ing Business in China For Dummies
8-0-470-04929-7

E-Mail Marketing For Dummies
978-0-470-19087-6

Job Interviews For Dummies, 3rd Edition*†
978-0-470-17748-8

Personal Finance Workbook For Dummies*†
978-0-470-09933-9

Real Estate License Exams For Dummies
978-0-7645-7623-2

Six Sigma For Dummies
978-0-7645-6798-8

Small Business Kit For Dummies,
2nd Edition*†
978-0-7645-5984-6

Telephone Sales For Dummies
978-0-470-16836-3

BUSINESS PRODUCTIVITY & MICROSOFT OFFICE

cess 2007 For Dummies
8-0-470-03649-5

cel 2007 For Dummies
8-0-470-03737-9

ffice 2007 For Dummies
8-0-470-00923-9

tlook 2007 For Dummies
8-0-470-03830-7

PowerPoint 2007 For Dummies
978-0-470-04059-1

Project 2007 For Dummies
978-0-470-03651-8

QuickBooks 2008 For Dummies
978-0-470-18470-7

Quicken 2008 For Dummies
978-0-470-17473-9

Salesforce.com For Dummies,
2nd Edition
978-0-470-04893-1

Word 2007 For Dummies
978-0-470-03658-7

EDUCATION, HISTORY, REFERENCE & TEST PREPARATION

rican American History For Dummies
8-0-7645-5469-8

gebra For Dummies
8-0-7645-5325-7

gebra Workbook For Dummies
8-0-7645-8467-1

t History For Dummies
8-0-470-09910-0

ASVAB For Dummies, 2nd Edition
978-0-470-10671-6

British Military History For Dummies
978-0-470-03213-8

Calculus For Dummies
978-0-7645-2498-1

Canadian History For Dummies, 2nd Edition
978-0-470-83656-9

Geometry Workbook For Dummies
978-0-471-79940-5

The SAT I For Dummies, 6th Edition
978-0-7645-7193-0

Series 7 Exam For Dummies
978-0-470-09932-2

World History For Dummies
978-0-7645-5242-7

FOOD, GARDEN, HOBBIES & HOME

idge For Dummies, 2nd Edition
8-0-471-92426-5

in Collecting For Dummies, 2nd Edition
8-0-470-22275-1

oking Basics For Dummies, 3rd Edition
8-0-7645-7206-7

Drawing For Dummies
978-0-7645-5476-6

Etiquette For Dummies, 2nd Edition
978-0-470-10672-3

Gardening Basics For Dummies*†
978-0-470-03749-2

Knitting Patterns For Dummies
978-0-470-04556-5

Living Gluten-Free For Dummies†
978-0-471-77383-2

Painting Do-It-Yourself For Dummies
978-0-470-17533-0

HEALTH, SELF HELP, PARENTING & PETS

ger Management For Dummies
8-0-470-03715-7

xiety & Depression Workbook
r Dummies
8-0-7645-9793-0

eting For Dummies, 2nd Edition
8-0-7645-4149-0

g Training For Dummies, 2nd Edition
8-0-7645-8418-3

Horseback Riding For Dummies
978-0-470-09719-9

Infertility For Dummies†
978-0-470-11518-3

Meditation For Dummies with CD-ROM,
2nd Edition
978-0-471-77774-8

Post-Traumatic Stress Disorder For Dummies
978-0-470-04922-8

Puppies For Dummies, 2nd Edition
978-0-470-03717-1

Thyroid For Dummies, 2nd Edition†
978-0-471-78755-6

Type 1 Diabetes For Dummies*†
978-0-470-17811-9

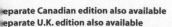

WILEY

INTERNET & DIGITAL MEDIA

AdWords For Dummies
978-0-470-15252-2

Blogging For Dummies, 2nd Edition
978-0-470-23017-6

Digital Photography All-in-One Desk Reference For Dummies, 3rd Edition
978-0-470-03743-0

Digital Photography For Dummies, 5th Edition
978-0-7645-9802-9

Digital SLR Cameras & Photography For Dummies, 2nd Edition
978-0-470-14927-0

eBay Business All-in-One Desk Reference For Dummies
978-0-7645-8438-1

eBay For Dummies, 5th Edition*
978-0-470-04529-9

eBay Listings That Sell For Dummies
978-0-471-78912-3

Facebook For Dummies
978-0-470-26273-3

The Internet For Dummies, 11th Edition
978-0-470-12174-0

Investing Online For Dummies, 5th Edition
978-0-7645-8456-5

iPod & iTunes For Dummies, 5th Edition
978-0-470-17474-6

MySpace For Dummies
978-0-470-09529-4

Podcasting For Dummies
978-0-471-74898-4

Search Engine Optimization For Dummies, 2nd Edition
978-0-471-97998-2

Second Life For Dummies
978-0-470-18025-9

Starting an eBay Business For Dummies, 3rd Edition†
978-0-470-14924-9

GRAPHICS, DESIGN & WEB DEVELOPMENT

Adobe Creative Suite 3 Design Premium All-in-One Desk Reference For Dummies
978-0-470-11724-8

Adobe Web Suite CS3 All-in-One Desk Reference For Dummies
978-0-470-12099-6

AutoCAD 2008 For Dummies
978-0-470-11650-0

Building a Web Site For Dummies, 3rd Edition
978-0-470-14928-7

Creating Web Pages All-in-One Desk Reference For Dummies, 3rd Edition
978-0-470-09629-1

Creating Web Pages For Dummies, 8th Edition
978-0-470-08030-6

Dreamweaver CS3 For Dummies
978-0-470-11490-2

Flash CS3 For Dummies
978-0-470-12100-9

Google SketchUp For Dummies
978-0-470-13744-4

InDesign CS3 For Dummies
978-0-470-11865-8

Photoshop CS3 All-in-One Desk Reference For Dummies
978-0-470-11195-6

Photoshop CS3 For Dummies
978-0-470-11193-2

Photoshop Elements 5 For Dummies
978-0-470-09810-3

SolidWorks For Dummies
978-0-7645-9555-4

Visio 2007 For Dummies
978-0-470-08983-5

Web Design For Dummies, 2nd Edition
978-0-471-78117-2

Web Sites Do-It-Yourself For Dummies
978-0-470-16903-2

Web Stores Do-It-Yourself For Dummies
978-0-470-17443-2

LANGUAGES, RELIGION & SPIRITUALITY

Arabic For Dummies
978-0-471-77270-5

Chinese For Dummies, Audio Set
978-0-470-12766-7

French For Dummies
978-0-7645-5193-2

German For Dummies
978-0-7645-5195-6

Hebrew For Dummies
978-0-7645-5489-6

Ingles Para Dummies
978-0-7645-5427-8

Italian For Dummies, Audio Set
978-0-470-09586-7

Italian Verbs For Dummies
978-0-471-77389-4

Japanese For Dummies
978-0-7645-5429-2

Latin For Dummies
978-0-7645-5431-5

Portuguese For Dummies
978-0-471-78738-9

Russian For Dummies
978-0-471-78001-4

Spanish Phrases For Dummies
978-0-7645-7204-3

Spanish For Dummies
978-0-7645-5194-9

Spanish For Dummies, Audio Set
978-0-470-09585-0

The Bible For Dummies
978-0-7645-5296-0

Catholicism For Dummies
978-0-7645-5391-2

The Historical Jesus For Dummies
978-0-470-16785-4

Islam For Dummies
978-0-7645-5503-9

Spirituality For Dummies, 2nd Edition
978-0-470-19142-2

NETWORKING AND PROGRAMMING

ASP.NET 3.5 For Dummies
978-0-470-19592-5

C# 2008 For Dummies
978-0-470-19109-5

Hacking For Dummies, 2nd Edition
978-0-470-05235-8

Home Networking For Dummies, 4th Edition
978-0-470-11806-1

Java For Dummies, 4th Edition
978-0-470-08716-9

Microsoft® SQL Server™ 2008 All-in-One Desk Reference For Dummies
978-0-470-17954-3

Networking All-in-One Desk Reference For Dummies, 2nd Edition
978-0-7645-9939-2

Networking For Dummies, 8th Edition
978-0-470-05620-2

SharePoint 2007 For Dummies
978-0-470-09941-4

Wireless Home Networking For Dummies, 2nd Edition
978-0-471-74940-0

PERATING SYSTEMS & COMPUTER BASICS

Iac For Dummies, 5th Edition
8-0-7645-8458-9

Iptops For Dummies, 2nd Edition
8-0-470-05432-1

nux For Dummies, 8th Edition
8-0-470-11649-4

lacBook For Dummies
8-0-470-04859-7

**lac OS X Leopard All-in-One
esk Reference For Dummies**
8-0-470-05434-5

Mac OS X Leopard For Dummies
978-0-470-05433-8

Macs For Dummies, 9th Edition
978-0-470-04849-8

PCs For Dummies, 11th Edition
978-0-470-13728-4

Windows® Home Server For Dummies
978-0-470-18592-6

Windows Server 2008 For Dummies
978-0-470-18043-3

**Windows Vista All-in-One
Desk Reference For Dummies**
978-0-471-74941-7

Windows Vista For Dummies
978-0-471-75421-3

Windows Vista Security For Dummies
978-0-470-11805-4

PORTS, FITNESS & MUSIC

aching Hockey For Dummies
8-0-470-83685-9

aching Soccer For Dummies
8-0-471-77381-8

tness For Dummies, 3rd Edition
8-0-7645-7851-9

otball For Dummies, 3rd Edition
8-0-470-12536-6

GarageBand For Dummies
978-0-7645-7323-1

Golf For Dummies, 3rd Edition
978-0-471-76871-5

Guitar For Dummies, 2nd Edition
978-0-7645-9904-0

**Home Recording For Musicians
For Dummies, 2nd Edition**
978-0-7645-8884-6

**iPod & iTunes For Dummies,
5th Edition**
978-0-470-17474-6

Music Theory For Dummies
978-0-7645-7838-0

Stretching For Dummies
978-0-470-06741-3

Get smart @ dummies.com®

- Find a full list of Dummies titles
- Look into loads of FREE on-site articles
- Sign up for FREE eTips e-mailed to you weekly
- See what other products carry the Dummies name
- Shop directly from the Dummies bookstore
- Enter to win new prizes every month!

eparate Canadian edition also available
eparate U.K. edition also available

ailable wherever books are sold. For more information or to order direct: U.S. customers visit www.dummies.com or call 1-877-762-2974.
. customers visit www.wileyeurope.com or call (0) 1243 843291. Canadian customers visit www.wiley.ca or call 1-800-567-4797.

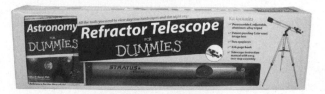